ZION & BRYCE

W. C. McRAE & JUDY JEWELL

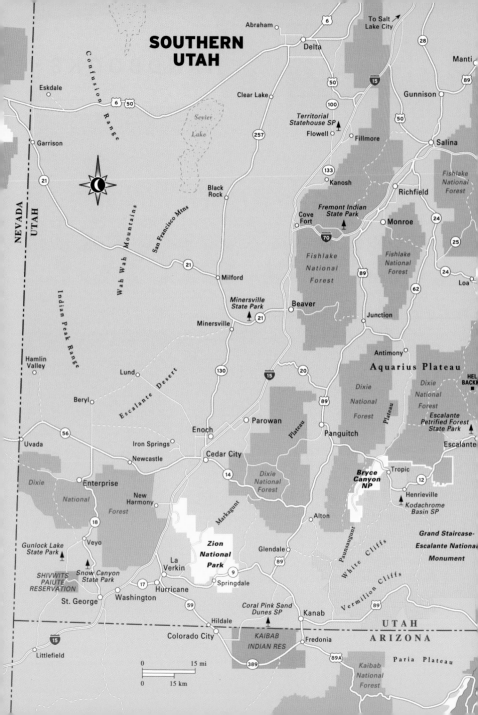

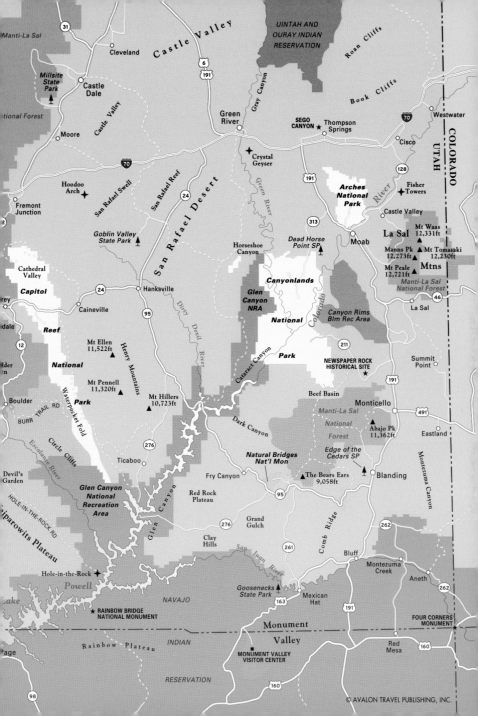

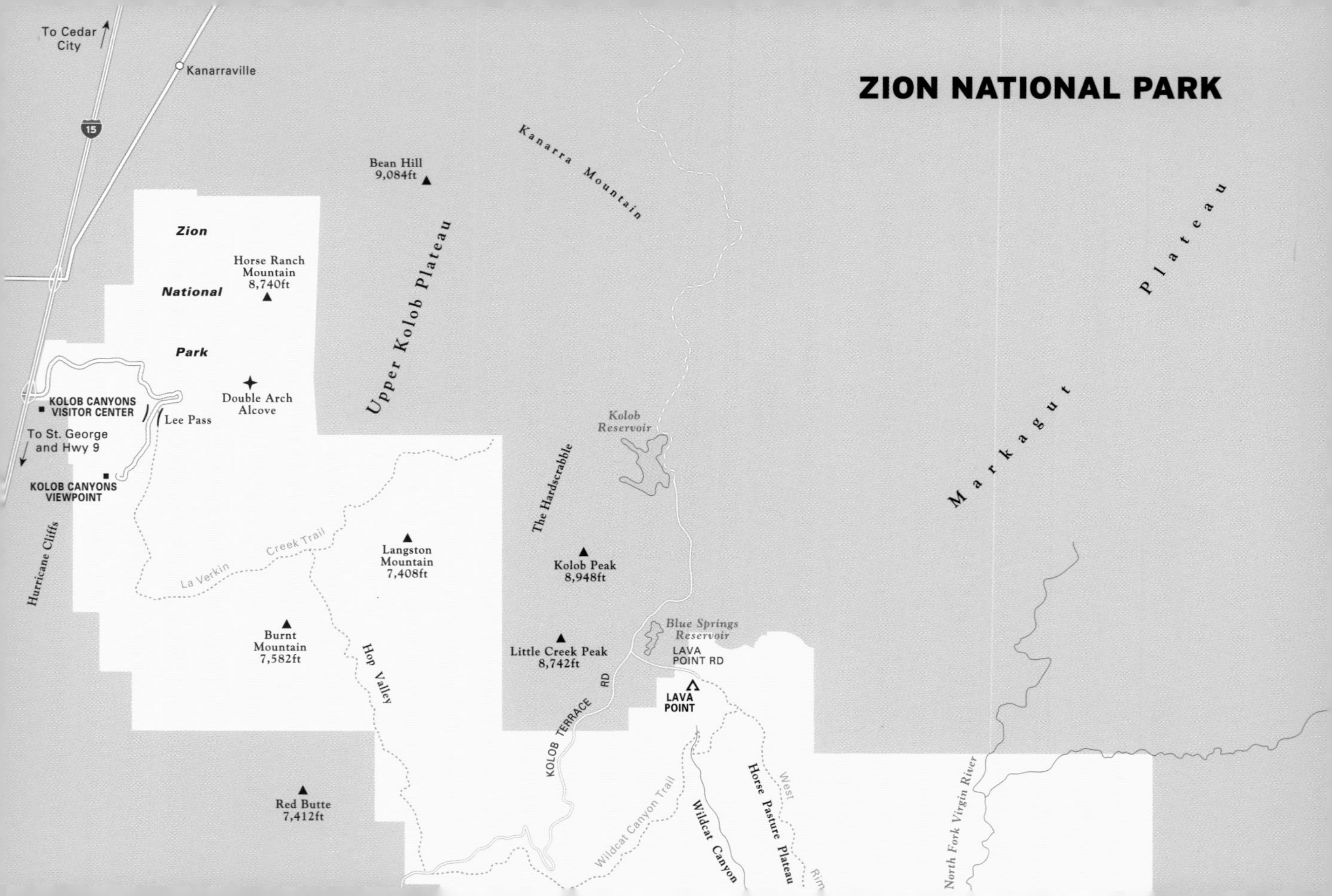

ZION NATIONAL PARK

Markagunt Plateau

Kanarra Mountain

Upper Kolob Plateau

Bean Hill
9,084ft

Horse Ranch
Mountain
8,740ft

Zion

National

Park

Double Arch
Alcove

Lee Pass

La Verkin Creek Trail

Kolob Reservoir

The Hardscrabble

Kolob Peak
8,948ft

Little Creek Peak
8,742ft

Langston
Mountain
7,408ft

Hop Valley

Burnt
Mountain
7,582ft

Red Butte
7,412ft

Blue Springs
Reservoir

LAVA
POINT RD

LAVA
POINT

KOLOB TERRACE RD

West Rim

Horse Pasture Plateau

Wildcat Canyon

Wildcat Canyon Trail

North Fork Virgin River

Kanarraville

To Cedar
City

15

To St. George
and Hwy 9

■ KOLOB CANYONS
VISITOR CENTER

■ KOLOB CANYONS
VIEWPOINT

Hurricane Cliffs

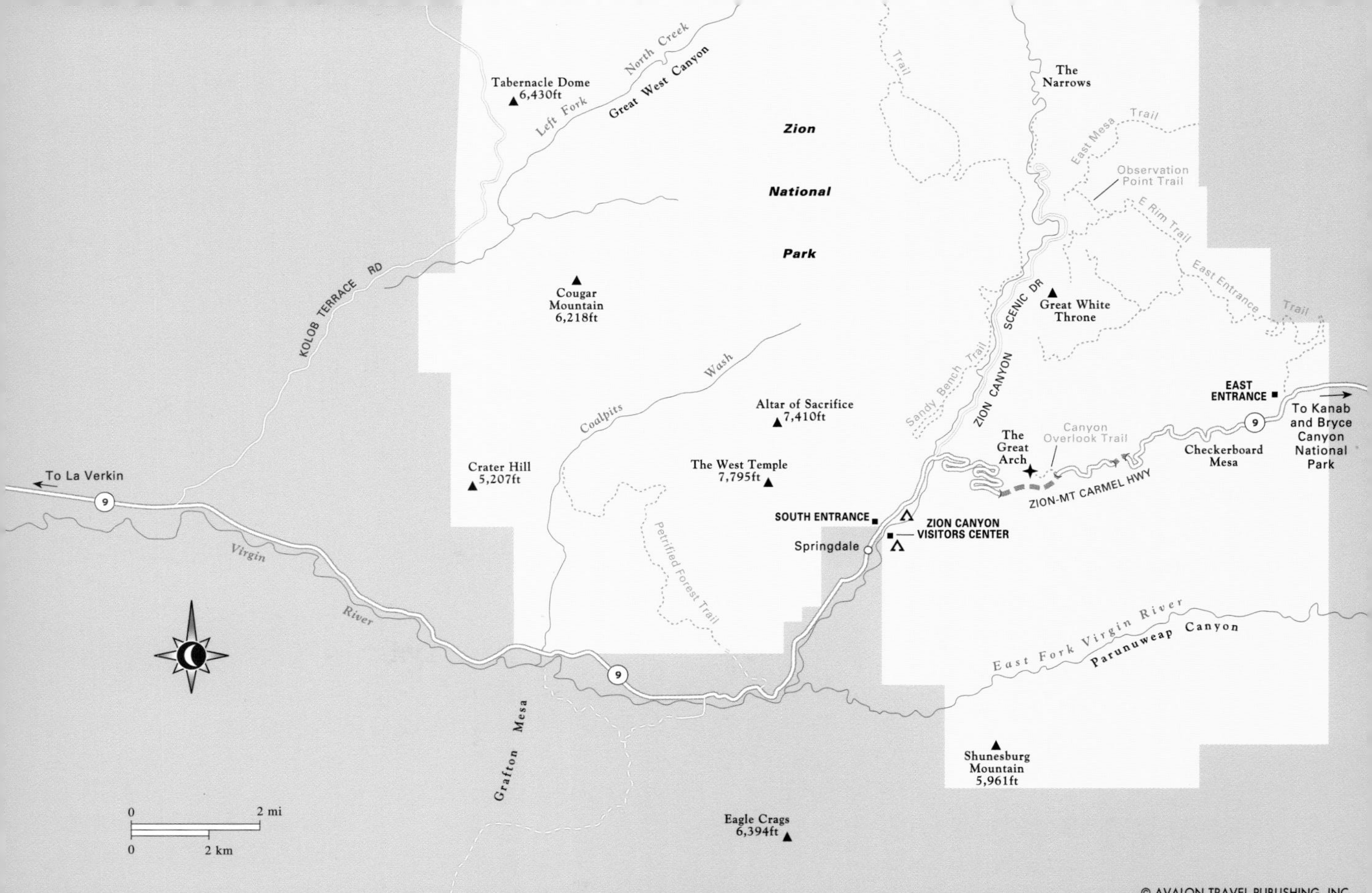

To Kanab and Bryce Canyon National Park

EAST ENTRANCE

9

Checkerboard Mesa

East Entrance Trail

Observation Point Trail

E Rim Trail

East Mesa Trail

The Narrows

Trail

▲ Great White Throne

Canyon Overlook Trail

ZION-MT CARMEL HWY

The Great Arch

ZION CANYON

SCENIC DR

Sandy Bench Trail

Trail

East Fork Virgin River

Parunuweap Canyon

Shunesburg Mountain 5,961ft ▲

ZION CANYON VISITORS CENTER

SOUTH ENTRANCE

Springdale

Zion National Park

Altar of Sacrifice 7,410ft ▲

The West Temple 7,795ft ▲

Wash

Coalpits

Petrified Forest Trail

9

Eagle Crags 6,394ft ▲

North Creek

Great West Canyon

Left Fork

Tabernacle Dome 6,430ft ▲

Cougar Mountain 6,218ft ▲

Crater Hill 5,207ft ▲

Grafton Mesa

KOLOB TERRACE RD

River

Virgin

2 mi

2 km

0

0

9

To La Verkin

© AVALON TRAVEL PUBLISHING, INC.

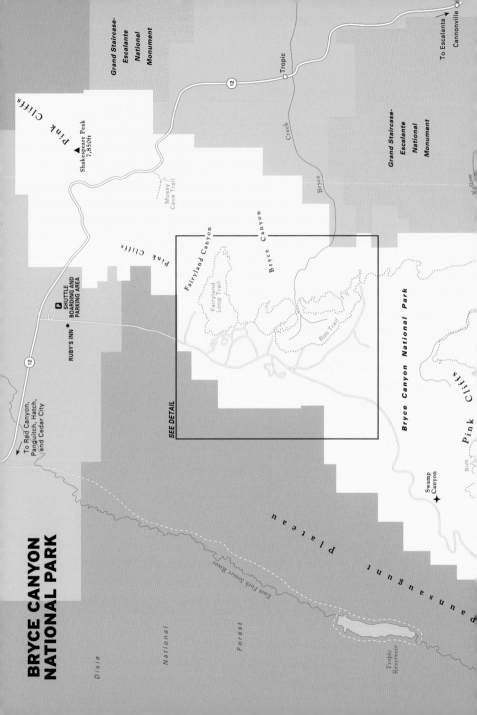

BRYCE CANYON NATIONAL PARK

Grand Staircase-
Escalante
National
Monument

Pink Cliffs

Shakespeare Peak
7,850ft

Mossy Cave Trail

Tropic

12

Creek

Bryce

Grand Staircase-
Escalante
National
Monument

Yellow

Pink Cliffs

Fairyland Canyon

Bryce Canyon

Fairyland
Loop Trail

Rim Trail

Bryce Canyon National Park

SHUTTLE
BOARDING AND
PARKING AREA

P

RUBY'S INN

SEE DETAIL

12

To Red Canyon,
Panguitch, Hatch,
and Cedar City

Rim

Pink Cliffs

Swamp
Canyon

Paunsaugunt Plateau

Dixie

National

Forest

East Fork Sewer River

To Escalante

Cannonville

Tropic Reservoir

DISCOVER
ZION & BRYCE

It's hard for most of us to get too excited about rocks. But then again, most of the rocks we encounter are usually covered with soil and plants, not to mention cement.

In southern Utah, all is laid bare – and the rocks are astoundingly diverse and beautiful. They take on fantastic shapes, as in Arches and Bryce Canyon National Parks; beautiful hues, notably at Kodachrome State Park and Bryce; and vast prominence, such as Zion's Patriarchs and Great White Throne. Sometimes the mere act of walking among the rocks takes on great significance, which, judging from the ancient petroglyphs, it also did for our predecessors.

The landscapes of southern Utah are so filled with stagger-ing beauty, drama, and power that it seems a place of myth. The canyons, arches, and mesas of Utah could serve as the backdrop for a film of the Old Testament or the journeys of Gilgamesh. Five

arch in Coyote Gulch, Grand Staircase-Escalante National Monument

spectacular national parks and several national monuments all lie within a day's drive of one another, sprawling over the highly eroded topography of an area larger than many European countries. Yet within this high, dry area is surprising diversity, and each park has its own characteristic landscape.

Zion National Park contains stunning contrasts, with barren, towering rock walls deeply incised by steep canyons containing a verdant oasis of cottonwood trees and wildflowers. As in many national parks, there are plenty of spectacular hikes; something a little different is the in-water hike up The Narrows of the Virgin River, which is not quite hiking, but a step less than full-on canyoneering.

Bryce National Park is famed for its abundance of red and pink hoodoos, delicate fingers of stone rising from a steep mountainside. A maze of hiking trails descends into this wonderland of towering

colorful hoodoos in Bryce Canyon National Park

formations, drawing adventurers away from the park's busy rim road. This is a place worth getting up for: Sunrise is when the lighting is magical, the air crisp and cool, and the trails empty. Return in winter to cross-country ski amid the silent, snow-draped pines and statue-like stones.

A large section of the Grand Staircase-Escalante National Monument preserves the dry washes and slot canyons trenched by the Escalante River and its tributaries as they drop toward the Colorado River. The sport of canyoneering was practically invented in these sinuously beautiful, high-rock-walled cathedrals of stone – long-distance hikers descend into the deep, narrow river channels to experience the near-mystical harmony of flowing water and stone. Day hikes lead across slickrock to waterfalls, sandstone arches, and narrow slot canyons.

The highlight of Capitol Reef National Park is Waterpocket Fold, an enormous wrinkle of rock rising from the desert. The Fremont River carves a magnificent canyon through the formation and of-

Balanced Rock, Arches National Park

fers hikers and explorers a leafy, well-watered sanctuary from the otherwise arid landscapes of southern Utah.

In vast Canyonlands National Park, the Colorado River begins to tunnel its mighty canyon through an otherworldly landscape of deep red sandstone. From overlooks in the Island in the Sky unit, expansive vistas take in hundreds of miles of canyon country, while white-water rafting the Colorado's Cataract Canyon is the wet and thrilling climax of many a vacation. The beauty is more serene and mystical at Arches National Park, where hundreds of delicate rock arches provide vast windows into the solid rock. Short trails draw hikers and photographers into an eerily beautiful land of slickrock promontories and high-flying stone arches. High-spirited Moab is the recreational mecca of southeastern Utah. It's a boisterous community known for its mountain-bike lifestyle and comfortable – even sophisticated – dining and lodging.

Southern Utah is more than a showcase of stunning erosion. Its cliffs and canyons have been home to Native Americans for thousands of years. The remains of ancient communities lie crumbling

cactus flower, Grand Staircase–Escalante National Monument

throughout the area and are particularly impressive at Hovenweep National Monument, a collection of near-millennia-old townsites for the ancient Anasazi. The haunting beauty of native rock art is on display at hundreds of locations in this part of Utah. An entire unit of Canyonlands National Park, in Horseshoe Canyon, is devoted to the Great Gallery, a magnificent rock art amphitheater where ghostly, life-size figures parade across a cliff face. A sacred, ceremonial shrine? A message board for passing Native Americans? No one has unlocked the secrets of the region's ancient petroglyphs and pictographs, but these mute messengers from prehistory cast a spell on all who view them.

Each park in southern Utah is distinctive, and each could provide the focus for a memorable, adventure-packed vacation. Although many people first visit this area as part of a "grand tour" of the Southwest, they often return to further explore a smaller and distinctive corner of this vast landscape. After getting a small glimpse of the magnificence and variety, some latch on to one special place and return year after year, growing to know it intimately.

Capitol Reef National Park

Contents

MAP CONTENTS

Salina

Cove Fort

70

24

Junction

15

89

Escalant

Cedar City

56

14

Bryce
Canyon
National
Park

12

Zion
National
Park

15

Grand Staircase-
Escalante Nationa
Monument

9

St. George

UTAH

Kanab

89

ARIZONA

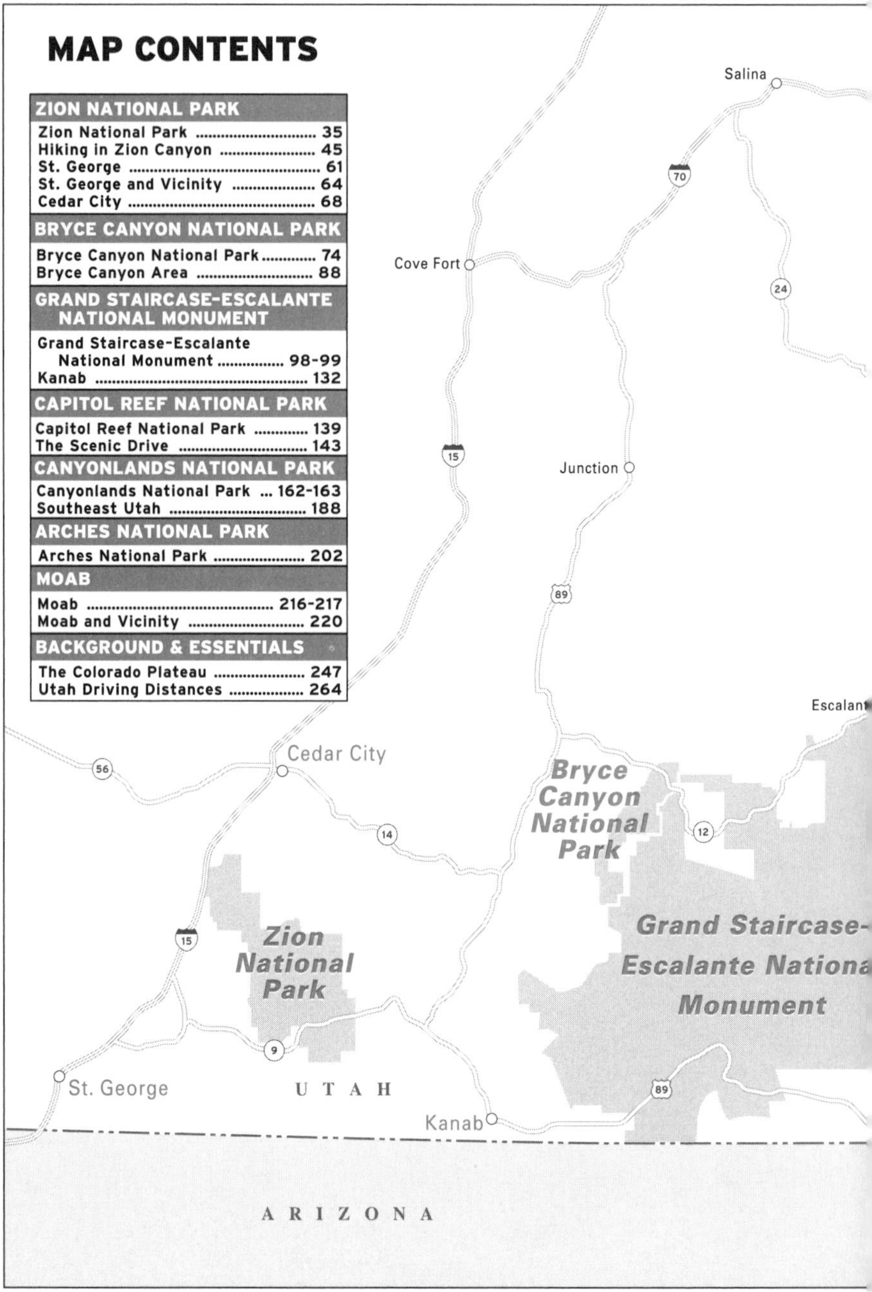

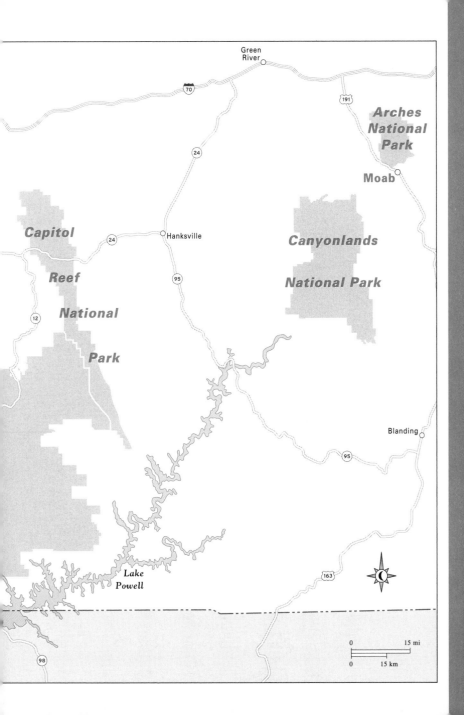

The Lay of the Land

The national parks of southern Utah are all part of the Colorado Plateau, a vast geologic province laid down as silt, sand, and salt beneath ancient seas many millions of years ago. Later, after forces deep in the earth lifted these sedimentary layers several miles above sea level, erosion cut vast canyons, arches, hoodoos, and chasms into the rock. Utah's national parks—each distinctly different—are a celebration of these astonishing geologic processes.

ZION NATIONAL PARK

Zion National Park is one of the most popular in the park system: Hiking trails lead up **narrow canyons cut into massive stone cliffs,** passing along quiet pools of water and groves of willows. Zion is so breathtaking and awe-inspiring that the early Mormons named these canyons for their vision of heaven. The park's main canyon, carved by the Virgin River, is a much quieter place to visit now that access is by shuttle bus; however, the rest of the park's canyons are the province of long-distance hikers.

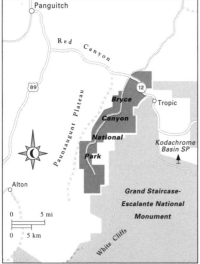

BRYCE CANYON NATIONAL PARK

Bryce Canyon National Park has famous vistas across an eroded amphitheater of **pink sandstone hoodoos.** One of the most popular parks, it's often just considered an extended photo opportunity for shutterbugs; however, you'll have quite a different experience from the amateur photographers along the rim if you venture into the park's backcountry. Short trails lead down from the canyon edge into a wonderland of fanciful formations and outcrops.

GRAND STAIRCASE-ESCALANTE NATIONAL MONUMENT

Grand Staircase–Escalante National Monument preserves some of the Southwest's best canyon hiking. Numerous long-distance hiking trails and an assortment of day hikes follow **the slot canyons of the Escalante River system.** Mountain bikers can head down the **Hole-in-the-Rock Road** or the **Burr Trail** to visit some of the same landscape via jeep road; even cruising scenic Highway 12 across Escalante country in a car is an eye-popping experience.

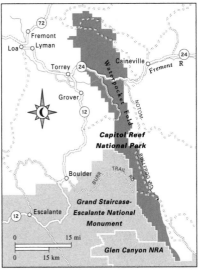

CAPITOL REEF NATIONAL PARK

Through no fault of its own, Capitol Reef National Park draws fewer crowds than Utah's other national parks. The park preserves a vast wrinkle of rock called **Waterpocket Fold** that buckles up into a vertical barricade across more than 100 miles of southeast Utah. Of the few canyons that penetrate Waterpocket Fold, the Fremont River Canyon is most accessible along Highway 24. Ancient petroglyphs, pioneer farms and orchards, and soaring rock formations extend the length of the canyon. A paved scenic highway explores more canyons along the fold's western face. The rest of the park is remote backcountry—just the way hikers and backpackers like it.

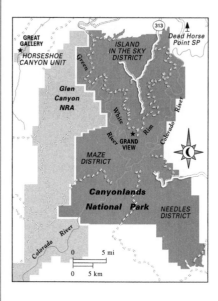

CANYONLANDS NATIONAL PARK

Canyonlands National Park is remote and otherworldly, with a wealth of rock art, Anasazi ruins, and vertical desert landscapes. There are four sections to the park: the **River District,** containing the canyons of the Colorado and Green Rivers; the **Needles District,** with a wealth of hiking trails and backcountry roads leading through a standing-rock desert; the **Maze District,** an extremely remote area filled with geologic curiosities and labyrinthine canyons; and the **Island in the Sky District,** a flat-topped mesa that overlooks all the rest. A separate area, the **Horseshoe Canyon Unit,** lies to the west and contains a significant cache of prehistoric rock art. Only the Island in the Sky and Needles Districts are easily accessible to casual travelers.

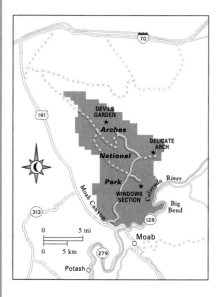

ARCHES NATIONAL PARK

Just up the road from Moab is Arches National Park, with its famous rock bridges. Arches is a great family park: It's not too large, and there are lots of medium-length, medium-difficulty hikes to explore. Unlike other Utah national parks, there's still plenty to see even if you can't get out and hike: You'll see some of the good stuff even if you're in a car. Be sure to hike to the **Windows Section,** a series of arches and rock fins at the center of the park, and to **Delicate Arch,** overlooking the Colorado River.

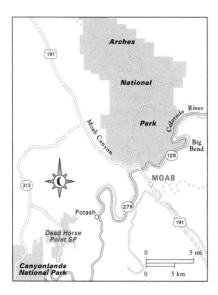

MOAB

At the heart of Utah's slickrock country, Moab is undeniably the recreation capital of southeastern Utah. Although mountain biking put Moab on the map, nowadays gonzo biking is just one of many sports and activities that draw the crowds—for instance, off-road-vehicle (ORV) exploration now seems to be the extreme sport of choice. Moab is also central to two of Utah's most popular parks. Arches is just minutes from downtown, and Canyonlands' many districts are an easy drive from Moab. But Moab is more than just a convenient place to stay when heading elsewhere. For many travelers, Moab is a destination in itself, a youthful, high-energy town in a stunning locale that also offers good restaurants, brewpubs, and coffee shops—in short, camaraderie. Add an overlay of old hippie, arty Bohemia, and you've got an unusual blend of cultures and energies that make Moab a unique destination in otherwise stuffy, reserved Utah.

Planning Your Trip

Although the national parks of Utah are located in a geographically compact area, connecting the dots and visiting each of them isn't as straightforward as it might seem. The extremely rugged topography of the area has made road building difficult, so visiting all of the parks requires a lot of driving. Maps often show unpaved back roads that can serve as shortcuts. Many of these are fine if you have a high-clearance vehicle, but check locally before setting out to determine current conditions: Rainstorms and snowmelt can render these roads impassable. Otherwise, sit back and enjoy the ride. These are some of the world's most scenic landscapes, and if you're in a hurry, you should stick to the freeway.

In general, the parks attract two kinds of visitors: tourists who come mostly to look and outdoor enthusiasts who come mostly to do. This book provides information for both kinds of traveler but advocates a middle ground between the two archetypes. Southern Utah has plenty of eye-popping scenery, and you'll want to see as much as possible, especially on your first trip through these desert canyons. This book also makes it easy to get out of the car and explore these landscapes up close. For each park, you'll find a selection of hikes rated from easy to challenging, plus information on mountain biking, horseback riding, four-wheel-drive exploring, white-water rafting, and other forms of recreation that let you get outdoors to explore the unique geology, natural history, and archaeology of these parks.

The entry fees for the national parks have gone up greatly in the past few years; admission to Zion is now $25 per vehicle. If you're planning on making the rounds of the Utah national parks, it's an excellent idea to purchase an America the Beautiful—National Parks and Federal Recreational Lands Pass ($80, good for one year from date of purchase), which provides access to federal recreation sites that charge an entrance or standard amenity fee. Senior passes ($10 for a lifetime pass) and free passes for residents with permanent disabilities are also available.

Don't ignore the areas outside national park boundaries, though. Chances are good that you'll drive right past these parks and monuments as you explore southern Utah. These areas are often less thronged than the national parks, but equally as compelling. The Cedar Breaks National Monument preserves an area with formations similar to Bryce Canyon, but without the crowds. Just below Bryce Canyon, Kodachrome Basin State Park is ringed by remarkable pink cliffs, plus odd rock pillars called sand pipes. Red Canyon, a national recreation area administered by the U.S. Forest Service, is immediately west of Bryce Canyon and shares its geology, but because it's not a national park, you can mountain bike and ride horses amid the red-rock formations. Hovenweep National Monument contains the ruins of ancient Anasazi stone villages. Natural Bridges National Monument contains formations that rival Arches National Park, but it lacks the crowds. Plus there are abundant Native American ruins, petroglyphs, and good hiking trails. Dead Horse State Park provides an eagle's-eye view over the Colorado River Canyon near Moab.

WHEN TO GO

The parks are all open year-round, although spring (April–early June) and fall (September–October) are the most pleasant times to visit. They're also the busiest, and springtime travelers may find that popular campgrounds and hotels are booked up well in advance.

Spring

The desert country shines with wildflowers in early spring, the choice time to visit. Each year's floral display depends on both the amount and timing of rains in the preceding winter. The same rain showers that bring spring flowers can also dampen trails for a few days. Especially in the higher elevations, clouds and rain can last for several days, so always have in mind a rainy-day alternative to hiking. (Arm yourself with insect repellent from late spring to midsummer.)

Late winter and early spring storms can play havoc with backcountry roads. Before setting out on a trip with the goal of backcountry exploration, call locally to determine if roads are open. It can take weeks for crews to repair roads after spring flood damage.

Summer

Summer travelers should look to the higher elevations to find relief from the heat that can envelop southern Utah. Bryce Canyon, at 6,600–9,100 feet, is a good bet. Consider spending a night on the way to or from the park in Cedar City, when summer brings the Utah Shakespeare Festival.

Plan to do your hiking early in the morning and spend the hot afternoons taking it easy. Thunderstorms are fairly common from late July through early September and bring the threat of flash flooding, especially in slot canyons. In Canyonlands, Arches, and Moab, summer temperatures can get into the 100s. Carrying (and drinking) water becomes critical then; carry at least one gallon per person per day.

Autumn

Nearly the entire state enjoys warm and dry weather, though hot temperatures can linger into October at the lowest elevations, and the possibility of snow gradually increases on the plateaus and mountains. Aspens turn to gold in the high country in late September and early October, followed by colorful displays of oaks, cottonwoods, and other deciduous plants in canyons lower down.

Winter

Visitors coming in winter should inquire about travel conditions because snow and ice occasionally close roads and trails at higher elevations. A few highways close for the winter, most notably the roads around Cedar Breaks National Monument.

Remember that Brigham Young established his winter home in St. George, near present-day Zion National Park. This southwest Utah town has become a retirement hot spot, with golf courses possibly outnumbering places of worship (and certainly far outnumbering bars and taverns).

Winter can be a great time to visit the high country around Bryce, where cross-county skiers take to the park roads. Around Escalante, the canyons can be quite nice in the winter during the days, but nights are freezing. In Canyonlands and Arches, winter days tend to be bright and sunny, but nighttime temperatures can dip into the teens or lower.

WHAT TO TAKE

No matter what time of year, remember to bring lots of sunscreen. Even in winter, the sun packs a wallop at high elevations. In summer, be prepared for blazing sun; unless you want to return from Utah looking like a leather hand-bag, buy and use a sunscreen with a high sun-protection level.

If you are planning on a lot of hiking, especially along slickrock trails or in rocky canyons, bring broken-in hiking shoes or boots. Light-weight sports or walking shoes won't provide much support in the rugged conditions of southern Utah.

Even in summer, there can be wide variations in temperature. Nights in the desert can be very chilly even when summer highs soar above 100 degrees. Especially if you're planning on hiking or backpacking, bring clothes that can be removed or put on in layers, as needed. Zip-off pants work especially well.

There's no need to pack clothes for "dress up." Nearly without exception, casual clothes are acceptable everywhere, even in what passes for a classy restaurant. You'll find it difficult to under-dress.

Alcohol presents another issue. If you think you'll want a drink, especially away from Moab or Springdale, pack a flask or a bottle of wine, especially if you have discerning tastes. While many restaurants in the towns around these parks now offer a selection of alcoholic beverages, including good wine and Utah microbrews, southern Utah is not a drinking culture, to put it mildly. If you're accustomed to a cocktail or a nightcap, you might want to bring a bottle along on your trip.

And sure, you can bring your cell phone, but don't count on it working over much of southern Utah.

Explore Zion & Bryce

THE BEST OF UTAH'S NATIONAL PARKS

Despite their proximity, visiting all of Utah's national parks is a bit complicated because of the rugged terrain. You must plan on a lot of driving. So get in a road trip frame of mind, cue up some good music, and head out. The following itinerary only scratches the surface of what there is to see, but after this sampler, you'll know where to focus your next Utah adventure.

Days 1–2

Start in Moab, a major center for recreation in southeast Utah. This small town is also the most convenient hub for visiting both **Arches** and **Canyonlands National Parks.** You can tour Arches in half a day if you take only short hikes to viewpoints; if you want to visit all of the sites along the park road and hike to famed Delicate Arch, you'll spend most of a day in the park. Devote day two to exploring **Canyonlands' Island in the Sky District,** taking in the astonishing vista points (particularly Grand View Point) and saving time for a hike to the cliff edge. In the evenings, enjoy the lively scene in Moab, with its good restaurants, brewpubs, and bicyclists.

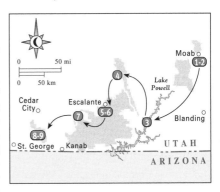

Day 3

From Moab, get an early start and drive south on U.S. 191. This day requires quite a bit of driving—roughly 200 miles. Pull off U.S. 191 40 miles south of Moab and drive toward the **Needles District** of Canyonlands. If you're short on time, you probably won't make the trip west to the park itself (it's 38 miles to the park gate), but at least follow the park access road for 10 miles to **BLM Newspaper Rock Historical Monument,** one of the finest and most accessible petroglyph sites in Utah. Return to U.S. 191 and continue south 78 miles, passing the ranching towns of Monticello and Blanding before turning west on Highway 95 to reach **Natural Bridges National Monument.** Often overlooked, this small park is a gem, with three massive rock bridges and an Anasazi cliff dwelling along a nine-mile loop highway. Back on Highway 95, continue eight miles to the junction of Highway 276, then follow this route 40 miles to Halls Crossing Marina on Lake Powell, which offers car-ferry service across the lake. After a half-hour crossing, you reach Bullfrog Marina on the west side of the lake, with excellent accommodations in Defiance House Lodge.

Day 4

From Bullfrog, you can follow the well-maintained Notom–Bullfrog backcountry road to Highway 24 and the entrance to **Capitol Reef National Park** (80 miles), or you can follow paved Highways 276 and 95 to Hanksville and enter the park along Highway 24 (117 miles). Either way, you'll end up in Capitol Reef. You'll want to explore the old pioneer town of Fruita, hike to see petroglyphs, and drive the scenic park road. Add a hike up the Chimney Rock Trail or along Capitol Wash. **Torrey,** a small town just west of the park, has a profusion of hotels and is the best base for exploring the Capitol Reef area.

Day 5

From Torrey, follow Highway 12 south through the **Grand Staircase-Escalante National Monument.** The 61-mile trip between Torrey and Escalante is one of the most scenic routes in all of Utah—don't plan to drive this in an hour! Take in all the scenery and sights, including a visit to the prehistoric ruins at **Anasazi State Park** and a hike up dramatic **Lower Calf Creek Falls Trail.** Spend the night in the town of Escalante at a motel or at the Escalante Petrified Forest State Park campground.

Day 6

Explore more of the Escalante River canyons. Drive 12.5 miles south from Highway 12 and turn onto the Hole-in-the-Rock Road to traipse around **Devils Garden.** You can also visit the canyons of **Dry Fork of Coyote Gulch,** 26 miles south of Highway 12. Return to Escalante for the night.

Day 7

From Escalante, continue west 42 miles on Highway 12 to **Bryce Canyon National Park.** Park the car and spend the day riding the park shuttle to vista points and exploring hoodoos from trailheads along the road. Camp in the park or stay at the historic park lodge or one of the motels just outside the park entrance.

Days 8-9

Get up in time to see the rising sun light up the hoodoos, then drive west on Highway 12 to U.S. 89, and south from there to Highway 9. At Highway 9, turn west and enter **Zion National Park** via the dramatic Zion–Mt. Carmel Highway (Bryce to Zion is 84 miles), then find a campsite or check into the lodge or a motel in Springdale. Ride the park shuttle for a quick overview of Zion Canyon. Spend a second day exploring the canyon and its many enchanting hikes, including the **Riverside Walk** or the **Emerald Pools trails.**

ANCIENT ROCK-ART LEGACY

The Colorado Plateau contains a rich tapestry of pictographs (drawings painted on rock using natural dyes) and petroglyphs (images carved into stone). Searching out rock-art panels can easily become an obsession, and it's a good one, since it will lead you far off the beaten path and deep into canyons that were once central for the area's ancient inhabitants. The earliest known images are in the Barrier Canyon Style, which may date back 8,000 years. Interestingly, these very early images are frequently of ghostly apparitions and horned, robed creatures, and seem to have had ritual significance. Rock art in the Fremont Style was created nearly 1,000 years ago and is more abstract and stylized, often with geometric shapes and ciphers. Ute Style images are comparatively recent—from the last 400 years—and often feature hunters on horseback, buffalo, and other game animals.

Zion

East of Cedar City, **Parowan Gap** is a narrow rock pass where ancient artists chiseled images over 1,000 years ago. Who knows what kinds of meanings these pictographs—of geometric designs, lizards, bear claws, and human figures—had for travelers through this pass?

Bryce

At Bryce, the rocks themselves are the art. There are no pictographs or petroglyphs of note here, at least not that anybody's telling about.

Grand Staircase-Escalante National Monument

Stop between the towns of Escalante and Boulder at the **Boynton Overlook** and scan the cliff face across the river to see a pictograph of many handprints. It's possible to scramble up for a closer look from the parking area where Highway 12 crosses the Escalante River.

Capitol Reef

Petroglyphs of horned mountain sheep and humans in headdresses are easily viewed from a parking area along Highway 24 in **Fremont River Canyon**. These are some of the most easily reached rock-art panels in Utah.

Canyonlands

One of the most important rock-art sites in the United States is the **Great Gallery** in Canyonlands' **Horseshoe Canyon Unit**. In fact, the park service created the unit specially to protect this trove of incomparable art. Human-sized images of ghost spirits cover the walls—this was clearly a sacred place for thousands of years. That it's reached after a day of backcountry driving and hiking only adds to the magic.

Newspaper Rock, near the Needles District, is another easily reached showcase of rock art. The immense rock face is a collage of fantastic creatures, footprints, abstract designs, hunters on horseback, and wild animals—in all, 2,000 years of art on a boulder.

In the southeast corner of Utah is **Hovenweep National Monument**, one of Utah's best-preserved Anasazi villages. There, among the ruins, you'll find many petroglyphs. The most interesting are in the **Holly Ruins**, where a series of spirals and concentric rings served as a calendar for ancient farmers. Shafts of light from the rising sun illuminate the petroglyphs. By aligning the designs, the Anasazi were able to mark the summer solstice and the fall and spring equinoxes.

Arches

On the hiking trial to **Delicate Arch** is an often-overlooked panel of Ute Style rock-art images. Images like these, of mounted horsemen hunting mountain sheep, are clearly from the historical period, since horses reached America from Spanish colonies.

Moab

A number of rock-art panels are found along the Colorado River near Moab, but for a vast gallery of prehistoric art, take the drive to Sego Canyon, an hour north of Moab off I-70, where you'll find hundreds of etched images, starting with ghostly, shamanic-looking creatures right out of sci-fi movies.

CAMP IT UP

Southern Utah is flush with campgrounds, including many great spots just outside national parks. This tour starts in the west, an easy drive from the Las Vegas airport, near Zion National Park.

Night 1

Snow Canyon State Park is a beautiful spot just outside busy St. George. Even though it's at a higher elevation than the town, this area gets very hot in the summer, and the campground is fairly lightly used then. But during spring, it's quite popular; reserve a site well in advance.

Nights 2 and 3

Head to Zion National Park, where you can find good spots in either of the two park-maintained campgrounds. If you're planning in advance, some sites in Watchman Campground can be reserved. Spend a couple of nights here to really see the park.

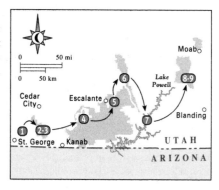

Night 4

The campgrounds at Bryce Canyon National Park are perfectly nice, but the high elevation of this park means cold nights in the spring and fall. (There are significant patches of snow on the ground in early May.) Find a warmer spot at Kodachrome Basin State Park, about 20 miles south of Bryce. Kodachrome is quite scenic in itself, with great campsites and several hiking trails.

Night 5

Two campgrounds near Escalante make a good base for exploring the northern edge of the Grand Staircase–Escalante National Monument. Of the two, the Calf Creek Campground, east of town, is more scenic, but Escalante Petrified Forest State Park, just west of town, has showers.

Night 6

Don't skip a visit to Capitol Reef. The most noteworthy thing about the park's Fruita Campground is its easy access to the local fruit trees (free for the picking in the right season) and hiking trails. Because no reservations are accepted, it's best to arrive here early in the day to claim a spot.

Night 7

Head south on Notom–Bullfrog Road, cross Lake Powell on the ferry, and pitch your tent at the Halls Crossing campground in Glen Canyon National Recreation Area. If you feel a need to drive farther, the main campground at Natural Bridges National Monument is perfectly nice, but it often fills up, leaving late-comers in the unappealing overflow site.

Or maybe it's time for a comfy mattress and a hot shower!

Night 8

Head east across Highway 95 to Blanding, then swing north on Highway 191 to Monticello. Drive north through Moab to Arches National Park where, if you planned your trip's details well in advance, a reserved campsite at the **Devils Garden Campground** will be waiting. If that's not the case, rest assured that there are many campsites in the Moab area.

Night 9

The next morning, get up early and head to the Needles District of Canyonlands National Park, where both loops of the **Squaw Flat Campground** have excellent sites. This place is popular, though, and it's easy to get skunked. If necessary, head east and camp either at the private Needles Outpost or at BLM sites near Newspaper Rock.

GOURMET DELIGHTS

Small-town Utah is not known for its cuisine. However, there are a few outposts of good food scattered around the parklands of southern Utah, where good chefs have unpacked their knives and whisks, and where the best local produce and meats are featured. Be sure to stop by and support these fine locally owned restaurants.

Springdale

Most likely, by the time you roll into the **Bit & Spur** (1212 Zion Park Blvd., 435/772-3498), you'll have been hiking all day, will be sunburned, hungry, and thirsty, and just about anything will taste good. But the food here really is the real deal: innovative Southwestern and Mexican food, where your poblano chile may be stuffed with shrimp and grits, your tamales with wild mushrooms, and your jalepeño peppers with cheese.

Kanab

It's a special surprise to wander across the **Rocking V Café** (97 W. Center, 435/644-8001), in a storefront on Kanab's main drag. As at most of southern Utah's best restaurants, chef-owners Victor and Vicky use local ingredients whenever possible to make Southwestern-style food, and they cater to everybody from vegans to steak lovers.

Boulder

The restaurant at the inviting Boulder Mountain Lodge, **Hell's Backbone Grill** (435/355-7460) offers incongruously fine dining in the little crossroads town of Boulder. The regularly changing menu features regionally based cuisine: a blend of Western Range, Pueblo Indian, and Southwestern flavors, with local organically grown vegetables and herbs and locally raised, natural meats.

Torrey

Inventive Southwestern cuisine is the specialty at **Cafe Diablo** (599 W. Main St., 435/425-3070) in Torrey. Chef-owner Gary Pankow, a graduate of the Culinary Institute of America, adds zest and finesse to locally grown organic meats and produce. In addition to freshly baked bread, desserts and ice cream are all homemade.

Moab

Moab's top dining destination is **Center Cafe** (60 North 100 West, 435/259-4295), with exciting globally inspired cuisine in a stylish wood-beamed dining room. The café offers both small plates and a fine-dining menu—everything from foie gras to house-made pierogi. The chefs use fresh, locally grown, organic produce in season, dry aged beef, and fresh seafood flown in from both coasts and the Gulf.

Seventeen miles northeast of Moab on Highway 128, the **River Grill** (435/259-4642) at

Sorrel River Ranch offers fine dining at a stunningly situated guest ranch and spa. Fresh seafood and steaks, plus a selection of Continental favorites, make this one of the top restaurants in southern Utah. Sunset dining on a deck overlooking the Colorado River and the back side of Arches National Park elevates dinner to a special occasion.

STANDING HIGH: THE BEST VISTAS

With a landscape characterized by mountain peaks and deep canyons, southern Utah is filled with big views. With a few exceptions, you won't need to hike uphill for miles to get a bird's-eye view—most of the vista points below are easily reached by a short hike or detour by car.

Zion

Okay, forget what we just said about not needing to hike uphill. If you really want the views, hike up to **Angels Landing.** But if you're not up for this stiff hike and just want an eyeful, jump off the shuttle bus at the **Court of the Patriarchs.**

Bryce

Don't dismiss **Sunrise Point** just because it's a cliché. The angle of the rising sun does make this viewpoint special. If you can't quite make it by sunrise, try a sunset view at **Sunset Point.** In fact, Bryce is so full of fantastic views that just about any pullout along the scenic drive is shockingly beautiful.

Grand Staircase-Escalante National Monument

Between Escalante and Boulder, Highway 12 climbs up a steep fin of rock called the **Hog's Back,** from where the slot canyons of the Escalante River and the cliffs of the Aquarius Plateau form a jaw-dropping 360-degree vista.

At the end of the 57-mile Hole-in-the-Rock Road, the road dead ends at a cliff over the Colorado River (you may have to walk the last mile or so, depending on conditions; ask before

you set out). Mormon pioneers blasted a trail down the 600-foot-high precipice, but views from the top, with the Colorado in a maze of red-rock canyons below, are enough for most modern explorers.

Capitol Reef

It's hard to get a handle on the fact that Waterpocket Fold is a vast wrinkle of rock over 100 miles long. Unless, of course, you climb up and look down on it. From **Navajo Knobs,** 1,500 feet above the Fremont River Canyon, reached after a six-mile climb from Hickman Natural Bridge Trailhead, you'll take in most of southern Utah and the snakelike ridge of Waterpocket Fold winding to the south.

Canyonlands

From the main access road into the Island in the Sky section of Canyonlands, two road-end vista points provide swallow-your-gum views over the incredible Colorado River Canyon. From **Dead Horse Point State Park,** a 30-foot-wide neck of land extends into the void over the twisting channels of the river 2,000 feet below. Continue to **Grand View Point,** above the confluence of the Colorado and the Green Rivers, for vistas of canyons, sheer rock walls, and pinnacles and distant mountains. This incredible vantage point displays hundreds of miles of the American Southwest.

Arches

In its sheer concentration of incredible scenery, it's hard to beat Arches for dramatic vistas.

Drive 16 miles from the park gates to Wolfe Ranch, then take the three-mile round-trip hike up a slickrock trail for the park's most incredible view. Looking across the Colorado River Canyon to the distant La Sal Mountains through **Delicate Arch** is a memory-of-a-lifetime experience.

BEST DAY HIKES

Zion

The **Emerald Pools trails** start from Zion Lodge and make good variable-length hikes. Depending on your stamina and the amount of time available, hike to Lower, Middle, or Upper Emerald Pool, or take more time and visit all three.

Bryce

Given the high elevation and the fact that all of Bryce's best hikes descend from the rim, meaning a climb back up to the rim at the hike's end, it's good to start with the relatively easy 1.5-mile trek to **Queen's Garden.** This will get you off the rim and down into the hoodoos and, unless you're acclimated to the 8,000-foot elevation, give you a bit of a workout. If you need a longer hike, connect with the Navajo Loop Trail to bring the total distance to about three miles.

Grand Staircase-Escalante National Monument

The hike up Calf Creek to **Lower Calf Creek Falls** is a delectable sampler of the kinds of sights that make the slickrock canyon country of Escalante such a compelling destination. From a trailhead right off Highway 12 (15 miles northeast of Escalante), a trail follows a desert canyon past rock art, ruins of an ancient Native American village, and beaver ponds, and terminates at a delicate, 126-foot

waterfall. The 5.5-mile round-trip trail is easy enough for families.

Capitol Reef

Many of the hikes in Capitol Reef involve quite a bit of climbing to reach high viewpoints over the Fremont River and Waterpocket Fold. However, hiking **Grand Wash** is easy and scenic. Grand Wash is one of only five canyons that cut through the rock reef, with walls up to 800 feet high and narrows of just 20 feet. Pick up the trail from Highway 24, five miles south of the visitors center, where Grand Wash enters Fremont Canyon. For a view over the wash, continue on the trail and climb up to Cassidy Arch (3.5 miles round-trip), named after outlaw Butch Cassidy, once a regular in these badlands.

Canyonlands

The hike into **Horseshoe Canyon** to view the phenomenal rock art at the **Great Gallery** is a near-mystical experience for many—this remote canyon has been a sacred destination for thousands of years. The 6.5-mile trail requires negotiating a steep canyon wall, but experiencing the stunning petroglyphs in a verdant canyon is well worth the effort. The trailhead is 30 miles east of Highway 24 on gravel roads.

In Canyonlands' **Island in the Sky District,** the landscape is nearly all vertical, and hiking trails explore the rock faces and canyon walls. The **Neck Spring Trail** drops from the Island in the Sky road down to a series of springs in Taylor Canyon, a tiny oasis with songbirds and luxuriant plantlife, then loops back up the canyon wall to complete the delightful, not-too-arduous five-mile hike.

Even though the Colorado River is responsible for trenching the incredible landscapes of Canyonlands, it's often difficult to see the river in its canyon. In the **Needles District,** the **Confluence Overlook Trail** allows hikers to look down on the confluence of the Green and Colorado Rivers from 1,000-foot cliffs. This fairly easy 11-mile round-trip trail starts from the end of Big Spring Canyon Overlook Scenic Drive.

Arches

The three-mile round-trip hike to **Delicate Arch** is a fantastic experience, a moderately demanding trail up a slickrock formation to the arch and transcendent views over the Colorado River Canyon. If you'd prefer a trail without the crowds, go to **Devils Garden,** at the end of the paved parkway, and hike the 7.2-mile loop trail past eight arches and the weird formations in Fin Canyon.

ZION NATIONAL PARK

Zion is a magnificent park, with stunning, soaring scenery. The canyon's naming is credited to Isaac Behunin, who believed this spot to be a refuge from religious persecution. When Brigham Young later visited the canyon, however, he found tobacco and wine in use and declared the place "not Zion"—which some dutiful followers then began calling it!

But the story here is really just all about rocks and water. Little trickles of water, percolating through massive chunks of sandstone, have created both dramatic canyons and markedly nondesertlike habitats, enabling an incredible variety of plants to find niches here.

When you visit Zion, the first thing to catch your attention will be the sheer cliffs and great monoliths of Zion Canyon reaching high into the heavens. Energetic streams and other forces of erosion created this land of finely sculptured rock. The large park spreads across 147,000 acres and contains eight geologic formations and four major vegetation zones. Elevations range from 3,666 feet, in lower Coalpits Wash, to 8,726 feet, atop Horse Ranch Mountain.

The highlight for most visitors is Zion Canyon, which is approximately 2,400 feet deep. Zion Canyon Scenic Drive winds through the canyon along the North Fork of the Virgin River past some of the most spectacular scenery in the park. (During the spring, summer, and early fall, a shuttle bus ferries visitors along this route.) Hiking trails branch off to lofty viewpoints and narrow side canyons. Adventurous souls can continue on foot past the road's end into the eerie depths of the Virgin River Narrows in upper Zion Canyon.

© EMILY ROTH

HIGHLIGHTS

(Zion Canyon Visitors Center: Sure, it's always a good idea to drop by a park's visitors center, but this one is an especially interesting place to explore. The highlights are the outdoor exhibits, the excellent bookstore, and the stop for the shuttle bus that will ferry you up the canyon (page 37).

(Court of the Patriarchs Viewpoint: Hop off the shuttle bus to spend a few moments trying to fit all three mountains into your camera's viewfinder. The Patriarchs, along with the Great White Throne, are emblematic of Zion's massive sandstone rocks (page 41).

(Weeping Rock: It's a short hike to this wet wall full of hanging gardens and moisture-loving plants, including the striking Zion shooting star. Weeping Rock also offers insight into the park's geology in a way that's simple enough and obvious enough for even nongeologists to understand (page 41).

(Emerald Pools Trails: A little bit like the Three Bears story, there's an Emerald Pool Trail that's right for just about everyone. The trail to the lower pool is paved (though non-electric-wheelchair users may need a push), the middle pool makes a good destination for a short hike, and the trail to the upper pool will make most hikers break a sweat. All three pools are, indeed, emerald green, and the trails are lined with wildflowers (page 46).

(West Rim Trail to Angels Landing: If you want to do one vigorous day hike, this one's a classic. Be prepared for spectacular views and some tenuous footing along the way – not for acrophobes or children (page 47).

(Riverside Walk: If you're a die-hard hiker, don't count this level paved path as a hiking trail – save it for an after-dinner stroll. But for those who aren't up to steep trails, this walk along the Virgin River is a good way to see the water, the plantlife, and the soaring canyon walls. At the end of the trail you can watch hikers set off up The Narrows (page 49).

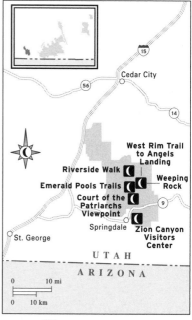

LOOK FOR **(** TO FIND RECOMMENDED SIGHTS, ACTIVITIES, DINING, AND LODGING.

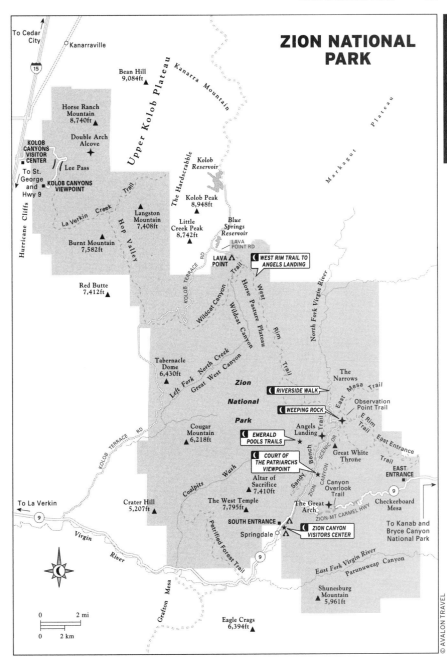

ZION NATIONAL PARK

To Cedar City

Kanarraville

Bean Hill
9,084ft

Upper Kolob Plateau

Kanarra Mountain

Horse Ranch
Mountain
8,740ft

Double Arch
Alcove

KOLOB
CANYONS
VISITOR
CENTER

Lee Pass

To St.
George
and
Hwy 9

KOLOB CANYONS
VIEWPOINT

The Hardscrabble

Kolob
Reservoir

Kolob Peak
8,948ft

Markagut Plateau

La Verkin Creek

Trail

Langston
Mountain
7,408ft

Hop Valley

Little
Creek Peak
8,742ft

Blue
Springs
Reservoir

LAVA
POINT RD

Hurricane Cliffs

Burnt Mountain
7,582ft

Red Butte
7,412ft

LAVA
POINT

☾ WEST RIM TRAIL TO
ANGELS LANDING

KOLOB TERRACE RD

Wildcat Canyon

Trail

Wildcat Canyon

Horse Pasture Plateau

West Rim Trail

North Fork Virgin River

Tabernacle
Dome
6,430ft

Left Fork North Creek

Great West Canyon

Zion

National

Park

The
Narrows

East Mesa Trail

☾ RIVERSIDE WALK

☾ WEEPING ROCK

Observation
Point Trail

E. Rim
Trail

Cougar
Mountain
6,218ft

☾ EMERALD
POOLS TRAILS

Angels
Landing

East Rim Trail

Bench Trail

East Entrance

☾ COURT OF
THE PATRIARCHS
VIEWPOINT

Great White
Throne

ZION CANYON SCENIC DR

Altar of
Sacrifice
7,410ft

EAST
ENTRANCE

KOLOB TERRACE RD

Wash

Sandy

Canyon
Overlook
Trail

Coalpits

Crater Hill
5,207ft

The West Temple
7,795ft

SOUTH ENTRANCE

The Great
Arch

ZION-MT CARMEL HWY

Checkerboard
Mesa

To La Verkin

9

Springdale

☾ ZION CANYON
VISITORS CENTER

To Kanab and
Bryce Canyon
National Park

Petrified Forest Trail

Virgin

River

9

East Fork Virgin River

Parunuweap Canyon

Grafton Mesa

Shunesburg
Mountain
5,961ft

0   2 mi

0   2 km

Eagle Crags
6,394ft

© AVALON TRAVEL

The spectacular Zion–Mt. Carmel Highway, with its switchbacks and tunnels, provides access to the canyons and high plateaus east of Zion Canyon. Two other roads enter the rugged Kolob section northwest of Zion Canyon. Kolob is a Mormon name meaning "the brightest star, next to the seat of God." The Kolob section includes wilderness areas rarely visited by humans.

Zion's grandeur extends all through the year. Even rainy days can be memorable as countless waterfalls plunge from every crevice in the cliffs above. Spring and autumn are the choice seasons for the most pleasant temperatures and the best chances of seeing wildlife and wildflowers. From about mid-October through early November, cottonwoods and other trees and plants blaze with color. Summer temperatures in the canyons can be uncomfortably hot, with highs hovering above 100°F. It's also the busiest season. In winter, nighttime temperatures drop to near freezing and weather tends to be unpredictable, with bright sunshine one day and freezing rain the next. Snow-covered slopes contrast with colorful rocks. Snow may block some of the high-country trails and the road to Lava Point, but the rest of the park is open and accessible year-round.

PLANNING YOUR TIME

Visitors short on time should drop in at the visitors center and ride the shuttle along Zion Canyon Scenic Drive, stopping for short walks on the Weeping Rock and Riverside Walk trails. If you have a full day, you can also include a hike to the Emerald Pools.

It's always worth spending a morning hiking with a park ranger. If you can hook up with a ranger hike, spend the morning of your second day going wherever the ranger leads you. In the afternoon, depending on your energy, hike to Weeping Rock (short) or Hidden Canyon (longer).

After this, it's time for longer hikes: Angels Landing is a classic for those who are in good shape and not afraid of heights. Or, if weather conditions and your own abilities dovetail favorably, the hike up the Virgin River (largely in the river) is a spectacular way to spend another full day.

For visitors with more time and a desire to leave busy Zion Canyon, the Kolob is great for longer hikes. It's also worth taking just a couple of hours to drive Kolob Canyons Road, which begins right off I-15. Motorists with more time may also want to drive Kolob Terrace Road to Lava Point for another perspective of the park; this drive is about 44 miles round-trip from the town of Virgin and has some unpaved sections.

Exploring the Park

Zion National Park (435/772-3256, www.nps .gov/zion, $25 per vehicle, $12 per person for pedestrians, bicyclists, and motorcyclists) is 43 miles northeast of St. George, 60 miles south of Cedar City, 41 miles northwest of Kanab, and 86 miles southwest of Bryce Canyon National Park. There are two entrances to the main section of the park: from Springdale you enter the south end of Zion Canyon, right near the visitors center and the Zion Canyon shuttle buses; from the east, you come in on the Zion–Mt. Carmel Highway, pass through a long tunnel, then pop into Zion Canyon a couple of miles north of the visitors center. There's a separate entrance for the Kolob Canyons area, in the park's northwest corner. A far-less-traveled part of the park is accessed by the Kolob Terrace Road, which heads north from Highway 9 at the tiny town of Virgin and goes to backcountry sites. (There's no entrance station on this road.)

Large RVs and bicycles must heed special regulations for the long tunnel on the Zion–Mt. Carmel Highway (see the sidebar *The Zion–Mt. Carmel Tunnel*).

Kolob Canyons Road, in the extreme northwestern section of the park, begins just off I-15 Exit 40 at the **Kolob Canyons Visitors Center** and climbs to an overlook for great views of the

© PAUL LEVY

The Great White Throne is a gleaming hunk of Navajo sandstone.

Finger Canyons of the Kolob; the drive is 10 miles round-trip.

◖ ZION CANYON VISITORS CENTER

The park's sprawling visitors center (8 A.M.–7 P.M. daily in summer, 8 A.M.–6 P.M. daily in spring and fall, 8 A.M.–5 P.M. daily in winter), between Watchman and South Campgrounds, is a hub of activity. The plaza outside the building features several interpretive plaques, including some pointing out environmentally sensitive design features of the visitors center. Inside, a large area is devoted to backcountry information; staff members can answer your questions about various trails, give you updates on the weather forecast, and help you arrange a shuttle to remote trailheads.

The busiest part of the visitors center is its bookstore, which is stocked with an excellent selection of books covering natural history, human history, and regional travel. Topographic and geologic maps, posters, slides, postcards, and film are sold here, too.

The best way by far to get a feel for Zion's impressive geology and variety of habitats is to take a hike with a park ranger. Many nature programs and hikes are offered from late March to November; check the posted schedule. From Memorial Day to Labor Day, children's programs are held at Zion Nature Center near South Campground; ask at the visitors center for details. A Backcountry Shuttle Board allows hikers to coordinate transportation between trailheads.

TOURS

With the exception of ranger-led hikes, Zion Canyon Field Institute classes, the horseback rides from Zion Lodge, and the running commentary from the more loquacious shuttle bus drivers, Zion is a do-it-yourself park. Outfitters are not permitted to lead trips within the park. If you'd like a guided tour outside park boundaries, there are several outfitters in Springdale (see *Springdale and Vicinity*) that lead biking, canyoneering, and climbing trips.

The **Zion Canyon Field Institute** (435/772-3264, www.zionpark.org) is authorized to run

ZION NATURAL HISTORY

GEOLOGY

Faulting has broken the Colorado Plateau into a series of smaller plateaus. At Zion you are on the Kolob Terrace of the Markagunt Plateau, whose rock layers are younger than those of the Kaibab Plateau at the Grand Canyon National Park and older than those exposed on the Paunsaugunt Plateau at Bryce Canyon National Park.

The rock layers at Zion began as sediments of oceans, rivers, lakes, or sand dunes deposited 65-240 million years ago. The soaring Navajo sandstone cliffs that form such distinctive features as the Great White Throne and the Three Patriarchs were originally immense sand dunes. Look for the slanting lines in these rock walls, which result from shifting winds as the sand dunes formed. Calcium carbonate in the sand piles acted as a glue to turn the dunes into rock, and it's also responsible for the white color of many of the rocks. The reddish rocks are also Navajo sandstone, but they've been stained by iron oxides – essentially rust.

Kayenta shale is the other main rock you'll see in Zion. For an up-close look, check out the streambed at Middle Emerald Pool. The rippled gray rock is Kayenta shale. This shale, found beneath the Navajo sandstone, is much less permeable than the sandstone. Water can easily trickle through the relatively porous sandstone, but when it hits the impermeable Kayenta shale, it runs along the top surface of the rock and seeps out on the side of the nearest rock face. Weeping Rock, with its lush cliffside springs, is a good place to see the junction between Navajo sandstone and Kayenta shale.

A gradual uplift of the Colorado Plateau, which continues today, has caused the formerly lazy rivers on its surface to pick up speed and knife through the rock layers. You

© EMILY ROTH

Sandstone walls rise precipitously from the valley floor.

can really appreciate these erosive powers during flash floods, when the North Fork of the Virgin River or other streams roar through their canyons. Erosion of some of the Virgin River's tributaries couldn't keep up with the main channel, and they were left as "hanging valleys" on the canyon walls. A good example is Hidden Canyon, which is reached by a steep trail up from Zion Canyon.

Although some erosive forces, like flash floods, are dramatic, the subtle freezing and thawing of water and the slow action of tree roots are responsible for most of the changes in the landscape. Water seeps into the Navajo sandstone, accumulating especially in the long, vertical cracks in the cliffs. The dramatic temperature changes, especially in the spring and fall, cause regular freezing and thawing, slowly enlarging the cracks and setting the stage for more dramatic rock falls. Erosion and rock fall continue to shape Zion Canyon. In 1995 a huge rockslide blocked the Zion Canyon Scenic Drive and left hundreds of people trapped at the lodge for several days until crews were able to clear a path.

FLORA AND FAUNA

Many different plant and animal communities live in the rugged terrain of deep canyons and high plateaus. Because the park lies near the meeting place of the Colorado Plateau, the Great Basin, and the Mojave Desert, species representative of all three regions can be found here.

Only desert plants can endure the long, dry spells and high temperatures found at Zion's lower elevations; they include cacti (prickly pear, cholla, and hedgehog), blackbrush, creosote bush, honey mesquite, and purple sage. Cacti and yucca are common throughout the park. Pygmy forests of piñon pine, Utah juniper, live oak, mountain mahogany, and the fragrant cliffrose grow between about 3,900 and 5,600 feet.

Once you get above the canyon floor, Zion's plants are not so different from what you'd find in the Pacific Northwest. Trees such as ponderosa pine and Douglas fir can thrive here thanks to the moisture they draw from the Navajo sandstone. White fir and aspen are also common on high, cool plateaus. Permanent springs and streams support a profusion of greenery such as cottonwood, box elder, willow, red birch, horsetail, and ferns. Watch out for poison ivy in moist, shady areas.

Colorful wildflowers pop out of the ground – indeed even out of the rocks – at all elevations from spring through autumn. In early spring, look for the Zion shooting star, a plant in the primrose family found only in Zion. Here, its nodding pink flowers are easily spotted along the Emerald Pools trails and at Weeping Rock. You're also likely to see desert phlox, a low plant covered with pink flowers, and, by mid-May, golden columbine.

Mule deer are common throughout the park. Also common is the bank beaver, which lives along the banks of the Virgin River rather than in log lodges, which would be too frequently swept away by flash floods. (Even though these beavers don't build log lodges, they still gnaw like crazy on trees – look near the base of riverside trees near Zion Lodge for their work.) Other wildlife includes elk, mountain lion, bobcat, black bear, bighorn sheep (reintroduced), coyote, gray fox, porcupine, ringtail cat, black-tailed jackrabbit, rock squirrel, cliff chipmunk, beaver, and many species of mice and bats.

Birders have spotted more than 270 species in and near the park, but most common are red-tailed hawks, turkey vultures, quail, mallard, great horned owls, hairy woodpeckers, ravens, scrub jays, black-headed grosbeaks, blue-gray gnatcatchers, canyon wrens, Virginia's warblers, white-throated swifts, and broad-tailed hummingbirds. Zion's high cliffs are good places to look for peregrine falcons; try spotting them from the cliffside at Angels Landing trail.

Hikers and campers will undoubtedly see northern sagebrush lizards, and hikers should watch for Western rattlesnakes, although these relatively rare reptiles are unlikely to attack unless provoked.

educational programs in the park. These programs range from animal tracking to photography to archaeology.

ZION NATURE CENTER

At the northern end of South Campground, this recently refurbished building houses programs for kids, including Junior Ranger activities for ages 6–12. Morning-long outdoor activities for kids run 9–11:30 A.M. daily Memorial Day through Labor Day (arrive 30 minutes early to register). The entire family can participate in afternoon activities, 1:30–3 P.M. daily Memorial Day through Labor Day. Programs focus on natural-history topics such as insects and bats in the park.

ZION CANYON SHUTTLE

By the late 1990s, visitors to Zion remembered the traffic nearly as vividly as they remembered the Great White Throne; throughout much of the summer, the canyon road was simply a parking lot for enormous RVs. To relieve the congestion, the National Park Service has instituted an April–October **shuttle-bus service** through the canyon.

There are actually two separate bus lines: One line travels between Springdale and the park entrance, stopping within a short walk of every Springdale motel and near several large visitor parking lots; the other bus line starts just inside the park entrance at the visitors center and runs the length of Zion Canyon Road, stopping at scenic overlooks, trailheads, and Zion Lodge. Lodge guests may obtain a pass authorizing them to drive to the lodge, but in general, private vehicles are no longer allowed to drive up Zion Canyon.

This is less of a pain than it might seem. It's still fine to drive to the campgrounds; in fact, the road between the park entrance and the Zion-Mt. Carmel Highway junction is open to all vehicles. Buses run frequently, so there's rarely much of a wait, and most of the bus drivers are friendly and well-informed, offering an engaging commentary on the sights that they pass (even pointing out rock climbers on the canyon walls).

If you get to Zion before 10 A.M. or after 3 P.M., there may be parking spaces available in the visitors-center lot. Midday visitors should just park in Springdale (at your motel or in a public lot) and catch a shuttle bus to the park entrance.

Riding the bus is free; its cost of operation is included in the park admission fee. Buses run as often as every six minutes 5:30 A.M.-11 P.M. (less frequently early in the morning and in the

oasis at the base of Zion Canyon

evening). No pets are allowed on the buses. November–March, private vehicles are allowed on all roads, and the buses are out of service.

Zion Canyon Scenic Drive is a six-mile road that follows the North Fork of the Virgin River upstream. Impressive natural formations along the way include the Three Patriarchs, Mountain of the Sun, Lady Mountain, Great White Throne, Angels Landing, and Weeping Rock. The bus stops at eight points of interest along the way; you can get on and off the bus as often as you wish at these stops. The road ends at Temple of Sinawava and the beginning of the Riverside Walk Trail.

MUSEUM OF HUMAN HISTORY

The old park visitors center has been retooled as a museum of southern Utah's cultural history, with a schmaltzy film introducing the park and fairly bare-bones exhibits focusing on Native American and Mormon history. The museum is open 8 A.M.–7 P.M. daily in summer, 10 A.M.–6 P.M. daily in spring and fall, 10 A.M.–5 P.M. daily in winter. It's at the first shuttle stop after the visitors center. This is a good place to visit when you're too tired to hike any farther, or if the weather forces you to seek shelter.

ZION CANYON

During the busy spring, summer, and fall seasons, you'll be traveling up and down Zion Canyon in a shuttle bus. Most visitors find this to be an easy and enjoyable way to visit the following sites.

◖ Court of the Patriarchs Viewpoint

A short trail from the parking area leads to the viewpoint. The Patriarchs, a trio of peaks to the west, overlook Birch Creek; they are (from left to right) Abraham, Isaac, and Jacob. Mount Moroni, the reddish peak on the far right, partly blocks the view of Jacob. Although the official viewpoint is a beautiful place to relax and enjoy the view, you'll get an even better view if you cross the road and head about half a mile up Sand Bench Trail.

Zion Lodge

Rustic Zion Lodge, with its big front lawn, spacious lobby (free but incredibly slow Internet access here), snack bar, restaurant, and restrooms, is a natural stop for most park visitors. You don't need to be a guest at the lodge to enjoy the ambiance of its public areas.

Cross the road from the lodge to catch the Emerald Pools trails, or walk a half mile north from the Zion Lodge shuttle stop to reach the Grotto.

The Grotto

The Grotto is a popular place for a picnic.

From here, a trail leads back to the lodge, and, across the road, the Kayenta Trail links up with the Emerald Pools trails.

Visible from several points along Zion Canyon Drive is the **Great White Throne.** Topping out at 6,744 feet, this bulky chunk of Navajo sandstone has become, along with the Three Patriarchs, emblematic of the park. Ride the shuttle in the evening to watch the rock change color as the setting sun lights it up.

◖ Weeping Rock

Several trails, including the short and easy Weeping Rock Trail, start here. Weeping Rock is home

NAVAJO SANDSTONE

Take a look anywhere along Zion Canyon, and you'll see 1,600-2,200-foot cliffs of Navajo sandstone. The big walls of Zion were formed from sand dunes deposited during a hot, dry period about 200 million years ago. Shifting winds blew the sand from one direction, then another – a careful inspection of the sandstone layer reveals the diagonal lines resulting from this "cross-bedding." Recent studies by researchers at the University of Nebraska-Lincoln, printed in *Nature* magazine, conclude that the vast dunes of southern Utah were formed when the landmass on which they sit was about 15 degrees north of the equator, about the same location as today's Honduras. The shift patterns apparent in the sandstone – the slanting striations easily seen in cliff-faces – were caused in part by intense monsoon rains, which served to compact and move the dunes each rainy season.

Eventually, a shallow sea washed over the dunes. Lapping waves left shells behind, and as the shells dissolved, their lime seeped down into the sand and cemented it into sandstone. After the Colorado Plateau lifted, rivers cut deeply through the sandstone layer. The formation's lower layers are stained red from iron oxides.

to hanging gardens and many moisture-loving plants, including the striking Zion shooting star. The rock "weeps" because this is a junction between porous Navajo sandstone and denser Kayenta shale. Water trickles down through the sandstone, and when it can't penetrate the shale, it moves laterally to the face of the cliff.

While you're at Weeping Rock, scan the cliffs for remains of cables and rigging that were used to lower timber from the top of the rim down to the canyon floor. During the early 1900s, this wood was used to build pioneer settlements in the area.

Big Bend

Look up! This is where you're likely to see rock climbers on the towering walls. Because outfitters aren't allowed to bring groups into the park, these climbers presumably are quite experienced and know what they're doing up there.

Temple of Sinawava

The last shuttle stop is at this canyon, where 2,000-foot-tall rock walls reach up from the sides of the Virgin River. There's not really enough room for the road to continue farther up the canyon, but it's plenty spacious for a fine paved walking path. The Riverside Walk heads a mile upstream to the Virgin Narrows, a place where the canyon becomes too narrow for even a sidewalk to squeeze through. You may see people hiking up The Narrows (in the river) from the end of the Riverside Walk. Don't join them unless you're properly outfitted.

EAST OF ZION CANYON

The east section of the park is a land of sandstone slickrock, hoodoos, and narrow canyons. You can see much of the dramatic scenery along the Zion–Mt. Carmel Highway (Highway 9) between the East Entrance Station and Zion Canyon. Most of this region invites exploration on your own. Try hiking a canyon or heading up a slickrock slope (the pass between Crazy Quilt and Checkerboard Mesas is one possibility). Highlights on the plateau include views of the White Cliffs and Check-

Checkerboard Mesa is a huge mound of Navajo sandstone on the east side of Zion.

© PAUL LEVY

erboard Mesa (both near the East Entrance Station) and a hike on the Canyon Overlook Trail (it begins just east of the long tunnel). Checkerboard Mesa's distinctive pattern is caused by a combination of vertical fractures and horizontal bedding planes, both accentuated by weathering. The highway's spectacular descent into Zion Canyon goes first through a 530-foot tunnel, then a 5,600-foot tunnel, followed by a series of six switchbacks to the canyon floor. Because the tunnel (completed in 1930) is narrow, any vehicle more than 7 feet, 10 inches wide, 11 feet, 4 inches high, or 40 feet long (50 feet with trailer) must go through in one-way traffic; a $15 fee (good for two passages) is charged at the tunnel to do this. Bicycles must be carried through the long tunnel on a car or truck (it's too dangerous to ride).

KOLOB CANYONS

North and west of Zion Canyon lies the remote backcountry of the Kolob. This area became a second Zion National Monument in 1937,

THE ZION-MT. CARMEL TUNNEL

If your vehicle is 7 feet 10 inches wide, 11 feet 4 inches tall, or larger, you will need a traffic-control escort through the narrow, mile-long Zion-Mt. Carmel Tunnel. Vehicles this size are too large to stay in their lane while traveling through the tunnel, which was built in the 1920s, when autos were not only small, but few and far between. Nearly all RVs, buses, trailers, fifth-wheels, and some camper shells require an "escort."

Visitors requiring an escort must pay a $15 fee per vehicle in addition to the entrance fee. Pay this fee at either park entrance before proceeding to the tunnel. The fee is good for two trips through the tunnel for the same vehicle during a seven-day period.

Though the park service persists in using the term "escort," you're really on your own through the tunnel. Park staff will stop oncoming traffic, allowing you enough time to drive down the middle of the tunnel, but you do not follow an escort vehicle. From April 1 through late October, traffic-control staff are present at the tunnel 8 A.M.-8 P.M. daily. During the winter season, oversized vehicle passage must be arranged at the entrance stations, Zion Canyon Visitors Center, Zion Lodge, or by phoning 435/772-3256. Bicycles and pedestrians are not allowed in the tunnel.

then was added to Zion National Park in 1956. You'll see all but one of the rock formations present in the park and evidence of past volcanic eruptions. Two roads lead into the Kolob. The paved five-mile Kolob Canyons Road begins at the Kolob Canyons Visitors Center just off I-15 and ends at an overlook and picnic area; it's open all year. Kolob Terrace Road is paved from the town of Virgin (15 miles west on Highway 9 from the South Entrance Station) to the turnoff for Lava Point; snow usually blocks the way in winter.

Kolob Canyons Visitors Center

Although it is small and has just a handful of exhibits, this visitors center (435/586-9548, 8 A.M.-5 P.M. daily in spring and summer, 8 A.M.-4:30 P.M. daily in fall and winter) is a good place to stop for information on exploring the Kolob region. Hikers can learn current trail conditions and obtain the permits required for overnight trips and Zion Narrows day trips. Books, topographic and geologic maps, posters, postcards, slides, and film are sold. The visitors center and the start of Kolob Canyons Road lie just off I-15 Exit 40.

Kolob Canyons Road

This five-mile scenic drive winds past the dramatic Finger Canyons of the Kolob to Kolob Canyons Viewpoint and a picnic area at the end of the road. The road is paved and has many pullouts where you can stop to admire the scenery. The first part of the drive follows the 200-mile-long Hurricane Fault, which forms the west edge of the Markagunt Plateau. Look for the tilted rock layers deformed by friction as the plateau rose nearly one mile. **Taylor Creek Trail,** which begins two miles past the visitors center, provides a close look at the canyons (see *Taylor Creek Trail* in the *Hiking in Kolob Canyons* section).

Lee Pass, four miles beyond the visitors center, was named after John D. Lee, who was the only person ever convicted of a crime in the infamous Mountain Meadows Massacre; he's believed to have lived nearby for a short time after the 1857 massacre, in which a California-bound wagon train was attacked by an alliance of Mormons and local Native Americans. About 120 people in the wagon train were killed. Only some small children too young to tell the story were spared. The close-knit Mormon community tried to cover up the incident and hindered federal attempts to apprehend the killers. Only Lee, who was in charge of Indian affairs in southern Utah at the time, was ever brought to justice—he was later executed.

La Verkin Creek Trail begins at Lee Pass Trailhead for trips to Kolob Arch and beyond. Signs at the end of the road identify the points, buttes, mesa, and mountains. The salmon-colored Navajo sandstone cliffs glow a deep red at sunset. **Timber Creek Overlook Trail** begins from the picnic area at road's end and climbs a half mile to the overlook (elevation 6,369 feet); views encompass the Pine Valley Mountains, Zion Canyons, and distant Mt. Trumbull.

KOLOB TERRACE

The Kolob Terrace section of the park is a high plateau roughly parallel to and west of Zion Canyon. From the town of Virgin, the road runs north through ranch land and up a narrow tongue of land, with drop-offs on either side, then the land widens into a high plateau. The Hurricane Cliffs rise from the gorge to the west, and the back side of Zion Canyon's big walls are to the east. The road passes in and out of the park and terminates at Kolob Reservoir, which is not in the park but is a popular boating and fishing destination. This section of the park is much higher than Zion Canyon, so it's a good place to explore when the canyon swelters in the summertime. It's also much less crowded than the busy canyon.

Lava Point

The panorama from Lava Point (elevation 7,890 feet) takes in the Cedar Breaks area to the north, the Pink Cliffs to the northeast, Zion Canyon Narrows and tributaries to the east, the Sentinel and other monoliths of Zion Canyon to the southeast, and Mt. Trumbull on the Arizona Strip to the south. Signs help identify features. Lava Point, which sits atop a lava flow, is a good place to cool off in summer—temperatures are about 20°F cooler than in Zion Canyon. Aspen, ponderosa pine, Gambel oak, and white fir grow here. A small, primitive **campground** near the point offers sites during warmer months; no water and no fee. From Virgin, take the Kolob Terrace Road about 21 miles north to the Lava Point turnoff; the viewpoint is 1.8 miles farther on a well-marked spur road.

Kolob Reservoir

This high-country lake north of Lava Point has good fishing for rainbow trout. An unpaved boat ramp is at the south end near the dam. People sometimes camp along the shore, although there are no facilities. Most of the surrounding land is private. To reach the reservoir, continue north 3.5 miles on Kolob Terrace Road from the Lava Point turnoff. The fair-weather road can also be followed past the reservoir to the Cedar City area. Blue Springs Reservoir, near the turnoff for Lava Point, is closed to the public.

Recreation

It's easy to explore Zion National Park, with hiking trails tailored to all abilities. The simplest approach is to ride the shuttle bus up Zion Canyon and hop off for short day hikes. These hikes past lush hanging gardens or up to vertiginous viewpoints may whet your appetite for extended backpacking trips or an in-water hike up the Virgin River Narrows.

Experienced hikers can do countless off-trail routes in the canyons and plateaus surrounding Zion Canyon; rangers can suggest areas. Rappelling and other climbing skills may be needed to negotiate drops in some of the more remote canyons. Groups cannot exceed 12 hikers per trail or drainage. Overnight hikers must obtain backcountry permits from either the Zion Canyon or Kolob Canyons visitors center. The permit fees are based on group size: $10 for 1–2 people, $15 for 3–7, and $20 for 8–12. Some areas of the park—mainly those near roads and major trails—are closed to overnight use. Ask about shuttles to backcountry trailheads outside Zion Canyon at the visitors center's backcountry desk. Shuttles are also available from Zion Rock and Mountain Guides (435/772-3303) and the Zion Adventure Company (435/772-0990) in Springdale.

HIKING IN ZION CANYON

The trails in Zion Canyon provide perspectives of the park that are not available from the roads. Many of the hiking trails require long ascents but aren't too difficult at a leisurely pace. Carry water on all but the shortest walks. Descriptions of the following trails are given in order from the mouth of Zion Canyon to the Virgin River Narrows.

Pa'rus Trail

- Distance: 2 miles one-way

- Duration: less than 1 hour

- Elevation gain: 50 feet

- Effort: easy

- Trailheads: South Campground and Canyon Junction

- Shuttle stops: Visitors Center and Canyon Junction

This paved trail runs from the South Campground to the Canyon Junction shuttle-bus stop. For most of its distance, it skirts the Virgin River and makes for a nice early morning or evening stroll. Listen for the trilling song of the canyon wren, then try to spot the small bird in the bushes. The Pa'rus Trail is the only trail in the park that's open to bicycles and pets.

Watchman Trail

- Distance: 1.2 miles one-way

- Duration: 2 hours

- Elevation gain: 370 feet

- Effort: easy–moderate

- Trailhead: just north of Watchman Campground

- Shuttle stop: Visitors Center

No, this hike doesn't go to the top of 6,555-foot Watchman Peak, but it does lead to a mesa with a good view of this prominent mountain southeast of the visitors center. The hike starts off fairly unspectacularly but then gets more interesting as it gains elevation. Be sure to look

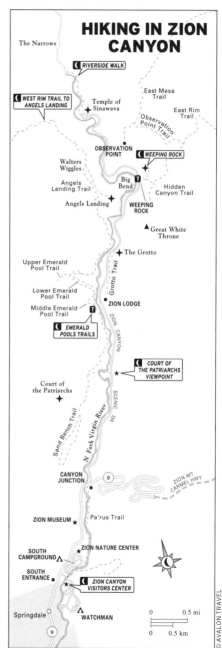

HIKING IN ZION CANYON

The Narrows

RIVERSIDE WALK

WEST RIM TRAIL TO ANGELS LANDING

Temple of Sinawava

East Mesa Trail

East Rim Trail

Observation Point Trail

OBSERVATION POINT

WEEPING ROCK

Walters Wiggles

Big Bend

Hidden Canyon Trail

Angels Landing Trail

Angels Landing

WEEPING ROCK

Great White Throne

The Grotto

Upper Emerald Pool Trail

Grotto Trail

Lower Emerald Pool Trail

Middle Emerald Pool Trail

ZION LODGE

EMERALD POOLS TRAILS

ZION CANYON

COURT OF THE PATRIARCHS VIEWPOINT

Court of the Patriarchs

SCENIC DR

Sand Bench Trail

N Fork Virgin River

CANYON JUNCTION

9

ZION-MT CARMEL HWY

ZION MUSEUM

Pa'rus Trail

SOUTH CAMPGROUND

ZION NATURE CENTER

SOUTH ENTRANCE

ZION CANYON VISITORS CENTER

Springdale

9

WATCHMAN

0   0.5 mi

0   0.5 km

© AVALON TRAVEL

© PAUL LEVY

Zion's Watchman Trail yields good views of the Watchman Peak, but doesn't lead to its summit. From the trail's end, there is also a bird's-eye view of the town of Springdale.

back over your shoulder for views of Zion Canyon's high walls.

At the mesa top, the Watchman pops into view. The short mesa-top loop trail is worth taking for its views of Springdale and its nice assortment of wildflowers, including barrel cacti.

During the middle of the day, this trail can bake in the sun. Try to hike it on a cool day, or early or late in the day. In fact, it's a good shakedown hike to do on the evening that you arrive at Zion. (As soon as the sun drops behind the canyon walls, set out—on long summer evenings, you'll have plenty of time to hike it before dark.)

Sand Bench Trail

- Distance: 1.7 miles loop

- Duration: 3 hours

- Elevation gain: 500 feet

- Effort: easy

- Trailhead: Zion Lodge

- Shuttle stops: Court of the Patriarchs or Zion Lodge

This loop trail has good views of the three Patriarchs, the Streaked Wall, and other monuments of lower Zion Canyon. During the main season, Zion Lodge organizes three-hour horseback rides on the trail. (The horses churn up dust and leave an uneven surface, though, so hikers usually prefer to go elsewhere.) The trail soon leaves the riparian forest along Birch Creek and climbs onto the dry benchland. Piñon pine, juniper, sand sage, yucca, prickly pear cactus, and other high-desert plants and animals live here. Hikers can get off the shuttle at the Court of the Patriarchs Viewpoint, walk across the scenic drive, then follow a service road to the footbridge and trailhead. A 1.2-mile trail along the river connects the trailhead with Zion Lodge. In warmer months, try to hike in early morning or late afternoon.

◖ Emerald Pools Trails

- Distance: 0.6 mile one-way to Lower Emerald Pool; 1 mile to Middle Emerald Pool; 1.4 miles to Upper Emerald Pool

- Duration: 1–3 hours

- Elevation gain: 70 feet to Lower Emerald Pool; 150 feet to Middle Emerald Pool; 350 feet to Upper Emerald Pool

- Effort: easy–moderate

- Trailhead: across footbridge from Zion Lodge

- Shuttle stop: Zion Lodge

Three spring-fed pools, small waterfalls, and views of Zion Canyon make this hike a favorite. You have a choice of three trails. The easiest is the paved trail to the Lower Pool; cross the footbridge near Zion Lodge and turn right. The Middle Pool can be reached by continuing 0.2 mile on this trail or by taking a totally different trail from the footbridge at Zion Lodge (after crossing the bridge, turn left, then right up the trail). Together these trails make a 1.8-mile round-trip loop. A third trail begins at the Grotto Picnic Area, crosses a footbridge, and turns left before continuing for 0.7 mile; the trail forks left to the Lower Pool and right to the Middle Pool. A steep 0.4-mile trail leads from the Middle Pool to Upper Emerald Pool. This magical spot has a white-sand beach and towering cliffs rising above. Don't expect to find solitude; these relatively easy trails are quite popular.

C West Rim Trail to Angels Landing

- Distance: 2.5 miles one-way

- Duration: 4 hours

- Elevation gain: 1,488 feet

- Effort: strenuous

- Trailhead: Grotto Picnic Area

- Shuttle stop: The Grotto

This strenuous trail leads to some of the best views of Zion Canyon. Start from Grotto Picnic Area (elevation 4,300 feet) and cross the footbridge, then turn right along the river. The trail climbs the slopes and enters the cool and shady depths of Refrigerator Canyon. Walter's Wiggles, a series of 21 closely spaced switchbacks, wind up to Scout Lookout and a trail junction—it's four miles round-trip and a 1,050-foot elevation gain if you decide to turn around here. Scout Lookout has fine views of Zion Canyon. The trail is paved and well graded to this point. Turn right at the junction and continue 0.5 mile to the summit of Angels Landing.

Angels Landing rises as a sheer-walled monolith 1,500 feet above the North Fork of the Virgin River. Although the trail to the summit is rough, chains provide security in the more exposed places. The climb is safe with care and good weather, but don't go if the trail is covered with snow or ice or if thunderstorms threaten. Children must be closely supervised, and people who are afraid of heights should skip this trail. Once on top, you'll see why Angels Landing got its name—the panorama makes all the effort worthwhile. It's most pleasant to do this hike during the cooler morning hours.

Energetic hikers can continue 4.8 miles on the main trail from Scout Lookout to **West Rim Viewpoint,** which overlooks the Right Fork of North Creek. This strenuous 12.8-mile round-trip hike from Grotto Picnic Area includes 3,070 feet in elevation gain. West Rim Trail continues through Zion's backcountry to Lava Point (elevation 7,890 feet), where there's a primitive campground. A car shuttle and one or more days are needed to hike the 13.3 miles (one-way) from Grotto Picnic Area. You'll have an easier hike by starting at Lava Point and hiking down to the picnic area; even so, be prepared for a *long* day hike. The trail has little or no water in some seasons.

Weeping Rock Trail

- Distance: 0.25 mile one-way

- Duration: 0.5 hour

- Elevation gain: 100 feet

- Effort: easy

- Trailhead: Weeping Rock parking area
- Shuttle stop: Weeping Rock

A favorite with visitors, this easy trail winds past lush vegetation and wildflowers to a series of cliffside springs above an overhang. Thousands of water droplets glisten in the afternoon sun. The springs emerge where water seeping through more than 2,000 feet of Navajo sandstone meets a layer of impervious shale. Signs along the way identify some of the trees and plants.

Observation Point Trail

- Distance: 3.6 miles one-way
- Duration: 6 hours
- Elevation gain: 2,150 feet
- Effort: strenuous
- Trailhead: Weeping Rock parking area
- Shuttle stop: Weeping Rock

This strenuous trail climbs to Observation Point (elevation 6,507 feet), on the edge of Zion Can-

© EMILY ROTH

Branch off from the Observation Point Trail to explore narrow Echo Canyon.

yon. Trails branch off along the way to Hidden Canyon, upper Echo Canyon, East Entrance, East Mesa, and other destinations. The first of many switchbacks begins a short way up from the trailhead at Weeping Rock parking area. You'll reach the junction for Hidden Canyon Trail after 0.8 mile. Several switchbacks later, the trail enters sinuous Echo Canyon. This incredibly narrow chasm can be explored for short distances upstream and downstream to deep pools and pour-offs. **Echo Canyon Trail** branches to the right at about the halfway point; this rough trail continues farther up the canyon and connects with trails to Cable Mountain, Deertrap Mountain, and the East Entrance Station (on Zion–Mt. Carmel Highway). The East Rim Trail then climbs slickrock slopes above Echo Canyon with many fine views. Parts of the trail are cut right into the cliffs (work was done in the 1930s by the Civilian Conservation Corps). You'll reach the rim at last after three miles of steady climbing. Then it's an easy 0.6 mile through a forest of piñon pine, juniper, Gambel oak, manzanita, sage, and some ponderosa pine to Observation Point. Impressive views take in Zion Canyon below and mountains and mesas all around. The **East Mesa Trail** turns right about 0.3 mile before Observation Point and follows the plateau northeast to a dirt road outside the park.

Hidden Canyon Trail

- Distance: 1.5 miles one-way
- Duration: 2–3 hours
- Elevation gain: 850 feet
- Effort: moderate
- Trailhead: Weeping Rock parking area
- Shuttle stop: Weeping Rock

See if you can spot the entrance to Hidden Canyon from below. Inside the narrow canyon are small sandstone caves, a little natural arch, and diverse plantlife. The high walls, rarely more than 65 feet apart, block sunlight except for a short time at midday. From the trailhead at the Weeping Rock parking area, follow the

East Rim Trail 0.8 mile up the cliff face, then turn right and go 0.7 mile on Hidden Canyon Trail to the canyon entrance. Footing can be a bit difficult in places, but chains provide handholds on the exposed sections. Steps chopped into the rock just inside Hidden Canyon help bypass some deep pools. After heavy rains and spring runoff, the creek forms a small waterfall at the canyon entrance. The canyon itself is about one mile long and mostly easy walking, although the trail fades away. Look for the arch on the right about half a mile up the canyon.

◖ Riverside Walk

- Distance: 1 mile one-way

- Duration: 1–2 hours

- Elevation gain: 57 feet

- Effort: easy

- Trailhead: Temple of Sinawava parking area

- Shuttle stop: Temple of Sinawava

This is one of the most popular hikes in the park, and except for the Pa'rus, it's the easiest.

At the end of Riverside Walk, the trail continues into the Virgin River.

© W. C. MCRAE

The nearly level paved trail begins at the end of Zion Canyon Scenic Drive and heads upstream along the Virgin River to The Narrows. Allow about two hours to fully take in the scenery—it's a good place to get a close-up view of Zion's lovely hanging gardens. Countless springs and seeps on the canyon walls support luxuriant plant growth and swamps. Most of the springs occur at the contact between the porous Navajo sandstone and the less-permeable Kayenta Formation below. The water and vegetation attract abundant wildlife; keep an eye out for birds and animals and their tracks. At trail's end, the canyon is wide enough for only the river. Hikers continuing upstream must wade and sometimes even swim (see entry for *The Narrows*). Late morning is the best time for photography. In autumn, cottonwoods and maples display bright splashes of color.

The Narrows

- Distance: 16 miles one-way

- Duration: 12 hours

- Elevation gain: 200 feet

- Effort: strenuous

- Trailheads: end of Riverside Walk or Chamberlain's Ranch

- Shuttle stop: Temple of Sinawava

Upper Zion Canyon is probably the most famous backcountry area in the park, yet it's also one of the most strenuous. There's no trail and you'll be wading much of the time in the river, which is usually knee- to chest-deep. In places, the high, fluted walls of the upper North Fork of the Virgin River are only 20 feet apart, and very little sunlight penetrates the depths. Mysterious side canyons beckon.

Hikers should be well prepared and in good condition—river hiking is more tiring than hiking over dry land. The major hazards are flash floods and hypothermia. Finding the right time to go through can be tricky: Spring runoff is too high, summer thunderstorms bring hazardous flash floods, and winter is too cold. That leaves just a part of early summer (mid-June–mid-July) and early autumn (mid-Sept.–mid-Oct.) as the best bets. You can get through the entire 16-mile (one-way) Narrows in about 12 hours, although two days is best to enjoy the beauty of the place. Children under 12 shouldn't attempt hiking the entire canyon.

Don't be tempted to wear river sandals or sneakers up The Narrows; it's easy to twist an ankle on the slippery rocks. If you have a pair of hiking boots that you don't mind drenching, they'll work, but an even better solution is available from the Zion Adventure Company (36 Lion Blvd., Springdale, 435/772-0990, www .zionadventures.com) and other Springdale outfitters. They rent specially designed river-hiking boots, along with neoprene socks, walking sticks, and, in cool weather, dry suits. They also provide a valuable orientation to hiking The Narrows. Boots, socks, and sticks rent for $17 per day, $26 for two days; with a dry suit the package costs $39 per day, $59 for two days.

Talk with rangers at the Zion Canyon Visitors Center before starting a trip; they also have a handout with useful information on planning a Narrows hike. You'll need a permit for hikes all the way through The Narrows—even on a day trip. No permit is needed if you're just going partway in and back in one day, although you must first check conditions and the weather forecast with rangers. Permits are required for overnight hikes; get them from the backcountry desk at the visitors center the day before you plan to hike or the morning of your hike (8 A.M.–noon). You will also be issued a plastic bag that's been specially designed to collect human waste. Only one-night stays are allowed. No camping is permitted below Big Springs. Group size for hiking and camping is limited to 12 along the *entire* route.

A downstream hike saves not only climbing but also the work of fighting the river currents. In fact, the length of The Narrows should only be hiked downstream. The upper trailhead is near Chamberlain's Ranch, reached by an 18-mile dirt road that turns north from Highway 9 east of the park. The lower trailhead is at the end of the Zion Canyon Scenic Drive. The elevation change is 1,280 feet.

A good half-day trip begins at the end of the Riverside Walk and follows The Narrows 1.5 miles (about two hours) upstream to Orderville Canyon, then back the same way. Orderville Canyon makes a good destination in itself; you can hike quite a ways up from Zion Canyon.

During the summer, Zion Rock and Mountain Guides (1458 Zion Park Blvd., 435/772-3303) offers a daily shuttle to Chamberlain's Ranch, leaving at 6 A.M. Make shuttle reservations between 9 A.M.–6 P.M. on the day before you want to ride. The fee is $28 per person, with a small discount if you rent gear from them. Zion Adventure Company (435/772-0990) has a similar service.

HIKING EAST OF ZION CANYON

You can't take the park shuttle bus to trailheads east of Zion Canyon, although the long-distance East Rim Trail, which starts just inside the park's eastern boundary, joins trails that lead down into Zion Canyon's Weeping Rock Trailhead.

Canyon Overlook Trail

- Distance: 0.5 mile one-way

- Duration: 1 hour

- Elevation gain: 163 feet

- Effort: easy

- Trailhead: parking area just east of the long (westernmost) tunnel on the Zion–Mt. Carmel Highway

This fun hike starts on the road east of Zion Canyon and features great views from the heights without the stiff climbs found on most other Zion trails. A booklet available at the start or at the Zion Canyon Visitors Center describes the geology, plantlife, and clues to the presence of wildlife. The trail winds in and out along the ledges of Pine Creek Canyon, which opens into a great valley. Panoramas at trail's end take in lower Zion Canyon in the distance. A sign at the viewpoint identifies Bridge Mountain, Streaked Wall, East Temple, and other features. The Great Arch of Zion—termed a "blind arch" because it's open on only one side—lies below; the arch is 580 feet high, 720 feet long, and 90 feet deep. The Canyon Overlook Trail begins across from the parking area just east of the longer (west) tunnel on the Zion–Mt. Carmel Highway.

East Rim Trail

- Distance: 10.6 miles one-way
- Duration: 6–8 hours
- Elevation loss: 1,340 feet
- Effort: strenuous
- Trailhead: east entrance of Zion National Park

This trail is best suited to a one-way trek. It's possible to do it as a long day hike but beautiful enough to encourage a slower-paced overnight trip. The great views start with a look at Checkerboard Mesa and continue as the big features of Zion Canyon come into view. The first half of the hike involves a steady climb, but then the trail tops out on a mesa and finishes by dropping into Zion Canyon. This downhill stretch is amazingly beautiful—even the slickrock that you walk on in places seems like a work of art. In the slickrock section, keep your eyes out for the rock cairns that mark the way.

The Observation Point trail joins in at nine miles; it's a steep two miles on this spur trail to Observation Point. The main trail continues down a paved path to Weeping Rock and the Zion Canyon shuttle bus.

The East Rim Trail tops out at 6,725 feet, high enough that snow may linger into the spring. Check with the staff at the visitors center's backcountry desk if you're hiking early in the season.

HIKING IN THE SOUTHWEST DESERT

During the summer, this area of the park can be extremely hot, and in the early spring, it's often too muddy to hike. These trails, which head north from Highway 9 west of the town of Springdale, are accessible without paying the park entrance fee.

Huber Wash

- Distance: 2.5 miles one-way
- Duration: 1 hour
- Elevation gain: 163 feet
- Effort: easy
- Trailhead: Highway 9, about 6 miles west of park entrance, near a power substation

From the parking area, this trail heads up Huber Wash, through painted desert and canyons. One of the highlights of hiking in this area, besides the desert scenery, is the abundance of petrified wood. There's even a logjam of petrified wood at the 2.5-mile mark, where the trail ends in a box canyon, decked with a hanging garden. If you're up to a tricky climb over the petrified logjam, you can climb up and catch the Chinle Trail, then hike five miles back to the road. The Chinle Trail emerges onto Highway 9 about 2.5 miles east of the Huber Wash Trailhead.

This is the ideal autumn hike. Even then, it'll be quite warm. Remember to bring plenty of water.

Coalpits Wash

- Distance: 1.6 miles one-way
- Duration: 2 hours
- Elevation gain: 100 feet
- Effort: easy
- Trailhead: Highway 9, about 7.3 miles west of park entrance
- Directions: The trailhead parking area may not be marked. It's between Rockville and Virgin, almost directly across Highway 9 from the turnoff to Grafton.

At 3,666 feet, the Coalpits Wash Trailhead is the lowest spot in Zion. This low elevation makes it an ideal winter hike, and it's also the best place to look for early spring wildflowers, including mariposa lilies, purple sagebrush, and pale evening primrose. (Birders also like this shrubby area.) If you have the opportunity to take a ranger-led tour up this wash, take it—you'll likely be introduced to many new plants.

The stream in this wash carries water for much of the year. After about a mile and a half, Coalpits joins Scroggins Wash. Though most hikers turn around at this point, it's possible to keep going up the ever-narrowing wash (the Chinle Trail joins in at 3.75 miles) and turn this into a good cool-season backpacking trip.

HIKING IN KOLOB CANYONS
Taylor Creek Trail

- Distance: 2.5 miles one-way

- Duration: 4 hours

- Elevation gain: 450 feet

- Effort: easy–moderate

- Trailhead: 2 miles east of Kolob Canyons Visitors Center, left side of road

This is an excellent day hike from Kolob Canyons Road heads upstream into the canyon of the Middle Fork of Taylor Creek. Double Arch Alcove is 2.7 miles from the trailhead; a dry fall 0.2 mile farther blocks the way (water flows over it during spring runoff and after rains). A giant rockfall occurred here in June 1990. From this trail you can also explore the North Fork of Taylor Creek. A separate trail along the **South Fork of Taylor Creek** leaves the drive at a bend 3.1 miles from the visitors center, then goes 1.2 miles upstream beneath steep canyon walls.

La Verkin Creek Trail to Kolob Arch

- Distance: 7 miles one-way

- Duration: 8 hours

- Elevation gain: 700 feet (drop)

- Effort: strenuous

- Trailhead: Lee Pass

Kolob Arch vies with Landscape Arch in Arches National Park as the world's longest natural rock span. Differences in measurement techniques have resulted in a controversy regarding which is longer: Kolob Arch's span has been measured variously at 292–310 feet, while Landscape Arch's measures at 291–306 feet. Kolob probably takes the prize because its 310-foot measurement was done using an accurate electronic method. Kolob's height is 330 feet and its vertical thickness is 80 feet. The arch makes a fine destination for a backpacking trip. Spring and autumn are the best seasons to go; summer temperatures rise into the 90s and winter snows make the trails hard to follow.

You have a choice of two moderately difficult trails. La Verkin Creek Trail begins at Lee Pass (elevation 6,080 feet) on Kolob Canyons Scenic Drive, four miles beyond the visitors center. The trail drops into Timber Creek (intermittent flow), crosses over hills to La Verkin Creek (flows year-round; some springs, too), then turns up side canyons to the arch. The 14-mile round-trip can be done as a long day-trip, but you'll enjoy the best lighting for photos at the arch if you camp in the area and see it the following morning. Carry plenty of water for the return trip; the 800-foot climb to the trailhead can be hot and tiring.

HIKING FROM KOLOB TERRACE ROAD

From the town of Virgin, Kolob Terrace Road runs north and passes several trailheads, including the Subway, a popular canyoneering spot, and a couple of great trails at Lava Point. These trails are far less traveled than those in Zion Canyon, and at about 7,000 feet, they stay fairly cool in the summer.

Snow blocks the access road to Lava Point for much of the year; the usual season is May or June through early November. Check road conditions with the Zion Canyon or Kolob Canyons Visitors Centers. From the South Entrance Station in Zion Canyon, drive west 15 miles on Highway 9 to Virgin, turn north 21 miles on Kolob Terrace Road (signed Kolob Reservoir), then turn right 1.8 miles to Lava Point.

The Subway

- Distance: 4.5 miles one-way
- Duration: 7 hours
- Elevation change: 2,000 feet
- Effort: strenuous
- Trailhead: Left Fork or Wildcat Canyon

A special semitechnical canyoneering hike for strong swimmers is the **Left Fork of North Creek,** a.k.a. "The Subway." This challenging day hike involves, at the very least, lots of route-finding, many stream crossings, and some rope work. Obviously, the Left Fork is not for everyone.

Like The Narrows, the Left Fork can be hiked either partway up, then back down (starting and ending at the Left Fork Trailhead) or, with a shuttle, from an upper trailhead at Wildcat Canyon downstream to the Left Fork Trailhead. The "top-to-bottom" route requires rappelling skills and at least 60 feet of climbing rope or webbing. It also involves swimming through several deep sections of very cold water.

Even though it is in a day-use-only zone, the Park Service requires a special permit, which, unlike other Zion backcountry permits, is available ahead of time through a somewhat convoluted lottery process. Prospective hikers should visit the park's website, www.nps.gov/zion, click on the "Backcountry Information" link, then click on "Reservations and Permits," followed by "Subway and Mystery Canyon Reservations." From there you will be introduced to the complicated lottery system of applying for a permit to hike the Subway. Lotteries are run monthly for hiking dates several months in the future. Each lottery entry costs $5, and each individual hiker can apply only once per month.

If you're planning this hike at the last minute, try calling 435/772-0170 to see if there are any openings. The Left Fork Trailhead is on Kolob Terrace Road 8.1 miles north of Virgin.

© PAUL LEVY

At the end of the Northgate Peaks Trail, in the Kolob Terrace, hikers can see the backside of Zion Canyon.

Hop Valley Trail to Kolob Arch

- Distance: 7 miles one-way
- Duration: 8 hours
- Elevation change: 1,050 feet
- Effort: strenuous
- Trailhead: Hop Valley Trailhead, 13 miles north of Virgin off the Kolob Terrace Road

Although most hikers reach Kolob Arch via the La Verkin Creek Trail, you can also hike to this scenic arch on the Hop Valley Trail from Kolob Terrace Road. The Hop Valley Trail is seven miles one-way to Kolob Arch with an elevation drop of 1,050 feet; water is available in Hop Valley and La Verkin Creek. You may have to do some wading in the creek, and the trail crosses private land (don't camp there).

Northgate Peaks Trail

- Distance: 2 miles one-way
- Duration: 2 hours
- Elevation change: 50 feet
- Effort: easy
- Trailhead: Wildcat Canyon Trailhead (southern end), 16 miles north of Virgin off Kolob Terrace Road

Most of the trails in this remote area of the park are long and challenging. Northgate Peaks is the exception: an easy family hike along a sandy trail. Hike out from the southern Wildcat Canyon Trailhead and pass the turnoff to the Hop Valley Trail; about 0.1 mile farther, turn right (south) onto the Northgate Peaks Trail. The trail passes through a pine-strewn meadow to a trail's end overlook of the Great West Canyon, surrounded by highly textured sandstone domes. Wildflowers, including the strikingly pretty shooting stars, are abundant near the end of the trail. This is also a good place to look for raptors.

West Rim Trail

- Distance: 13.3 miles one-way
- Duration: 8 hours or overnight
- Elevation change: 3,600 feet
- Effort: strenuous
- Trailhead: Lava Point Trailhead

The West Rim Trail goes southeast to Zion Canyon, 13.3 miles one-way with an elevation drop of 3,600 feet (3,000 of them in the last six miles). This is the western end of the same trail that takes hikers from Zion Canyon to Angels Landing. Water can normally be found along the way at Sawmill, Potato Hollow, and Cabin Springs.

From its start on the edge of the Kolob Plateau to its end in Zion Canyon, the West Rim Trail passes through a wide range of ecosystems, including sandstone domes and an unexpected pond at Potato Hollow, and many great views. The trail is most often done as a two-day backpacking trip, which gives hikers time to explore and enjoy the area.

You can also reach the Lava Point Trailhead by hiking the one-mile **Barney's Trail** from Site 2 in Lava Point Campground.

Wildcat Canyon Trail

- Distance: 5 miles one-way
- Duration: 5 hours
- Elevation change: 450 feet
- Effort: moderate
- Trailhead: Lava Point Trailhead

The Wildcat Canyon Trail heads southwest from Lava Point to a trailhead on Kolob Terrace Road (16 miles north of Virgin), so if it's possible to arrange a shuttle, you can do this as a one-way hike in about three hours. The trail, which travels across slickrock, through forest, and past cliffs, has views of the Left Fork North Creek drainage but lacks a reliable water source. You can continue north and west toward Kolob Arch by taking the four-mile **Connector Trail** to **Hop Valley Trail.**

You can also reach the Lava Point Trailhead by hiking the one-mile **Barney's Trail** from Site 2 in Lava Point campground.

© PAUL LEVY

Horse and mule rides leave from Zion Lodge and travel along the Sand Bench Trail.

BIKING

One of the fringe benefits of the Zion Canyon shuttle bus is the great bicycling that's resulted from the lack of automobile traffic. It used to be way too scary to bike along the narrow, traffic-choked Zion Canyon Scenic Drive, but now it's a joy.

On the stretch of road where cars are permitted—between the visitors center and Canyon Junction (where the Zion–Mt. Carmel road meets Zion Canyon Scenic Drive)—the two-mile, paved Pa'rus Trail is open to bikers as well as pedestrians, and makes for easy, stress-free pedaling.

If you decide you've had enough cycling, every shuttle bus has a rack that can hold two bicycles. Bike parking is plentiful at the visitors center, Zion Lodge, and most trailheads.

Outside the Zion Canyon area, Kolob Terrace Road is a good place to stretch your legs; it's 22 miles to Kolob Reservoir.

There's really no place to mountain bike within the park, but there are good mountain-biking spots, including places to practice slickrock riding, just outside the park boundaries. It's best to stop by one of the local bike shops for advice and a map of your chosen destination.

Bike rentals and maps are available in Springdale at Bike Zion (1458 Zion Park Blvd., 435/772-3303, www.bikingzion.com) and at Zion Cycles (868 Zion Park Blvd., 435/772-0400).

HORSEBACK RIDING

Trail rides on horses and mules leave from the corral near Zion Lodge (435/772-3810) and head down the Virgin River. A one-hour trip ($30) goes to the Court of the Patriarchs, and a half-day ride ($65) follows the Sand Bench Trail. Riders must be at least seven years old for the short ride and 10 for the half-day ride, and weigh no more than 220 pounds.

CLIMBING

Rock climbers come to scale the high Navajo sandstone cliffs; after Yosemite, Zion is the nation's most popular big-wall climbing area. However, Zion's sandstone is far more fragile than Yosemite's granite, and it has a tendency to crumble and flake, especially when wet. Beginners should avoid these walls—experience with crack climbing is a must.

For route descriptions, pick up a copy of *Desert Rock*, by Eric Bjørnstad, or *Rock Climbing Utah*, by Stewart M. Green. Both books are sold at the visitors center bookstore. The backcountry desk in the visitors center also has a notebook full of route descriptions supplied by past climbers. Check here to make sure your climbing area is open—some are closed to protect nesting peregrine falcons—and remember to bring a pair of binoculars to scout climbing routes from the canyon floor.

If you aren't prepared to tackle the 2,000-foot-high canyon walls, you may want to check out a couple of bouldering sites, both quite close to the south entrance of the park. One huge boulder is 40 yards west of the park entrance; the other is a large slab with a crack, located 0.5 mile north of the entrance.

During the summer, it can be intensely hot on unshaded walls. The best months for climbing are March–May and September–early November.

If watching the climbers at Zion gives you a hankering to scale a wall, the Zion Adventure Company in Springdale (36 Lion Blvd., 435/772-1001, www.zionadventures.com) runs half-day and day-long climbing clinics for beginning and experienced climbers. Similar offerings are provided by Zion Rock and Mountain Guides (1458 Zion Park Blvd., 435/772-3303, www.zionrockguides.com). Because no outfitters are permitted to operate inside the park, these classes are held near St. George.

OUTFITTERS

Several good outfitters have shops in Springdale, just outside the park. Here you can buy all manner of gear and outdoor clothing. You can also pick up canyoneering skills, take a guided mountain-bike ride (outside the park, of course), or learn to climb big sandstone walls.

Campers who left that crucial piece of equipment at home should visit **Zion Outdoors** (868 Zion Park Blvd., 435/772-0630), as should anybody who needs to spruce up their wardrobe with some stylish outdoor clothing.

Zion Cycles (868 Zion Park Blvd., 435/772-0400, www.zioncycles.com) and **Bike Zion** (1458 Zion Park Blvd., 435/772-3303, www.bikingzion.com) both offer rentals of all sorts of bikes, from kids' bikes ($10 for a half-day rental) to road bikes ($25 half day) to full-suspension mountain bikes ($35 half day).

Canyoneering supplies, including gear to hike The Narrows or the Subway, are available from Zion Adventure Company (36 Lion Blvd., 435/772-1001, www.zionadventures.com) and Zion Rock and Mountain Guides (1458 Zion Park Blvd., 435/772-3303, www.zionrockguides.com).

Accommodations

Within the park, lodging is limited to Zion Lodge and the two park campgrounds. Look to Springdale or the east entrance of the park for more options.

ZION LODGE

This rustic lodge (435/772-7700 or 888/297-2757, www.zionlodge.com) sits in the heart of Zion Canyon, three miles up Zion Canyon Scenic Drive. Zion Lodge provides the only accommodations and food options within the park. It's open year-round; reservations for rooms can be made up to 13 months in advance. During high season, all rooms are booked months in advance. Double rooms begin at $151; cute cabins are $161.

The lodge restaurant offers a southwestern and Mexican-influenced menu daily for breakfast, lunch, and dinner (435/772-7760, dinner reservations required, most dinner entrées around $15). A snack bar serves decent fast food, including salads (closes in winter).

The lodge also has evening programs, a post office (open Mon.–Sat.), and a gift shop.

CAMPGROUNDS
Zion Canyon Campgrounds

Campgrounds in the park often fill up on Easter and other major holidays. During the summer, they're often full by early afternoon, so it's best to arrive early in the day. The **South** and **Watchman Campgrounds,** both just inside the south entrance, have sites for $16 with water but no showers. Watchman has some sites with electrical hookups for $18; prime riverside spots are $20. Reservations can be made in advance for some sites at Watchman Campground (877/444-6777, www.recreation.gov). One of the campgrounds stays open in winter.

South Campground is a bit smaller than Watchman, with a few choice walk-in sites and easy access to the Pa'rus Trail, but tenters shouldn't eschew Watchman; loops C and D are for tents, and these sites are more spacious than those at South.

Some of the pioneers' fruit trees in the campgrounds are still producing; you're free to pick your own. Private campgrounds lie just outside the park in Springdale (see *Springdale and Vicinity*) and just east of the park's east entrance.

It should be noted that camping in Zion's two big campgrounds can be pretty laid back; indeed, it can be luxurious. Campers have easy access, via the park's free shuttles, to good restaurants in Springdale. It's also simple enough to find showers in Springdale; just outside the park, the privately owned Zion Canyon Campground has showers ($4).

Other Campgrounds

Up the Kolob Terrace Road, find **Lava Point Campground,** a small, primitive campground that offers sites during warmer months; no water and no fee. The **Red Ledge Campground** in Kanarraville (435/586-9150) is the closest commercial campground to the Kolob Canyons area (there's no campground in this area of the park); go two miles north on I-15, take Exit 42, and continue 4.5 miles into downtown Kanarraville. The campground is open year-round with a tent and RV sites, cabins, a store, showers, and a laundry room. The tiny agricultural community here was named after a local Paiute chief. A low ridge south of town marks the southern limit of prehistoric Lake Bonneville. Hikers can explore trails in Spring and Kanarra Canyons within the **Spring Canyon Wilderness Study Area** just east of town.

Springdale and Vicinity

Mormons settled this tiny town (pop. 493) in 1862, but with its location just outside the park's south entrance, Springdale is geared more toward serving park visitors than the typical Mormon settlement. Its many high-quality motels and B&Bs, as well as frequent shuttle-bus service to the park's entrance, make Springdale an appealing base for a visit to Zion. Farther down the road toward Hurricane are the little towns of Rockville and Virgin, both of which are quickly becoming B&B suburbs of Springdale.

ZION CANYON GIANT SCREEN THEATRE

You *know* you should be in the park itself, not looking at movies of it on a six-story-tall screen (145 Zion Park Blvd., 435/772-2400 or 888/256-3456, films start on the hour, 11 A.M.–8 P.M. summer, winter hours vary, $8 adults, $5.50 children under 12). But, assuming you've been out hiking all day and need a little rest, come here to meet the Anasazi, watch Spanish explorers seek golden treasure, witness the hardships of pioneer settlers, enter remote slot canyons, and join rock-climbers hundreds of feet up vertical cliff faces. The feature program is *Treasure of the Gods,* but there's nearly always a big-screen version of a Hollywood movie showing as well (don't expect to see current hits; all the movies are a few years old).

O.C. TANNER AMPHITHEATER

The summer highlight at this open-air theater (435/652-7994) is a series of musical concerts held on Saturday evenings throughout the summer. The amphitheater is just outside the park entrance.

ACCOMMODATIONS

The quality of lodgings in the area just outside Zion National Park is quite high. Springdale offers a wide range of accommodations. Just down the road, Rockville has several B&Bs. The next town west of the park, Hurricane, has all the standard chain motels.

$50-75

The least expensive lodgings in Springdale are the motel rooms at the **Terrace Brook Lodge** (990 Zion Park Blvd., 435/772-3237, terracebrooklodge.com, $60 and up) and the **El Rio Lodge** (995 Zion Park Blvd., 888/772-3205 or 435/772-3205, www.elriolodge.com, $52 and up), which offers rooms in a green, shady location with a sundeck. Both are about a mile from the park entrance. If you want to be closer to the park entrance, **Zion Canyon Campground** (479 Zion Park Blvd., 435/772-3237, www.zioncanyoncampground.com, $65 and up) has motel rooms as well as tent and RV sites. The **Canyon Ranch Motel** (668 Zion Park Blvd., 435/772-3357 or 866/946-6276, www.canyonranchmotel.com, $64 and up) is another good value, with small units—some with kitchenettes—scattered around a grassy, shaded lawn.

The hosts at the **Bunkhouse at Zion B&B** (149 E. Main St., Rockville, 435/772-3393, www.bunkhouseatzion.com, $55–80) are dedicated to living sustainably, and they bring this ethic into their two-room B&B. The views are remarkable from this quiet spot in Rockville.

$75-100

The **Driftwood Lodge** (1515 Zion Park Blvd., 435/772-3262 or 800/528-1234, www.driftwoodlodgeandsuites.com, $72 and up) has a pool and a spa, and is a step up from the budget motels. Another midrange choice is the **Zion Park Motel** (865 Zion Park Blvd., 435/772-3251, www.zionparkmotel.com, $79) with clean basic rooms and a small pool.

In Springdale, **Under the Eaves B&B** (980 Zion Park Blvd., 435/772-3457, www.under-the-eaves.com, $80 and up) features homey guest rooms, two with shared bath, in a vintage home. It's also possible to pay a bit more for a gorgeous kitchenette suite. Children over seven are welcome.

Down the road in Rockville, **Rockville Rose Inn** (125 E. Main St., Rockville, 435/772-0800, www.rockvillerose.com, $75–100) has rooms in a large Victorian set back from the road.

Over $100

(**Flanigan's Inn** (428 Zion Park Blvd., 435/772-3244 or 800/765-7787, www.flanigans.com, $109 and up) is a quiet and convenient place to stay. Rooms are set back off the main drag and face onto a pretty courtyard. Up on the hill behind the inn, a labyrinth provides an opportunity to take a meditative walk in a stunning setting. An excellent restaurant, a pool, and spa services make this an inviting place to spend several days.

Probably the most elegant place to stay in Springdale is the **(** **Desert Pearl Inn** (707 Zion Park Blvd., 888/828-0898 or 435/772-8888, www.desertpearl.com, $143 and up), a very handsome lodgelike hotel perched above the Virgin River. (Some rooms have views of the river; others face the pool.) Much of the wood used for the beams and the finish moldings was salvaged from a railroad trestle made of century-old Oregon fir and redwood that once spanned the north end of the Great Salt Lake. The rooms are all large and beautifully furnished, with a modern look.

Another attractive newer motel is **Best Western Zion Park Inn** (1215 Zion Park Blvd., 435/772-3200 or 800/934-7275, www.zionparkinn.com, $115 and up), part of a complex with a good restaurant, a swimming pool, a gift shop, and some of the nicest rooms in Springdale. In addition to regular rooms, there are also various suites and kitchen units available.

Just outside the south gates to Zion, the **(Cliffrose Lodge** (281 Zion Park Blvd., 435/772-3234 or 800/243-8824, www.cliff roselodge.com, $139 and up) sits in five acres of lovely, well-landscaped gardens with riverfront access. The rooms are equally nice, and there's a pool and a laundry room. The Cliffrose is favored by many longtime Zion fans.

For a place with a bit of personality (or perhaps more accurately, with multiple personalities), try the **Novel House Inn at Zion** (73 Paradise Rd., 435/772-3650 or 800/711-8400, www.novelhouse.com, $129–149), a B&B with 10 guest rooms, each decorated with a literary theme and named after an author (including Mark Twain, Rudyard Kipling, and Louis L'Amour). All rooms have private baths and great views, and the B&B is tucked off the main drag.

Red Rock Inn (998 Zion Park Blvd., 435/772-3139, www.redrockinn.com, $112 and up) offers accommodations in newly constructed individual cabins, all with canyon views. Full-breakfast baskets are delivered to your door.

Campgrounds

The **Zion Canyon Campground** (479 Zion Park Blvd., 435/772-3237) offers cabins, new motel rooms, tent sites (no dogs allowed in tent sites), and RV sites. Though the sites are pretty close together, a few are situated right on the bank of the Virgin River. Facilities include a store, pizza parlor, game room, laundry room, and showers.

FOOD

Just outside the park entrance, near the Springdale shuttle stop, **Sol Foods** (95 Zion Park Blvd., 435/772-0277, 7 A.M.–10 P.M. daily) is a short walk from either park campground and a good place for a salad or sandwich ($6.50–9). There's also a computer with Internet access.

Mean Bean Coffee (932 Zion Park Blvd., 435/772-0654, 6:30 A.M.–afternoon daily) is the hip place to hang in the morning. Besides coffee drinks, they serve breakfast burritos and a few pastries. For a more substantial meal,

head across the way to **Oscar's Café** (948 Zion Park Blvd., 435/772-3232, $8–15, 8 A.M.–two hours after sunset daily), where you can get a good burger or a Mexican-influenced breakfast or lunch. The patio here is set back off the main road and is especially pleasant.

An old gas station has become the **(Whiptail Grill** (445 Zion Park Blvd., 435/772-0283, lunch and early dinner daily, $8–13), a casual spot serving innovative homemade food such as spaghetti squash enchiladas. There's very little seating inside, so plan to eat at the outdoor tables or take your meal to-go.

Also good, and reasonably priced, is **Zion Pizza and Noodle** (868 Zion Park Blvd., 435/772-3815), housed in an old church and serving a good selection of microbrews. The American-style menu at the **Bumbleberry Inn** (897 Zion Park Blvd., 435/772-3224, breakfast, lunch, and dinner Mon.–Sat.) includes bumbleberry pies (just ask them what a bumbleberry is!) and pancakes.

The following restaurants all offer full liquor service: The **(Spotted Dog Café** (at Flanigan's Inn, 428 Zion Park Blvd., 435/772-3244, breakfast, lunch, and dinner daily, dinner $12–24) is one of Springdale's top restaurants; it has varied Southwestern and traditional American offerings, including a surprisingly good pumpkin-seed pizza. Be sure to order a salad with (or for) your dinner—the house salad is superb. If you want to eat outside, try to get a table on the back patio, which is quieter and more intimate than the dining area out front.

The other really good place for dinner in Springdale is the **(Bit & Spur Restaurant** (1212 Zion Park Blvd., 435/772-3498, dinner nightly, $10–25, reservations recommended during busy season), a lively Mexican place with a menu that goes far beyond the usual south-of-the-border concoctions. (Keep your fingers crossed that sweet-potato tamales will be the evening's special!)

Across the street from the Bit & Spur, the **Switchback Grille** (1215 Zion Park Blvd., 435/772-3200, breakfast, lunch, and dinner daily, $14–25 dinner) offers steaks, wood-fired pizza, rotisserie chicken, and seafood in a pleasantly bland atmosphere. There's patio seating in good weather.

INFORMATION AND SERVICES

People traveling with their dogs are in a bit of a dilemma when it comes to visiting Zion. No pets are allowed on the trails (except the Pa'rus Trail) or in the shuttle buses, and it's absolutely unconscionable to leave a dog inside a car here in the warmer months. Fortunately, the **Doggy Dude Ranch** (435/772-3105, www.doggydude ranch.com) provides conscientious daytime and overnight pet care on Highway 9 in Rockville.

The **Zion Canyon Medical Clinic** (120 Lion Blvd., 435/772-3226) provides urgent-care services. The **post office** is in the center of town on Zion Park Boulevard (435/772-3950). You may also want to check out the art galleries along Zion Park Boulevard; some of them have high-quality merchandise.

St. George

Southern Utah's largest town lies between lazy bends of the Virgin River on one side and rocky hills of red sandstone on the other. Although it has gained a reputation as a retirement haven (thanks in part to its warm winter climate and its plethora of golf courses), it is not particularly appealing to most travelers. In order to appreciate St. George, it may be necessary to visit its outskirts, where Snow Canyon State Park and a couple of spas can be found.

In 1861, more than 300 Mormon families in the Salt Lake City area answered the call to go south to start the Cotton Mission, of which St. George became the center (hence the frequently used term "Dixie" to describe the area). The settlers overcame great difficulties to farm and to build an attractive city in this remote desert. Brigham Young chose the city's name to honor George A. Smith, who had served as head of the Southern (Iron) Mission during the 1850s. (The title "Saint" means simply that he was a Mormon—a Latter-Day Saint.) Visits to some of the historic sites will add to your appreciation of the city's past; ask for the *St. George Historic Walking Tour* brochure at the chamber of commerce. The warm climate, dramatic setting, and many year-round recreation opportunities have helped make St. George (pop. about 50,000) the fastest-growing city in the state.

Visitors can see the **St. George Temple** (250 East 400 South, 435/673-5181) from the outside and stop in its visitors center, or tour **Brigham Young's winter home** (67 West 200 North, 435/673-2517), but if your eye is set on Zion, you'll most likely just use St. George as a jumping-off point.

DINOSAUR TRACKWAYS

Back in the Early Jurassic, when the supercontinent of Pangaea was just beginning to break up, lakes covered this part of present-day Utah, and dinosaurs were becoming the earth's dominant vertebrates. Two sites southeast of St. George preserve dinosaur tracks from this era. Of the two, the more recently discovered site at Johnson Farm is more impressive and much easier to get to; indeed, it's been called one of the world's 10 best dinosaur track sites. The Fort Pearce site is good if you're hankering for some back-road travel and scouting dino tracks and petroglyphs in remote washes.

St. George Dinosaur Discovery Site at Johnson Farm

Tracks at the Johnson Farm site (2180 E. Riverside Dr., 435/574-3466, www.dinotrax.com, 10 A.M.–6 P.M. Mon.–Sat., $3 adults, $2 children 3–11) were discovered in 2000 by a retired optometrist. Since then, a vast number of tracks, including those of three species of theropods (meat-eating dinosaurs), and impor-

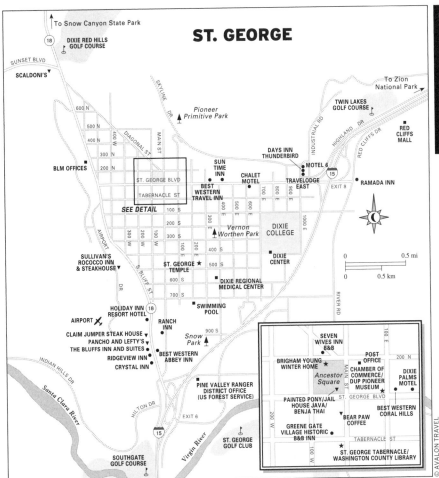

tant "trace fossils" of pond scum, plants, invertebrates, and fish have also been uncovered.

Excavation work is ongoing, but a new visitors center provides a good look at some of the most exciting finds, including a wall-sized slab of rock with footprints going to and fro. Also quite remarkable are the "swim tracks," which settled a long-standing argument over whether or not dinosaurs actually swam.

The track site is on the outskirts of St. George, about two miles south of Exit 10 from I-15.

Fort Pearce Dinosaur Tracks

A scenic back-road drive through the desert between St. George and Hurricane passes the ruins of Fort Pearce and more dinosaur tracks. Much of the road is unpaved and has rough and sandy spots, but it's usually suitable for cautious drivers in dry weather.

This group of tracks documents the passage of at least two different dinosaur species more than 200 million years ago. The well-preserved tracks, in the Moenave Formation, were made

© PAUL LEVY

The St. George Dinosaur Discovery Site at Johnson Farm is one of the best places in the world to view dinosaur footprints.

by a 20-foot-long herbivore weighing an estimated 8–10 tons and by a carnivore half as long. No remains of the dinosaurs themselves have been found here.

In 1861, ranchers arrived in Warner Valley to run cattle on the desert grasslands. Four years later, however, Indian troubles threatened to drive the settlers out. The Black Hawk War and periodic raids by Navajos made life precarious. Springs in Fort Pearce Wash—the only reliable water for many miles—proved the key to domination of the region. In December 1866, work began on a fort overlooking the springs. The stone walls stood about eight feet high and were more than 30 feet long. No roof was ever added. Much of the fort and the adjacent corral (built in 1869) have survived to the present. Local cattlemen still use the springs for their herds. Petroglyphs can be seen in various places along the wash, including a quarter mile downstream from the fort along ledges on the north side of the wash.

To reach this somewhat remote site from St. George, head south on River Road, cross the Virgin River Bridge, and turn left on 1450 South. Continue on main road and keep bearing east through several 90-degree left and right turns. Turn left (east) onto a dirt road at the Fort Pearce sign and continue 5.6 miles to a road that branches right along a small wash to the Fort Pearce parking lot. The dinosaur tracks are in a wash about two miles farther down the road from Fort Pearce; the parking area is marked by a sign.

SNOW CANYON STATE PARK

If St. George's outlet stores and chain restaurants threaten to close in on you, head a few miles north of town to the red-rock canyons, sand dunes, volcanoes, and lava flows of Snow Canyon. Walls of sandstone 50–750 feet high enclose the five-mile-long canyon. Hiking trails trace the canyon bottom and lead into the backcountry for a closer look at the geology, flora, and fauna. Common plants are barrel, cholla, and prickly pear cacti; yucca; Mormon tea; shrub live oak; cliffrose; and cottonwood. Delicate wildflowers bloom

© PAUL LEVY

Snow Canyon State Park trails are convenient to spa-goers.

mostly in the spring and autumn, following the wet seasons, but cacti and the sacred datura (see the sidebar *Datura: A Plant with a Past* in *Capitol Reef* chapter) can flower in the heat of summer.

Wildlife includes sidewinder and Great Basin rattlesnakes, Gila monsters, desert tortoises, kangaroo rats, squirrels, cottontails, kit foxes, coyotes, and mule deer. You may find some Native American rock art, arrowheads, bits of pottery, and ruins. Many of the placenames in the park honor Mormon pioneers. Snow Canyon was named for Lorenzo and Erastus Snow—not for the rare snowfalls.

Summers are too hot for comfortable hiking except in early morning. Highway 18 leads past an overlook on the rim of Snow Canyon and to the paved park road (Highway 300) that drops into the canyon and follows it to its mouth and the small town of Ivins. Snow Canyon is about 12 miles northwest of St. George. It's reached either by Highway 18—the faster way—or via Santa Clara and Ivins. Each vehicle is charged a $5 day-use fee.

GOLF

With 10 golf courses in the area, St. George enjoys a reputation as Utah's winter golf capital. Red sandstone cliffs serve as the backdrop for **Dixie Red Hills** (1250 North 645 West, 435/634-5852) on the northwest edge of town, a nine-hole, par-34 municipal course. **Green Spring Golf Course** (588 N. Green Spring Dr., 435/673-7888), just west of I-15 Washington Exit 10, has 18 holes (par 71) and a reputation as one of the finest courses in Utah.

Professionals favor the cleverly designed **Sunbrook Golf Course** (2366 Sunbrook Dr., 435/634-5866) off Dixie Downs Road, between Green Valley and Santa Clara: 27 holes, par 72. The **St. George Golf Club** (2190 South 1400 East, 435/634-5854) has a popular 18-hole, par-73 course south of town in Bloomington Hills. The **Southgate Golf Course** (1975 S. Tonaquint Dr., 435/628-0000), on the southwest edge of town, has 18 holes. The adjacent Southgate Game Improvement Center (435/674-7728) can provide golfers with computerized golf-swing analyses plus plenty of indoor practice space and lots of balls.

Entrada (2511 W. Entrada Trail, 435/674-7500) is a newer 18-hole private course that's fast on its way to becoming St. George's most respected. The Johnny Miller–designed course is northwest of St. George at beautiful Snow Canyon and incorporates natural lava flows, rolling dunes, and arroyos (dry riverbeds) into its design. The 18-hole, par-72 **Sky Mountain** (1030 North 2600 West, 435/635-7888) is northeast of St. George in nearby Hurricane.

ACCOMMODATIONS

St. George offers many places to stay and eat. Motel prices stay about the same year-round, although they may drop if business is slow in summer. Considering the popularity of this destination, prices are reasonable. Golfers should ask about golf-and-lodging packages. You'll find most lodgings along the busy I-15 business route of St. George Boulevard (Exit 8) and Bluff Street (Exit 6). As for food, you'll find almost every fast-food place known to humanity just off the interstate on St. George Boulevard.

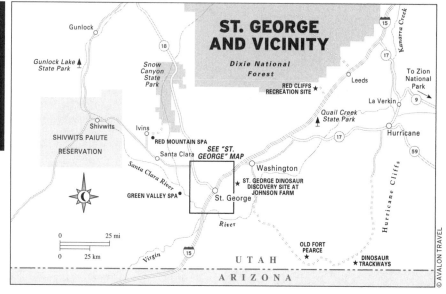

Under $50

Many of St. George's less expensive lodging choices operate at Exit 8 off I-15 or on St. George Boulevard as it heads west to downtown. Right at the freeway exchange you'll find **Motel 6** (205 North 1000 East, 435/628-7979 or 800/466-8356, $41–59), with a pool; pets are okay.

Near downtown, the **Chalet Motel** (664 E. St. George Blvd., 435/628-6272, $30–60) offers some efficiency kitchens, two three-bed rooms, and a pool.

Dixie Palms Motel (185 E. St. George Blvd., 435/673-3531, $30–50) is a classic old-fashioned courtyard motel on the main strip right downtown, with an outdoor pool and fridges and microwaves in the rooms. The **Sun Time Inn** (420 E. St. George Blvd., 435/673-6181 or 800/237-6253, $35–60, higher in winter) has kitchenettes and a pool.

Near Exit 6 off I-15, the **Ridgeview Inn** (1230 S. Bluff St., 435/628-5234 or 800/275-3494, $40–50) offers a pool and a spa.

$50-75

The **Days Inn Thunderbird** (150 North 1000 East, 435/673-6123 or 800/527-6543, $50 and up) has a pool, hot tub, sauna, fitness center, and free continental breakfast; pets are okay.

In the downtown area, the Spanish-style **Best Western Travel Inn** (316 E. St. George Blvd., 435/673-3541 or 800/528-1234, $65–83) is a relatively small motel with an outdoor pool and an indoor spa.

Leave the freeway at Exit 6 off I-15 to find another selection of motels. Most rooms at **The Bluffs Inn and Suites** (1140 S. Bluff St., 435/628-6699 or 800/832-5833, $50–90) are suites with efficiency kitchens. Facilities include a pool and a spa; pets are okay.

$75-100

Close to downtown is one of St. George's best: the **Best Western Coral Hills** (125 E. St. George Blvd., 435/673-4844 or 800/542-7733, www.coralhills.com, $80–120), a very attractive property with indoor and outdoor pools and two spas, an exercise room, and a complimentary continental breakfast.

Look for more motels at Exit 6 off I-15. The **Holiday Inn Resort Hotel & Convention**

Center (850 S. Bluff St., 435/628-4235 or 800/457-9800, www.histgeorgeutah.com, $80 and up) is a large complex with a "Holidome" complete with indoor and outdoor pools, whirlpool, recreation/fitness facilities, tennis court, and putting green. At the **Best Western Abbey Inn** (1129 S. Bluff St., 888/222-3946 or 435/652-1234, www.bwabbeyinn.com, $85–95), all rooms have microwaves and refrigerators. There's an outdoor pool, an indoor spa, recreation/fitness facilities, and a free hot breakfast. Both of these lodgings are near Exit 6 off I-15.

Just across from Brigham Young's winter home, the [(**Seven Wives Inn Bed & Breakfast** (217 North 100 West, 435/628-3737 or 800/600-3737, www.sevenwivesinn .com, $90 and up) offers rooms in two historic homes (including one that served as a safe house for polygamists after the practice was banned in the 1880s) and a cute cottage. All guest rooms have private baths and are decorated with antiques. Children and pets are wel-

come, there's an outdoor pool, and in-room massages are available.

You'll find an entire compound of pioneer-era homes at the **Greene Gate Village Historic Bed & Breakfast Inn** (76 W. Tabernacle, 435/628-6999 or 800/350-6999, www.greengatevillage .com, $89 and up). Nine beautifully restored homes offer a variety of lodging options—groups or families can rent an entire home. Many rooms come with kitchens and private baths, some with private whirlpools. There's also a pool shared by all guests. Children are welcome.

East of the Exit 8 interchange, right beside the Factory Outlet Mall, is the **Ramada Inn** (1440 E. St. George Blvd., 435/628-2828 or 800/713-9435, $75–89). Facilities include an outdoor pool and a hot tub; a complimentary continental breakfast is also included.

Over $100
The **Crystal Inn** (1450 S. Hilton Inn Dr., 435/688-7477 or 800/662-2525, www.crystal inns.com, $115) is located on a golf course and

© PAUL LEVY

Just a few miles from downtown St. George, you'll find beautiful campsites at Snow Canyon State Park.

has beautiful public areas and nicely appointed guest rooms. Facilities include a pool, a sauna, and private tennis courts.

Campgrounds

The best camping in the area is at **Snow Canyon State Park** (435/628-2255 or 800/322-3770, www.reserveamerica.com for reservations, necessary in spring). Sites are in a pretty canyon and include showers. From downtown St. George, go 12 miles north on Highway 18, then left two miles ($15 without hookups, $18 with hookups).

The other public campgrounds in the area are **Quail Creek State Park** (435/879-2378, www.stateparks.utah.gov) and the BLM's **Red Cliffs Recreation Site** (435/688-3200), both north of town off I-15 (Exit 16 when coming from the south, Exit 23 when approaching from the north). Quail Creek is on a reservoir and is a good option if you have a boat. Red Cliffs is a little more scenic and has trails.

Right in St. George, **McArthur's Temple View RV Resort** (975 S. Main, 435/673-6400 or 800/776-6410) is near the temple district and has a pool, laundry room, and showers. East of town, near Exit 8 off I-15, is **Settlers RV Park** (1333 East 100 South, 435/628-1624), with a pool and showers. The park accepts RVs only.

Spas

St. George is home to two large spa resorts and recreation centers in gorgeous natural settings. The **Green Valley Spa** (1871 W. Canyon View Dr., 435/628-8060 or 800/237-1068, www.greenvalleyspa.com, from $112 per person, double occupancy, for room only to $564 per person per night for a package with all meals and lots of treatments and activities) is a fitness, sports, health, and beauty spa with all-inclusive rates. Facilities include three pools, racquetball courts, a fully equipped gym with an array of fitness, yoga, and meditation classes as well as tennis instruction, golf privileges, plus hiking and climbing in neighboring canyons. There's also a whole catalog of beauty and rejuvenation treatments (which may be in-cluded in a package deal or tacked on at extra cost), ranging from massage, wraps, and aromatherapy to more spiritual renewals such as personal meditation guidance. Rooms flank a parklike pool and garden area. Three spa meals daily are served; they're included in the cost of most packages. Rates vary widely; summer is the least expensive time to visit.

Slightly less swanky, the **Red Mountain Spa** (202 N. Snow Canyon Rd., 800/407-3002, www.redmountainspa.com) focuses even more intently on outdoor adventure and fitness. Facilities include numerous swimming and soaking pools, a fitness center and gym, tennis courts, a salon, a spa, conference rooms, plus access to lots of hiking and biking trails. Prices, which include all meals, lodging, and use of most spa facilities and recreation, start at about $240 per person per day, double occupancy, with special deals often available online. Spa services, including massage, facials, body polishing, and aromatherapy, cost extra.

FOOD

For a major recreation and retirement center, St. George is curiously lacking in unique places to eat. Almost every chain restaurant can be found here, but don't expect a bevy of local fine-dining houses. You'll also find it bizarrely difficult to find restaurants that stay open late; even in high season, most restaurants close by 9 P.M.

The best place to head for lunch or dinner is Ancestor's Square, a trendy shopping development at the intersection of St. George Boulevard and Main Street. **◖ Painted Pony** (435/634-1700, lunch and dinner, dinners $21–31) puts Southwestern and, in some cases, Asian touches on American standards; try salmon rolls with a carrot orange sauce or, for lunch, a pulled pork sandwich with poblano aioli ($9). Downstairs from the Painted Pony is another pretty good restaurant, **Benja Thai and Sushi** (435/628-9538, lunch and dinner Tues.–Sat., dinners about $10–12), one of the very few Thai restaurants in southern Utah. Also in Ancestor's Square is the tiny **Jail House Java** (435/668-1819).

Just across St. George Boulevard, **Bear Paw Coffee** (75 N. Main St., 435/634-0126) is another of the few places in town to hang out and drink coffee. Breakfasts are large and delicious.

For formal dining and spectacular views, head west toward the airport for **Sullivan's Rococo Inn & Steak House** (511 Airport Rd., 435/628-3671, lunch and dinner daily, dinners $15–28), where prime rib, steak, and seafood are the specialties. The best Italian food in town is at **Scaldoni's Gourmet Grill** (Phoenix Plaza Mall, 929 W. Sunset Blvd., 435/674-1300, lunch Mon.–Fri., dinner nightly, dinner $10–28), with some delicious pasta dishes (including the rich Bolognese) and a variety of meat and seafood entrées.

INFORMATION AND SERVICES

The **St. George Chamber of Commerce** (97 E. St. George Blvd., 435/628-1658, www .stgeorgechamber.com, 9 A.M.–5 P.M. Mon.–Fri. and 9 A.M.–1 P.M. Sat.), in the old county courthouse (built 1866–1876), can tell you about the sights, events, and services of southwestern Utah; it has brochures of accommodations, restaurants, a historic walking tour, and area ghost towns. Another good online source of information is www.utahsdixie.com.

For recreation, see the **Pine Valley Ranger District office** (196 E. Tabernacle, 435/688-3246, www.fs.fed.us/r4/dixie, 8 A.M.–5 P.M. Mon.–Fri.) for information on fishing, hiking, and camping in the Dixie National Forest north of town. Maps of the forest and Pine Valley Wilderness are available. The **Bureau of Land Management** (345 E. Riverside, 435/688-3200, www.ut.blm.gov/stgeorge_fo/, 8 A.M.–4:30 P.M. Mon.–Fri.) oversees vast lands in Utah's southwest corner and the Arizona Strip.

The **post office** is at 180 North Main (435/673-3312). The **Dixie Regional Medical Center** provides hospital care (544 South 400 East, 435/688-4000).

GETTING THERE

United and **Delta** (represented by Skywest) both fly into the St. George Municipal Airport (SGU, 317 S. Donlee Dr., 435/634-5822).

Several of the usual rental-car companies operate at the St. George airport: **Budget** (435/673-6825 or 800/527-0700), **Avis** (435/627-2002 or 800/230-4898), and **Hertz** (435/652-9941 or 800/654-3131).

Skywest Airlines, in partnership with Delta, has several daily direct flights to Salt Lake City and Las Vegas. United Express flies to Los Angeles. It's an easy drive from Las Vegas to St. George, so travelers may want to consider flying into Vegas and renting a car there.

Greyhound buses (435/673-2933) depart from McDonald's (1235 S. Bluff St.) for Salt Lake City, Denver, Las Vegas, and other destinations. The **St. George Shuttle** (435/628-8320 or 800/933-8320, www.stgshuttle.com) will take you to Las Vegas in a 15-passenger van for $30. Trips depart from the Shuttle Lodge Inn (915 S. Bluff St.).

Cedar City

Cedar City (pop. around 24,000), known for its scenic setting and its summertime Utah Shakespearean Festival, is a handy base for exploring a good chunk of southern Utah. Just east of town rise the high cliffs of the Markagunt Plateau—a land of panoramic views, colorful rock formations, desolate lava flows, extensive forests, and flower-filled meadows.

Also on the Markagunt Plateau is the Cedar Breaks National Monument, an immense amphitheater eroded into the vividly hued underlying rock.

Within an easy day's drive are Zion National Park to the south and Bryce Canyon National Park and Grand Staircase–Escalante National Monument to the east. Cedar City is just east

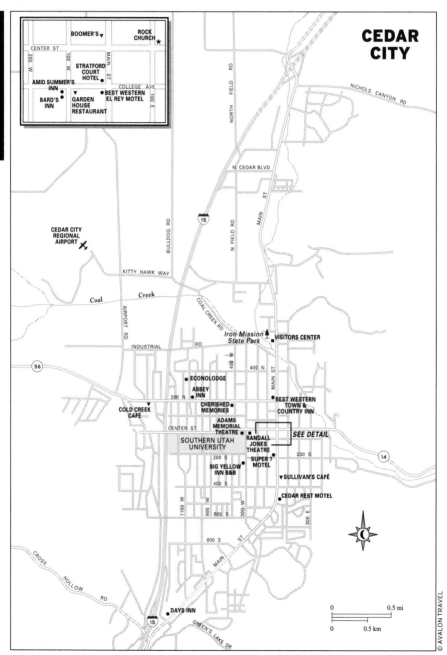

CEDAR CITY

Detail inset (upper left):
- BOOMER'S
- ROCK CHURCH
- CENTER ST
- 200 W
- 100 W
- MAIN ST
- STRATFORD COURT HOTEL
- 100 E
- AMID SUMMER'S INN
- COLLEGE AVE
- BARD'S INN
- GARDEN HOUSE RESTAURANT
- BEST WESTERN EL REY MOTEL

Main map labels:
- NICHOLS CANYON RD
- NORTH FIELD RD
- N CEDAR BLVD
- MAIN ST
- 15
- CEDAR CITY REGIONAL AIRPORT
- BULLDOG RD
- N FIELD RD
- KITTY HAWK WAY
- Coal Creek
- AIRPORT RD
- COAL CREEK RD
- Iron Mission State Park
- VISITORS CENTER
- INDUSTRIAL RD
- 400 W
- 400 N
- 56
- ECONOLODGE
- ABBEY INN
- 200 N
- CHERISHED MEMORIES
- BEST WESTERN TOWN & COUNTRY INN
- COLD CREEK CAFÉ
- CENTER ST
- ADAMS MEMORIAL THEATRE
- SOUTHERN UTAH UNIVERSITY
- RANDALL JONES THEATRE
- SEE DETAIL
- 200 S
- 200 S
- 14
- BIG YELLOW INN B&B
- SUPER 7 MOTEL
- 400 S
- SULLIVAN'S CAFÉ
- 1100 W
- 800 W
- 600 S
- 300 W
- CEDAR REST MOTEL
- 300 E
- 800 S
- MAIN ST
- CROSS HOLLOW RD
- 15
- DAYS INN
- GREEN'S LAKE DR

| 0 | 0.5 mi |
| 0 | 0.5 km |

© AVALON TRAVEL

of I-15, 52 miles northeast of St. George and 253 miles southwest of Salt Lake City; take I-15 Exit 57, 59, or 62.

UTAH SHAKESPEAREAN FESTIVAL

Cedar City's lively festival (435/586-7880 general info, 435/586-7878 or 800/752-9849 box office, www.bard.org) presents three Shakespearean plays each season, choosing from both well-known and rarely performed works. Most of the action centers on the Adams Shakespeare Theatre, an open-air theater in the round, which is closely designed after the original Globe Theatre from Elizabethan London. The indoor Randall Jones Theatre presents the "Best of the Rest"—works by other great playwrights such as Chekhov, George Bernard Shaw, and Arthur Miller. A total of nine plays are staged each season from late June through mid-October.

Costumed actors stage the popular free Greenshow each evening (7 P.M. Mon.–Sat.) before the performances with a variety of Elizabethan comedy skits, Punch and Judy shows, period dances, music, juggling, and other good-natured 16th-century fun. Backstage tours of the costume shop, makeup room, and stage show you how the festival works. At literary seminars each morning, actors and Shakespearean scholars discuss the previous night's play. Production seminars, held daily except Sunday, take a close look at acting, costumes, stage props, special effects, and other details of play production.

The Greenshow and seminars are free, but you'll have to pay for most other events. Tickets cost $20–48, and it's wise to purchase them well in advance; however, last-minute theater-goers can usually find tickets to *something*.

The theaters are on the Southern Utah University campus near the corner of Center and 300 West. Rain occasionally dampens the performances (the Elizabethan theater is open to the sky), and plays may move to a conventional theater next door, where the box office is located.

OLD IRON TOWN STATE PARK

This newly developed state park (635 N. Main, 435/586-9290, $3) focuses on history rather than recreation. The iron works here had their start in 1850, when Brigham Young, hoping to increase Utah's self-sufficiency, sent workers to develop an "iron mission." The iron works eventually became a private company, and though it never really prospered financially, the area has become Iron County. Here, indoor and outdoor exhibits focus on the iron foundry and other aspects of local history.

SCENIC DRIVES
Parowan Gap

Ten miles west of the small I-15 town of Parowan is a pass where Native Americans have pecked many designs into the rocks. People and wildlife hunting the Red Hills commonly passed through this gap, and it may have served as an important site for hunting rituals. The rock art's meaning hasn't been deciphered, but it probably represents the thoughts of many different tribes over the past 1,000 or more years. Geometric designs, snakes, lizards, mountain sheep, bear claws, and human figures are all still recognizable. You can get here on a good gravel road from Parowan by going north on Main and turning left 10.5 miles on the last street (400 North). Or, from Cedar City, go north on Main (or take I-15 Exit 62), follow signs for Highway 130 north 13.5 miles, then turn right 2.5 miles on a good gravel road (near Milepost 19). You'll find an interpretive brochure and map at the Bureau of Land Management (BLM) offices in Cedar City.

Markagunt Scenic Byway

Starting at Cedar City's eastern boundary, Highway 14 plunges into a narrow canyon flanked by steep rock walls before climbing up to the top of the Markagunt Plateau. This is a scenic route, passing dramatic rock cliffs and pink-rock hoodoos that echo the formations at Zion and Bryce Canyon National Parks. Although it's not a quick drive—especially if you get caught behind a lumbering RV—the scenic qualities of the canyon and the incredible vistas, which extend across Zion and down into Arizona, will amply repay your patience. The route also passes several wooded campgrounds and small mountain resorts. Because of their elevations—mostly 8,000–9,000 feet—these high mountain getaways are popular when the temperatures in the desert basin towns begin to bake. The route ends at the Long Valley Junction, at U.S. 89, 41 miles east of Cedar City.

ACCOMMODATIONS

During the Shakespeare Festival, Cedar City is a popular destination, so it's best to reserve a room at least a day or two in advance during the summer. There are two major concentrations of motels. A half dozen large chain hotels cluster around the I-15 exits, together with lots of fast-food restaurants and strip malls. Downtown, along Main Street, are even more motels, ranging from classy new places to budget motels. You can easily walk from most of the downtown motels to the Shakespeare Festival. Most of Cedar City's B&Bs are also within a stroll of the festival grounds.

Note that the following prices are for the high summer festival season. Outside of high season, expect rates to drop about a third.

Under $50

Cedar City has few mom-and-pop budget motels. Downtown, the **Super 7 Motel** (190 S. Main, 435/586-6566, $35 and up) has a bit of a budget ambiance, but it's a good deal.

$50-75

Along Main Street in downtown Cedar City, the **Cedar Rest Motel** (479 S. Main, 435/586-9471, $55 and up) is one of the best values in town; it offers free breakfasts, and small pets are okay.

At I-15 Exit 57, the **Days Inn** (1204 S. Main, 888/556-5637 or 435/867-8877, $64 and up) is a well-kept place with an indoor pool and complimentary continental breakfast.

At I-15 Exit 52, the **Econolodge** (333 North 1100 West, 888/326-6613 or 435/867-4700, $59 and up) is a newer motel with an outdoor pool and a hot tub.

$75-100

One of the best places to stay in Cedar City is the **Stratford Court Hotel** (18 S. Main, 435/586-2433 or 877/688-8884, www.stratford courthotel.com, $79 and up); this nice hotel has an outdoor pool, free passes to a local gym, and a complimentary continental breakfast. The on-site restaurant is one of the better places in town.

Another good choice is **Abbey Inn** (940 West 200 North, 435/586-9966 or 800/325-5411, www.abbeyinncedar.com, $83 and up), with recently redone rooms, an indoor pool, and a good free breakfast.

The **Best Western El Rey Inn** (80 S. Main, 435/586-6518 or 800/528-1234, www.bwelrey .com, $79 and up) offers suites, a restaurant, pool, sauna, and spa.

Bed-and-breakfast inns and Shakespeare seem to go hand-in-hand. The **Bard's Inn Bed & Breakfast** (150 South 100 West, 435/586-6612, www.bardsbandb.com, $85 and up), two blocks from the Shakespearean Festival, has seven guest rooms, all with private bath, plus there's a two-bedroom cottage. It's open during festival season only. Right next door, the antique-filled **Amid Summer's Inn** (140 South 100 West, 435/867-4691, www.amid summersinn, $99 and up) has five sumptuously decorated rooms, including one suite, all with private bathrooms in a restored 1930s cottage. Also near the Shakespeare Festival, at the edge of the Southern Utah University campus, the **Big Yellow Inn** (234 South 300 West, 435/586-0960, www.bigyellowinn .com, $79 and up) is easy to spot; rooms are packed full of antiques and have high-speed Internet hookups. Several rooms are in a house directly across the street from the main inn. **Cherished Memories** (170 North 400 West, 888/867-6498 or 435/867-6498, www .cherishedmemoriesbnb.com, $105) is an antique-furnished Victorian home with four guest rooms, located two blocks from the Shakespearean Festival.

For a more rural touch, the **Willow Glen Inn Bed & Breakfast** (3308 N. Bulldog Rd., 435/586-3275, www.willowgleninn.com, $67–195) has 10 units in four separate buildings, including an old "pony barn," located on a 10-

acre farm five miles north of downtown Cedar City, I-15 Exit 62.

Campgrounds

East of Cedar City on Highway 14 are a handful of campgrounds in the Dixie National Forest. The closest, **Cedar Canyon** (635/865-3200, www.fs.fed.us/r4/dixie), is 12 miles from town in a pretty canyon along Cow Creek. It's at 8,100 feet and open with water from early June to mid-September. **Cedar City KOA** (1121 N. Main, 435/586-9872 or 800/562-9873) is open all year with cabins, showers, a playground, and a pool, and can accommodate tents as well as RVs. **Country Aire RV Park** (1700 N. Main, 435/586-2550) is open all year with showers and a pool.

FOOD

Family restaurants dominate Cedar City's cuisine. **Sullivan's Cafe** (301 S. Main, 435/586-6761, breakfast, lunch, and dinner daily) is a favorite for casual family dining. **Boomer's** (5 N. Main St., 435/865-9665) serves burgers, shakes, fries, and American standards. Upstairs is **Boomer's Pasta Garden,** a sister restaurant with a selection of pasta dishes.

At the **◖ Pastry Pub** (86 W. Center, 435/867-1400) you'll find pastries, good sandwiches, and coffee.

The following fine-dining restaurants each serve wine and cocktails. The **Garden House Restaurant** (164 South 100 West, 435/586-6110, lunch and dinner Mon.–Sat. summers, call for hours off-season) is housed in a charming cottage off the main drag with fine dining (try the trout quesadilla for lunch, $9). Don't worry when you see that **Cold Creek Cafe** (1575 West 200 North, 435/586-1700, $8–25) is attached to a hotel; it's one of the best restaurants in town.

East of Cedar City on Highway 14 is a dramatic desert canyon with two of the area's finest restaurants; both open for dinner only. The steakhouse atmosphere is casual and welcoming at **Rusty's Ranch House,** two miles east of town on Highway 14 (2275 E. Highway 14, 435/586-3839, dinner Mon.–Sat., $12–28), serving good steak and seafood dinners in a dramatic canyon setting. Two miles farther up the same road is the Western-style **Milt's Stage Stop** (3560 E. Hwy. 14, 435/586-9344, dinner nightly, $12–25), serving steak, prime rib, and seafood.

INFORMATION AND SERVICES

The **Iron County Visitors Center** (581 N. Main, 435/586-5124 or 800/354-4849, 9 A.M.–5 P.M. Mon.–Fri., 9 A.M.–1 P.M. Sat., www.scenicsouthernutah.com) is a big, new place just south of the Iron Mission State Park with a raft of information and free Internet access. The **Cedar City Ranger District office** of Dixie National Forest (1789 Wedgewood Ln., 435/865-3700) has information on recreation and travel on the Markagunt Plateau.

The **BLM's Cedar City District office** is just off Main (176 E. DL Sargent Dr., 435/586-2401, 7:45 A.M.–4:30 P.M. Mon.–Fri.) on the north edge of town.

The **Mountain West Bookstore** (77 N. Main, 435/586-3828) offers a selection of Utah history, travel, general reading, and LDS titles.

GETTING THERE

America West (800/235-9292, www.usairways.com) has flights between the Cedar City Municipal Airport and Salt Lake City (800/453-9417). Rent a car from **Enterprise** (435/865-1435) or **Avis** (435/867-9898) at the airport.

BRYCE CANYON NATIONAL PARK

In Bryce Canyon, a geologic fairyland of rock spires rises beneath the high cliffs of the Paunsaugunt Plateau. This intricate maze, eroded from a soft limestone, now glows with warm shades of reds, oranges, pinks, yellows, and creams. The rocks provide a continuous show of changing color through the day as the sun's rays and cloud shadows move across the landscape.

Looking at these rock formations is like looking at puffy clouds in the sky; it's easy to find images in the shapes of the rocks. Some see the natural rock sculptures as Gothic castles, others as Egyptian temples, subterranean worlds inhabited by dragons, or vast armies of a lost empire. The Paiute tale of the Legend People relates how various animals and birds once lived in a beautiful city built for them by Coyote; when the Legend People began behav-

ing badly toward Coyote, he transformed them all into stone.

Bryce Canyon isn't a canyon at all, but the largest of a series of massive amphitheaters cut into the Pink Cliffs. In Bryce Canyon National Park, you can gaze into the depths from viewpoints and trails on the plateau rim or hike down moderately steep trails and wind your way among the spires. A 17-mile scenic drive traces the length of the park and passes many overlooks and trailheads. Off-road, the nearly 36,000 acres of Bryce Canyon National Park offers many opportunities to explore spectacular rock features, dense forests, and expansive meadows.

The park's elevation ranges 6,600–9,100 feet, so it's usually much cooler here than at Utah's other national parks. Expect pleasantly warm days in summer, frosty nights in spring

© W. C. MCRAE

HIGHLIGHTS

◖ Sunrise and Sunset Points: At their appointed hours, these overlooks are irresistible, especially if you have a camera in hand. Unless you are utterly jaded, don't pass these off as mere clichés (page 78).

◖ Inspiration Point: From Sunset Point, walk south along the Rim Trail to see a fantastic maze of hoodoos in the "Silent City." Vertical joints in the rocks have weathered to form many rows of narrow gullies, some more than 200 feet deep (page 79).

◖ Yovimpa and Rainbow Points: Really, all of Bryce's viewpoints are pretty spectacular, but this 9,115-foot-high spot at the end of the scenic road is particularly dramatic. From this spot you can start a day hike, a backpacking trip, or a stroll along a nature trail (page 80).

◖ Queen's Garden Trail: This, the easiest hike below the rim, can still leave flatlanders huffing and puffing. The trail drops from Sunrise Point through impressive features in the middle of Bryce Amphitheater to a hoodoo resembling a portly Queen Victoria (page 81).

◖ Navajo Loop Trail: From Sunset Point, hike down through a narrow canyon. At the bottom, the loop leads into deep, dark Wall Street – an even narrower canyon – then returns to the rim. From the bottom you can hook up with other trails, including one leading to the town of Tropic (page 82).

◖ Red Canyon Bike Trails: As lovely as Bryce Canyon is, sometimes the crowds, the tour buses, and all the synchronized oohing and aahing can begin to close in on you. In that case, put rubber to the road on the wonderful paved bike trail that parallels Highway 12 through Red Canyon. If the paved path is too tame, take a mountain bike up Red Canyon's trails (page 89).

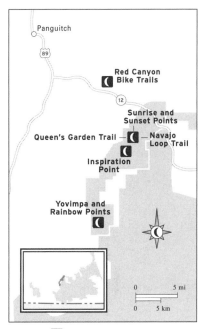

LOOK FOR ◖ TO FIND RECOMMENDED SIGHTS, ACTIVITIES, DINING, AND LODGING.

and autumn, and snow at almost any time of year. The visitors center, scenic drive, and a campground stay open throughout the year.

PLANNING YOUR TIME

Allow a full day to see the visitors center exhibits, enjoy the viewpoints along the scenic drive, and take a few short walks. Because of the layout of the park, with viewpoints all on the east side of the scenic drive, rangers recommend driving all the way south to Rainbow Point, and then stopping at viewpoints on your way back toward the park entrance; this means you won't constantly be needing to turn left across oncoming traffic.

The hike into Queen's Garden is a good, relatively short hike, and is easy to fit into a one-day tour of the park. If you have more time to hike, the Navajo Loop Trail is also good; it can be combined with the Queen's Garden for a pretty substantial trek. Another good bet for strong hikers is the outstanding Peekaboo

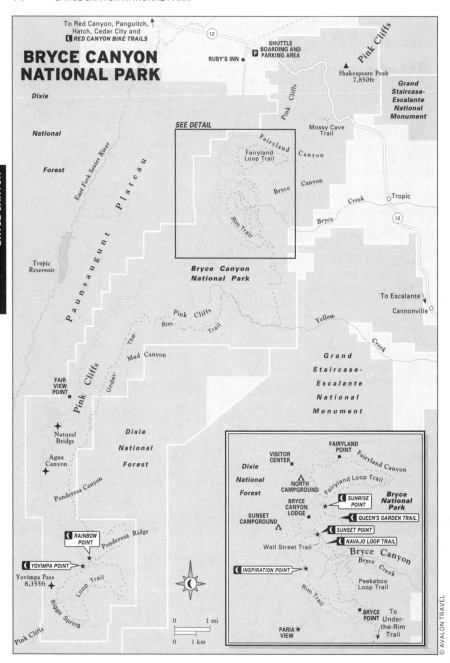

© AVALON TRAVEL

© EMILY ROTH

Not actually a canyon, Bryce Canyon is instead an eroded amphitheater at the edge of the Paunsaugunt Plateau.

Loop. These trails are often crowded near the rim, but less so the farther out you head. But if the crowds begin to get to you, it's time to visit the Fairyland Loop Trail, which is off the main drag and is less trafficked.

If you're interested in photographing the hoodoos (and it's hard to resist the urge), it makes sense to spend the night in or near the park. Photographers usually obtain the best results early and late in the day when shadows set off the brightly colored rocks.

Memorable sunsets and sunrises reward visitors who stay overnight. Moonlit nights reveal yet another spectacle.

If you want to travel into the backcountry, be sure to consult with a ranger about your plans. Remember that winter can last a long time at this elevation, and many trails can be blocked by snow and ice into the spring. The weather can also take a toll on the trails, and it's not uncommon to learn that your selected trail has been closed by rock fall.

Exploring the Park

Bryce Canyon National Park (435/834-5322, www.nps.gov/brca, $25 per vehicle or $12 per bicyclist, pedestrian, or motorcyclist, admission good for seven days and unlimited shuttle use) is just south of the incredibly scenic Highway 12, between Bryce Junction and Escalante. To reach the park from Bryce Junction (at the intersection of U.S. 89 and Hwy.

12, seven miles south of Panguitch), head 14 miles east on Highway 12, then south three miles on Highway 63. From Escalante, it's about 50 miles west on Highway 12 to the turnoff for Bryce; turn south onto Highway 63 for the final three miles into the park (winter snows occasionally close this section). Both approaches have spectacular scenery.

BRYCE CANYON NATURAL HISTORY

GEOLOGY

As the top step of the Grand Staircase, Bryce's rocks are young by geologic standards. The park's Pink Cliffs lie on top of older rock layers, which are exposed in stairstep form as you head south toward the Grand Canyon.

This fantastic landscape got its start about 60 million years ago as sediment dropped to the bottom of a large body of water – named Lake Flagstaff by geologists. Silt and calcium carbonate and other minerals settled on the lake bottom, then consolidated and became the Claron Formation – a soft, silty limestone with some shale and sandstone.

Lake Flagstaff had long since disappeared when the land began to rise as part of the Colorado Plateau uplift about 16 million years ago. Uneven pressures beneath the plateau caused it to break along fault lines into a series of smaller plateaus at different levels known as the "Grand Staircase." Bryce Canyon National Park occupies part of one of these plateaus – the Paunsaugunt.

The spectacular Pink Cliffs on the east edge of the Paunsaugunt Plateau contain the famous erosional features known as "hoodoos," which are carved in the Claron Formation. Variations in hardness of the rock layers result in these strange features, which seem almost alive. Water flows through cracks, wearing away softer rock around hard, erosion-resistant caps. Finally, a cap becomes so undercut that the overhang allows water to drip down, leaving a "neck" of rock below the harder cap. Traces of iron and manganese provide the distinctive coloring. The hoodoos continue to change – new ones form and old ones fade away. Despite appearances, wind plays little role in creation of the landscape; it's the freezing and thawing, snowmelt, and rainwater that dissolve weak layers, pry open cracks, and carve out the forms. The plateau cliffs, meanwhile, recede at a rate of about one foot every 50-65 years; look for trees on the rim that now overhang the abyss. Listen, and you might hear the sounds of pebbles falling away and rolling down the steep slopes.

FLORA AND FAUNA

Bryce's plantlife changes considerably with elevation; higher elevations are moister than the lowlands and can support relatively lush vegetation. The warm, dry slopes beneath the canyon's rim, below about 7,000 feet, are dominated by piñon pine, Utah juniper, and Gambel oak.

Between 7,000-8,500 feet, Ponderosa pines rise majestically over greenleaf manzanita and other shrubs. You'll find these species in the area around the visitors center, campground, and lodge.

Blue spruce, white fir, Douglas fir, limber pine, bristlecone pine, and aspen thrive in the cool, moist conditions above 8,500 feet. It's easy to see these trees at Rainbow and Yovimpa Points, which are just above 9,100 feet.

Wildflowers put on a showy display from spring to early autumn. Springs and seeps below

---

Special hazards you should be aware of include crumbly ledges and lightning strikes. People who have wandered off trails or gotten too close to the drop-offs have had to be pulled out by rope. Avoid cliffs and other exposed areas during electrical storms, which are most common in late summer.

VISITORS CENTER

From the turnoff on Highway 12, follow signs past Ruby's Inn to the park entrance; the visitors center (open daily except Thanksgiving and Christmas, 8 A.M.–8 P.M. summer, 8 A.M.–6 P.M. spring and fall, 8 A.M.–4:30 P.M. winter) is a short distance farther on the right. A brief slide show, shown every half hour, introduces the park. Geologic exhibits illustrate how the land was formed and how it has changed. Historic displays cover the Paiutes, early explorers, and the first settlers. Trees, flowers, and wildlife are identified. Rangers present a variety of naturalist programs, including short hikes, from mid-May through early September; see the posted schedule.

© EMILY ROTH

a tree against a sandstone wall, Bryce Canyon National Park

the rim support pockets of water birch, bigtooth maple, willows, and narrow-leaf cottonwood.

Larger wildlife visit the higher elevations in summer, then move down out of the park as winter snows arrive. It's no shock that mule deer frequent Bryce's meadows, especially in morning and evening, but it's a little more surprising to see wild turkeys grazing there. Other residents include mountain lions, black bears,

coyotes, bobcats, gray foxes, striped skunks, badgers, porcupines, Utah prairie dogs, yellow-bellied marmots, Uinta chipmunks, and golden-mantled ground squirrels. Beavers live near the park on the East Fork of the Sevier River. (*Paunsaugunt* is Paiute for "home of the beaver.") Despite the cool climate, you can find a few reptiles; look for the short-horned lizard, skink, and Great Basin rattlesnake.

Birds appear in greatest numbers May-October. Violet-green swallows and white-throated swifts dive and career among the hoodoos in hot pursuit of flying insects. Other summer visitors are the golden eagle, red-tailed hawk, Western tanager, and mountain bluebird. Year-round residents include woodpeckers, owls, ravens, Steller's jays, Clark's nutcrackers, and blue grouse.

Bryce's cliffs have become home to a thriving population of California condors. Six condors were released in the Vermilion Cliffs south of Bryce in 1996, and the population has grown to about 100. Peregrine falcons are another avian success story here; at least two pairs of these raptors nest in the park. Look for them from Paria View.

Although some wild creatures may seem quite tame, they must not be fed or handled – rodents may have diseases, and young deer contaminated with human scent might be abandoned by their mothers. Also, animals who become dependent on humans may die in winter when left to forage for themselves after the summer crowds have left.

TOURS

The most basic tour of the park, which comes with the price of admission, is a ride on the park shuttle bus. Shuttle buses run every 12 minutes, and the trip through the park takes 50 minutes. Of course, the beauty of the shuttle is that you can get off at any stop, hike for a while, then catch another bus. Shuttle season runs from Memorial Day through Labor Day.

Beyond a shuttle ride, **Ruby's Inn,** a hotel, restaurant, and recreation complex at the park entrance, is a good place to take measure of the opportunities for organized recreation and sightseeing excursions around Bryce Canyon. The lobby is filled with outfitters who are anxious to take you out on the trail; you'll find each of the following there, along with other vendors who organize hayrides, barn dances, and chuck-wagon dinners. **Ruby's Horseback Rides** (435/834-5341 or 866/782-0002, www .horserides.net, Apr.–Oct.) has horseback riding near Bryce Canyon. There's a choice of half-day ($65) and whole-day ($100 including lunch) trips, as well as a 1.5-hour trip

BRYCE CANYON SHUTTLE

When rangers and visitors alike began to complain seriously about the "Bryce Canyon national parking lot," park administrators took note. But bigger parking lots, obviously, weren't the environmentally friendly solution.

In 2000, the National Park Service instituted a shuttle service through Bryce Canyon Park. Buses run during the peak summer season from the Shuttle Parking and Boarding Area at the intersection of Highways 12 and 63 to the visitors center, with stops at Ruby's Inn and Ruby's Campground. From the visitors center, the bus travels to the park's developed areas, including all the main amphitheater viewpoints, Sunset Campground, and the Bryce Canyon Lodge. Passengers can take as long as they like at any viewpoint, then catch a later bus. The shuttle-bus service also makes it easier for hikers, who don't need to worry about car shuttles between trailheads.

Use of the shuttle-bus system is not mandatory; you can still bring in your own vehicle. However, even if you do drive into the park, don't plan to pull a trailer all the way to Rainbow Point. Trailers aren't allowed past Sunset Campground. Trailer parking is available at the visitors center.

($45). Short rides (as well as half- and full-day trips) are offered by **Scenic Rim Trail Rides** (435/679-8761 or 800/679-5859, www.bryce canyonhorseback.com), which also operates out of Ruby's. An hour-long ride is $30. Horseback rides are also offered by a concessionaire inside the park (Canyon Trail Rides, Bryce Canyon Lodge, 435/679-8665, www.canyonrides. com); a two-hour ride ($40) goes to the canyon floor. During the summer, Ruby's also sponsors a rodeo every Wednesday through Saturday at 7 P.M. across from the inn ($9 adults, $6 children 3–12).

You can also explore the area around Bryce Canyon on a noisier steed. Guided all-terrain-vehicle (ATV) tours of Red Canyon are offered by **Great Western ATV** (866/866-6616, $35 for a one-hour trip).

If you'd like to get a look at Bryce and the surrounding area from the air, you can choose to take a scenic flightseeing tour from **Bryce Canyon Airlines** (Ruby's Inn, 435/834-8060), which offers both plane and helicopter tours. There's quite a range of options, but a 35-minute airplane tour costs $139 per person (two-fare minimum) and gives a good look at the surroundings.

SCENIC DRIVES

From elevations of about 8,000 feet near the visitors center, the park's scenic drive gradually winds 1,100 feet higher to Rainbow Point. About midway you'll notice a change in the trees from largely ponderosa pine to spruce, fir, and aspen. On a clear day, you can enjoy vistas of more than 100 miles from many of the viewpoints. Because of parking shortages on the drive, trailers must be left at the visitors center or campsite. Visitors wishing to see all of the viewpoints should take a walk on the Rim Trail.

Note that even though we have presented the viewpoints in north-to-south order, when the park is bustling it's better to drive all the way to the southern end of the road and visit the viewpoints from south to north, thus avoiding left turns against traffic. (Of course, if you're just heading to one viewpoint or trailhead, it's fine to drive directly to it!)

Fairyland Point

To reach the turnoff (just inside the park boundary), go north 0.8 mile from the visitors center, then east one mile. Whimsical forms line Fairyland Canyon a short distance below. You can descend into the "fairyland" on the **Fairyland Loop Trail,** or follow the **Rim Trail** for other panoramas.

◀ Sunrise and Sunset Points

These overlooks are off to the left about one mile past the visitors center; they're connected by a half-mile paved section of the **Rim Trail.**

It's easy to imagine Sunrise Point's hoodoos as statues or fanciful characters.

Panoramas from each point take in large areas of Bryce Amphitheater and beyond. The lofty Aquarius and Table Cliff Plateaus rise along the skyline to the northeast; you can see the same colorful Claron Formation in cliffs that faulting has raised about 2,000 feet higher. A short walk down either the **Queen's Garden Trail** or the **Navajo Loop Trail** from Sunset Point will bring you close to Bryce's hoodoos and provide a totally different experience from what you get atop the rim.

Inspiration Point

It's well worth the 0.75-mile walk south along the **Rim Trail** from Sunset Point to see a fantastic maze of hoodoos in the "Silent City." (It's also accessible by car, from a spur road near the Bryce Point turnoff.) Weathering along vertical joints has cut many rows of narrow gullies, some more than 200 feet deep. It's a short but steep 0.2-mile walk up to Upper Inspiration Point.

Bryce Point

This overlook at the south end of Bryce Am-

phitheater has expansive views to the north and east. It's also the start for the **Rim, Peekaboo Loop,** and **Under-the-Rim trails.** From the turnoff two miles south of the visitors center, follow signs 2.1 miles in.

Paria View

Cliffs drop precipitously into the headwaters of Yellow Creek, a tributary of the Paria River. You can see a section of Under-the-Rim Trail winding up a hillside near the mouth of the amphitheater below. Distant views take in the Paria River Canyon, White Cliffs (of Navajo sandstone), and Navajo Mountain. The plateau rim in the park forms a drainage divide. Precipitation falling west of the rim flows gently into the East Fork of the Sevier River and the Great Basin; precipitation landing east of the rim rushes through deep canyons in the Pink Cliffs to the Paria River and on to the Colorado River and the Grand Canyon. Take the turnoff for Bryce Point, then keep right at the fork.

Farview Point

This sweeping panorama takes in a lot of geology. You'll see levels of the Grand Staircase that include the Aquarius and Table Cliff Plateaus to the northeast, Kaiparowits Plateau to the east, and White Cliffs to the southeast. Look beyond the White Cliffs to see a section of the Kaibab Plateau that forms the north rim of the Grand Canyon in Arizona. The overlook is on the left nine miles south of the visitors center.

Natural Bridge

This large feature lies just off the road on the left, 1.7 miles past Farview Point. The span is 54 feet wide and 95 feet high. Despite its name, this is an arch formed by weathering from rain and freezing, not by stream erosion like a true natural bridge. Once the opening reached ground level, runoff began to enlarge the hole and to dig a gully through it.

Agua and Ponderosa Canyons

You can admire sheer cliffs and hoodoos from the Agua Canyon overlook on the left, 1.4

BRYCE CANYON

© W. C. MCRAE

HOODOOS

Though many visitors assume that wind shaped Bryce Canyon's hoodoos, they were, in fact, formed by water, ice, and gravity, and the way those elements and forces have interacted over the years on rocks of varying hardness.

When the Colorado Plateau uplifted, vertical breaks – called joints – formed in the plateau. Joints allowed water to flow into the rock. As water flowed through these joints, erosion widened them into rivulets, gullies, and, eventually, deep slot canyons. Even more powerful than water, the action of ice freezing, melting, then freezing again (as it does about 200 days a year at Bryce) causes ice wedges to form within the rock joints, eventually breaking the rock.

Bryce Canyon is composed of layers of limestone, siltstone, dolomite, and mudstone. Each rock type erodes at a different rate, carving the strange shapes of the hoodoos. The word *hoodoo* derives from the same sources as *voodoo;* both words are sometimes used to describe folk beliefs and practices. Early Spanish explorers transferred the mystical sense of the word to the towering, vaguely humanoid rock formations that rise above Southwestern landscapes. The Spaniards believed that Native Americans worshipped these statuelike "enchanted rocks." In fact, while early Indians considered many hoodoo areas sacred, there is no evidence that they worshipped the stones themselves.

miles past Natural Bridge. With a little imagination, you may be able to pick out the Hunter and the Rabbit below. Ponderosa Canyon overlook, on the left 1.8 miles farther, offers a panorama similar to that at Farview Point.

◖ Yovimpa and Rainbow Points

The land drops away in rugged canyons and fine views at the end of the scenic drive, 17 miles south of the visitors center. At an elevation of 9,115 feet, this is the highest area of the park. Yovimpa and Rainbow Points lie only a short walk apart yet offer different vistas. The **Bristlecone Loop Trail** is an easy one-mile loop from Rainbow Point to ancient bristlecone pines along the rim. The **Riggs Spring Loop Trail** makes a good day hike; you can begin from either Yovimpa Point or Rainbow Point and descend into canyons in the southern area of the park. The **Under-the-Rim Trail** starts from Rainbow Point and winds 22.5 miles to Bryce Point; day hikers can make a 7.5-mile trip by using the Agua Canyon Connecting Trail and a car shuttle.

Recreation

Although it's possible to have an entirely pleasant visit to Bryce by just riding the shuttle and hopping off to snap pictures at various viewpoints, a short hike or horseback ride down off the rim will give you an entirely different perspective of the hoodoos, native plants, and, perhaps, wildlife of the park.

HIKING

Hikers enjoy close-up views of the wonderfully eroded features and gain a direct appreciation of Bryce's geology. Because almost all of the trails head down off the canyon's rim, they're moderately difficult, with many ups and downs, but the paths are well graded and signed. Hikers not accustomed to the 7,000- to 9,000-foot elevation will find the going relatively strenuous and should allow extra time. Be sure to carry water and drink frequently—staying well hydrated will give you more energy.

Wear a hat and sunscreen to protect against sunburn, which can be a problem at these elevations. Don't forget rain gear because storms can come up suddenly. Always carry water for day trips because only a few natural sources exist. Ask at the visitors center for current trail conditions and water sources; you can also pick up a free hiking map at the visitors center. Snow may block some trail sections in winter and early spring. Horses are permitted only on Peekaboo Loop. Pets must stay above the rim; they're allowed on the Rim Trail only between Sunset and Sunrise Points.

Overnight hikers can obtain the required $5 backcountry permit at the visitors center (camping is allowed only on the Under-the-Rim and Riggs Spring Loop trails). Backpack stoves must be used for cooking; wood fires are prohibited. Although there are several isolated springs in Bryce's backcountry, it's prudent to carry at least one gallon of water per person per day. Ask about the location and flow of springs when you register for the backcountry permit.

Don't expect much solitude during the summer on the popular Rim, Queen's Garden, Navajo, and Peekaboo Loop trails. Fairyland Loop Trail is less used, and the backcountry trails are almost never crowded. September and October are the choice hiking months—the weather is best and the crowds smallest, although nighttime temperatures in late October can dip well below freezing.

Rim Trail

- Distance: 5.5 miles one-way

- Duration: 5–6 hours round-trip

- Elevation gain: 540 feet

- Effort: easy

- Trailheads: Fairyland Point, Bryce Point

- Shuttle stop: Fairyland Point, Bryce Point

This easy trail follows the edge of Bryce Amphitheater. Most people walk short sections of the rim in leisurely strolls or use the trail to connect with five other trails that head down beneath the rim. The half-mile stretch of trail near the lodge between Sunrise and Sunset

Points is paved and nearly level; other parts are gently rolling.

Fairyland Loop Trail

- Distance: 8-mile loop

- Duration: 4–5 hours

- Elevation loss: 900 feet

- Effort: strenuous

- Trailhead: Fairyland Point or Sunrise Point

- Shuttle stop: Fairyland Point or Sunrise Point

This trail winds in and out of colorful rock spires in the northern part of Bryce Amphitheater, a somewhat less-visited area one mile off the main park road. Although the trail is well graded, remember the 900-foot climb you'll make when you exit. You can take a loop hike of eight miles from either Fairyland Point or Sunrise Point by using a section of the **Rim Trail;** a car shuttle saves three hiking miles. The whole loop is too long for many visitors, who enjoy short trips down and back to see this "fairyland."

◖ Queen's Garden Trail

- Distance: 0.75 mile one-way

- Duration: 1.5 hours

- Elevation loss: 320 feet

- Effort: moderate

- Trailhead: Sunrise Point

- Shuttle stop: Sunrise Point

A favorite of many people, this trail drops from Sunrise Point through impressive features in the middle of Bryce Amphitheater to a hoodoo resembling a portly Queen Victoria. This is the easiest excursion below the rim. Queen's Garden Trail also makes a good loop hike with the **Navajo Loop** and **Rim Trails;** most people who do the loop prefer to descend the steeper Navajo and climb out on Queen's Garden Trail for a 3.5-mile hike. Trails also connect with the **Peekaboo Loop Trail** and go to the town of Tropic.

◖ Navajo Loop Trail

- Distance: 1.3-mile loop
- Duration: 1.5 hours
- Elevation drop: 520 feet
- Effort: moderate
- Trailhead: Sunset Point
- Shuttle stop: Sunset Point

From Sunset Point, you'll drop 520 feet in 0.75 mile through a narrow canyon. At the bottom, the loop leads into deep, dark **Wall Street**—an even narrower canyon half a mile long—then returns to the rim. Other destinations from the bottom of Navajo Trail are **Twin Bridges, Queen's Garden Trail, Peekaboo Loop Trail,** and the town of Tropic. The 1.5-mile trail to Tropic isn't as scenic as the other trails, but it does provide another way to enter or leave the park; ask at the visitors center or in Tropic for directions to the trailhead.

© W. C. MCRAE

Hike down on Navajo Loop Trail to get up close and personal with the hoodoos.

Peekaboo Loop Trail

- Distance: 5.5-mile loop
- Duration: 4 hours
- Elevation change: 800 feet
- Effort: moderate–strenuous
- Trailhead: Bryce Point
- Shuttle stop: Bryce Point

This enchanting walk is full of surprises at every turn—and there are lots of turns! The trail is in the southern part of Bryce Amphitheater, which has some of the most striking rock features. You can start from Bryce Point (6.5 miles round-trip), from Sunset Point (5.5 miles round-trip via Navajo Trail), or from Sunrise Point (seven miles round-trip via Queen's Garden Trail). The loop segment itself is 3.5 miles long with many ups and downs and a few tunnels. The elevation change is 500–800 feet, depending on the trailhead you choose. This is the only trail in the park where horses are permitted; remember to give horseback travelers the right-of-way and, if possible, to step to higher ground when you allow them to pass.

Under-the-Rim Trail

- Distance: 22.5 miles one-way
- Duration: 2 days or longer
- Elevation change: 1,500 feet
- Effort: strenuous
- Trailhead: Bryce Point, Rainbow Point
- Shuttle stop: Bryce Point, Rainbow Point

The longest trail in the park winds 22.5 miles below the Pink Cliffs between Bryce Point to the north and Rainbow Point to the south. Allow at least two days to hike the entire trail; the elevation change is about 1,500 feet with many ups and downs. Four connecting trails from the scenic drive make it possible to travel the Under-the-Rim Trail as a series of day hikes, too. Another option is to combine the Under-the-Rim and **Riggs Spring Loop** trails for a total of 31.5 miles.

GREENLEAF MANZANITA

© JUDY JEWELL

greenleaf manzanita

One of the easiest plants to identify at Bryce is greenleaf manzanita. The leaves on this low-lying shrub are dark green and leathery; the bark is cinnamon-colored. Look closely, and you may see fine hairs on the stems. Pink urn-shaped flowers dangle from the stems in May, followed in late summer by fruit that resembles tiny cream-colored apples (*manzanita* is a Spanish word for little apple). Manzanita, which is common in California and the inland Pacific Northwest, easily survives snowy winters, though parts of the plant that aren't covered by an insulating blanket of snow may die from the cold. To conserve water during the hot summers, manzanita leaves stand straight up in a vertical position, reducing the surface area exposed to the sun and slowing transpiration.

Native Americans brewed a diuretic tea from manzanita leaves and made cider from its ripe fruits. They also used the crushed leaves and fruit as a poultice for poison ivy. Patient (or lucky) visitors may spot wildlife browsing on the manzanita – both mule deer and wild turkeys are fond of it.

The **Hat Shop,** an area of delicate spires capped by erosion-resistant rock, makes a good day-hiking destination; begin at Bryce Point and follow the Under-the-Rim Trail for about two miles. Most of this section is downhill (elevation change of 900 feet); you'll have to climb it on the way out.

Swamp Canyon Loop

- Distance: 4.3-mile loop
- Duration: 2 hours
- Elevation loss: 628 feet
- Effort: moderate
- Trailhead: Swamp Canyon
- Shuttle stop: Swamp Canyon

This loop comprises three trails: the Swamp Canyon Connecting Trail, a short stretch of the Under-the-Rim Trail, and the Sheep Creek Connecting Trail. Drop below the rim on the Swamp Canyon trail to a smaller, sheltered canyon that is, by local standards, a wetland. Swamp Canyon's two tiny creeks and a spring provide enough moisture for a lush growth of grass and willows. Salamanders live here, as do a variety of birds (this is usually a good trail for bird-watching).

Bristlecone Loop Trail

- Distance: 1-mile loop
- Duration: 0.5 hours
- Elevation gain: 150 feet
- Effort: easy
- Trailhead: Rainbow Point, Yovimpa Point
- Shuttle stop: Rainbow Point

This easy one-mile loop begins from either Rainbow or Yovimpa Point and goes to viewpoints and ancient bristlecone pines along the rim. These hardy trees survive fierce storms

---

BRISTLECONE PINE

Somewhere on earth, a bristlecone pine tree may one of the planet's oldest living organisms. The trees here, while not the world's oldest, are up to 1,700 years old. (A bristlecone in California is nearly 4,800 years old.) These twisted, gnarly trees are easy to spot in the area around Rainbow Point because they *look* their age.

What makes a bristlecone live so long? For one, its dense, resinous wood protects it from insects, bacteria, and fungi that kill many other trees. It grows in a harsh, dry climate, where there's not a lot of competition from other plants. During droughts that would kill most other plants, the bristlecone can slow down its metabolism until it's practically dormant, then spring back to life when conditions are less severe. Although the dry desert air poses its own set of challenges, it also keeps the tree from rotting.

Besides its ancient look, a bristlecone pine can be recognized by its distinctive needles – they're packed tightly, five to a bunch, with the bunches running along the length of a branch, giving it a bottle-brushlike appearance.

---

and extremes of hot and cold that no other tree can. Some of the bristlecone pines here are 1,700 years old.

Riggs Spring Loop

- Distance: 8.5-mile loop
- Duration: 5 hours
- Elevation loss: 1,625 feet
- Effort: strenuous
- Trailhead: Rainbow Point
- Shuttle stop: Rainbow Point

One of the park's more challenging day hikes or a leisurely overnighter, this trail begins from Rainbow Point and descends into canyons in the southern area of the park. The loop is about nine miles long, with an elevation change of 1,625 feet. Of the three backcountry campgrounds along the trail, the Riggs Spring site is most conveniently located; it's about halfway around the loop. Great views of the hoodoos, lots of aspen trees, a couple of pretty meadows, and good views off to the east are some of the highlights of this hike. Day hikers often take a shortcut that bypasses Riggs Spring and saves 0.75 mile.

Mossy Cave Trail

- Distance: 0.5 mile one-way
- Duration: 0.5 hour
- Elevation gain: 209 feet
- Effort: easy
- Trailhead: Highway 12, between Mileposts 17 and 18

This easy trail is just off Highway 12, northwest of Tropic, near the east edge of the park. (This means that park entrance fees aren't required.) Hike up Water Canyon to a cool alcove of dripping water and moss. Sheets of ice and icicles add beauty to the scene in winter. The hike is only one mile round-trip with a small elevation gain. A side trail just before the cave branches right a short distance to a little waterfall; look for several small arches in the colorful canyon walls above. Although the park lacks perennial natural streams, the stream in Water Canyon flows even during dry spells. Mormon pioneers labored three years to channel water from the East Fork of the Sevier River through a canal and down this wash to the town of Tropic. Without this irrigation, the town might not even exist. From the visitors center, return to Highway 12 and turn east 3.7 miles toward Escalante; the parking area is on the right just after a bridge (between Mileposts 17 and 18). Rangers schedule guided walks to the cave and the waterfall during the main season.

MOUNTAIN BIKING

Although mountain biking is prohibited on trails inside the national park, just a few miles west of the park entrance, Red Canyon's bike trails are spectacularly scenic and exhilarating to ride. For more information, see the *Red Canyon* section under *Vicinity of Bryce Canyon.*

Ruby's Inn provides a shuttle service for Red Canyon mountain bikers.

HORSEBACK RIDING

If you'd like to get down among the hoodoos but aren't sure you'll have the energy to hike back up to the rim, consider letting a horse help you along. Canyon Trail Rides (Bryce Canyon Lodge, 435/679-8665, www.canyonrides.com), a park concessionaire, offers guided rides near Sunrise Point, and both two-hour ($40) and half-day ($65) trips are offered. Both rides descend to the floor of the canyon; the longer ride follows the Peekaboo Loop Trail. Riders must be at least seven years old and weigh no more than 220 pounds; the horses and wranglers are accustomed to novices.

OUTFITTERS

You guessed it: If there's a piece of gear or clothing that you need, the **General Store** at Ruby's is the best place to look for it. Here you'll find a large stock of groceries, camping and fishing supplies, film and processing, Native American crafts, books, souvenirs,

---

VISITING BRYCE CANYON IN WINTER

Though Bryce is most popular during the summer months, it is especially beautiful and otherworldly during the winter, when the rock formations are topped with snow. Because Bryce is so high (the elevation ranges 8,000–9,000 feet), winter lasts a long time, often into April.

The main park roads and most viewpoints are plowed, and the Rim Trail is an excellent, easy snowshoe or cross-country ski route. **Paria Ski Trail** (5-mile loop) and **Fairyland Ski Trail** (2.5-mile loop) are marked for snowshoers and cross-country skiers. Whenever snow depth measures 18 inches or more, snowshoes are loaned free of charge at the visitors center (the deposit of a credit card is required). Rent cross-country ski equipment just outside the park at Ruby's Inn (866/866-6616 or 435/834-5341, www.rubysinn.com). Miles of snowmobile trails are groomed outside the park.

During the winter, most of the businesses around the park entrance shut down. The notable exception is Ruby's Inn, which is a wintertime hub of activity. During the winter months, rates drop precipitously – most rooms go for less than $60 January–March.

Ruby's Inn hosts the Bryce Canyon Winter Festival during Presidents Day weekend in February. The three-day festival includes free cross-country skiing and snowshoeing clinics, demos, and tours. This is also the time and place to pick up tips on ski archery and winter photography.

---

and a post office. Horseback rides, helicopter tours, and airplane rides are arranged in the lobby just outside the store. In winter, cross-country skiers can rent gear and use trails located near the inn as well as in the park. Snowmobile trails are available (snowmobiles may not be used within the park). Western-fronted shops across from Ruby's Inn offer trail rides, chuck-wagon dinners, mountain-bike rentals, souvenirs, and a petting farm.

Inside the park, there's another general store, with groceries, camping supplies, and coin-operated showers and a laundry room. It's open from mid-April through late September and is located between North Campground and Sunrise Point.

If you need specialized outdoor gear, you're more likely to find it 50 miles east in the town of Escalante than in the Bryce Canyon neighborhood.

Accommodations and Food

Travelers may have a hard time finding accommodations and campsites from April to October in both the park and nearby areas. Advance reservations at lodges, motels, and the park campground are a good idea; otherwise, plan to arrive by late morning. Bryce Canyon Lodge is the only lodge in the park itself, and you'll generally need to make reservations months in advance to get a room in this historic landmark. (But it doesn't hurt to ask about vacancies.) Other motels are clustered near the park entrance road, but many do not offer much for the money. The quality of lodgings is somewhat better in Tropic, 11 miles east on Highway 12, and in Panguitch, 25 miles to the northwest.

One of the park's two large campgrounds has 32 sites available for reservation (877/444-6777, www.recreation.gov, $10 per night, plus a $10 reservation fee). The rest of the sites are first-come, first-served; arrive by noon in the main season for a better chance of finding a spot.

UNDER $75

During the winter, it's easy to find inexpensive accommodations in this area; even rooms at Ruby's Inn start at about $60. Several motels are clustered on Highway 12, right outside the park boundary. Many of these have seen a lot of use over the years, usually without a lot of attendant upkeep. **Foster's Motel** (1150 Hwy. 12, 435/834-5227 or 800/372-4750, www .fostersmotel.com, $50) has plain-vanilla motel rooms best suited for budget travelers who don't want to camp and don't plan to spend a lot of time in their room. It's four miles west of the park entrance in a small complex with a restaurant and a supermarket.

$75-100

One of the newest hotels, and a good value for the area, is the **Bryce View Lodge** (991 S. Hwy. 63, 888/279-2304 or 435/834-5180, www.bryceviewlodge.com, $78 and up), which has rooms in handsome buildings near the park entrance, across the road from Ruby's Inn. (It's owned by Ruby's.)

Six miles west of the park turnoff, **Bryce Canyon Pines Motel** (Hwy. 12, Milepost 10, 435/834-5441 or 800/892-7923, www.bryce canyonmotel.com, $75–90) is an older motel with both motel rooms and cottages, a seasonal covered pool, horseback rides, an RV park, and a restaurant open daily for breakfast, lunch, and dinner from early April to late October.

$100-125

Set among ponderosa pines a short walk from the rim, **Bryce Canyon Lodge** (435/834-5361 for same-day reservations or 888/297-2757, www.brycecanyonlodge.com, open Apr.–Oct., $115–140) was built in 1923 by a division of the Union Pacific Railway; a spur line once terminated at the front entrance. The lodge has lots of charm and is listed on the National Register of Historic Places. It also has by far the best location of any Bryce-area accommodation; it's the only lodging in the park itself.

Activities at the lodge include horseback rides, park tours, evening entertainment, and ranger talks; a gift shop sells souvenirs, while food can be found at both a restaurant and a snack bar. Try to make reservations as far in advance as possible.

The sprawling **Best Western Ruby's Inn** (435/834-5341 or 800/468-8660, www.rubys inn.com, $130 and up) offers many year-round services on Highway 63 just north of the park boundary; winter rates are about half of high-season rates. The hotel features an indoor pool and a hot tub and all the bustling activity you could ever want. Kitchenettes and family rooms are also available; pets are allowed. Ruby's Inn is more than just a place to stay, however. This is one of the area's major centers for all manner of recreational outfitters, dining, entertainment, and shopping. Many tour bus groups bed down here. Although it is kind of a zoo, the quality of the rooms at Ruby's is generally higher than what you'll find at other lodgings in the immediate area. If you want something more sumptuous and relaxing, consider staying at a B&B in nearby Tropic.

CAMPGROUNDS

The park's two campgrounds both have water and some pull-through spaces. Reservations are accepted at North Campground; make them at least two days in advance (877/444-6777, www.recreation.gov, $10 per night, plus a $10 reservation fee). Otherwise, try to arrive early for a space during the busy summer season because both campgrounds usually fill by 1 or 2 P.M. The **North Campground** is on the left just past the visitors center. The best sites here are just a few yards downhill from the Rim Trail, with easy hiking access to other park trails. The **Sunset Campground** is about 2.5 miles farther on the right, across the road from Sunset Point. Sunset has campsites accessible to people with disabilities.

Basic groceries, camping supplies, and coin-operated showers and a laundry room are available from mid-April through late September at the **General Store,** between North Campground and Sunrise Point. During the rest of the year, you can go outside the park to Ruby's Inn for these services.

The Dixie National Forest has three Forest Service **campgrounds** located in scenic set-tings among ponderosa pines. They'll often have room when campgrounds in the park are full. Sites can be reserved at Pine Lake, King Creek, and Red Canyon Campgrounds (877/444-6777, www.recreation.gov, $9–18, water available). The **Pine Lake Campground** lies at 7,700 feet just east of its namesake lake in a forest of ponderosa pine, spruce, and juniper. Sites are open mid-May through mid-September. From the highway junction north of the park, head northeast 11 miles on Highway 63 (gravel), then turn southeast six miles.

King Creek Campground is on the west shore of Tropic Reservoir, which has a boat ramp and fair trout fishing. Sites are at 8,000 feet and are usually open May through late September. Head seven miles south of Highway 12 down the gravel East Fork Sevier River Road, 2.8 miles west of the park turnoff. **Red Canyon Campground** is just off Highway 12 four miles east of U.S. 89. It's at 7,400 feet, below brilliantly colored cliffs, and stays open late May through late September. Contact the Powell Ranger District office in Panguitch (435/676-9300) for more information on Kings and Red Canyon Campgrounds. Contact the Escalante Ranger District office in Escalante (435/826-5400) for information on Pine Lake.

A little farther away is beautiful **Kodachrome State Park.** From Bryce, take Highway 12 east to Cannonville, then head south to the park. (See the *Grand Staircase–Escalante National Monument* chapter for details.)

Private campgrounds in the area are $20 and up per night. The **Ruby's Inn Campground** (435/834-5301, open early Apr.–late Oct.) is at the park junction and has spaces for tents ($20) and RVs ($28–31); showers and a laundry room are open all year. They've also got a few tepees (starting at $28 per day) and bunkhouse-style cabins ($50 per day, no bedding provided). All of the considerable facilities at Ruby's are available to camping patrons. **Bryce Canyon Pines Campground,** four miles west of the park entrance (435/834-5441 or 800/892-7923), has an indoor pool, game room, groceries, and shaded sites.

BRYCE CANYON

FOOD

The dining room at the **Bryce Canyon Lodge** (435/834-5361, dinner entrées $12–22) is atmospheric and offers food that's as good as you're going to find in the area. It's open daily in season for breakfast, lunch, and dinner (reservations advised for dinner). For lunch, the snack bar is a good bet in nice weather; the only seating is outside on the patio or in the hotel lobby. With 12 hours advance notice, you can order a box lunch from the dining room.

If you really want a high-volume dining experience, Ruby's Inn **Cowboy Buffet and Steak Room** (435/834-5341, $10–25) is an incredibly busy place. It's also one of Bryce Canyon's better restaurants and is open for breakfast, lunch, and dinner daily. Casual lunch and dinner fare

is served in the inn's snack bar, the **Canyon Diner,** April through October.

Bryce Canyon Resort (435/834-5351 or 800/834-0043), near the turnoff for the park, has an on-site restaurant that features steak and barbecue and is open daily for breakfast, lunch, and dinner.

Two long-established restaurants west of the park entrance have a low-key, noncorporate atmosphere and pretty good food. The small family-run restaurant attached to **Bryce Canyon Pines** (Hwy. 12, Milepost 10, 435/834-5441 or 800/892-7923) is a homey place to stop for burgers, soup ($3.25), or sandwiches. Two miles west of the park turnoff is **Foster's** (435/834-5227), with steaks and old-fashioned diner food.

Vicinity of Bryce Canyon

Sometimes the bustle at Bryce's rim and at the large commercial developments right at the entrance to the park can be a little off-putting. It's easy to escape the crowds by heading just a few miles west on scenic Highway 12.

RED CANYON

The drive on Highway 12 between U.S. 89 and the turnoff for Bryce Canyon National Park passes through this well-named canyon. Because Red Canyon is not part of Bryce, many of the trails here are open to mountain biking and ATV riding. In fact, this canyon has become very popular as other Utah mountain-biking destinations become crowded.

Staff members at the **Red Canyon Visitors Center** (Hwy. 12 between Mileposts 3 and 4, 435/676-2676, 9 A.M.–6 P.M. daily Memorial Day–Labor Day, 9 A.M.–6 P.M. Fri.–Mon. during spring and fall) can tell you about the trails and scenic backcountry roads that wind through the area. Books and maps are available here. (For details about Red Canyon Campground, see the *Campgrounds* section under *Accommodations and Food.*)

The U.S. Forest Service maintains many

scenic hiking trails that wind back from the highway for a closer look at the geology. The following trails are open to hikers only. Be-

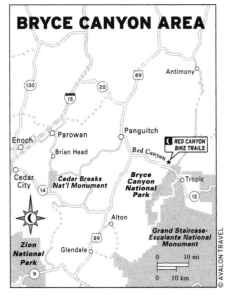

BRYCE CANYON AREA

cause this is not part of the national park, dogs are permitted on these trails.

Pink Ledges Trail

• Distance: 1-mile loop

• Duration: 0.5 hour

• Elevation gain: 100 feet

• Effort: easy

• Trailhead: Red Canyon Visitors Center

The Pink Ledges Trail, the easiest and most popular trail in the area, loops past intriguing geological features. Signs identify some of the trees and plants.

Birdseye Trail

• Distance: 0.75 mile one-way

• Duration: 1 hour

• Elevation gain: 150 feet

• Effort: easy–moderate

• Trailhead: Red Canyon Visitors Center

The Birdseye Trail winds by red-rock formations, including a supposedly bird-shaped rock, and connects the visitors center with the Photo Trail and its parking area on Highway 12 just inside the forest boundary.

Buckhorn Trail

• Distance: 0.9 mile one-way

• Duration: 1.5 hour

• Elevation gain: 250 feet

• Effort: moderate–strenuous

• Trailhead: Red Canyon Campground, site 23

This trail climbs to views of the interesting geology of Red Canyon. It's a good choice if you'd like to burn off a little energy and get a sense of the surrounding country. The campground is on the south side of Highway 12 between Mileposts 3 and 4.

For a longer hike (four miles one-way), turn left off the Buckhorn Trail after about 0.6 mile onto the Golden Wall Trail. Follow the Golden Wall Trail south past yellow limestone walls, then north again back to Highway 12, where it comes out across from the visitors center. A short spur, the Castle Bridge Trail, climbs to a ridge overlooking the Golden Wall before rejoining the Golden Wall Trail.

Tunnel Trail

• Distance: 0.7 mile one-way

• Duration: 1.5 hours

• Elevation gain: 300 feet

• Effort: moderate

• Trailhead: Highway 12 pullout just west of tunnels

The Tunnel Trail ascends to fine views of the canyon and the two highway tunnels. The trail crosses a streambed and then climbs a ridge to access excellent views.

◖ Red Canyon Bike Trails

A rather wonderful paved bike trail parallels Highway 12 for five miles through Red Canyon. Parking lots are located at either end of the trail, at the Thunder Mountain Trailhead and Coyote Hollow Road.

True mountain bikers will eschew the pavement and head to **Casto Canyon Trail,** a 5.5-mile one-way trail that winds through a variety of red-rock formations and forest. This ride starts west of the visitors center, about two miles east of U.S. 89. Turn north from Highway 12 onto Forest Road 118, and continue about three miles to the Casto Canyon parking lot. For part of the way, the trail is shared with ATVs, but then the bike trail splits off to the right. The usual turnaround point is at Sanford Road.

This ride can be linked with other trails to form a 17-mile one-way test of biking skills and endurance, with the route starting and ending along Highway 12. If you don't have a shuttle vehicle at each of the trailheads, you'll need to

The Red Canyon bike trail, just north of Bryce Canyon National Park, provides smooth sailing for road bikers.

pedal back another eight miles along the paved roadside trail to retrieve your vehicle. Start at Tom Best Road, just east of Red Canyon. You'll climb through forest, turning onto Berry Spring Creek Road and then Cabin Hollow Road. Once the trail heads into Casto Canyon, you'll have five downhill miles of wonderful red-rock scenery. When you reach the Casto Canyon Trailhead, you can choose to return to Highway 12 or pedal out to U.S. 89 and Panguitch. Much of the trail is strenuous, and you must take water along because there's no source along the way. There are several side trails you could use to make this into a shorter ride; stop by the visitors center for more information.

PAUNSAUGUNT WILDLIFE MUSEUM

The Paunsaugunt Wildlife Museum (1945 W. Hwy. 12, 435/834-5555 summer, 702/877-8664 winter, www.brycecanyonwildlifemuseum .com, 9 A.M.–10 P.M. daily April 1–Nov. 15, $8 adults, $5 children 6–12), formerly located in the town of Panguitch, is housed in a large new

building just west of the turnoff to Bryce Canyon. This taxidermy collection depicts more than 450 animals from around the world displayed in dioramas resembling their natural habitats. It's actually quite well done, and kids seem to love it. There's also a good collection of Native American artifacts and a beautiful butterfly display.

CEDAR BREAKS NATIONAL MONUMENT

If you're driving between Zion and Bryce National Parks, consider stopping at Cedar Breaks. But take note: This is high country, and the road is closed from mid-October through late May.

Cedar Breaks is much like Bryce Canyon, but it's on a different high plateau and lacks the crowds that flock to Bryce. Here, on the west edge of the Markagunt Plateau, a giant amphitheater 2,500 feet deep and more than three miles across has been eroded into the stone. A fairyland of forms and colors appears below the rim. Ridges and pinnacles extend like buttresses from the steep cliffs. Cottony patches of clouds often drift through the craggy landscape. Traces of iron, manganese, and other minerals have tinted the normally white limestone a rainbow of warm hues. The intense colors blaze during sunsets and glow even on a cloudy day. Rock layers look much like those at Bryce Canyon National Park, but here they're 2,000 feet higher. Elevations range from 10,662 feet at the rim's highest point to 8,100 feet at Ashdown Creek. In the distance, beyond the amphitheater, is Cedar City and the desert's valleys and ranges. Dense forests broken by large alpine meadows cover the rolling plateau country away from the rim. More than 150 species of wildflowers brighten the meadows during summer; the colorful display peaks during the last two weeks in July.

Two easy trails near the rim give an added appreciation of the geology and forests here. Allow extra time while on foot—walking can be tiring at high elevations. Regulations prohibit pets on the trails.

A five-mile scenic drive leads past four spectacular overlooks, each with a different perspective. Avoid overlooks and other exposed areas during thunderstorms, which are common on summer afternoons. Heavy snows close the road for much of the year. You can drive in only from about late May (or later) until the first big snowstorm of autumn—usually in October. Winter visitors can travel by snowmobile (unplowed roads only), ski, or snowshoe from Brian Head (two miles north of the monument) or Highway 14 (2.5 miles south).

Cedar Breaks National Monument is 24 miles east of Cedar City, 17 miles south of Parowan, 30 miles southwest of Panguitch, and 27 miles northwest of Long Valley Junction. The nearest accommodations and restaurants are two miles north in Brian Head, where **Cedar Breaks Lodge** (223 Hunter Ridge Rd., 435/677-3000 or 888/282-3327, www.cedar breakslodge.com, $70 and up, summer) has fairly posh rooms, a day spa, and good deals during the summer (Brian Head is busiest during the ski season).

Visitors Center and Campground

A log cabin visitors center (435/586-0787 summer, 435/586-0787 winter, www.nps.gov/cebr, 8 A.M.–6 P.M. daily June 1–mid-Oct., $4-per-vehicle park-entrance fee) includes exhibits, an information desk, and a bookstore. The exhibits provide a good introduction to the Markagunt Plateau and identify local rocks, wildflowers, trees, animals, and birds. Staff members offer nature walks, geology talks, and campfire programs; see the schedules posted in the visitors center and at the campground. An entrance fee of $4 per vehicle is collected near the visitors center; there's no charge if you're just driving through the monument without stopping. The small campground to the east has water and a $14 fee; camping is first-come, first-served. The campground is open from about mid-June through late September. (If you plan to visit in June or September, it's best to call ahead to check the campground's status; some years its season is remarkably short.) There's a picnic area near the campground.

Spectra Point/Ramparts Trail

- Distance: 2 miles one-way
- Duration: 2 hours
- Elevation gain: 400 feet
- Effort: moderate–strenuous
- Trailhead: visitors center

The Spectra Point/Ramparts Trail begins at the visitors center, then follows the rim along the south edge of the amphitheater to an overlook. Hikers who are short on time, or feeling the effects of the 10,000-foot elevation, can cut the distance in half by stopping after one mile at Spectra Point, where weather-beaten bristlecone pines grow. The trail's end is marked by an overlook.

Alpine Pond Trail

- Distance: 2-mile loop
- Duration: 1 hour

- Elevation loss: 20 feet
- Effort: easy
- Trailhead: visitors center

The Alpine Pond Trail drops below the rim into one of the few densely wooded areas of the amphitheater. The trail winds through enchanting forests of aspen, subalpine fir, and Engelmann spruce. You can cut the hiking distance in half with a car shuttle between the two trailheads or by taking a connector trail that joins the upper and lower parts of the loop near Alpine Pond. Begin from either Chessmen Ridge Overlook or the trailhead pullout 1.1 miles farther north. A trail guide is available at the start or at the visitors center.

Tropic

Mormon pioneer Ebenezer Bryce homesteaded near the town site of Tropic in 1875, but the work of scratching a living from the rugged land became too hard. He left five years later for more promising areas in Arizona. The name of the park commemorates his efforts. He is remembered as saying of the area, "Well, it's a hell of a place to lose a cow." Other pioneers settled six villages near the upper Paria River between 1876 and 1891. The towns of Tropic, Cannonville, and Henrieville still survive. Tropic lies just 11 miles east of Bryce Canyon National Park and is visible from many of the park's viewpoints. Travelers think of Tropic primarily for its cache of motels lining Main Street (Highway 12), but several pleasant B&Bs also grace the town. A **log cabin** built by Ebenezer Bryce has been moved to a site beside the Bryce Pioneer Village Motel; ask to see the cabin's small collection of pioneer and Native American artifacts. A **tourist booth** in the center of town is open 11 A.M.–7 P.M. daily from early May through late October.

Bryce Valley, east of the park, is visible from the town of Tropic.

ACCOMMODATIONS
$50-75

Aside from a couple of nice B&Bs, the best place to stay in Tropic is in the **Bryce Country Cabins** (320 N. Hwy. 12, 888/679-8643 or 435/679-8643, www.brycecountrycabins.com, $75). The cabins overlook a meadow, and each has a private bath. On the south end of town, the **Bryce Pioneer Village Motel** (80 S. Main, 435/679-8546 or 800/222-0381, www.bpvillage .com, $55 and up) has typical budget-level rooms and several cabins (one with kitchen); there's also a campground with sites for tents and RVs.

$75-100

Up on a bluff on the outskirts of town, the **Buffalo Sage B&B** (980 N. Hwy. 12, 435/679-8443 or 866/232-5711, www.buffalosage.com, $90 s, $95 d) has great views and rooms decorated in an upscale Southwestern style. At the other end of town, the **Bullberry Inn B&B** (435/679-8820 or 800/249-8126, www.bull berryinn.com, $75 s, $105 d) has wraparound porches, and guest rooms contain private baths and rustic-style furniture.

At the **Bryce Canyon Inn** (21 N. Main, 435/679-8502 or 800/592-1468, www.bryce canyoninn.com, open Mar.–Oct., $60 motel rooms, $85 cabins), the tidy new cabins are nicely furnished and one of the more appealing options in the Bryce neighborhood.

America's Best Value Bryce Valley Inn (199 N. Hwy. 12, 435/679-8811 or 800/442-1890, www.brycevalleyinn.com, $85) has conventional motel rooms in an attractive wood-fronted, Western-look motel with an adjoining restaurant. Pets are permitted but are charged an extra fee.

Over $100

The **Stone Canyon Inn** (435/679-8611 or 866/489-4680, www.stonecanyoninn.com, $110–175 rooms, $295 cottages), just west of Tropic with views of Bryce, has comfortable, uncluttered rooms. Stone Canyon also has brand-new two-bedroom "cabin cottages," which can be divided to provide smaller units. The owners are happy to point you toward their favorite trails. At **Bryce Canyon Livery B&B** (660 West 50 South, 888/889-8910 or 435/679-8780, www.brycecanyonbandb.com, $105), every room has a private bath; several have balconies with views of Bryce Canyon.

Campgrounds

In town, you can find RV camping at **Bryce Pioneer Village Motel** (80 S. Main, 435/679-8546 or 800/222-0381, www.bpvillage.com). Head east to Cannonville for a **KOA** (175 N. Red Rock Dr., 435/679-8988 or 888/562-4710, www.koa.com), or continue south from Cannonville to Kodachrome Basin State Park (see the *Grand Staircase–Escalante National Monument* chapter for details on this lovely park).

FOOD

There are a few adequate restaurants in town. **Clarke's** (141 N. Main, 435/679-8633, breakfast, lunch, and dinner daily) is an all-around place that serves Mexican food, pasta, and steaks. **Bryce Pioneer Village Motel** (80 S. Main, 435/679-8546 or 800/222-0381, dinner some nights, 6–9 P.M., $13–16, call for reservation) has a restaurant specializing in Dutch-oven cooking. Because it's only open when they have 20 or more confirmed customers, it's critical to call ahead.

Panguitch

BRYCE CANYON

Pioneers arrived here in 1864, but angry Utes forced evacuation just two years later. A second attempt by settlers in 1871 succeeded, and Panguitch (the Paiute word for "big fish") is now the largest town in the area.

Panguitch is one of the more pleasant towns in this part of Utah, and there is an abundance of reasonably priced motels, plus a couple of good places to eat. It's a good stopover on the road between Zion and Bryce National Parks.

The early 20th-century commercial buildings downtown have some of their original facades. On side streets you can see sturdy brick houses built by the early settlers. Stop by the **Daughters of Utah Pioneers Museum** (125 E. Center St., 4–8 P.M. Mon.–Sat. Memorial Day–Labor Day) in the old bishop's storehouse to see historic exhibits of Panguitch. During the off-season, the museum is open by appointment; phone numbers of volunteers are on the door.

The **city park** on the north edge of town has picnic tables, a playground, tennis courts, and a tourist-information cabin. A **swimming pool** (250 E. Center, 435/676-2259) is by the high school.

Travelers in the area during the second weekend in June should try to swing by for the annual **Quilt Walk,** an all-out festival with historic home tours, quilting classes, and lots of food. The Quilt Walk commemorates a group of seven pioneers who trudged through snow to bring food back to starving townspeople— they spread quilts on the deep, soft snow and walked on them in order not to sink.

ACCOMMODATIONS
Under $50

Panguitch is the best place in greater Bryce Canyon to find a budget motel room. Of these, the **Color Country Motel** (526 N. Main St., 435/676-2386 or 800/225-6518, www.color

Panguitch has a small, old-fashioned downtown with classic red-brick storefronts.

© PAUL LEVY

countrymotel.com, $40 s, $52 d) is the most attractive, with an outdoor pool and clean, well-maintained rooms.

$50-75

A good midrange pick is the **Canyon Lodge** (210 N. Main St., 435/676-8292 or 800/440-8292, www.color-country.net, $75). The **Panguitch Inn** (50 N. Main St., 435/676-8871 or 800/331-7407, www.panguitchinn.com, $75) is an old downtown hotel open April through October.

Along U.S. 89, the **New Western** (180 E. Center St., 435/676-8876 or 800/528-1234, $75) has a swimming pool and hot tub, plus laundry facilities. Some rooms are in an older building—you may want to assess room quality and noise level before handing over your credit card.

The **Adobe Sands** (390 N. Main St., 435/676-8874 or 800/497-9261, $75) is a perfectly acceptable standard motel, open May through October.

$75-100

Stay in one of the landmark red-brick homes: the tidy **Red Brick Inn of Panguitch B&B** (161 North 100 West, 435/676-2141 or 866/733-2745, www.redbrickinnutah.com, $89 and up) has distinctive barnlike architecture and includes cozy bedrooms and a three-bedroom apartment. If you like B&Bs, this is definitely the best place in town to stay.

If you'd rather go with a standard motel room, the **Marianna Inn Motel** (699 N. Main St., 435/676-8844 or 800/331-7407, $85) is an attractive place that allows pets.

Campgrounds

Open year-round, **Hitch-N-Post Campground** (420 N. Main, 435/676-2436) offers spaces for tents and RVs and has showers and a laundry room. The **Big Fish KOA Campground** (555 S. Main, 435/676-2225, mid-Apr.–mid-Oct.) on the road to Panguitch Lake includes a pool, recreation room, laundry, and showers; rates start at $24 for tents, $30 for RVs, and $49 for cabins. The closest public campground is on Highway 12 in Red Canyon.

FOOD

The culinary high point of a visit to Panguitch will likely be the mesquite-grilled meats at **Cowboy's Smokehouse Bar-B-Q** (95 N. Main St., 435/676-8030, lunch and dinner Mon.–Sat. mid-Mar.–mid-Oct.), where live country music and Western atmosphere are regulars on the menu. Then again, it may be a traditional Utah scone, from **Grandma Tina's** (523 N. Main St., 435/676-2377, breakfast, lunch, and dinner daily summer, lunch and early dinner Thurs.–Sun. winter). (The scones are deep fried and are very tasty, like not-too-sweet doughnuts.) For dinner, Tina's serves Italian favorites, with several vegetarian options. The **Flying M Restaurant** (580 N. Main, 435/676-8008, three meals daily) is a favorite for its hearty breakfasts and standard American comfort-food dinners, including homemade turkey potpies. All three places serve beer and wine, and you'll find it hard to spend more than $20 on dinner in Panguitch.

INFORMATION AND SERVICES

Contact the **Garfield County Travel Council** (55 S. Main St., 435/676-1160 or 800/444-6689, www.brycecanyoncountry.com) for information on Panguitch and the nearby area. The **Powell Ranger District office** of the Dixie National Forest (225 E. Center, 435/676-9300, 8 A.M.–4:30 P.M. Mon.–Fri.) has information on campgrounds, hiking trails, fishing, and scenic drives in the forest and canyons surrounding Bryce Canyon National Park.

The **post office** is at 65 North 100 West. **Garfield Memorial Hospital** (200 North 400 East) can be reached at 435/676-8811 (hospital) or 435/676-8842 (clinic). It's the main hospital in this part of the state.

GRAND STAIRCASE-ESCALANTE NATIONAL MONUMENT

The 1.9-million-acre Grand Staircase–Escalante National Monument (GSENM, 435/644-4600, www.ut.blm.gov/monument) contains a vast and wonderfully scenic collection of slickrock canyonlands and desert, prehistoric village sites, Old West ranch land, and arid plateaus, and miles of back roads linking stone arches, mesas, and abstract rock formations. The monument even preserves a historic movie set! (Think vintage Westerns.)

The monument contains essentially three separate districts: On the eastern third are the narrow wilderness canyons of the Escalante River and its tributaries. In the center of the monument is a vast swath of arid rangeland and canyons called the Kaiparowits Plateau, with few developed destinations—before use of all-terrain vehicles (ATVs),

dune buggies, and dirt bikes was limited, these canyons and bluffs were a popular playground for off-road enthusiasts. The western third of the monument edges up against the Gray, White, and Pink Cliffs of the Grand Staircase. These thinly treed uplands are laced with former Forest Service roads. The GSENM is the largest land grouping designated as a national monument in the lower 48 states.

There's little dispute that the **Escalante canyons** are the primary reason people visit the monument. The river and its tributaries cut deep and winding slot canyons through massive slickrock formations, and hiking these canyon bottoms is an extremely popular adventure. A multiday trek is a rite of passage for many devoted hikers, but you don't

© EMILY ROTH

HIGHLIGHTS

◖ Kodachrome Basin State Park:
Strange-looking rock pillars or "sand pipes" are the attraction at this state park on the edge of the Grand Staircase-Escalante National Monument. Hiking trails and a campground make this a good base for exploring Cottonwood Canyon Road south into the monument (page 104).

◖ Grosvenor Arch: In a remote, yet drivable, location off Cottonwood Canyon Road lies the magnificent Grosvenor Arch (actually two sandstone arches). Photographers, including those from a National Geographic expedition in the 1940s, are invariably drawn to it (page 104).

◖ Anasazi State Park: In addition to the good indoor exhibits at this park's museum, there's an excavated Anasazi village out back displaying a wide range of Anasazi building styles. This is an excellent opportunity to learn about the Anasazi (page 108).

◖ Burr Trail Road: From its start in Boulder, through the astounding Long Canyon, to views of the Waterpocket Fold, the Circle Cliffs, and distant mountains, the Burr Trail Road is a treat to drive. Don't expect a fast trip; if the weather has been wet, inquire about the condition of the unpaved section (page 109).

◖ Lower Calf Creek Falls: Easy enough for families, accessible with a regular car, and with a different highlight every half mile or so, this hike is definitely worth including. Expect to see desert varnish, beaver ponds, Native American ruins, pictographs, and the misty 126-foot-high Lower Calf Creek Falls (page 120).

◖ Dry Fork of Coyote Gulch: To explore the enchanting slot canyons of this area, it's necessary to drive 26 miles along the bumpy dirt Hole-in-the-Rock Road. If you and your vehicle are up for such a drive, don't miss it! The slot canyons are easy enough for reasonably fit people to explore, and they'll give you a taste of canyoneering (page 122).

LOOK FOR ◖ TO FIND RECOMMENDED SIGHTS, ACTIVITIES, DINING, AND LODGING.

GRAND STAIRCASE

have to be a hardened backcountry trekker to enjoy this landscape: Two backcountry roads wind through the area, and some day hikes are possible.

The other districts offer less-well-defined opportunities for adventure. Backcountry drivers and long-distance mountain bikers will find mile after mile of desert and canyon to explore. **Grosvenor Arch,** with double windows, is a popular back-road destination. At the southern edge of the park, along the Arizona border, is another rugged canyon system that's popular with long-distance hikers. The **Paria River Canyon** is even more remote than the Escalante, and hiking these slot canyons requires experience and preparation.

PLANNING YOUR TIME

If you only have one day, plan to drive across the stunning Highway 12. The Lower Calf Creek Falls hike begins right off the highway between Escalante and Boulder, and hiking it is a great way to spend half a day.

If you have an additional day or two, it makes sense to base yourself either in Escalante (convenient camping and moderately priced accommodations) or in Boulder (where it's possible to sleep and eat in luxury). Spend your second day here exploring Hole-in-the-Rock Road, where you can hike slot canyons in the Dry Fork of Coyote Gulch and explore Devils Garden. It's possible to stay in this area of the monument for several days, either backpacking along the Escalante River or exploring its various canyons as day hikes. If you're at all up to backpacking, it's only a one-nighter to hike from the town of Escalante along the river to the river's highway crossing.

If you have more time, drive between the Kanab area and Cannonville on Cottonwood Road. Stop and walk up through the Cottonwood Narrows and, at the north end of the road, visit Grosvenor Arch and Kodachrome State Park. If you want to make a loop drive, return on the Johnson Canyon and Skutumpah Roads, with a hike along Lick Wash.

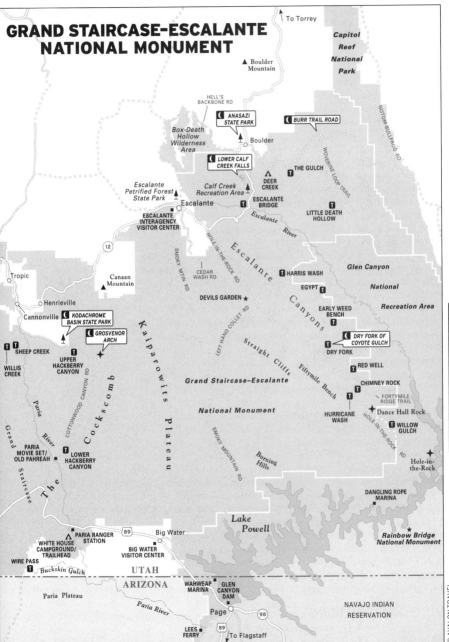

GRAND STAIRCASE-ESCALANTE NATIONAL MONUMENT

To Torrey

Capitol Reef National Park

Boulder Mountain

HELL'S BACKBONE RD

ANASAZI STATE PARK

BURR TRAIL ROAD

Box-Death Hollow Wilderness Area

Boulder

LOWER CALF CREEK FALLS

THE GULCH

Escalante Petrified Forest State Park

Calf Creek Recreation Area

DEER CREEK

WOLVERINE LOOP TRAIL

Escalante

ESCALANTE BRIDGE

LITTLE DEATH HOLLOW

ESCALANTE INTERAGENCY VISITOR CENTER

Escalante River

12

Tropic

Canaan Mountain

SMOKY MTN. RD

CEDAR WASH RD

HOLE-IN-THE-ROCK RD

Escalante Canyons

HARRIS WASH

EGYPT

Glen Canyon

National

Henrieville

DEVILS GARDEN

EARLY WEED BENCH

Recreation Area

Cannonville

KODACHROME BASIN STATE PARK

LEFT HAND COLLET RD

DRY FORK OF COYOTE GULCH

GROSVENOR ARCH

DRY FORK

SHEEP CREEK

UPPER HACKBERRY CANYON

COTTONWOOD CANYON RD

Straight Cliffs

Fiftymile Bench

RED WELL

CHIMNEY ROCK

WILLIS CREEK

Kaiparowits Plateau

Grand Staircase-Escalante

FORTYMILE RIDGE TRAIL

Dance Hall Rock

HURRICANE WASH

HOLE-IN-THE-ROCK RD

WILLOW GULCH

Paria River

National Monument

SMOKY MOUNTAIN RD

Burning Hills

Hole-in-the-Rock

The Cockscomb

PARIA MOVIE SET/ OLD PAHREAH

LOWER HACKBERRY CANYON

DANGLING ROPE MARINA

Grand Staircase

Lake Powell

Rainbow Bridge National Monument

PARIA RANGER STATION

89

Big Water

WHITE HOUSE CAMPGROUND/ TRAILHEAD

BIG WATER VISITOR CENTER

WIRE PASS

Buckskin Gulch

UTAH

ARIZONA

WAHWEAP MARINA

GLEN CANYON DAM

Paria Plateau

Paria River

Page

98

NAVAJO INDIAN RESERVATION

LEES FERRY

89

To Flagstaff

GRAND STAIRCASE

Exploring the Park

There is currently no entrance fee for visiting the monument. Free permits are required for all overnight backcountry camping or backpacking. There is a fee to camp in the monument's three developed campgrounds.

Hikers in the Paria Wilderness area are required to buy a permit (this includes Paria Canyon and Coyote Buttes), as are hikers at the Calf Creek Recreation Area.

It's best to have a travel strategy when visiting this huge national monument. Just as important, especially for a visit of more than a couple of days, is a vehicle that can take on some rugged roads. (A Subaru wagon proved perfectly adequate in dry weather, but when the clay was wet and muddy, the back roads were virtually impassable in all but four-wheel-drive vehicles with significantly higher clearance than a station wagon.)

Only two paved roads pass through the monument, both in an east–west trajectory. Highway 12, on the northern border of the park, links Bryce Canyon and Capitol Reef National Parks with access to the Escalante canyons. This is one of the most scenic roads in Utah—in fact, *Car and Driver* magazine rates this route as one of the 10 most scenic in all of the United States. Its innumerable swallow-your-gum vistas and geologic curiosities will keep you on the edge of your seat.

U.S. 89, which travels along the southern edge of the monument between Kanab and Lake Powell, is no scenery slouch either. It is also the access road for the North Rim of the Grand Canyon in Arizona. Three fair-weather dirt roads, each with a network of side roads and trails, cut through the rugged heart of the monument, linking the two paved roads. Before heading out on these back roads, check with a visitors center for conditions; high-clearance vehicles are recommended.

VISITORS CENTERS

The administrative headquarters of the GSENM is in Kanab (190 E. Center St.,

435/644-4300, www.ut.blm.gov/monument, 7:30 A.M.–5:30 P.M. daily Mar. 15–Nov. 15, 8 A.M.–4:30 P.M. Mon.–Fri. Nov. 15–Mar. 15), about 15 miles from the southwestern edge of the monument, but the regional visitors centers, listed below, are the best places to contact for practical travel information.

Escalante Interagency Visitors Center (755 W. Main St., Escalante, 435/826-5499, 7:30 A.M.–5:30 P.M. daily mid-Mar.–mid-Nov., 8 A.M.–4:30 P.M. Mon.–Fri. mid-Nov.–mid-Mar.) is housed in a sprawling building at the west end of the town of Escalante. Staff here are very knowledgeable and helpful, and exhibits focus on the monument's ecology and biological diversity.

Kanab Visitor Center (745 E. U.S. 89, Kanab, 435/644-4680, 8 A.M.–5 P.M. daily mid-Mar.–mid-Nov., 8 A.M.–4:30 P.M. Mon.–Fri. mid-Nov.–mid-Mar.) is the place to stop if you're planning to drive Cottonwood or Johnson Canyon and Skutumpah Roads from the south. Staff can give you updates on the road conditions and suggest driving and hiking strategies. Exhibits at this visitors center concentrate on geology and archaeology.

Cannonville Visitors Center (10 Center St., Cannonville, 435/826-5640, 8 A.M.–4:30 P.M. daily mid-Mar.–mid-Nov.) is an attractive building at the north end of Cottonwood and Johnson Canyon/Skutumpah Roads. Even if the office is closed, stop by to look at the outdoor exhibits, which depict the different cultures that have lived in the area.

Big Water Visitors Center (100 Upper Revolution Way, Big Water, 435/675-3200, 8 A.M.–5 P.M. daily mid-Mar.–mid-Nov.), a spiral-shaped building designed to resemble an ammonite, is home to a small but distinctive collection of dinosaur bones and a wild mural depicting Late Cretaceous life in the area. Stop here to learn about local paleontology.

Anasazi State Park (460 N. Highway 12, Boulder, 435/335-7382, www.stateparks.utah .gov, 9 A.M.–5 P.M. daily mid-Mar.–mid-Nov.,

GRAND STAIRCASE-ESCALANTE NATURAL HISTORY

© PAUL LEVY

the amazing landscape of the Grand Staircase-Escalante National Monument

GEOLOGY

About 300 million years ago, this land was at times a great Sahara-like desert with dunes towering hundreds of feet high. At other times, the land sank below sea level and was covered by water. Thick layers of sediment built up one on top of the other. During the last 50 million years, powerful forces within the earth slowly pushed the entire region one mile upward. The ancestral Colorado River began to carve the deep gorges seen today at the Grand Canyon. In turn, the tributaries of the Colorado, such as the Escalante, were also forced to trench deeper and deeper in order to drain their watershed.

The most characteristic rocks in the monument are the ancient dunes, turned to stone called slickrock, which make up many of the sheer canyon cliffs, arches, and spires of the region. Delicate cross-bedded lines of the former dunes add grace to these features. Forces within the restless plateau have also buckled and folded rock layers into great reefs as long as 100 miles. Weathering then carved them into rainbow-hued rock monuments. The aptly named Cockscomb, visible from the Cottonwood Canyon Road, which cuts through the center of the monument, is an example of these massive rock wrinkles.

FLORA AND FAUNA

The dry conditions and thin or nonexistent soils limit both plantlife and wildlife in the Escalante region. Annual plants simply wait for a wet year before quickly flowering and spreading their seeds. Piñon pines, junipers, and other plants often adapt by growing in rock cracks that concentrate moisture and nutrients. Small mammals such as mice, wood rats, rock squirrels, and chipmunks find food and shelter in these outposts of vegetation. Even meager soils permit growth of hardy shrubs like blackbrush, greasewood, sagebrush, rabbitbrush, and Mormon tea. Prickly pear and other types of cacti do well in the desert, too.

Perhaps the most unusual plant communities are the cryptobiotic crusts found on sandy soils. Mosses, lichens, fungi, algae, and diatoms live together in a gray-green or black layer up to several inches thick. Microclimates surrounding canyon seeps and springs provide a haven for hanging gardens of grasses, ferns, orchids, columbines, mosses, and other water-loving plants. River and stream banks have their own vegetation, including river willows, cattails, tamarisks, and cottonwoods.

Wildlife you might see in the semiarid desert are mule deer, desert bighorn sheep, pronghorns, coyotes, bobcats, foxes, skunks, porcupines, and many species of rodents. Ravens, eagles, hawks, owls, falcons, magpies, and smaller birds fly overhead. Watch out for poisonous rattlesnakes and scorpions, although these shy creatures won't attack unless provoked.

GRAND STAIRCASE

© PAUL LEVY

The Grand Staircase-Escalante National Monument Visitors Center in Cannonville is worth a stop.

$3 per person to visit park) has a ranger on duty at an information desk inside the museum. The museum itself is worth a visit, so don't be stingy with your three bucks!

Paria Contact Station (U.S. 89, 44 miles east of Kanab, no phone, 8:30 A.M.–4:15 P.M. daily Mar. 15–Nov. 15) is a small visitors center, but an important stop for anyone planning to hike Paria Canyon.

TOURS

For **guided tours** of the Escalante canyons, contact **Utah Canyons Outback Adventures** (325 W. Main St., 435/826-4967 or 877/777-7988, www.utahcanyons.com). Trips focus on day hikes ($80 for a full day), with popular trips going to slot canyons and scenic Phipps Arch. They also offer hiker shuttles and run a good gear shop in the salmon-colored building in downtown Escalante.

The guides at **Excursions of Escalante** (125 E. Main St., Escalante, 800/839-7567, www.excursionsofescalante.com) lead trips into more remote canyons, including some

that require some technical canyoneering to explore and some multiday backpacking trips. A day of basic canyoneering costs $135, including instruction.

Many local outfitters use pack animals. With **Escape Goats** (435/826-4652, www.utahpackgoats.com), you'll hike with goats (and a friendly, goat-loving human guide) into canyons. This is a good bet for families with kids.

Hike into the canyon backcountry (let horses pack your gear) and spend a few days exploring with **Escalante Canyon Outfitters** (888/326-4453 or 435/335-7311, www.ecohike.com). Four-day trips run just over $1,200.

Red Rock 'n Llamas (877/955-2627 or 435/559-7325, www.redrocknllamas.com) offers a variety of fully outfitted hiking adventures in the Escalante area. Llamas will carry most of the gear, leaving you to explore in comfort. Most trips are for three or four nights and cost $800–900.

The Boulder-based **Earth Tours** (435/691-1241, www.earth-tours.com) offers half-day ($50 per person) to six-day (price varies ac-

GRAND STAIRCASE

cording to number of guests) tours of the area. Most trips are led by a geologist with a wide-ranging interest in natural history; lodging for the longer trips is at the luxurious Boulder Mountain Lodge.

ALONG HIGHWAY 12

This tour proceeds west to east, from Bryce Canyon National Park and Tropic along the north edge of the monument to the towns of Escalante and Boulder. Stop at the **Cannonville Visitors Center** (10 Center St., 435/826-5640) for information about back-road conditions and hikes in this part of the monument. Two backcountry roads depart from Cannonville and lead to remote corners of the monument.

Johnson Canyon/Skutumpah Road

This northern end of this route is in Cannonville; its southern terminus is at U.S. 89 just east of Kanab (46 miles one-way). From the northernmost stretch of this road, Bryce Canyon rises to the west; about six miles from the southern end, and off to the east on private land (look from the road, don't trespass), is the set from the TV show *Gunsmoke*.

The unpaved portions of the road are usually in good condition, except after rains, when the bentonite soils that make up the roadbed turn to goo. In good weather, cars can usually make the journey. The road follows the Pink and White Cliff terraces of the Grand Staircase, with access to some excellent and comparatively undersubscribed-to hiking trails. Several steep slot canyons make for excellent canyoneering. The lower 16 miles of Johnson Canyon Road are paved.

Cottonwood Canyon Scenic Backroad

This 46-mile route also connects Cannonville with U.S. 89, but passes through quite different terrain and landscapes. One of the most scenic backcountry routes in the monument, the Cottonwood Canyon road not only offers access to dramatic Grosvenor Arch, but it also passes along the Cockscomb, a soaring buckle of rock that divides the Grand Stair-

DOWN THE GRAND STAIRCASE

The broad, tilted terraces of the Grand Staircase step down through time. Some 200 million years of sedimentation are visible here: pink in the north, then traveling through gray, white, and into vermilion cliffs.

A freshwater lake deposited the limey siltstones that became the Pink Cliffs (see these same rocks in Bryce National Park). This layer formed on top of the shale of the Gray Cliffs, deposited when an ocean covered the area, and rich with marine fossils and coal, formed from ancient wetland plants. The next older step, the White Cliffs, is composed of Navajo sandstone, one of the main rocks seen in Zion National Park. On the bottom step, the bright Vermilion Cliffs (visible around Kanab) are also sandstone, laden with fossils of fish and dinosaurs. At the base of the whole staircase, the striped, brick-colored Chinle badlands form the bed for the Paria River.

These sandstone steps are stacked like pancakes. As in much of the Colorado Plateau region, the erosional activity of water and wind produces amazing geological displays, including the intricate network of deep canyons, uplifted plateaus, sheer cliffs, beautiful sandstone arches and natural bridges, water pockets, sandstone monoliths, pedestals and balanced rocks, domes, and buttes.

GRAND STAIRCASE

case and the Kaiparowits Plateau. Cottonwood Creek, which this road parallels, is a normally dry streambed that cuts through the angular rock beds of the Cockscomb. Several excellent hikes lead into the canyons and narrows, where Paria River, Hackberry Canyon, and Cottonwood Creek all meet, about 20 miles south of Cannonville.

Check at the Cannonville or Big Water visitors center for information about road conditions. Although the road is sometimes passable for cars, several road crossings are susceptible to washouts after rainstorms, and the northern portion is impassable even to four-wheel-drive vehicles when wet because of the extremely unctuous nature of the roadbed. Check conditions before setting out if you plan to go beyond Grosvenor Arch.

Kodachrome Basin State Park

Visitors come to Kodachrome Basin State Park (435/679-8562, www.stateparks.utah.gov, $6 day use, $15 camping), located in a basin southeast of Bryce, to see not only colorful cliffs but also strange-looking rock pillars that occur nowhere else in the world. Sixty-seven rock pillars (here called "sand pipes") found in and near the park range in height from 6 to nearly 170 feet. One theory of their origin is that earthquakes caused sediments deep underground to be churned up by water under high pressure. The particles of calcite, quartz, feldspar, and clay in the sand pipes came from underlying rock formations, and the pipes

appeared when the surrounding rock eroded away. Most of the other rocks visible in the park are Entrada sandstone: The lower orange layer is the Gunsight Butte Member, and the white layer with orange bands is the Cannonville Member.

Signs name some of the rock features. "Big Stoney," the phallus-shaped sand pipe overlooking the campground, is so explicit that it doesn't need a sign! An article, "Motoring into Escalante Land," by Jack Breed, in the September 1949 issue of *National Geographic,* brought attention to the scenery and renamed the area "Kodachrome Flat," for the then-experimental Kodak film used by the expedition. The state park is a worthwhile stop, both as a day trip to see the geology and as a pleasant spot to camp. The park also offers several good half-day hiking trails and a host of shorter hikes.

To reach the park, drive to Cannonville and follow signs for nine miles along paved Cottonwood Canyon Road. Adventurous drivers can also approach the park from U.S. 89 to the south via Cottonwood Canyon Road (35 miles) or Skutumpah Road through Bull Valley Gorge and Johnson Canyon (48 miles). These routes may be impassable in wet weather but are generally okay in dry weather for cars with good clearance.

You can arrange horseback rides at **Trailhead Station** (435/679-8787, www.brycecanyoninn .com), a small store in the park that sells groceries and camping supplies from early April to late October. It also rents several cabins ($75); call ahead or reserve online.

The state park's **campground** (435/679-8562, reservations at 800/322-3770 or www .reserveamerica.com) sits in a natural amphitheater at an elevation of 5,800 feet. It's open all year and has restrooms, showers, and a dump station. During the winter, restrooms and showers may close, but pit toilets are available. The campground usually has room except on summer holidays.

GRAND STAIRCASE

© JUDY JEWELL

Kodachrome Basin State Park has outstanding scenery, a fairly extensive trail system, and a good campground.

Grosvenor Arch

Just one mile off Cottonwood Canyon Road, a side road leads to the magnificent Grosvenor

© JUDY JEWELL

Though Grosvenor Arch is spectacular, bad weather frequently closes the unpaved access road.

Arch. It takes a bit of effort to get here (the 10-mile dirt road between the turnoff to Kodachrome Basin State Park and the arch can be bumpy and, in wet weather, should be avoided), so a visit to the arch can take on the qualities of a pilgrimage. There are actually two arches here, which is a rare occurrence for such erosion-formed arches. Their position, jutting like flying buttresses out of a soaring cliff, is also quite stunning. The larger of the two openings is 99 feet across. A 1949 National Geographic Society expedition named the double arch in honor of the society's president. The turnoff is 10 miles from the Kodachrome Basin State Park turnoff and 29 miles from U.S. 89.

Escalante Petrified Forest State Park

This pleasant park (435/826-4466, www.state parks.utah.gov, $5 day use, $15 camping) just northwest of the town of Escalante offers camping, boating, fishing, picnicking, hiking, a visitors center with displays of petrified wood and dinosaur bones, and a chance to see petri-

fied wood along trails. Rivers of 140 million years ago carried trees to the site of present-day Escalante and buried them in sand and gravel. Burial prevented decay as crystals of silicon dioxide gradually replaced the wood cells. Mineral impurities added a rainbow of colors to the trees as they turned to stone. Weathering has exposed this petrified wood and the water-worn pebbles and sand of the Morrison Formation. For a look at some colorful petrified wood, follow the **Petrified Forest Trail** from the campground up a hillside wooded with piñon pine and juniper. At the top of the 240-foot-high ridge, continue on a loop trail to the petrified wood; allow 45–60 minutes for the one-mile round-trip hike. The steep **Rainbow Loop Trail** (0.75 mile) branches off the Petrified Forest Trail to more areas of petrified wood.

The **campground** (reservations at 800/322-3770, www.reserveamerica.com) stays open all year and offers drinking water and showers but no hookups. The adjacent 139-acre Wide Hollow Reservoir offers fishing, boating, and bird-watching. Canoe rentals are $5 per hour, or $10 for four hours. The park is 1.5 miles west of Escalante on Highway 12, then 0.7 mile north on a gravel road.

Town of Escalante

The town of Escalante, 38 miles east of Bryce Canyon and 23 miles south of Boulder, has all services and is headquarters for explorations of the Escalante River canyons. The Escalante Interagency Office (755 W. Main St., 435/826-5499) provides information on local hikes and road conditions. For more information, see the *Escalante* section later in this chapter.

Smokey Mountain Road

From Escalante, it's 78 miles south to U.S. 89 at Big Water, just shy of Lake Powell, along Smokey Mountain Road. This road is rougher than other cross-monument roads. Be sure to check on conditions before setting out; four-wheel-drive vehicles are required. As this route passes across the Kaiparowits Plateau, the landscape is bleak and arid. Then, the road drops precipitously down onto a bench where side roads lead through badlands to Lake Powell beaches. Big Water is 19 miles from Page, Arizona, and 57 miles from Kanab.

Hole-in-the-Rock Road

The building of this road by determined Mormons was one of the great epics in the colonization of the West. Church leaders organized the Hole-in-the-Rock Expedition to settle the wild lands around the San Juan River of southeastern Utah, believing that a Mormon presence would aid in ministering to the Native Americans there and prevent non-Mormons from moving in. In 1878, the Parowan Stake issued the first call for a colonizing mission to the San Juan, even before a site had been selected.

Preparations and surveys took place the following year as the 236 men, women, and children received their calls. Food, seed, farming and building tools, 200 horses, and more than 1,000 head of cattle would be taken along. Planners ruled out lengthy routes through northern Arizona or eastern Utah in favor of a

---

A PIONEER ACCOUNT OF ESCALANTE TRAVEL

Mormon pioneer Elizabeth Morris Decker described the descent from Hole-in-the-Rock Road in a letter to her parents on February 22, 1880:

If you ever come this way it will scare you to death to look down it. It is about a mile from the top down to the river and it is almost strait [sic] down, the cliffs on each side are five hundred feet high and there is just room enough for a wagon to go down. It nearly scared me to death. The first wagon I saw go down they put the brake on and rough locked the hind wheels and had a big rope fastened to the wagon and about ten men holding back on it and then they went down like they would smash everything. I'll never forget that day. When we was walking down Willie looked back and cried and asked me how we would get back home.

---

straight shot via Escalante that would cut the distance in half. The expedition set off in the autumn of 1879, convinced that they were part of a divine mission.

Yet hints of trouble to come filtered back from the group as they discovered the Colorado River crossing to be far more difficult than first believed. Lack of springs along the way added to their worries. From their start at Escalante, road builders progressed rapidly for the first 50 miles, then slowly over rugged slickrock for the final six miles to Hole-in-the-Rock. A sheer 45-foot drop below this narrow notch was followed by almost a mile of extremely steep slickrock to the Colorado River. The route looked impossible, but three crews of workers armed with picks and blasting powder worked simultaneously to widen the notch and construct a precarious wagon road down to the river and up the cliffs on the other side.

The job took six weeks. Miraculously, all of the people, animals, and wagons made it down and were ferried across the Colorado River without a serious accident. Canyons and other obstacles continued to block the way as the weary group pressed on. Only after six months of exhausting travel did they stop at the present-day site of Bluff on the San Juan River.

Today, on a journey from Escalante, you can experience a bit of the same adventure the pioneers knew. Except for scattered signs of ranching, the land remains unchanged. If the road is dry, vehicles with good clearance can drive to within a short distance of Hole-in-the-Rock. The rough conditions encountered past Dance Hall Rock require more clearance than most cars allow. Bring sufficient gas, food, and water for the entire 126-mile round-trip from Escalante.

The turnoff from Highway 12 is five miles east of Escalante. In addition to rewarding you with scenic views, Hole-in-the-Rock Road passes many side drainages of the Escalante River to the east and some remote country of the Kaiparowits Plateau high above to the west. Staff at the information center just west of Escalante can give current road conditions and suggest hikes.

Metate Arch and other rock sculptures decorate **Devils Garden,** 12.5 miles down Hole-in-the-Rock Road. Turn west 0.3 mile at the sign to the parking area because you can't really see the "garden" from the road. Red- and cream-colored sandstone formations sit atop pedestals or tilt at crazy angles. Delicate bedding lines run through the rocks. There are no trails or markers—just wander about at your whim. The Bureau of Land Management has provided picnic tables, grills, and outhouses for day use. No overnight camping is permitted at Devils Garden.

Dance Hall Rock (38 miles down Hole-in-the-Rock Road) jumped to the fiddle music and lively steps of the expedition members in 1879. Its natural amphitheater has a relatively smooth floor and made a perfect gathering spot when the Hole-in-the-Rock group had to wait three weeks at nearby Fortymile Spring for road work to be completed ahead. Dance Hall Rock is an enjoyable place to explore and only a short walk from the parking area. Solution holes, left from water dissolving in the rock, pockmark the sandstone structure.

At road's end (57 miles from Highway 12), continue on foot across slickrock to the notch and views of the blue waters of Lake Powell below. Rockslides have made the descent impossible for vehicles, but hikers can scramble down to the lake and back in about one hour. The elevation change is 600 feet. The half-mile round-trip is strenuous. After a steep descent over boulders, look for steps of Uncle Ben's Dugway at the base of the notch. Below here the grade is gentler. Drill holes in the rock once held oak stakes against which logs, brush, and earth supported the outer wagon wheels. The inner wheels followed a narrow rut 4–6 inches deep. About two-thirds of the route down is now under water, although the most impressive road work can still be seen.

Boynton Overlook and Hundred Hands Pictograph

Be sure to pull off Highway 12 at the Boynton Overlook and scan the walls on the far side of the Escalante River for the Hundred Hands pictograph. (Binoculars help immensely.) For a closer look, hike up from the parking lot just at the bottom of the hill, at the Escalante River crossing. Rather than hike along the river, go up above the house (don't stray onto fenced-in private property), scramble up the face of the first cliff, and follow faint trails and rock cairns across the bench. (It's easiest if you've located the pictographs first from the overlook.) The Hundred Hands are high up on a cliff face that's larger than the one you scrambled up. Follow the cliff to the right, where pictographs of goats are lower on the wall.

Back down at river level, head downstream a few hundred yards and look up to the left to see Anasazi ruins, known as the "Moki house."

Calf Creek Recreation Area

This stunning canyon and park offers the most

© PAUL LEVY

It takes binoculars and a little looking, but the Hundred Hands pictograph is visible from the Boynton Overlook.

accessible glimpse of what Escalante canyon country is all about. The trailhead to 126-foot **Lower Calf Creek Falls** is here, and you should definitely make plans for the half-day hike, especially if you have no time for further exploration of this magical landscape. Otherwise, stop here to picnic in the shade of willows and cottonwoods. This is also the most convenient and attractive **campsite** for dozens of miles. The 13 campsites have water, fire pits, and picnic tables.

The Million-Dollar Road

Highway 12 between Escalante and Boulder was completed in 1935 by workers from the Civilian Conservation Corps. The cost was a budget-busting $1 million. Before then, mules carried supplies and mail across this wilderness of slickrock and narrow canyons. The section of Highway 12 between Calf Creek and Boulder is extraordinarily scenic—even jaded travelers used to the wonders of Utah will have to pull over and ogle the views from the **Hog's Back,** where the road crests a fin of rock above

the canyons of the Escalante. Be here for sunset on a clear evening and you'll have a memory to carry for the rest of your life.

Boulder

Boulder is a tiny community in a lovely location at the base of Boulder Mountain, where the alpine air mixes with the desert breezes. The single best lodging choice in the Escalante region—the Boulder Mountain Lodge—is here, so plan accordingly. (See the *Boulder* section later in this chapter for more information.)

◖ Anasazi State Park

At this excellent state park (Hwy. 12 one mile north of Boulder, 435/335-7308, www.stateparks.utah.gov, 8 A.M.–6 P.M. daily, $3 per person), museum exhibits, an excavated village site, and a pueblo replica provide a look into the life of these ancient people. The Anasazi stayed here for 50–75 years sometime between A.D. 1050 and 1200. They grew corn, beans, and squash in fields nearby. The village population peaked at about 200, with an esti-

© W. C. MCRAE

Anasazi State Park features excavated Anasazi structures.

mated 40–50 dwellings. Why the Anasazi left or where they went isn't known for sure, but a fire swept through much of the village before the Anasazi abandoned it. Perhaps they burned the village on purpose, knowing they would move on. University of Utah students and faculty excavated the village, known as the Coombs Site, in 1958 and 1959. You can view pottery, axe heads, arrow points, and other tools found at the site in the museum, along with delicate items like sandals and basketry that came from more protected sites elsewhere. A diorama shows how the village might have appeared in its heyday. You can see video programs on the Anasazi and modern tribes upon request.

The self-guided tour of the ruins begins behind the museum, which is on Highway 12, 28 miles northeast of Escalante and 38 miles south of Torrey. You'll see a whole range of Anasazi building styles—a pit house, masonry walls, *jacal* walls (mud reinforced by sticks), and combinations of masonry and jacal. Replicas of habitation and storage rooms behind the museum show complete construction details.

Burr Trail Road

Burr Trail Road, originally a cattle trail blazed by stockman John Atlantic Burr, extends from the town of Boulder on Highway 12 to the Notom–Bullfrog Road, which runs between Highway 24 near the eastern entrance to Capitol Reef National Park and Bullfrog Marina on Lake Powell, off Highway 276. Starting at Boulder, the road is paved until the boundary between the GSENM and Capitol Reef National Park (31 miles), where the route traverses the Circle Cliffs, as well as spectacular canyon areas such as Long Canyon and the Gulch. As the route meets Waterpocket Fold, in Capitol Reef National Park, breathtaking switchbacks rise some 800 feet in just half a mile. These switchbacks are not considered suitable for RVs or vehicles towing trailers. The unpaved sections of the road may be impassable in poor weather. Visitors should inquire about road and weather conditions before setting out. Also inquire about hiking trails that depart from side roads.

Burr Trail Road joins Notom–Bullfrog Road

THE POLITICS OF ESTABLISHING THE NATIONAL MONUMENT

In September 1996, President Bill Clinton declared 1.9 million acres of south-central Utah a national monument, ending a decades-old debate about preserving the wilderness canyons in this part of the Southwest. The federal government's move sought to prevent the establishment of coal mines in the area, which had been planned by a Dutch resource-extraction consortium. The monument was formed by combining existing public land into a single administrative unit: The land now preserved as Grand Staircase–Escalante National Monument consists of land formerly supervised by the Bureau of Land Management (BLM), the Forest Service, and the state of Utah. The responsibility for administering the new monument was assigned to the BLM.

Preservation of the canyons as a national monument angered the Republican Utah legislative delegation and many others in this deeply conservative state. They were angry that they were not consulted about the formation of the monument, and they argued that the federal government should not interfere with local agriculture and the existing community. The move pleased environmentalists and backcountry recreationists, however, who feared that the existence of a mining operation, no matter how environmentally sound, would destroy the area's unique scenic splendor and ancient Anasazi art and ruins.

Feelings pro and con about the monument can still run deep around Escalante and southern Utah, but a whole new breed of business is springing up to address the needs of the tourists and recreationists who flock here. For people who have adapted to the changing economic and environmental forces, hostility to the monument and the crowds it attracts is subsiding, though certain issues, especially concerning the size of the monument and activities permitted within its boundaries, are still being litigated, and may be for years.

The irony in all of this is that so far, in terms of land usage, very little has changed for either the farmers and ranchers who have leased these federal lands for generations or for the hikers and bikers who want to explore the wilds of this canyon country. The BLM has moved slowly to reassess access to the land and is trying to preserve the land's tradition as a multiuse area (with ranchers retaining grazing leases on federal land). Certain restrictions are in place, but these mostly affect the use of all-terrain vehicles (ATVs) and non-street-legal vehicles (off-road vehicles, dune buggies, and certain kinds of dirt bikes).

just before it exits Capitol Reef National Park. For information on Notom–Bullfrog Road, see the *Capitol Reef National Park* chapter.

ALONG U.S. 89

This tour proceeds from Kanab to the Utah–Arizona border. From Kanab to Page, Arizona, at the Colorado River's Glen Canyon Dam, is 80 miles.

Johnson Canyon Road

Eight miles east of Kanab, Johnson Canyon Road heads north along the western border of the monument before joining Skutumpah Road and Glendale Bench Road. This road system links up with several more remote backcountry roads in the monument, and eventually leads to Cannonville along Highway 12. From U.S. 89, Johnson Canyon Road is paved for its initial miles. The road passes an abandoned movie set, where the TV series *Gunsmoke* was sometimes filmed. The road then climbs up through the scenic Vermilion and then White Cliffs of the Grand Staircase. The road eventually passes over Skutumpah Terrace, a rather featureless plateau covered with scrub.

Paria Townsite Road

This road has several names, including Paria Valley Road. It turns north off U.S. 89 at Milepost 31. The five-mile dirt road is passable to cars when dry. It passes some towering and colorful canyons and mesas, among which the remains of a **1930s Western movie set** are slowly decaying. From the parking area, walking trails lead to the abandoned bleached wood buildings, which make for great photo opportunities against the rugged backdrop. Farther along the road, as it approaches the Paria River, are the remains of Pareah, although there's not much left of this ghost town.

Paria Canyon and Vermilion Cliffs National Monument

Paria Canyon—a set of magnificent slot canyons that drain from Utah down through northern Arizona to the Grand Canyon—is the focus of popular multiday canyoneering expeditions. Paria Canyon and 293,000 acres of surrounding desert grasslands are now protected as Vermilion Cliffs National Monument. Although the monument spreads south from the Utah-Arizona border, access to the monument's most famous sites is through from back roads in Utah. In addition to the long Paria Canyon backpacking route, some shorter but strenuous day hikes explore this area (see *Recreation*). For more information, contact the Kanab Visitors Center (745 E. U.S. 89, Kanab, 435/644-4680, 8 A.M.–5 P.M. daily mid-Mar.–mid-Nov., 8 A.M.–4:30 P.M. Mon.–Fri. mid-Nov.–mid-Mar.) or stop at the Paria Contact Station, near Milepost 21 on U.S. 89.

Cottonwood Canyon Road

A few miles east of the ranger station, Cottonwood Canyon Road leads north. The unpaved road's lower portions, usually passable with a car in dry weather, pass through scenic landscapes as the road pushes north. The route climbs up across a barren plateau before dropping down onto the Paria River. Several good hikes lead from roadside trailheads into steep side canyons. The route continues north along the Cockscomb, a long wrinkle of rock ridges that run north and south across the desert. At the northern end of this route are Grosvenor Arch, Kodachrome State Park, and Highway 12 (46 miles).

Big Water and Smoky Mountain Road

At the little crossroads of Big Water, the GSENM has built a new visitors center (100 Upper Revolution Way, Big Water, 435/675-3200, 8 A.M.–5 P.M. daily mid-Mar.–mid-Nov.) to serve the needs of travelers to the monument and to Glen Canyon National Recreation Area (NRA), which is immediately adjacent to this area. The visitors center is definitely worth a stop—it houses bones from a 75 million-year-old, 30-foot-long duck-billed dinosaur. The backbone bearing toothmarks from a tyrannosaur and the 13-foot-long dino tail are especially impressive.

Joining U.S. 89 at Big Water is Smoky Mountain Road. This long and rugged road links Big Water to Highway 12 at Escalante, 78 miles north. The southern portions of the route pass through Glen Canyon NRA, and side roads lead to remote beaches and flooded canyons. The original *Planet of the Apes* was shot here, before the area was inundated by Lake Powell.

From Big Water, it's 19 miles to Page, Arizona, on U.S. 89.

GRAND STAIRCASE

Recreation

The monument preserves some of the best long-distance hiking trails in the American Southwest, but it also has shorter trails for travelers who want to sample the wonderful slot canyons and backcountry without venturing too far afield.

Be sure to check at local visitors centers for road and trail conditions, up-to-date maps, and, if you're backpacking, a free backcountry pass, which is required for overnight stays. Many of the following hikes require extensive travel on backcountry roads, which can be impassable after rains and rough the rest of the time. In summer, these trails are hot and exposed; always carry plenty of water and sunscreen and wear a hat.

Hiking the **Escalante River Canyon** is one of the world's greatest wilderness treks. Most people devote 4–6 days to exploring these slickrock canyons, which involve frequent scrambling (if not rock climbing), stream fording (if not swimming), and exhausting detours around rock falls and logjams. Most of the day hikes are along side canyons of the Escalante River and can be reached by trailheads off Hole-in-the-Rock Road or Burr Trail. A couple of shorter hikes—Lower Calf Creek Falls and Escalante Natural Bridge—start quite conveniently from Highway 12. Another good jumping-off point for day hikers is the Dry Fork Coyote Gulch Trailhead, 26 miles south of Highway 12 on Hole-in-the-Rock Road; trails here lead to two fascinating and beautifully constricted slot canyons.

The **Paria Canyon** is another famed long-distance slickrock canyon hike that covers 37 miles between the border of Utah and the edge of the Colorado River's Marble Canyon. Several long day hikes leave from trailheads on the Paria Plateau, along the border with Arizona.

Other areas with developed hiking trails include the Skutumpah Road area and Cottonwood Canyon, in the center of the park. Otherwise, hiking in the monument is mostly on unmarked routes. Although the park is de-

veloping more day-hiking options, the rangers encourage hardy adventurers to consider extended hikes across the rugged and primitive outback, beyond the busy canyon corridors. Call one of the visitors centers and ask for help from the rangers to plan a hiking adventure where there are no trails.

HIKING ALONG JOHNSON CANYON/SKUTUMPAH ROAD

The northern portions of this road pass through the White Cliffs area of the Grand Staircase, and several steep and narrow can-

WALKING SOFTLY

Only great care and awareness can preserve the pristine canyons of the Escalante. You can help if you pack out all trash, avoid trampling on the fragile cryptobiotic soils (dark areas of symbiotic algae and fungus on the sand), travel in groups of 12 or fewer, don't disturb Native American artifacts, and protect wildlife by leaving your dogs at home. Most important, bury human waste well away from water sources, trails, and camping areas; unless there's a fire hazard, burn toilet paper to aid decomposition. Campfires in developed or designated campgrounds are allowed only in fire grates, fire pits, or fire pans. Wood collection in these areas is not permitted. The use of backpacking stoves is recommended by the National Parks Service and the Bureau of Land Management. Visitors are encouraged to maximize efforts to "leave no trace" of their passage in the area.

Leave No Trace, Inc. is a national organization dedicated to awareness, appreciation, and respect for our wildlands. The organization also promotes education of outdoor recreation that is environmentally responsible. More information about Leave No Trace is available at www.lnt.org.

yons are trenched into these terraces. Rough hiking trails explore these slot canyons. As when hiking any slot canyon, be sure to check the weather report before venturing up-canyon, and beware of changes in weather; flash floods can strike fast, and they are especially common in mid- to late summer.

Willis Creek Narrows

- Distance: 2.2 miles one-way
- Duration: 3–4 hours
- Elevation change: 40 feet
- Effort: easy
- Trailhead: 9 miles south of Cannonville along Skutumpah Road

This relatively easy trail follows a small stream as it etches a deep and narrow gorge through the sandstone. From the parking area, where Skutumpah Road crosses Willis Wash, walk downstream along the wash. Follow the streambed, which quickly descends between slickrock walls. The canyon is at times no more than 6–10 feet across, while the walls rise 200–300 feet. The trail follows the streambed through the canyon for nearly 2.5 miles. To return, backtrack up the canyon. Use caution when hiking during flash flood season.

Bull Valley Gorge

- Distance: 1 mile one-way
- Duration: 1–2 hours
- Elevation change: 850 feet
- Effort: moderate–strenuous
- Trailhead: 10.5 miles south of Cannonville along Skutumpah Road

Approximately 1.5 miles south of Willis Creek on Skutumpah Road, a narrow bridge vaults over the Bull Valley Gorge. Like the Willis Creek Narrows, this is a steep and narrow cleft in the slickrock; however, scrambling along the canyon bottom is a greater challenge. From the bridge, walk upstream along a faint trail on the north side of the crevice until the walls are low enough to scramble down. From here, the canyon deepens quickly, and you'll have to negotiate several dry falls along the way (a rope will come in handy). When you reach the area below the bridge, look up to see a 1950s-model pickup truck trapped between the canyon walls. Three men died in this 1954 mishap; their bodies were recovered, but the pickup was left in place. The canyon continues another mile from this point; after that the valley widens out a bit. There is no loop trail out of the canyon, so turn back when you've seen enough.

Lick Wash

- Distance: 4 miles one-way to Park Wash
- Duration: 4–5 hours
- Elevation change: 200 feet
- Effort: easy
- Trailhead: 20 miles south of Cannonville along Skutumpah Road

From Lick Wash, trails lead downstream into slot canyons to a remote arroyo (dry riverbed) surrounded by rock-topped mesas. One of these lofty perches contains a preserve of now-rare native grasses. Although this area can be reached in a day's hike, this is also a good place to base a multiday camping trip. The trail starts just below the road crossing on Lick Wash and follows the usually dry streambed as it plunges into a narrow slot canyon. The canyon bottom is mostly level and easy to hike. After one mile, the canyon begins to widen; after four miles, Lick Wash joins Park Wash, a larger desert canyon.

Looming above this canyon junction are mesas topped with deep sandstone terraces. Rising to the east is **No Mans Mesa,** skirted on all sides by steep cliffs. The 1,788 acres atop the mesa were grazed by goats for six months in the 1920s, but since then the pristine grassland has been protected by the BLM as an Area of Critical Environmental Concern. Hardy hikers can scramble up a steep

GRAND STAIRCASE

trail—used by the aforementioned goats—to visit this wilderness preserve. The ascent of No Mans Mesa is best considered an overnight trip from Lick Wash Trailhead.

HIKING ALONG COTTONWOOD CANYON ROAD

The northerly portions of this route pass by **Kodachrome Basin State Park,** with a fine selection of hiking trails through colorful rock formations. The first five hikes in this section are in Kodachrome Park. For a brief introduction to the park's ecology, follow the short **Nature Trail.**

Panorama Trail

- Distance: 3-mile loop
- Duration: 2 hours
- Elevation change: 350 feet
- Effort: easy

© JUDY JEWELL

The hike up Cottonwood Narrows is one of the few easy hikes in the Grand Staircase-Escalante backcountry.

- Trailhead: west side of park road, south of Trailhead Station

The Panorama Trail loops through a highly scenic valley with sand pipes and colorful rocks. The trail then leaves the valley and climbs up the rocks, offering good views of the park's formations. The most spectacular views are found at Panorama Point, which requires a short, steep climb up a few switchbacks. If the three-mile loop leaves you thirsty for more hiking (and you're carrying an adequate supply of water), several spur trails offer the opportunity for a longer loop. Be sure to pick up a map of the park's hiking trails before you begin. (They're available in several locations, including the Trailhead Station.)

Angel's Palace Trail

- Distance: 1-mile loop
- Duration: 0.5–0.75 hour
- Elevation change: 300 feet
- Effort: easy–moderate
- Trailhead: Kodachrome Basin State Park, just east of group campground

From the trailhead, hike up the butte to its top, where you're rewarded with fine views of the park and surrounding area, including Bryce Canyon. Once on top of the butte, the trail is level, and the hike becomes an easy amble. It's easy to spend quite a bit of time exploring the plateau. Take note that horseback riders share this trail.

Grand Parade Trail

- Distance: 1.5-mile loop
- Duration: 1.5 hours
- Elevation change: 100 feet
- Effort: easy
- Trailhead: Kodachrome Basin State Park, Trailhead Station

The Grand Parade Trail makes a loop with good views of rock pinnacles. It stays on the floor of the canyon, so it's much gentler than some of the park's other hikes. But it's not dull—it visits a couple of box canyons and rock formations that supposedly look like marchers in a parade. Horses are permitted on this trail.

Eagle's View Trail

• Distance: 0.5 mile one-way

• Duration: 0.5 hour

• Elevation change: 1,000 feet

• Effort: moderate–strenuous

• Trailhead: north of Kodachrome Basin State Park campground

Eagle's View Trail, a segment of a historic cattle trail, climbs steep cliffs above the campground. The highest overlook is a steep quarter-mile ascent from the campground, but if you just want a good view, hike just to the top of the second set of stairs—after this point, the trail gets very narrow and exposed. Because this trail is so steep and has significant exposure, it's not good for young children. It's also best to avoid it in gusty winds.

Shakespeare Arch Trail

• Distance: 0.5 mile one-way

• Duration: 0.5 hour

• Elevation change: 50 feet

• Effort: easy

• Trailhead: From the main park road, head east past the Arch group campground, turn right (south), and follow signs to Shakespeare Arch.

Though the arch is the destination of this trail, the trailside plants and excellent views are other highlights of this easy hike. Pick up a brochure at the trailhead to help with plant identification. The arch, which is 20 feet across and 90 feet high, is tucked into a small, out-of-the-way cove and was not discovered until 1976, when a ranger searching for a coyote den

© JUDY JEWELL

Discovered in 1976, Shakespeare Arch is at the end of an easy hike.

GRAND STAIRCASE

stumbled across it. Note: Just because you've seen this arch doesn't mean you should skip Grosvenor Arch. Think of Shakespeare Arch as an appetizer for the main course down the road at Grosvenor.

Hackberry Canyon

• Distance: 22 miles one-way

• Duration: 3 days

• Elevation change: 1,300 feet

• Effort: strenuous

• Trailhead: southern end of BLM Road 422

• Directions: Head south on Cottonwood Canyon Road for 7.5 miles from where the pavement ends at Kodachrome Basin State Park to the crossing of Round Valley Draw. From here, turn south on BLM Road 422.

Hikers can travel the 22-mile length of this scenic canyon in three days or make day hikes from either end of the trail. The lower canyon meets Cottonwood Canyon at an elevation of

4,700 feet, just above the mouth of the Paria River. Cottonwood Canyon Road provides access to both ends. A small spring-fed stream flows down the lower half of Hackberry; hikers should expect to get their feet wet. Many side canyons invite exploration. One of them, Sam Pollock Canyon, is on the west side about 4.5 miles upstream from the junction of Hackberry and Cottonwood Canyons; follow it 1.75 miles up to **Sam Pollock Arch** (60 feet high and 70 feet wide). Available topographic maps include the metric 1:100,000 Smoky Mountain or the 7.5-minute Slickrock Bench and Calico Peak. Michael Kelsey's *Hiking and Exploring the Paria River* contains trail and trailhead information and a history of the Watson homestead, located a short way below Sam Pollock Canyon.

Cottonwood Narrows

- Distance: 1.5 miles one-way

- Duration: 2 hours

- Elevation change: minimal

- Effort: easy

- Trailhead: From pavement's end at Kodachrome Basin State Park, head south on Cottonwood Canyon Road. The northern end of the Cottonwood Narrows is 15 miles down the dirt road; the southern end is a mile farther south. Access is easier from the southern end.

This hike through a narrow, high-walled Navajo sandstone canyon is good for casual hikers. The sandy-bottomed wash offers an easy path through the Cockscomb and a good look at the layers of warped rocks. Several side canyons join into the wash; if you're up for some scrambling, they can make for good exploring. Even on this short hike, remember to bring water. Use caution during flash flood season.

Box of the Paria River

- Distance: 3.5 miles one-way

- Duration: 4–5 hours

- Elevation change: 500 feet

- Effort: strenuous

- Trailhead: at the confluence of Cottonwood Creek and Paria River, 2.5 miles south of lower Hackberry Canyon Trailhead (29 miles south of the pavement's end at Kodachrome State Park or, from the south, 11.5 miles north of U.S. 89)

The confluence of Paria, Hackberry, and Cottonwood Canyons provides the backdrop to an excellent if strenuous day hike. The Box of the Paria River involves some steep climbs up rocky slopes as it traverses a tongue of slickrock between the mouth of the Hackberry and Paria Canyons. The route then follows the Paria River through its "box" or cliff-sided canyon in the Cockscomb Formation. The trail returns to the trailhead by following Cottonwood Canyon upstream to the trailhead. For an easier hike up the box, start at the Old Paria town site, at the northern end of Movie Set Road. Hike a mile down the Paria River, then turn east into the box. Inquire at visitors centers for maps and about conditions.

HIKING ALONG THE ESCALANTE RIVER

The maze of canyons that drain the Escalante River presents exceptional hiking opportunities. You'll find everything from easy day hikes to challenging backpacking treks. The Escalante's canyon begins just downstream from the town of Escalante and ends at Lake Powell about 85 miles beyond. In all this distance, only one road (Highway 12) bridges the river. Many side canyons provide additional access to the Escalante, and most are as beautiful as the main gorge. The river system covers such a large area that you can find solitude even in spring, the busiest hiking season. The many eastern canyons remain virtually untouched.

The Escalante canyons preserve some of the quiet beauty once found in Glen Canyon, which is now lost under the waters of Lake Powell. Prehistoric Anasazi and Fremont people have left ruins, petroglyphs, pictographs, and artifacts in many locations. These archaeological resources are protected by federal law. *Please don't collect or disturb them.*

Before setting out, visit the rangers at the information center on the west edge of Escalante for the required free permit to backpack overnight in the GSENM, and to check on the latest trail and road conditions. Restrictions on group size may be in force on some of the more popular trails. You can also obtain topographic maps and literature that show trailheads, mileages, and other information that may be useful in planning trips. Some of the more popular trailheads have self-registration stations for permits.

The best times for a visit are early March to early June and mid-September to early November. Summertime trips are possible, too, but be prepared for higher temperatures and greater flash-flood danger in narrow canyons. Travel along the Escalante River involves frequent crossings, and there's always water in the main canyon, usually ankle- to knee-deep. Pools in The Narrows between Scorpion Gulch and Stevens Canyon can be up to chest-deep in spots (which you can bypass), but that's the exception. Occasional springs, some tributaries, and the river itself provide drinking water. Always purify it first; the BLM warns of the unpleasant disease giardiasis, which is caused by an invisible protozoan. Don't forget insect repellent—mosquitoes and deer flies seek out hikers in late spring and summer. Long-sleeved shirts and long pants also discourage biting insects and protect against the brush.

For guided day hikes and hiker shuttles into the Escalante canyons, contact **Utah Canyons** (325 W. Main St., 435/826-4967, www.utah canyons.com).

Escalante Canyon Trailheads

The many approaches to the area allow all sorts of trips. Besides the road access at Escalante and the Highway 12 bridge, hikers can reach the Escalante River through western side canyons from Hole-in-the-Rock Road or eastern side canyons from Burr Trail Road. The western-canyon trailheads on Hole-in-the-Rock Road can be more easily reached by car,

thus facilitating vehicle shuttles. To reach eastern-canyon trailheads, with the exceptions of Deer Creek and the Gulch on Burr Trail Road, you'll need lots of time and, if the road is wet, a sturdy four-wheel-drive vehicle. You must carry water for these more remote canyons. With the exception of Deer Creek, they're usually dry.

Town of Escalante to Highway 12 Bridge

- Distance: 15 miles one-way

- Duration: overnight

- Elevation loss: 500 feet

- Effort: moderate–strenuous

- Trailhead: near town of Escalante

- Directions: Follow signs from Highway 12 on the east side of town, by the high school, to the trailhead.

This section of the Escalante River offers easy walking and stunning canyon scenery. Tributaries and sandstone caves invite exploration. You'll find good camping areas the entire way. (Be sure to get a permit for overnight camping.) Usually the river here is only ankle deep. Almost immediately, the river knifes its way through the massive cliffs of the Escalante Monocline, leaving the broad valley of the upper river behind. Although there is no maintained trail along this stretch of the east-flowing river, it's relatively easy to pick your way along the riverbank.

Death Hollow, which is far prettier than the name suggests, meets the Escalante from the north after 7.5 miles. Several good swimming holes carved in rock lie a short hike upstream from the Escalante; watch for poison ivy among the greenery. Continue farther up Death Hollow to see more pools, little waterfalls, and outstanding canyon scenery. You can bypass some pools, but others you'll have to swim—bring a small inflatable boat, air mattress, or waterproof bag to ferry packs.

Sand Creek, on the Escalante's north side 4.5 miles downstream from Death Hollow, is also worth exploring; deep pools begin a short way up from the mouth. Another half mile down the Escalante, a natural arch appears high on the canyon wall. Then Escalante Natural Bridge comes into view, just two miles from the Highway 12 bridge.

Escalante Natural Arch and Bridge

• Distance: 2 miles one-way

• Duration: 2 hours

• Elevation change: 100 feet

• Effort: easy

• Trailhead: Highway 12 bridge over the Escalante River, between Escalante and Boulder

This hike upstream from the highway gives day hikers a taste of the Escalante River. After about 1.5 miles of hiking, you'll see the arch (look up) and then the 130-foot-high natural bridge. Hike upstream from the bridge for better views of the arch. Continue the hike for another half mile beyond the arch to the point where Sand Creek enters the Escalante. Hotweather hikers may want to head a short distance up Sand Creek to find deep pools.

Phipps Wash

• Distance: 2 miles one-way to Maverick Bridge

• Duration: 3 hours

• Elevation change: 300 feet

• Effort: easy

• Trailhead: Highway 12 bridge over the Escalante River, between Escalante and Boulder

Start this hike from the highway crossing and follow the Escalante River downstream to Phipps Wash, a lovely side canyon. (A sign will direct you to cross the Escalante River; heed it.) Highlights of the hike are Maverick Bridge, about half a mile up the wash in a side canyon, and Phipps Arch, visible high on the canyon wall above the wash. If you want to continue up the wash, the streambed trail gives

way to a sandy wash, then slickrock. The head of Phipps Wash is about four miles from the Escalante River.

Highway 12 Bridge to Harris Wash

• Distance: 26.5 miles one-way

• Duration: 4–6 days

• Elevation change: 700 feet

• Effort: moderate

• Trailhead: Highway 12 bridge over the Escalante River

This is where many long-distance trekkers begin their exploration of the Escalante canyons. In this section, the Escalante Canyon offers a varied show: In places the walls close in to make constricted narrows; at others they step back to form great valleys. Side canyons filled with lush greenery and sparkling streams contrast with dry washes of desert, yet all can be fun to explore. A good hike of 4–6 days begins at the highway bridge, goes down the Escalante to Harris Wash, then up Harris to a trailhead off Hole-in-the-Rock Road (37 miles total).

From the Highway 12 bridge parking area, a trail leads to the river. Canyon access goes through private property; cross the river at the posted signs. **Phipps Wash** comes in from the south (right side) after 1.5 miles and several more river crossings. Turn up its wide mouth for half a mile to see Maverick Bridge in a drainage to the right. To reach Phipps Arch, continue another 0.75 mile up the main wash, turn left into a box canyon, and scramble up the left side (see the 7.5-minute Calf Creek topographic map).

Bowington (Boynton) Arch is an attraction in a north side canyon known locally as Deer Creek. Look for this small canyon on the left one mile beyond Phipps Wash; hike up it for about a mile, past three deep pools, and then turn left into a tributary canyon. In 1878, gunfire resolved a quarrel between local ranchers John Boynton and Washington Phipps. Phipps was killed, but both their names live on.

Waters of **Boulder Creek** come rushing into the Escalante from the north in the next major side canyon, 5.75 miles below the Highway 12 bridge. The creek, along with its Dry Hollow and Deer Creek tributaries, provides good canyon walking; deep areas may require swimming or climbing up on the plateau. (You could also start down Deer Creek from Burr Trail Road, where they meet, 6.5 miles southeast of Boulder at a primitive BLM campground; starting at the campground, follow Deer Creek 7.5 miles to Boulder Creek, then 3.5 miles down Boulder to the Escalante.) Deer and Boulder Creeks have water year-round.

High, sheer sandstone walls constrict the Escalante River in a narrow channel below Boulder Creek, but the canyon widens again above the **Gulch** tributary, 14 miles below the highway bridge. Hikers can head up the Gulch on a day hike.

Alternatively, hikers can descend the Gulch from Burr Trail Road to join the Escalante Canyon at this point (the Gulch Trailhead is 10.8 miles southeast of Boulder). The hike from the road down to the Escalante is 12.5 miles, but there's only one difficult spot: a 12-foot waterfall in a section of narrows about halfway down. When Rudi Lambrechtse, author of *Hiking the Escalante,* tried friction climbing around the falls and the pool at their base, he fell and broke his foot. That meant a painful three-day hobble out. Instead of taking the risk, Rudi recommends backtracking about 300 feet from the falls and climbing out from a small alcove in the west wall (look for a cairn on the ledge above). Climb up Brigham Tea Bench, walk south, then look for cairns leading back east to the narrows, and finally descend to the streambed (a rope helps to lower packs in a small chimney section).

Most springs along the Escalante are difficult to spot. One that's easy to find is in the first south bend after the Gulch; water comes straight out of the rock a few feet above the river. Escalante Canyon becomes wider as the river lazily meanders along. Hikers can cut off some of the bends by walking in the open desert between canyon walls and riverside willow thickets. A bend cut off by the river itself loops to the north just before Horse Canyon, three miles below the Gulch. Along with its tributaries **Death Hollow** and **Wolverine Creek, Horse Canyon** drains the Circle Cliffs to the northeast. Floods in these mostly dry streambeds wash down pieces of black petrified wood. (Vehicles with good clearance can reach the upper sections of all three canyons from a loop road off Burr Trail Road.) Horse and Wolverine Creek Canyons offer good easy-to-moderate hiking, but if you really want a challenge, try Death Hollow (sometimes called "Little Death Hollow" to distinguish it from the larger one near Hell's Backbone Road). Starting from the Escalante River, go about two miles up Horse Canyon and turn right into Death Hollow; rugged scrambling over boulders takes you back into a long section of twisting narrows. Carry water for Upper Horse Canyon and its tributaries. Lower Horse Canyon usually has water.

About 3.5 miles down the Escalante from Horse Canyon, you'll enter Glen Canyon NRA and come to Sheffield Bend, a large, grassy field on the right. Only a chimney remains from Sam Sheffield's old homestead. Two grand amphitheaters lie beyond the clearing and up a stiff climb in loose sand. Over the next 5.5 river miles to Silver Falls Creek, you'll pass long bends, dry side canyons, and a huge slope of sand on the right canyon wall. Don't look for any silver waterfalls in **Silver Falls Creek**—the name comes from streaks of shiny desert varnish on the cliffs. You can approach Upper Silver Falls Creek by a rough road from Burr Trail Road, but a car shuttle between here and any of the trailheads on the west side of the Escalante River would take all day. Most hikers visit this drainage on a day hike from the river. Carry water with you.

Harris Wash is to the right (west) side of the Escalante River almost opposite Silver Falls Creek. When the Hole-in-the-Rock route proved so difficult, pioneers figured there had to be a better way to the San Juan Mission. Their new wagon road descended Harris Wash to the Escalante River, climbed part of Silver Falls Creek, crossed the Circle Cliffs,

GRAND STAIRCASE

descended Muley Twist Canyon in the Waterpocket Fold, then followed Hall's Creek to Hall's Crossing on the Colorado River. Charles Hall operated a ferry there 1881–1884. Old maps show a jeep road through Harris Wash and Silver Falls Creek Canyons, used before the National Park Service closed off the Glen Canyon NRA section. Harris Wash lies just half a mile downstream and across the Escalante from Silver Falls Creek.

C Lower Calf Creek Falls

- Distance: 2.75 miles one-way

- Duration: 4 hours

- Elevation gain: 250 feet

- Effort: easy–moderate

- Trailhead: Calf Creek Campground, on Highway 12, 16 miles east of Escalante ($2 day-use parking fee)

Calf Creek is a tributary to the Escalante River, entering it right near Highway 12. The hike to Lower Calf Creek Falls is quite accessible for ordinary folks and is, for many people, the highlight of their first trip to the Escalante area. It's the dazzling enticement that brings people back for longer and more remote hiking trips. From the trailhead and park just off Highway 12, the trail winds between high cliffs of Navajo sandstone streaked with desert varnish, where you'll see beaver ponds, Native American ruins and pictographs, and the misty 126-foot-high Lower Calf Creek Falls. A brochure available at the trailhead next to the campground identifies many of the desert and riparian plant species along the way. Bring water and perhaps a lunch. Summer temperatures can soar, but the falls and the crystal-clear pool beneath stay cool. Sheer cliffs block travel farther upstream.

Calf Creek Campground, near the road, has 13 sites ($10) with drinking water from early April through late October. Reserve group sites through the Escalante Visitors Center.

Upper Calf Creek Falls

- Distance: 1 mile one-way

- Duration: 1.5 hours

- Elevation gain: 500 feet

- Effort: moderate

- Trailhead: just east of Milepost 81 on Highway 12

- Directions: From Escalante, drive about 20.5 miles east on Highway 12. Turn left onto a dirt road between Mileposts 80 and 81; the road may be marked by a black boulder with a white stripe. Drive 0.25 mile up the bumpy dirt road to the trailhead. (Park low-clearance vehicles at the turnoff and walk to the trailhead.)

The hike to Upper Calf Creek Falls is more strenuous and less populated than the trail to the lower falls. It's also entirely different in nature, so don't feel that, if you've hiked to the lower falls, the upper-falls trip will be a mere repeat. This hike starts with a fairly steep descent across slickrock then continues

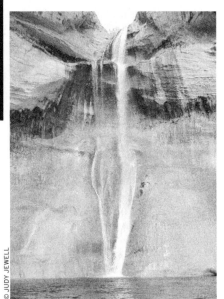

© JUDY JEWELL

Lower Calf Creek Falls

GRAND STAIRCASE

along a sandy trail. At a fork, you can choose to hike down to the base of the 87-foot-high falls or stay high and continue across more slickrock to the top of the falls and some deep pools in the stream. Near the bottom of the falls are hanging gardens and thick vegetation. At the top, paintbrush grows out of cracks in the slickrock.

Harris Wash

- Distance: 10.25 miles one-way from trailhead to Escalante River
- Duration: 2 days round-trip
- Elevation change: 700 feet
- Effort: moderate
- Trailhead: Harris Wash Trailhead off Hole-in-the-Rock Road
- Directions: From Highway 12 turn south on Hole-in-the-Rock Road for 10.8 miles, then left 6.3 miles on a dirt road (keep left at the fork near the end).

Clear, shallow water glides down this gem of a canyon. High cliffs streaked with desert varnish are deeply undercut and support lush hanging gardens. Harris Wash provides a beautiful route to the Escalante River, but it can also be a destination in itself; tributaries and caves invite exploration along the way. The sand and gravel streambed makes for easy walking. Don't be dismayed by the drab appearance of upper Harris Wash. The canyon and creek appear a few miles downstream. The Harris Wash Trailhead has a restriction of 12 persons per group.

Harris Wash to Lake Powell

- Distance: 42.75 miles one-way
- Duration: 8–9 days
- Elevation change: 1,000 feet
- Effort: moderate
- Trailhead: Harris Wash Trailhead off Hole-in-the-Rock Road
- Directions: From Highway 12 turn south on Hole-in-the-Rock Road for 10.8 miles, then left 6.3 miles on a dirt road (keep left at the fork near the end).

The Escalante continues its spectacular show of wide and narrow reaches, side canyons, and intriguing rock formations. A trip all the way from Harris Wash Trailhead to the Escalante, down the Escalante to near Lake Powell, then out to the Hurricane Wash Trailhead is 66.25 miles and requires 8–10 days. Many shorter hikes using other side canyons are possible, too.

Still in a broad canyon, the Escalante flows past **Fence Canyon** (on the west), 5.5 miles from Harris Wash. Fence Canyon has water and is a strenuous 3.5-mile cross-country route out to the end of Egypt Road. Get trail directions from a ranger and bring a topographic map. (Adventurous hikers could do a three-day, 20-mile loop via Fence Canyon, the Escalante River, and the northern arm of Twentyfive Mile Wash.) To reach the trailheads, take Hole-in-the-Rock Road 17.2 miles south of Highway 12, then turn left (east) 3.7 miles on Egypt Road to Twentyfive Mile Wash Trailhead or 9.1 miles to Egypt Trailhead.

Twentyfive Mile Wash, on the west side 11.5 miles below Harris Wash, is a good route for entering or leaving the Escalante River. The moderately difficult hike is 13 miles one-way from trailhead to river. Scenery changes from an uninteresting dry wash in the upper part to a beautiful canyon with water and greenery in the lower reaches. To get to the trailhead, take Hole-in-the-Rock Road 17.2 miles south of Highway 12, then turn left and drive 3.7 miles on Egypt Road.

Moody Creek enters the Escalante six meandering river miles below Twentyfive Mile Wash (or just 2.25 miles as the crow flies). A rough road off Burr Trail Road gives access to Moody Creek, Purple Hills, and other eroded features. The distance from trailhead to river is seven miles one-way (moderately strenuous), although most hikers find it more convenient to hike up from the Escalante. **Middle Moody Creek** enters Moody Creek three miles above the Escalante. Moody and Middle Moody Canyons feature colorful rock layers, petrified wood, a narrows, and solitude. Carry water because springs and waterpockets cannot be counted on. Canyons on the east side of the Escalante tend to be much drier than those on the west side.

East Moody Canyon enters the Escalante 1.5 miles downstream from Moody Canyon, and it, too, makes a good side trip. There's often water about half a mile upstream. Continuing down the Escalante, look on the left for a *rincón,* a meander cut off by the river.

Scorpion Gulch enters through a narrow opening on the right, 6.5 miles below Moody Canyon. A strenuous eight-mile climb up Scorpion Gulch over rockfalls and around deep pools brings you to a trailhead on Early Weed Bench Road. Experience, directions from a ranger, and a topographic map are needed. A challenging four-day, 30-mile loop hike uses Fox Canyon, Twentyfive Mile Wash, the Escalante River, and Scorpion Gulch. Water is found only in lower Twentyfive Mile Wash, the river, and lower Scorpion Gulch. The Early Weed Bench turnoff is 24.2 miles south on Hole-in-the-Rock Road from Highway 12; head in 5.8 miles to Scorpion Gulch Trailhead.

In the next 12 miles below Scorpion Gulch, Escalante Canyon is alternately wide and narrow. Then the river plunges into **The Narrows,** a five-mile-long section choked with boulders; plan on spending a day picking a route through this stretch. Watch out for chest-deep water here! Remote and little-visited **Stevens Canyon** enters from the east near the end of The Narrows; Stevens Arch stands guard 580 feet above the confluence. The upper and lower parts of Stevens Canyon usually have water.

Coyote Gulch, on the right 1.5 miles below Stevens Canyon, marks the end of the Escalante for most hikers. In some seasons, Lake Powell comes within one mile of Coyote Gulch and occasionally floods the canyon mouth. Coyote can stay flooded for several weeks, depending on the release flow of Glen Canyon Dam. The river and lake don't have a pretty meeting place—quicksand and dead trees are

found here. Logjams make it difficult to travel in from the lake by boat.

Coyote Gulch has received more publicity than other areas of the Escalante, and you're more likely to meet other hikers here. Two arches, a natural bridge, graceful sculpturing of the streambed and canyon walls, deep undercuts, and a cascading creek make a visit well worthwhile. The best route in starts where Hole-in-the-Rock Road crosses Hurricane Wash, 34.7 miles south of Highway 12. It's 12.5 miles one-way from the trailhead to the river, and the hike is moderately strenuous. Coyote Gulch, which has water, is 5.25 miles from the trailhead. Another way into Coyote Gulch begins at the Red Well Trailhead; it's 31.5 miles south on Hole-in-the-Rock Road, then 1.5 miles east (keep left at the fork). Starting from Red Well adds almost a mile to the hike, but this route is also less crowded.

◖ Dry Fork of Coyote Gulch

- Distance: 3.5-mile loop

- Duration: 5 hours

- Elevation change: 300 feet

- Effort: moderate

- Trailhead: Dry Fork of Coyote Gulch

- Directions: From Highway 12, turn south on Hole-in-the-Rock Road for 26 miles. Turn left at the sign for Dry Fork and continue 1.7 miles along a rutted dirt road to the trailhead.

Twenty-six miles south of Highway 12 is a series of narrow, scenic, and exciting slot canyons reached by a moderate day hike. The canyons feed into the Dry Fork of Coyote Gulch, reached from the Dry Fork Trailhead. These three enchanting canyons are named **Peek-a-boo, Spooky,** and **Dry Creek.** Exploring these slots requires basic canyoneering skills and the ability to pass through some fairly narrow (12-inch) spaces. From the trailhead parking lot, follow cairns down into the sandy bottom of the Dry Fork of Coyote Gulch. The slot canyons all enter the gulch from the north; watch for cairns and trails because the openings can be easy to miss.

©PAUL LEVY

It takes a little scrambling to enter Peek-a-boo Canyon.

You'll have to scramble up some rocks to get into Peek-a-boo. The slots sometimes contain deep pools of water; chockstones and pour-offs can make access difficult. No loop trail links the three slot canyons; follow each until the canyon becomes to narrow to continue, then come back out. To make a full circuit of these canyons requires about 3.5 miles of hiking.

HIKING IN PARIA CANYON AND VERMILION CLIFFS

The wild and twisting canyons of the Paria River and its tributaries offer a memorable experience for experienced hikers. Silt-laden waters have sculpted the colorful canyon walls, revealing 200 million years of geologic history. *Paria* means "muddy water" in the Paiute language. You enter the 2,000-foot-deep gorge of the Paria in southern Utah, then hike 37 miles downstream to Lee's Ferry in Arizona, where the Paria empties into the Colorado River. A handful of shorter but rugged day hikes lead to superb scenery and geologic curiosities.

Ancient petroglyphs and campsites show that Pueblo people traveled the Paria more than 700 years ago. They hunted mule deer and bighorn sheep while using the broad, lower end of the canyon to grow corn, beans, and squash. The Dominguez-Escalante Expedition stopped at the mouth of the Paria in 1776, and these were the first white men to see the river. John D. Lee and three companions traveled through the canyon in 1871 to bring a herd of cattle from the Pahreah settlement to Lee's Ferry. After Lee began a Colorado River ferry service in 1872, he and others farmed the lower Paria Canyon. Prospectors came here to search for gold, uranium, and other minerals, but much of the canyon remained unexplored. In the late 1960s, the BLM organized a small expedition whose research led to protection of the canyon as a primitive area. The Arizona Wilderness Act of 1984 designated Paria Canyon a wilderness, along with parts of the Paria Plateau and Vermilion Cliffs. In 2000, Vermilion Cliffs National Monument was created. For more information, see www.az.blm .gov/vermilion/vermilion.htm.

The **BLM Paria Canyon Ranger Station** is in Utah, 43 miles east of Kanab on U.S. 89 near Milepost 21. It's on the south side of the highway, just east of the Paria River. Permits are required for hiking in Paria Canyon and to visit other sites in Vermilion Cliffs National Monument.

Hiking Paria Canyon

- Distance: 38.5 miles one-way

- Duration: 4–6 days

- Elevation change: 1,300 feet

- Effort: moderate

- Trailhead: Whitehouse Campground

- Directions: The trailhead is two miles south of the Paria ranger station on a dirt road near a campground and old homestead site called White House Ruins. The exit trailhead is in Arizona at Lonely Dell Ranch of Lee's Ferry, 44 miles southwest of Page via U.S. 89 and 89A (or 98 miles southeast of Kanab on U.S. 89A).

GRAND STAIRCASE

Allow plenty of time to hike Paria Canyon—there are many river crossings and you'll want to make side trips up at least some of the tributary canyons. Hikers should have enough backpacking experience to be self-sufficient as help may be days away. Flash floods can race through the canyon, especially during summer. Rangers close the Paria if they think a danger exists. Because the upper end is narrowest (between miles 4.2 and 9.0), rangers require that all hikers start here so they have up-to-date weather information for their passage

You must register at a trailhead or the Kanab BLM office (318 North 100 East, Kanab, UT, 435/644-2672, 8 A.M.–4:30 P.M. Mon.–Fri. year-round). Permits to hike the canyon are $5 per day per person; backpackers should get a permit at the ranger station, but day hikers can just register and pay the fee at the trailhead. The visitors center and the office both provide weather forecasts and brochures with map and hiking information. The visitors center always has the weather forecast posted at an outdoor information kiosk.

The hike requires a 150-mile round-trip car shuttle. For a list of shuttle services, check the BLM website or ask at the Arizona Strip Interpretive Association (345 E. Riverside Dr., St. George, UT, 435/688-3246), Paria Contact Station, or Kanab Field Office. Expect to pay about $100 for this service.

All visitors should take special care to minimize their impact on this beautiful canyon. Check the BLM's "Visitor Use Regulations" for the Paria before you go. Regulations include no campfires in the Paria and its tributaries, a pack-in/pack-out policy, and that latrines be made at least 100 feet away from river and campsite locations. Also, remember to take some plastic bags to carry out toilet paper; the stuff lasts years and years in this desert climate. You don't want to haunt future hikers with TP flowers!

The Paria rangers recommend a maximum group size of six, though regulations specify a 10-person limit. No more than 20 people per day can enter the canyon for overnight trips. The best times to travel along the Paria are from about mid-March through June and October through November. May, especially Memorial Day weekend, tends to be crowded. Winter hikers often complain of painfully cold feet. Wear shoes suitable for frequent wading; canvas shoes are better than heavy leather hiking boots. You can get good drinking water from springs along the way (see the BLM hiking brochure for locations); it's best not to use the river water because of possible chemical pollution from farms and ranches upstream. Normally the river's only ankle-deep, but in spring or after rainy spells, it can become much deeper. During thunderstorms, levels can rise to more than 20 feet deep in the Paria Narrows, so heed weather warnings! Quicksand, which is most prevalent after flooding, is more a nuisance than a danger—usually it's just knee-deep. Many hikers carry a walking stick to probe the opaque waters for good crossing places.

Wrather Canyon Arch, one of Arizona's largest natural arches, lies about one mile up a side canyon of the Paria. The massive structure has a 200-foot span. Turn right (southwest) at mile 20.6 on the Paria hike. (The mouth of Wrather Canyon and other points along the Paria are unsigned; you need to follow your map.)

Buckskin Gulch and Wire Pass

- Distance: 1.7 miles one-way

- Duration: 3 hours

- Elevation change: 300 feet

- Effort: moderate

- Trailhead: Wire Pass Trailhead

- Directions: From Kanab, head 37 miles east on U.S. 89 to BLM Road 700 (also called House Rock Valley Rd.), between Mileposts 25 and 26. Turn south for 8.5 bumpy miles to the trailhead.

Buckskin Gulch is an amazing slot-canyon tributary of the Paria, with convoluted walls reaching hundreds of feet high and narrowing to as little as four feet in width. In places the walls block out so much light that it's like walking in a cave. Be *very* careful to avoid flash floods.

Day hikers can get a taste of this incredible canyon country by driving to the Wire Pass Trailhead. From the trailhead, a relatively easy trail leads into Wire Pass, a narrow side canyon that joins Buckskin Gulch. The trail travels the length of Wire Pass to its confluence with Buckskin Gulch. From here, you can explore this exceptionally narrow canyon, or follow Buckskin Gulch to its appointment with Paria Canyon (12.5 miles).

For the full experience of Buckskin Gulch, long-distance hikers can begin at Buckskin Gulch Trailhead, 4.5 miles south of U.S. 89 off BLM Road 700. From here, it's 16.3 miles (one-way) to Paria Canyon. Hikers can continue down the Paria or turn upstream and hike six miles to exit at the White House Trailhead near the ranger station. Hiking this gulch can be strenuous, with rough terrain, deep pools of water, and log and rock jams that may require the use of ropes. Conditions vary considerably from one year to the next. Regulations mandate packing your waste out of this area.

Hiking permits are $5 per day per person; backpackers should get a permit at the ranger station, but day hikers can just register and pay the fee at the trailhead.

Coyote Buttes

You've probably seen photos of these dramatic rock formations: towering sand dunes frozen into rock. These much-photographed buttes are located on the Paria Plateau, just south of Wire Pass. Access is strictly controlled, and you can only enter the area with advanced reservation and by permit. The number of people allowed into the area is also strictly limited; however, the permit process, fees, and restrictions are exactly the same as for Paria Canyon. See the Vermilion Cliffs Monument website for information (www.az.blm .gov/vermilion/vermilion.htm).

The BLM has divided the area into Coyote North and Coyote South, with a limit of 10 people per day in each. No dogs are allowed. The Wave—the most photographed of the buttes—is in Coyote North, so this region is the most popular (and easiest to reach from Wire Pass Trailhead); BLM staff will give you a map and directions when you get your permit. After the trailhead, you're on your own because the wilderness lacks signs. Permits are more difficult to obtain in spring and autumn— the best times to visit—and on weekends. The fragile sandstone can break if climbed on, so it's important to stay on existing hiking routes and wear soft-soled footwear.

MOUNTAIN BIKING

Mountain bikes are allowed on all roads in the monument, but not on hiking trails. Mountain bikers are not allowed to travel cross-country off roads, or to make their own routes across slickrock; however, there are hundreds of miles of primitive road in the monument, with dozens of loop routes available for cyclists on multiday trips. In addition to following the scenic **Burr Trail** from Boulder to Waterpocket Fold in Capitol Reef National Park, cyclists can loop off this route and follow the Circle Cliffs/Wolverine trail. This 45-mile loop traverses the headwaters of several massive canyons as they plunge to meet the Escalante River.

Hole-in-the-Rock Road is mostly a one-way-in, one-way-out affair, but cyclists can follow side roads to hiking trailheads and big vistas over the Escalante canyons. Popular side roads include a 10-mile round-trip road to the area known as Egypt, and the Fifty Mile Bench Road, a 27-mile loop from Hole-in-the-Rock Road that explores the terrain above Glen Canyon. Left Hand Collet Road, a rough jeep trail that a mountain bike can bounce through easily enough, links Hole-in-the-Rock Road with the Smoky Mountain Road system, with links to both Escalante in the north and Big Water in the south.

Other popular routes in the **Big Water area** include the Nipple Butte loop and the steep loop around Smoky Butte and Smoky Hollow, with views over Lake Powell. **Cottonwood Canyon Road,** which runs between U.S. 89 and Cannonville, is another long back road with access to a network of less-traveled trails.

Request more information on mountain biking from the visitors centers. They have handouts and maps and can help cyclists plan backcountry bike adventures. This country is remote and primitive, so cyclists must carry everything they are likely to need. Also, there are no clean water sources in the monument, so cyclists must transport all drinking water or be prepared to purify it.

FOUR-WHEEL-DRIVE EXPLORATION

Without a mountain bike or a pair of hiking boots, the best way to explore the backcountry of the GSENM is with a four-wheel-drive high-clearance vehicle; however, the scale of the monument, the primitive quality of many of the roads, and the extreme weather conditions common in the desert mean that you shouldn't head into the backcountry unless you are confident in your skills as a mechanic and driver. Choose roads that match your vehicle's capacity and your driving ability, and you should be okay. Some roads that appear on maps are slowly going back to nature: rather than close some roads, park officials are letting the desert reclaim them. Other roads are being closed, so it's best to check on access and road conditions before setting out. Remember that many of the roads in the monument are *very* slow going. If you've got somewhere to be in a hurry, these corrugated, boulder-dodging roads may not get you there in time. Be sure to take plenty of water—not only for drinking, but also for overheated radiators. It's also wise to carry wooden planks or old carpet scraps for help in gaining traction should your wheels be mired in the sand.

RAFTING

Most of the year, shallow water and rocks make boat travel impossible on the Escalante River, but for two or three weeks during spring runoff, which peaks in early April and late May,

river levels rise high enough to be passable. (In some years there may not be enough water in any season.) Contact the information center in Escalante for ideas on when to hit the river at its highest. Shallow draft and maneuverability are essential, so inflatable canoes or kayaks work best (also because they are easier to carry out at trip's end or if water levels drop too low for floating). Not recommended are rafts (too wide and bulky) and hard-shelled kayaks and canoes (they get banged up on the many rocks). The usual launch is the Highway 12 bridge. Coyote Gulch—a 13-mile hike—is a good spot to get out, as is Crack in the Wall, which is a 2.75-mile hike on steep sand from the junction of Coyote and Escalante Canyons to Forty-Mile Ridge Trailhead; four-wheel drive is needed, and a rope is required to negotiate the vessel over the canyon rim. Hole-in-the-Rock is another pullout (a 600-foot ascent over boulders; rope suggested). You could also arrange for a friend to pick you up by boat from Halls Crossing or Bullfrog Marina. River boaters must obtain a free backcountry permit from either the BLM or the National Park Service.

OUTFITTERS

There aren't many places to shop for gear in this remote area. The most centrally located shops are in the town of Escalante, where you'll find **Utah Canyons Desert Adventure Store** (325 W. Main St., 435/826-4967), which stocks books, maps, and some outdoor gear. Right across the street, **Escalante Outfitters** (310 W. Main St., 435/826-4266) has a little bit of everything (including a small liquor store) and is a good place to pick up a warm jacket or a stylish tank top.

Another shop with a good selection of clothing and gear is in Kanab. **Willow Canyon Outdoor** (263 South 100 East, 435/644-8884) also serves coffee and has an excellent book shop.

Escalante

Escalante is a natural hub for exploration of the GSENM. Even if you don't have the time or the inclination to explore the rugged canyon country that the monument protects, you'll discover incredible scenery just by traveling Highway 12 through Escalante country.

At first glance, Escalante looks like a town that time has passed by. Only 744 people live here, in addition to the resident cows, horses, and chickens that you'll meet just one block off Main Street. Yet this little community is the biggest place for more than 60 miles around and a center for ranchers and travelers. Escalante (elevation 5,813 feet) has the neatly laid-out streets and trim little houses typical of Mormon settlements.

One caveat: Drive slowly through town! The local police officer seems to have a refined eye for out-of-towners exceeding the speed limit.

THE PETRIFIED FOREST

Trees fall into water, are washed downstream, and are buried by mud, silt, and ash. Minerals and elements like silica (from volcanic ash) enter the wood either from water or the ground, filling in the "pores." When the pores of the wood have been filled, its color changes, depending on the minerals present. This mineral-loaded wood is resistant to rotting and is often quite beautiful, displaying the original cellular structure and grain of the wood.

Two especially good places to see petrified wood are along Huber Wash, in the western section of Zion National Park just west of Springdale, and at Escalante Petrified Forest State Park, just west of the town of Escalante.

Although it should go without saying that the petrified wood in these places should stay there – and not travel home in a hiker's pack or pocket – this general ethical guideline is backed up by a potent mythology of misfortune befalling people who steal petrified wood. Posted on a bulletin board at the base of the Petrified Forest Trail in the state park are many letters from people who decided to return bits of petrified wood they'd secreted away from the park, and the tales of how their lives went down the tubes after they'd stolen the wood.

ACCOMMODATIONS

Accommodations in Escalante range from simple to luxurious, but they all must add a hefty 12.5 percent room tax to the fees listed here.

Under $50

The seven small but comfy log cabins at **Escalante Outfitters** (310 W. Main St., 435/826-4266, www.escalanteoutfitters.com, $45) share men's and women's bathhouses and a common grassy area. Tucked behind the store (which also houses a casual pizza and espresso restaurant and a tiny liquor store), these cabins are convenient to all the action the town has to offer, including wireless Internet access. If you'd rather sleep in your own tent, camping is permitted on the lawn ($14), which is sheltered from the street. Dogs are permitted for a small fee in the cabins and are free if they stay in your tent.

The following are basic but perfectly acceptable: The **Moqui Motel** (480 W. Main St., 435/826-4210, www.go-utah.com/moqui-motel/, $30–50) has rooms and some kitchenettes and an RV park ($15 with hookups; no tents). The **Padre Motel** (20 E. Main St., 435/826-4276, www.padremotel.com, open Mar.–Nov., $30–75) has standard rooms as well as five minisuites with two bedrooms each.

$50-100

Just a shade more expensive than the rock-bottom places is the **Circle D Motel** (475 W. Main St., 435/826-4297, www.utahcanyons.com/circled.htm, $60 d), which reaches out to bicyclists and hikers. Pets are welcome in some rooms. In the winter, rates drop to as low as $30.

Another pleasant and modern establishment is **Rainbow Country B&B** (586 East 300 South, 435/826-4567 or 800/252-8824, www.bnbescalante.com, $59–89), with four guest rooms sharing 2.5 baths; guests have the use of a hot tub, a pool table, and a TV lounge.

The **Prospector Inn** (380 W. Main St., 435/826-4653, www.prospectorinn.com, $62 d) is Escalante's largest and most modern motel; there's a restaurant and lounge on the premises. If you usually stay at Best Westerns or comparable motels, this is the only standard motel in town that's even close to that quality.

Over $100

Head east from Escalante on Highway 12 to the landmark ◖ **Kiva Koffeehouse** (Milepost 73.86 on Hwy. 12, 435/826-4550, www.kivakoffeehouse.com, $160 includes breakfast), a quirky hilltop restaurant just east of the Boynton Overlook high above the Escalante River. The two spacious and beautifully decorated rooms each include a remarkable view of the surrounding country. The comfortable rooms with their grand views, fireplaces, and big, deep, jetted bathtubs make this a wonderful place to relax after a day of exploring, and the absence of TV and telephone makes it all the better. The Kiva is just above the spot where the Escalante River crosses Highway 12 and is a good base for hikers.

Right in the center of town, but tucked back away from the main drag, rooms at **Escalante's Grand Staircase B&B** (280 W. Main St., 435/826-4890 or 866/826-4890, www.escalantebnb.com, $135) are some of the nicest in the area. Rooms are individually decorated—several have rather bold murals—and are separate from the main house.

Another downtown Escalante B&B is **Canyons B&B** (120 E. Main St., 435/826-4747 or 866/526-9667, www.canyonsbnb.com, $105–115, Mar.–Nov.), where a modern "bunkhouse" has been built behind an old

farmhouse. There's nothing rustic about the three guest rooms; all are attractively decorated and equipped with TV, telephones, and wireless Internet access.

If you're traveling with a family or group of friends, consider renting the architecturally striking, solar-heated **LaLuz Desert Retreat** (888/305-4705, www.laluz.net, $150 and up), in a private setting just south of town. Two houses, designed in the Usonian tradition of Frank Lloyd Wright, are available. Each house sleeps up to six.

Campgrounds

Escalante Petrified Forest State Park (435/826-4466, www.stateparks.utah.gov, reservations at 800/322-3770, www.reserveamerica.com, $15 camping, open year-round) just northwest of the town of Escalante is conveniently located and full of attractions of its own, including most notably trails passing big chunks of petrified wood. Drinking water and showers are available, but the park has no hookups.

In town, you can stay at **Broken Bow RV Camp** (495 W. Main St., 888/241-8785 or 435/826-4959), which has simple cabins and sites for tents and RVs, plus showers and laundry services. It's closed in winter.

Calf Creek Recreation Area lies in a pretty canyon 15.5 miles east of Escalante on Highway 12; sites run $10 and are open from early April through late October; you can reserve group sites through the BLM office. **Lower Calf Creek Falls Trail** (5.5 miles round-trip) begins at the campground and follows the creek upstream to the 126-foot-high falls.

Campgrounds at **Posey Lake** (16 miles north, $8) and **Blue Spruce** (19 miles north, $7) sit atop the Aquarius Plateau in Dixie National Forest. Sites open around Memorial Day weekend and close in mid-September. Take Hell's Backbone Road (dirt) from the east edge of town.

FOOD

The **Esca-Latte Coffee Shop and Pizza Parlor,** part of Escalante Outfitters (310 W.

Main St., 435/826-4266, breakfast, lunch, and dinner daily), is a reliable place to eat in this little town. It serves espresso, handmade pizza ($17–21), and microbrew beer. The smoked trout plate ($9) is a special treat. The café has a couple of computers where customers can check email.

The **Trailhead Café** (125 E. Main St., 435/826-4714, 11:30 A.M.–4 P.M. Wed.–Mon. Apr.–Nov.) has the best burgers in town. For sandwiches or the town's best Mexican food, stop in at **Georgie's** (190 W. Main St., 435/826-4784, lunch and dinner Tues.–Sat., less than $10).

Other dining spots are more traditional small-town restaurants. The **Golden Loop Cafe** (39 W. Main St., 435/826-4433, breakfast, lunch, and dinner daily) is a typical Main Street diner with plenty of local color and homemade food.

East of town, **Kiva Koffeehouse** (Milepost 73.86 on Hwy. 12, 435/826-4550, 8:30 A.M.–4:30 P.M. Wed.–Mon.) is worth a stop, for a latte or for lunch (delicious food, much of it organic), and for a look at the view.

INFORMATION AND SERVICES

The Escalante Interagency office (755 W. Main St., 435/826-5499, 7:30 A.M.–5:30 P.M. daily mid-Mar.–mid-Nov., 8 A.M.–4:30 P.M. Mon.–Fri. mid-Nov.–mid-Mar.) on the west edge of town has an **information center** for visitors to Forest Service, BLM, and National Park Service areas around Escalante; this is also one of the best spots for information on the GSENM (open). Hikers or bikers headed for overnight trips in the monument system can obtain permits at the information center.

Kazan Memorial Clinic (65 N. Center St., 435/826-4374) offers medical care on Mondays, Wednesdays, and Fridays. The nearest hospital is 70 miles away, in Panguitch.

AROUND ESCALANTE
Hell's Backbone Scenic Drive

This scenic 38-mile drive climbs high into the forests north of Escalante with excellent views of Death Hollow and Sand Creek Canyons and the distant Navajo, Fifty Mile, and Henry Mountains.

Hell's Backbone Road reaches an elevation of 9,200 feet on the slopes of Roger Peak before descending to Hell's Backbone, 25 miles from town. Mule teams used this narrow ridge, with precipitous canyons on either side, as a route to Boulder until the 1930s. At that time, a bridge built by the Civilian Conservation Corps allowed the first vehicles to make the trip. You can still see the old mule path below the bridge. After 38 miles, the road ends at Highway 12; turn right 24 miles to return to Escalante or turn left three miles to Boulder. Cars can usually manage the gravel and dirt Hell's Backbone Road when it's dry. Snows and snowmelt, however, block the way until about late May. Check with the Interagency office in Escalante for current conditions. Trails and rough dirt roads lead deeper into the backcountry to more vistas and fishing lakes.

Posey Lake Campground (elevation 8,700 feet) offers sites amid aspen and ponderosa pines and is open with drinking water Memorial Day weekend through mid-September ($8). Rainbow and brook trout swim in the adjacent lake. A hiking trail (two miles round-trip) begins near space number 14 and climbs 400 feet to an old fire-lookout tower, with good views of the lake and surrounding country. Posey Lake is 14 miles north of Escalante, then two miles west on a side road.

Blue Spruce Campground (elevation 7,860 feet) is another pretty spot, but it has only six sites. Anglers can try for pan-sized trout in a nearby stream. The campground, surrounded by blue spruce, aspen, and ponderosa pine, has drinking water from Memorial Day weekend to mid-September ($7); go north 19 miles from town, then turn left and drive half a mile.

Boulder

About 180 people live in this farming community at the base of Boulder Mountain. Ranchers began drifting in during the late 1870s, although not with the intent that they'd form a town. By the mid-1890s, Boulder had established itself as a ranching and dairy center. Remote and hemmed in by canyons and mountains, Boulder remained one of the last communities in the country to rely on pack trains for transportation. Motor vehicles couldn't drive in until the 1930s. Today Boulder is worth a visit to see an excavated Anasazi village and the spectacular scenery along the way. Take paved Highway 12 either through the canyon and slickrock country from Escalante or over the Aquarius Plateau from Torrey (near Capitol Reef National Park). Burr Trail Road connects Boulder with Capitol Reef National Park's southern district via Waterpocket Fold and Circle Cliffs. A fourth way in is from Escalante on the dirt Hell's Backbone Road, which comes out three miles west of Boulder at Highway 12.

ACCOMMODATIONS

You wouldn't expect to find one of Utah's nicest places to stay in tiny Boulder, but the **Boulder Mountain Lodge,** along Highway 12 right in town (435/355-7460 or 800/556-3446, www.boulder-utah.com, $72 and up winter, $97 and up high season) offers the kinds of facilities and setting that make this one of the few destination lodgings in the state. The lodge's buildings are grouped around the edge of a private, 15-acre pond that serves as an ad hoc wildlife refuge. You can sit on the deck or wander paths along the pond, watching and listening to the amazing variety of birds that make this spot their home. The guest rooms and suites are in a handsome and modern Western-style lodge facing the pond; rooms are nicely decorated with quality furniture and beddings, and there's a central great room with a fireplace and library and a large outdoor hot tub. One of Utah's best restaurants, Hell's Backbone Grill, is on the premises.

More modest accommodations are available at **Pole's Place** (435/335-7422 or 800/730-7422, www.boulderutah.com/polesplace, closed in winter), across the road from the state park. It has a well-maintained motel, café, and gift shop. The **Hills and Hollows Mini-Mart** (435/335-7349, on the hill above Hwy. 12) rents bunkhouse cabins for $24 a night.

Guest Ranches

Cowboy up at the **Boulder Mountain Ranch,** seven miles from Boulder on Hell's Backbone Road (435/355-7480, www.boulderutah.com/bmr). Guests have a choice of simple B&B accommodations in the lodge or free-standing cabins ($62–84). Options include daily trail rides, multiday horse-packing trips, and two- to five-day riding and lodging packages based out of the ranch.

Campgrounds

The best bet for tent campers is **Deer Creek Campground,** 6.5 miles from Boulder on Burr Trail Road. During the summer, another alternative is to head north on Highway 12 up Boulder Mountain to a cluster of Forest Service campgrounds (see *Around Boulder*). In town, RV campers can stay at the **Boulder Exchange** (next to Anasazi State Park, 435/335-7304).

FOOD

The Boulder Mountain Lodge restaurant, the **Hell's Backbone Grill** (435/355-7460 or 800/556-3446, $12–26 dinner entrées) has gained something of a cult following across the West. Run by two American Buddhist women, the restaurant has a menu that changes with the seasons, but you can count on finding fresh fish, chipotle-rubbed meat, outstanding meatloaf, tasty *posole,* and excellent desserts. For simpler but good fare, the **Burr Trail Cafe** (435/335-7432, lunch and dinner, Memorial Day weekend–autumn, lunch about $8, dinner about $15) is at the intersection of Highway 12 and Burr Trail Road.

© W. C. MCRAE

Hell's Backbone Grill in tiny and remote Boulder offers some of the finest dining in Utah.

INFORMATION AND SERVICES

A good stop for **visitor information** is the Anasazi State Park Museum, where there's an info desk for the GSENM. The two gas stations in Boulder sell groceries and snack food; at Hills and Hollows Mini-Mart, you'll find provisions as diverse as soy milk and organic cashews.

AROUND BOULDER
Boulder Mountain Scenic Drive

Utah 12 climbs high into forests of ponderosa pine, aspen, and fir on Boulder Mountain between the towns of Boulder and Torrey. Travel in winter is usually possible, although heavy snows can close the road. Viewpoints along the drive offer sweeping panoramas of Escalante canyon country, Circle Cliffs, Waterpocket Fold, and the Henry Mountains. Hikers and anglers can explore the alpine country of Boulder Mountain and seek out the 90 or so trout-filled lakes. The Great Western Trail, which was built with ATVers in mind, runs over Boulder Mountain to the west of the highway. The Dixie National Forest map (Escalante and Teasdale Ranger District offices) shows the back roads, trails, and lakes.

The U.S. Forest Service has three developed campgrounds about midway along this scenic drive: **Oak Creek** (18 miles from Boulder, elevation 8,800 feet), **Pleasant Creek** (19 miles from Boulder, elevation 8,600 feet), and **Singletree** (the largest of the three and the best pick for larger RVs, 24 miles from Boulder, elevation 8,200 feet). The season (with water) lasts from about late May through mid-September; sites cost $9–10. Campgrounds may also be open in spring and autumn without water. **Lower Bowns Reservoir** (elevation 7,000 feet) has primitive camping (no water or fee) and fishing for rainbow and cutthroat trout; turn east five miles on a rough dirt road (not recommended for cars) just south of Pleasant Creek Campground.

Contact the the **Escalante Ranger District office** (755 W. Main St., Escalante, 435/826-5400) for information about camping or recreation on Boulder Mountain. **Wildcat Information Center,** near Pleasant Creek Campground, has forest information and is open in the summer with irregular hours.

Kanab

Striking scenery surrounds this small town in Utah's far south. The Vermilion Cliffs to the west and east glow with a fiery intensity at sunrise and sunset. Streams have cut splendid canyons into surrounding plateaus. The Paiutes knew the spot as *Kanab,* meaning "place of the willows," which still grow along Kanab Creek. Mormon pioneers arrived in the mid-1860s and tried to farm along the unpredictable creek. Irrigation difficulties culminated in the massive floods of 1883, which in just two days gouged

a section of creek bed 40 feet below its previous level. Ranching proved better suited to this rugged and arid land.

Hollywood discovered this dramatic scenery in the 1920s and has filmed more than 150 movies and TV series here since. Famous films shot hereabouts include movies as different as *My Friend Flicka, The Lone Ranger,* and *The Greatest Story Ever Told.* The TV series *Gunsmoke* and *F Troop* were shot locally. Film crews have constructed several Western sets near Kanab, but

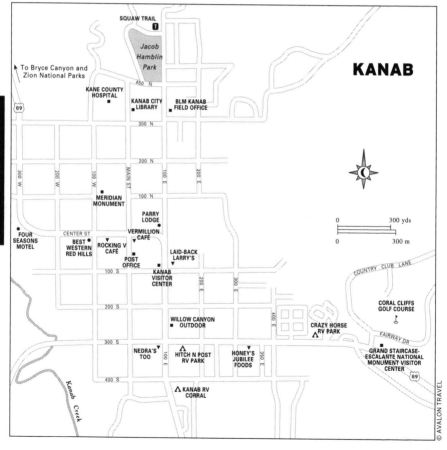

most lie on private land and are difficult to visit. The Paria set east of town, however, is on BLM land and open to the public.

If, while exploring Kanab, you see what looks like a family reunion, it might be just a man and his wives from the nearby polygamist settlement of Colorado City or Hildale! Visitors may also want to note that in 2006, the Kanab mayor and city council passed a resolution declaring "We envision a local culture that upholds the marriage of a woman to a man, and a man to a woman, as ordained of God.… We see our homes as open to a full quiver of children, the source of family continuity and social growth. We envision young women growing into wives, homemakers, and mothers; and we see young men growing into husbands, home-builders, and fathers."

While most park visitors see Kanab (pop. 3,500) as a handy stopover on trips to Bryce, Zion, and Grand Canyon National Parks and the southern reaches of the GSENM, a few interesting sites around town may warrant more than a sleep–eat–dash-out-of-town visit.

SQUAW TRAIL

- Distance: 1.5 miles one-way

- Duration: 2 hours

- Elevation gain: 800 feet

- Effort: moderate

- Trailhead: north end of 100 East, near the city park

This well-graded trail provides a close look at the geology, plantlife, and animals of the Vermilion Cliffs just north of town. To cut the hike down by a mile and cut the elevation gain in half, turn around at the first overlook, where views to the south take in Kanab, Fredonia, Kanab Canyon, and the vast Kaibab Plateau. At the top, look north to see the White, Gray, and Pink Cliffs of the Grand Staircase. Pick up a trail guide at the information center (brochures may also be available at the trailhead or BLM office). Bring water with you. Try to get a very early start in summer.

MOQUI CAVE

This natural cave (five miles north of Kanab on U.S. 89, 435/644-8525, www.moquicave.com, 9 A.M.–7 P.M. Mon.–Sat. Memorial Day–Labor Day, 10 A.M.–4 P.M. Mon.–Sat. off-season; $4.50 adults, $4 seniors, $3 ages 13–17, $2.50 ages 6–12) has been turned into a tourist attraction with a large collection of Native American artifacts. Most of the arrowheads, pottery, sandals, and burial items on display have been excavated locally. A diorama re-creates an Anasazi ruin located five miles away in Cottonwood Wash. Fossils, rocks, and minerals are exhibited, too, including what's claimed to be one of the largest fluorescent mineral displays in the country. The collections and a gift shop lie within a spacious cave that stays pleasantly cool even in the hottest weather.

CORAL PINK SAND DUNES STATE PARK

Churning air currents funneled by surrounding mountains have deposited huge sand dunes in this valley west of Kanab. The ever-changing dunes reach heights of several hundred feet and cover about 2,000 of the park's 3,700 acres. Different areas in the park (435/648-2800 or 800/322-3770 for reservations, www.stateparks.utah.gov, $5 per vehicle day use, $15 per vehicle camping) have been set aside for hiking, off-road vehicles, and a campground.

From Kanab, the shortest drive is to go north eight miles on U.S. 89 (to between Mileposts 72 and 73), turn left 9.3 miles on the paved Hancock Road to its end, then turn left (south) one mile on a paved road into the park. From the north, you can follow U.S. 89 3.5 miles south of Mount Carmel Junction, then turn right (south) 11 miles on a paved road. The back road from Cane Beds in Arizona has about 16 miles of gravel and dirt with some sandy spots; ask a park ranger for current conditions.

The canyon country surrounding the park has good opportunities for hiking and off-road-vehicle travel; the BLM office in Kanab can supply maps and information. Drivers with four-wheel-drive vehicles can turn south

BEST FRIENDS ANIMAL SANCTUARY

Best Friends Animal Sanctuary in Kanab is a popular place to visit. Some folks stay to volunteer.

© PAUL LEVY

GRAND STAIRCASE

If anybody else owned these 35,000 acres in the canyon north of town, there would be expensive McMansions sprawling across the hills. Instead, there are giant octagonal doghouses filled with animals no one else wants: former research animals, aggressive dogs, old dogs, sick dogs, dogs who have been abused or neglected. There are also plenty of cats, rabbits, birds, pot-bellied pigs, and horses (including one that's over 40 years old).

Best Friends Animal Sanctuary, the largest no-kill animal shelter in the country, takes in unwanted or abused animals and provides whatever rehabilitation is possible. Many animals are adopted out, but even the unadoptable ones are given homes for life, with plenty of care and attention from the sanctuary's fleet of employees and volunteers.

The shelter's origins date back to the 1970s, when a group of animal lovers began trying to prevent the euthanization of unadoptable animals. They began rescuing animals who were about to be put to sleep by shelters, re-

habilitated them as necessary, and found them homes. In the early 1980s, this group of dedicated rescuers bought land in Angel Canyon just north of Kanab and, with their motley crew of unadoptable animals, established this sanctuary. Now, some 1,800 animals live here at any given time, and the shelter is the county's largest employer, with over 200 staff members caring for the animals and the grounds.

But even this large staff can't take care of all of the animals' needs. The shelter's fleet of volunteers is constantly changing; each volunteer spends anywhere from a couple of days to a couple of months feeding, walking, petting, and cleaning up after the animals. Volunteers also give the animals the attention and socialization necessary for them to become good companions.

Best Friends (www.bestfriends.org) runs tours several times a day. Call 435/644-2001 for reservations or to learn more about volunteering at the shelter. There's no charge for a tour, although donations are gladly accepted.

on Sand Springs Road (1.5 miles east of Ponderosa Grove Campground) and go one mile to Sand Springs and another four miles to the South Fork Indian Canyon Pictograph Site in a pretty canyon. Visitors may not enter the Kaibab-Paiute Indian Reservation, which is south across the Arizona state line, from this side.

ENTERTAINMENT AND EVENTS

In summer, free musical concerts are held at the city park gazebo, at the center of town. Wednesdays bring an ongoing local talent show. The GSENM office (435/644-4680, www.ut.blm.gov/monument) sponsors regular ranger talks through the spring. A unique Kanab event is the **Greyhound Gathering** (mid-May of most years, 435/644-2903, www.greyhoundgang.com), when hundreds of greyhound owners converge on the town. Events include a parade, a race, and a howl-in. The Greyhound Gang, a nonprofit organization dedicated to the rescue, rehabilitation, and adoption of ex-racing greyhounds, hosts this unlikely festival.

SUPPLIES

Find a good selection of books, camping gear, and clothing, along with a little coffee bar, at **Willow Canyon Outdoor** (263 South 100 East, 435/644-8884). **Terry's Cameras** (19 W. Center, 435/644-5981) supplies film and camera needs (including repairs for film cameras) beyond what you would expect in a town of this size. The shop almost qualifies as an antique camera museum.

Denny's Wigwam (78 E. Center, 435/644-2452) is a landmark Old West trading post with a broad selection of Western jewelry, cowboy hats and boots, and souvenirs.

ACCOMMODATIONS

Most of the lodgings in Kanab are in modest family-run motels. Reservations are a good idea during the busy summer months. All of the motels and campgrounds are on U.S. 89, which follows 300 West, Center, 100 East, and 300 South through town.

Under $50

The **Quail Park Lodge** (125 U.S. 89 N., 435/644-5094 or 866/702-8099, www.quailparklodge.com, $45 and up) has a pool and accepts pets. It's one of the nicer budget motels in town. The **Bob-Bon Inn** (236 U.S. 89 N., 435/644-5094, $45 and up) is a renovated family-run motel. The **Sun-N-Sand Motel** (347 South 100 East, 435/644-5050 or 800/654-1868, $42 and up) has a pool, spa, and kitchenettes.

$50-75

One place in Kanab that varies from the usual motor-court formula is the **Parry Lodge** (89 E. Center, 435/644-2601 or 800/748-4104, $57 and up). Built during Kanab's heyday as a movie-making center, the Parry Lodge was where the stars stayed; 60 years later, this is still a pleasantly old-fashioned place to spend the night. At the very least, you'll want to stroll through the lobby, where lots of photos of the celebrities who once stayed here are displayed. There are several two-bedroom units, a pool, and a restaurant.

A good midrange choice is the **Four Seasons Motel** (36 North 300 West, 435/644-2635, $60 and up), which has a pool and accepts pets. Another good bet is **Aiken's Lodge** (79 W. Center, 435/644-2625 or 800/790-0380, www.aikenslodge.com, $65), also with a pool. It's closed in January and February.

$75-100

The rooms at **Best Western Red Hills Motel** (125 W. Center, 435/644-2675 or 800/830-2675, www.bestwesternredhills.com, $90 and up) are a step up in comfort from Kanab's lower-priced digs. It has a pool and is within a short walk of restaurants. Rates drop substantially during summer, fall, and winter.

North of Kanab, at Mount Carmel Junction, is another Best Western. The **Best Thunderbird Resort** (435/648-2203, www.bestwestern.com, $92 and up) is convenient if you're heading to Zion or Bryce Canyon National Parks.

GRAND STAIRCASE

Over $100

Especially nice if you're traveling with a group are the **Kanab Garden Cottages** (various locations, 435/644-2020, www.kanabcottages. com, $150 and up, three-night minimum). The three houses can easily sleep five or six people, are all within walking distance of town, and are pet-friendly.

Northwest of Kanab, just a few miles east of Zion National Park, are the very appealing cabins of the **Zion Mountain Resort** (E. Hwy. 9, 435/648-2555 or 866/648-2555, www.zion mountainresort.com, $120 and up weekdays, $145 and up weekends). The cabins have anywhere from one bedroom with microwave and fridge to two bedrooms with kitchens. The setting is great, with expansive views and a decent on-site restaurant. Rates drop by about $40 in the off-season.

Campgrounds

The campground at **Coral Pink Sand Dunes State Park** has restrooms with showers, paved pull-through sites, and a dump station. It's a pleasant, shady spot, but it can hum with ATV traffic. It's open all year, but the water is shut off from late October until Easter; winter campers must bring their own. Reservations are recommended for the busy Memorial Day–Labor Day season. It's about 10 miles due west of Kanab, but the two are not directly connected by a road. Reach the campground by turning west off U.S. 89 about 10 miles north of Kanab onto Hancock Road, and follow it 12 miles to the campground. The route is well-marked by signs.

Just north of the state park, the BLM maintains **Ponderosa Grove Campground** on the north edge of the dunes. There's no water here. From Kanab, head eight miles north on U.S. 89, turn west on Hancock Road (between Mileposts 72 and 73), and continue 7.3 miles to the campground.

The **Kanab RV Corral** (483 South 100 East, 435/644-5330) has RV sites (no tents) with hot showers, a pool, and laundry service open all year. The **Hitch'n Post RV Park** (196 East 300 South, 435/644-2142 or 800/458-3516) has sites for both RVs and tents, and has showers. It's open all year. The **Crazy Horse Campark** (625 East 300 South, 435/644-2782, mid-Apr.–late Oct.) has a pool, store, game room, and showers; tents are permitted.

FOOD

Find the best food in town at 🄲 **Rocking V Café** (97 W. Center, 435/644-8001, lunch and dinner daily, $14–27 dinner). The setting is casual and the food has a modern Southwest flair. Rocking V, which caters to both vegans and steak-lovers, pays homage to the "slow food" movement and makes everything from scratch. Be sure to check out the art gallery upstairs.

Drop by **Laid-Back Larry's** (98 South 100 East, 435/644-3636) for espresso or a smoothie. True to its name, this place has a tropical beach-hut ambiance. The **Vermilion Café** (4 E. Center, 435/644-3886) is another good place for espresso drinks, pastries, and deli sandwiches.

If you're hankering for a good spinach enchilada or other Mexican food, settle into the friendly **Nedra's Too** (300 South 100 East, 435/644-2030, lunch and dinner daily, $8–10 full dinner).

Travelers setting out into the GSENM from Kanab should note that this is the best place for many miles around to stock up on groceries. **Honey's Food Jubilee** (260 East 300 South, 435/644-5877) is a good grocery store on the way out of town to the east.

INFORMATION

Staff members at the **Kanab Visitor Center** (78 South 100 East, 435/644-5033, www.kane utah.com, 8 A.M.–8 P.M. Mon.–Sat.) offer literature and advice for services in Kanab and travel in Kane County. The **Grand Staircase-Escalante National Monument** has a visitors center (745 E. U.S. 89, Kanab, 435/644-4680, 8 A.M.–5 P.M. daily mid-Mar.–mid-Nov., 8 A.M.–4:30 P.M. Mon.–Fri. mid-Nov.–mid-Mar.) on the east edge of town.

CAPITOL REEF NATIONAL PARK

Though Capitol Reef gets far less attention than the region's other national parks, it is a great place to visit, with excellent hiking and splendid scenery. Wonderfully sculpted rock layers in a rainbow of colors put on a fine show here. Although you'll find these same rocks throughout much of the Four Corners region, their artistic variety has no equal outside Capitol Reef National Park. About 70 million years ago, gigantic forces within the earth began to uplift, squeeze, and fold more than a dozen rock formations into the central feature of the park today—the Waterpocket Fold, so named for the many small pools of water trapped by the tilted strata. Erosion has since carved spires, graceful curves, canyons, and arches. The Waterpocket Fold extends 100 miles between Thousand Lake Mountain to the north and Lake Powell to the south. (Look for it if you ever fly south from Salt Lake City—we never really grasped its magnitude until we flew over it on the way to Mexico!) The most spectacular cliffs and rock formations of the Waterpocket Fold form Capitol Reef, located north of Pleasant Creek and curving northwest across the Fremont River toward Thousand Lake Mountain. The reef was named by explorers who found the Waterpocket Fold a barrier to travel and likened it to a reef blocking passage on the ocean. One particular rounded sandstone hill reminded them of the Capitol Dome in Washington, D.C.

Roads and hiking trails in the park provide access to the colorful rock layers and to the plants and wildlife that live here. You'll also see remnants of the area's long human history—

© W. C. MCRAE

HIGHLIGHTS

◖ **The Scenic Drive:** Capitol Reef's 25-mile round-trip Scenic Drive encompasses not only scenery and all its attendant geology, but also human history, pioneer sites, and even free fruit in season (page 143).

◖ **Notom-Bullfrog Road:** You'll pass nearly 80 miles of the Waterpocket Fold's eastern side while traveling along this road, which exposes the fold's geologic wonders. Distinctive panoramas are your reward, and scenic side canyons beckon hikers (page 144).

◖ **Chimney Rock Trail:** The trail to Chimney Rock starts right on Highway 24, and even if you weren't meaning to visit Capitol Reef, it's worth taking a couple of hours to hike it. Panoramic views from the top take in the face of Capitol Reef (page 148).

◖ **Grand Wash Trail:** Hike from the trailhead on Highway 24 into The Narrows, where the canyon walls close in and rise to 200 feet. Grand Wash offers easy hiking, great scenery, and an abundance of wildflowers (page 151).

◖ **Capitol Gorge:** Hike through another wash past Fremont rock art and a Mormon "pioneer register" to a turnoff for a spur trail leading to natural water tanks called waterpockets. Listen for the lovely song of the canyon wren (page 153).

LOOK FOR ◖ TO FIND RECOMMENDED SIGHTS, ACTIVITIES, DINING, AND LODGING.

petroglyphs and storage bins of the prehistoric Fremont people, a schoolhouse and other structures built by Mormon pioneers, and several small uranium mines from the 20th century. Legends tell of Butch Cassidy and other outlaw members of the "Wild Bunch" who hid out in these remote canyons in the 1890s.

Even travelers short on time will enjoy a quick look at visitors center exhibits and a drive on Highway 24 through an impressive cross section of Capitol Reef cut by the Fremont River. You can see more of the park on the Scenic Drive, a narrow paved road that heads south from the visitors center. The drive passes beneath spectacular cliffs of the reef and enters Grand Wash and Capitol Gorge

Canyons; allow at least 1.5 hours for the 21-mile round-trip and any side trips. The fair-weather Notom–Bullfrog Road (paved as far as Notom) heads south along the other side of the reef for almost 80 miles with fine views of Waterpocket Fold. Burr Trail Road (dirt inside the park) in the south actually climbs over the fold in a steep set of switchbacks, connecting Notom Road with Boulder. Only drivers with high-clearance vehicles can explore Cathedral Valley in the park's northern district. All of these roads provide access to viewpoints and hiking trails.

Expect hot summer days (highs in the upper 80s and low 90s) and cool nights. Late-afternoon thunderstorms are common in July and August;

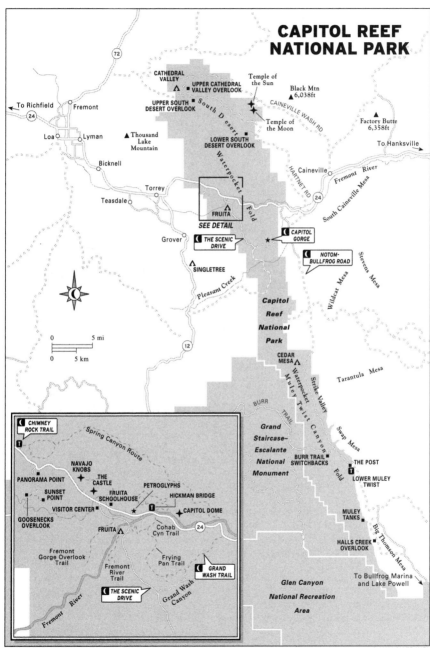

CAPITOL REEF

be alert for impending storms, which can bring flash flooding. Winter brings cool days (highs in the 40s) and night temperatures in the low 20s and teens. Snow accents the colored rocks while rarely hindering traffic on the main highway. Winter travel on the back roads and trails may be halted by snow, but it soon melts when the sun comes out. Annual precipitation averages only seven inches, peaking in the late-summer thunderstorm season.

PLANNING YOUR TIME

Many southern Utah travelers treat Capitol Reef as a pass-through, and indeed it's easy to get a feel for the park by taking a short hike off Highway 24 (perhaps just the walk out to Goosenecks and Sunset Point). But a short visit here may leave you longing for more. On a one-day visit, be sure to stop in the visitors center for the slide show (it's less schmaltzy than many national-park slide shows and explains the geology quite nicely), hike either Grand Wash or Capitol Gorge, and spend some time exploring the park's human history, from Fremont petroglyphs to the Fruita blacksmith shop. It's easy to spend two or three days camping at the park campground or staying in nearby Torrey and taking day hikes in the park's core district. But if you've got the proper vehicle, after a couple of days you'll want to explore the Notom–Bullfrog Road. If you're just driving, this is easy to do in a day; if you get out of the car to explore every canyon, it can take all the time you have to give it.

Exploring the Park

The most accessible part of Capitol Reef National Park (435/425-3791, www.nps.gov/care, $5 per vehicle) is along Highway 24, about 11 miles east of Torrey. In fact, several trails start right off the highway, which means that it's not necessary to pay admission fees in order to get a tiny taste of this park.

VISITORS CENTER

Start with a good 10-minute slide show, which is shown on request, introducing Capitol Reef's natural wonders and history. In the main room of the visitors center, a giant relief map offers a bird's-eye view of the entire park. Rock samples and diagrams illustrate seven of the park's geologic formations, and photos identify local plants and birds. Prehistoric Fremont artifacts on display include petroglyph replicas, sheepskin moccasins, pottery, basketry, stone knives, spear and arrow points, and bone jewelry. Other historic exhibits outline exploration and early Mormon settlement.

Hikers can pick up a map of trails that are near the visitors center and of longer routes in the southern park areas; naturalists will want the checklists of plants, birds, mammals, and other wildlife, while history buffs can learn more about the area's settlement and the founding of the park. Rangers offer nature walks, campfire programs, and other special events from Easter to mid-October; the bulletin board outside the visitors center lists what's on. The visitors center is on Highway 24 at the turnoff for Fruita Campground and the Scenic Drive (open 8 A.M.–7 P.M. daily June–Sept., 8 A.M.–4:30 P.M. daily the rest of the year).

ALONG HIGHWAY 24

From the west, Highway 24 drops from the broad mountain valley near Torrey onto Sulphur Creek, with dramatic rock formations soaring into the horizon. A huge amphitheater of stone rings the basin, with formations such as Twin Rocks, Chimney Rock, and the Castle glowing in deep red and yellow tones. Ahead, the canyon narrows as the Fremont River slips between the cliffs to carve its chasm through Waterpocket Fold.

Panorama Point

Take in the incredible view from Panorama Point, 2.5 miles west of the visitors center on

CAPITOL REEF NATURAL HISTORY

GEOLOGY

Exposed rocks at Capitol Reef reveal wind-swept deserts, rivers, mud flats, and inland seas of long ago. Nearly all the layers date from the Mesozoic era (65-230 million years ago), when dinosaurs ruled the earth. Later uplift and twisting of the land, which continues to this day, built up the Colorado Plateau of southern Utah and the Rocky Mountains to the east. Immense forces squeezed the rocks until they bent up and over from east to west in the massive crease of Waterpocket Fold.

FLORA AND FAUNA

Ponderosa pine and other cool-climate vegetation grow on the flanks of Thousand Lake Mountain (7,000-9,000 feet high) in the northwest corner of the park. Most of the Waterpocket Fold, however, is at 5,000-7,000 feet, covered with sparse junipers and piñon pines that cling precariously in cracks and thin soils of the slickrock. The soil from each rock type generally determines what will grow. Mancos Shale forms a poor clay soil supporting only saltbush, shadscale, and galleta grass. On Dakota sandstone you'll see mostly sage and rabbitbrush. Clays of the Morrison Formation repel nearly all plants, while its sandstone nurtures mostly juniper, piñon pine, and cliffrose; uranium prospectors discovered that astragalus and prince's plume commonly grow near ore deposits. Sands of the Summerville Formation nourish grasses and four-wing saltbush. The Fremont River and several creeks provide a lush habitat of cottonwood, tamarisk, willow, and other water-loving plants.

Streamside residents include beavers, muskrats, minks, tree lizards, Great Basin spadefoot toads, Rocky Mountain toads, and leopard frogs. Spadefoot toads, fairy shrimp, and insects have adapted to the temporary waterpockets by completing the aquatic phase of their short life cycles in a hurry. Near water or out in the drier country, you might see mule deer, coyotes, gray foxes, porcupines, spotted and striped skunks, badgers, black-tailed jackrabbits, desert cottontails, yellow-bellied marmots, rock squirrels, Colorado chipmunks,

© W. C. MCRAE

Capitol Gorge is one of only five canyons cut through Waterpocket Fold.

Ord's kangaroo rats, canyon mice, and five known species of bats. With luck, you may sight a relatively rare (and suitably distant) mountain lion or black bear.

Although you can't miss seeing the many small lizards along the trails, snakes tend to be more secretive; those in the park include the striped whipsnake, Great Basin gopher snake, wandering garter snake, and the rarely seen and quite venomous midget faded rattlesnake. Some common birds are the sharp-shinned hawk, American kestrel, chukar, mourning dove, white-throated swift, black-chinned and broad-tailed hummingbirds, violet-green swallow, common raven, piñon and scrub jays, canyon and rock wrens, and rufous-sided towhee. Most wildlife, except birds, wait until evening to come out, and they disappear again the following morning.

During the springtime, Capitol Reef-area bird-watchers may want to drive south of Highway 24 through Teasdale to look for the roadside bald eagle's nest. The large nest is a couple of miles south of the highway and is easy to spot. Don't disturb the eagles!

the south side of the highway. Follow signs south for 0.15 mile to Panorama Point and views of Capitol Reef and the distant Henry Mountains to the east and looming Boulder Mountain to the west. The large black basalt boulders were swept down from Boulder Mountain to the reef as part of giant debris flows between 8,000 and 200,000 years ago.

Goosenecks

Continue past Panorama Point one mile on a gravel road to the **Goosenecks of Sulphur Creek.** A short trail leads to Goosenecks Overlook on the rim (elevation 6,400 feet) for dizzying views of the creek below. Canyon walls display shades of yellow, green, brown, and red. Another easy trail leads a third of a mile to **Sunset Point** and panoramic views of the Capitol Reef cliffs and the distant Henry Mountains.

Fruita Schoolhouse

Remnants of the pioneer community of Fruita stretch along the narrow Fremont River Canyon. The **Fruita Schoolhouse** is just east of the visitors center on the north side of the highway. Early settlers completed this one-room log structure in 1896. Teachers struggled at times with rowdy students, but the kids learned their three Rs in grades one through eight. Mormon church meetings, dances, town meetings, elections, and other community gatherings took place here. A lack of students caused the school's closing in 1941. Rangers are on duty some days in summer (ask at the visitors center). At other times, you can peer inside the windows and listen to a recording of a former teacher recalling what school life was like.

Fremont Petroglyphs

Farther down the canyon, 1.2 miles east of the visitors center on the north side of the highway, are several panels of Fremont petroglyphs (watch for road signs). Several human figures with headdresses and mountain sheep decorate the cliff. You can see more petroglyphs by walking to the left and right along the cliff face. Stay on the trail and *do not* climb the talus slope.

Fremont petroglyphs along Highway 24

CAPITOL REEF

Behunin Cabin

Behunin Cabin is 6.2 miles east of the visitors center on the south side of the highway. Elijah Cutlar Behunin used blocks of sandstone to build this cabin in about 1882. For several years, Behunin, his wife, and 11 of their 13 children shared this sturdy but quite small cabin. (The kids slept outside.) He moved on, though, when floods made life too difficult. Small openings allow a look inside the dirt-floored structure, but no furnishings remain.

Fremont River Waterfall

Near the end of the narrow sandstone canyon, a small waterfall in the Fremont River attracts photographers and impromptu swimming parties. The river twists through a narrow human-made crack in the rock before making its final plunge into a pool below. A sign warns of hazardous footing above the falls. Take the sandy path from the parking area to where you can safely view the falls from below. Use extreme caution if you intend to cool off in the pool at the base of the waterfall because the undertow is strong and dangerous. Parking is 6.9 miles east of the visitors center on the north side of the highway.

◖ THE SCENIC DRIVE

Turn south from Highway 24 at the visitors center to experience some of the reef's best scenery and to learn more about its geology. An illustrated pamphlet, available on the drive or in the visitors center, has keyed references to numbered stops along the 25-mile (round-trip) drive. Descriptions identify rock layers and explain how they were formed. A quick tour requires about 1.5 hours, but several hiking trails may tempt you to extend your stay. The Scenic Drive is paved, although side roads have gravel surfaces.

Fruita

You'll first pass orchards and several of Fruita's buildings. A **blacksmith shop** (0.7 mile from the visitors center on the right) displays tools, harnesses, farm machinery, and Fruita's first tractor. The tractor didn't arrive until 1940—long after the rest of the country had modern-

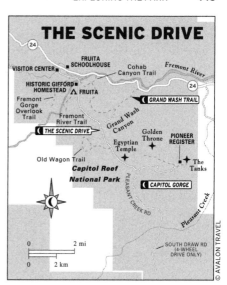

ized. In a recording, a rancher tells about living and working in Fruita.

The **Historic Gifford Homestead,** one mile south on the Scenic Drive, is typical of rural Utah farmhouses of the early 1900s. Cultural demonstrations and handmade items are available. A picnic area is just beyond; with fruit trees and grass, this is a pretty spot for lunch. A short trail crosses orchards and the Fremont River to the Fruita schoolhouse.

Grand Wash

The Scenic Drive leaves the Fremont River valley and climbs up a desert slope, with the rock walls of the Waterpocket Fold rising to the east. Turn east into Grand Wash, a dry channel etched through the sandstone. A dirt road follows the twisting gulch one mile, with sheer rock walls rising along the sandy streambed. At the road's end, an easy hiking trail follows the wash 2.5 miles to its mouth along Highway 24.

Past Slickrock Divide, the rock lining the reef deepens into a ruby red and forms itself into odd columns and spires that resemble statuary. Called the **Egyptian Temple,** this is one of the most striking and colorful areas along the road.

CAPITOL REEF

Capitol Gorge

The Capitol Gorge is the end of the Scenic Drive, 10.7 miles from the visitors center. Capitol Gorge is a dry canyon through Capitol Reef much like Grand Wash. Believe it or not, the narrow, twisting Capitol Gorge was the route of the main state highway through south-central Utah for 80 years! Mormon pioneers laboriously cleared a path so wagons could go through, a task they repeated every time flash floods rolled in a new set of boulders. Cars bounced their way down the canyon until 1962, when Highway 24 opened, but few traces of the old road remain today. Walking is easy along the gravel riverbed, but don't enter if storms threaten. An easy one-mile saunter down the gorge will take day hikers past **petroglyphs** and a "register" rock where pioneers carved their names. For other Capitol Gorge hikes, see *Recreation*.

Pleasant Creek Road

Turn right 8.3 miles from the visitors center, where the Scenic Drive curves east toward Capitol Gorge, onto Pleasant Creek Road, which continues south below the face of the reef. After three miles, the sometimes rough dirt road passes Sleeping Rainbow/Floral Ranch (closed to the public) and ends at Pleasant Creek. A rugged four-wheel-drive road continues on the other side but is much too rough for cars. Floral Ranch dates back to Capitol Reef's early years of settlement. In 1939 it became the Sleeping Rainbow Guest Ranch, from the translation of the native name for Waterpocket Fold. Now the ranch belongs to the park, but the former owners still live here. Pleasant Creek's perennial waters begin high on Boulder Mountain to the west and cut a scenic canyon completely through Capitol Reef. Hikers can head downstream through the three-mile-long canyon and then return the way they went in, or they can continue another three miles cross-country to Notom Road.

NORTH DISTRICT

Only the most adventurous travelers enter the remote canyons and desert country of the north. The few roads *cannot* be negotiated by four-wheel-drive vehicles, let alone ordinary cars, in wet weather. In good weather, high-clearance vehicles (good clearance is more important than four-wheel drive) can enter the region from the east, north, and west. The roads lead through stately sandstone monoliths of Cathedral Valley, volcanic remnants, badlands country, many low mesas, and vast sand flats. Foot travel allows closer inspection of these features or lengthy excursions into the canyons of Polk, Deep, and Spring Creeks, which cut deeply into the flanks of Thousand Lake Mountain.

Mountain bikers enjoy these challenging roads as well, but they must stay on established roads. Much of the north district is good for horseback riding, too. **Cathedral Valley Campground's** five sites provide a place to stop for the night; rangers won't permit car camping elsewhere in the district. The campground is on the four-wheel-drive Cathedral Valley loop road about 36 miles from the visitors center (from the park entrance, head 12 miles east on Highway 24, then turn north and ford the Fremont River and follow Hartnet Road about 24 miles to the campground); check on road conditions at the visitors center before heading out. The **Upper Cathedral Valley Trail,** just below the campground, is an enjoyable one-mile walk offering excellent views of the Cathedrals. Hikers with a backcountry permit must camp at least half a mile from the nearest road. Guides to the area can be purchased at the visitors center.

SOUTH DISTRICT
◖ Notom-Bullfrog Road

Capitol Reef is only a small part of the Waterpocket Fold. By taking the Notom–Bullfrog Road, you'll see nearly 80 miles of the fold's eastern side. This route crosses some of the younger geologic layers, such as those of the Morrison Formation, which form colorful hills. In other places, eroded layers of the Waterpocket Fold jut up at 70-degree angles. The Henry Mountains to the east and the many canyons on both sides of the road add to the

© W. C. MCRAE

Waterpocket Fold is a vast rock wrinkle nearly 100 miles long.

memorable panoramas. The road has been paved as far as Notom, and about 25 miles are paved on the southern end near Bullfrog. The rest of the road is dirt and gravel. Most cars should have no trouble negotiating this road in good weather. Keep an eye on the weather before setting out, though; the dirt-and-gravel surface is usually okay for cars when dry but can be dangerous for *any* vehicle when wet. Sandy spots and washouts may present a problem for low-clearance vehicles; contact the visitors center to check current conditions. Have a full gas tank and carry extra water and food because no services are available between Highway 24 and Bullfrog Marina. Purchase a small guide to this area at the visitors center. Features and mileage along the drive from north to south include the following:

Mile 0.0: The turnoff from Highway 24 is 9.2 miles east of the visitors center and 30.2 miles west of Hanksville (another turnoff from Highway 24 is three miles east).

Mile 2.2: Pleasant Creek; the mouth of the canyon is 5–6 miles upstream, although it's only about three miles away if you head cross-country from south of Notom. Hikers can follow the canyon three miles upstream through Capitol Reef to Pleasant Creek Road (off the Scenic Drive).

Mile 4.1: Notom Ranch is to the west; once a small town, Notom is now a private ranch.

Mile 8.1: Burrow Wash; hikers can explore the narrow canyon upstream.

Mile 9.3: Cottonwood Wash; another canyon hike just upstream.

Mile 10.4: Five Mile Wash; yet another canyon hike.

Mile 13.3: Sheets Gulch; a scenic canyon lies upstream here, too.

Mile 14.1: Sandy Ranch Junction; high-clearance vehicles can turn east 16 miles to the Henry Mountains.

Mile 14.2: Oak Creek Access Road; the creek

CAPITOL REEF

WATERPOCKET FOLD

About 65 million years ago, well before the Colorado Plateau uplifted, sedimentary rock layers in south-central Utah buckled, forming a steep-sided monocline, a rock fold with one very steep side in an area of otherwise nearly horizontal layers. A monocline is a "step-up" in the rock layers along an underlying fault. The rock layers on the west side of the Waterpocket Fold have been lifted more than 7,000 feet higher than the layers to the east. The 100-mile-long fold was then subjected to millions of years of erosion, which slowly removed the upper layers to reveal the warped sedimentary layers at its base. Continued erosion of the sandstone has left many basins, or "waterpockets," along the fold. These seasonal water sources, often called water "tanks," are used by desert animals, and they formed a water source for prehistoric people. Erosion of the tilted rock layers continues today, forming colorful cliffs, massive domes, soaring spires, stark monoliths, twisting canyons, and graceful arches. Getting a sense of the Waterpocket Fold requires some off-pavement driving. The best viewpoint is along Burr Trail Road, which climbs up the fold between Boulder and Notom-Bullfrog Road.

cuts a two-mile-long canyon through Capitol Reef and makes a good day hike. Backpackers sometimes start upstream at Lower Bowns Reservoir (off Highway 12) and hike the 15 miles to Oak Creek Access Road. The clear waters of Oak Creek flow all year but are not potable.

Mile 14.4: Oak Creek crossing.

Mile 20.0: Entering Capitol Reef National Park; a small box has information sheets.

Mile 22.3: Cedar Mesa Campground is to the west; the small five-site campground is surrounded by junipers and has fine views of Waterpocket Fold and the Henry Mountains. Free sites have tables and grills; there's an outhouse but no drinking water. Red Canyon Trail begins here, heads west into a huge box canyon in Waterpocket Fold, and is four miles round-trip.

Mile 26.0: Bitter Creek Divide; streams to the north flow to the Fremont River; Halls Creek on the south side runs through Strike Valley to Lake Powell, 40 miles away.

Mile 34.1: Burr Trail Road Junction; turn west up the steep switchbacks to ascend Waterpocket Fold and continue to Boulder and Highway 12 (36 miles). Burr Trail is the only road that actually crosses the top of the fold, and it's one of the most scenic in the park. Driving conditions are similar to the Notom–Bullfrog Road—okay for cars when dry. Pavement begins at the park boundary and continues to Boulder. Although paved, the Burr Trail still must be driven slowly because of its curves and potholes. The section of road through Long Canyon has especially pretty scenery.

Mile 36.0: Surprise Canyon Trailhead; a hike into this narrow, usually shaded canyon takes 1–2 hours.

Mile 36.6: The Post; a small trading post here once served sheepherders and some cattlemen, but today this spot is just a reference point. Park here to hike to Headquarters Canyon. A trailhead for Lower Muley Twist Canyon via Halls Creek lies at the end of a half-mile-long road to the south.

Mile 37.5: Leaving Capitol Reef National Park; a small box has information sheets. Much of the road between here and Glen Canyon National Recreation Area has been paved.

Mile 45.5: Road junction; turn right (south) to continue to Bullfrog Marina (25 miles) or go straight (east) for Starr Springs Campground (23 miles) in the Henry Mountains.

CAPITOL REEF

Mile 46.4: The road to the right (west) goes to Halls Creek Overlook. This turnoff is poorly signed and easy to miss; look for it 0.9 mile south of the previous junction. Turn in and follow the road three miles, then turn right at a fork 0.4 mile to the viewpoint. The last 0.3 mile may be too rough for low-clearance cars. A picnic table is the only "facility" here. Far below in Grand Gulch, Halls Creek flows south to Lake Powell. Look across the valley for the double Brimhall Bridge in the red sandstone of Waterpocket Fold. A steep trail descends to Halls Creek (1.2 miles one-way), and it's possible to continue another 1.1 miles up Brimhall Canyon to the bridge. A register box at the overlook has information sheets on this route. Note, however, that the last part of the hike to the bridge requires difficult rock-scrambling and wading or swimming through pools! Hikers looking for another adventure might want to follow Halls Creek 10 miles downstream to the narrows. Here, convoluted walls as high as 700 feet narrow to little more than arm's-length apart. This beautiful area of water-sculpted rock sometimes has deep pools that require swimming.

Mile 49.0: Colorful clay hills of deep reds, creams, and grays rise beside the road. This clay turns to goo when wet, providing all the traction of axle grease.

Mile 54.0: Beautiful panorama of countless mesas, mountains, and canyons. Lake Powell and Navajo Mountain can be seen to the south.

Mile 65.3: Junction with paved Highway 276; turn left (north) for Hanksville (59 miles) or right (south) to Bullfrog Marina (5.2 miles).

Mile 70.5: Bullfrog Marina (see *Glen Canyon National Recreation Area* in the *Canyonlands National Park* chapter).

Lower Muley Twist Canyon

"So winding that it would twist a mule pulling a wagon," said an early visitor. This canyon has some of the best hiking in the southern district of the park. In the 1880s, Mormon pioneers used the canyon as part of a wagon route between Escalante and new settlements in southeastern Utah, replacing the even more difficult Hole-in-the-Rock route.

Unlike most canyons of the Waterpocket Fold, Muley Twist runs lengthwise along the crest for about 18 miles before finally turning east and leaving the fold. Hikers starting from Burr Trail Road can easily follow the twisting bends down to Halls Creek, 12 miles away. Two trailheads and the Halls Creek route allow a variety of trips.

You could start from Burr Trail Road near the top of the switchbacks (2.2 miles west of Notom–Bullfrog Road) and hike down the dry gravel streambed. After four miles, you have the options of returning the same way, taking the Cut Off route east 2.5 miles to Post Trailhead (off Notom–Bullfrog Road), or continuing eight miles down Lower Muley Twist Canyon to its end at Halls Creek. Upon reaching Halls Creek, turn left (north) five miles up the creek bed or the old jeep road beside it to the Post. This section of creek lies in an open, dry valley. With a car shuttle, the Post would be the end of a good two-day, 17-mile hike, or you could loop back to Lower Muley Twist Canyon via the Cut Off route and hike back to Burr Trail Road for a 23.5-mile trip. It's a good idea to check the weather beforehand and avoid the canyon if storms threaten.

Cream-colored sandstone cliffs lie atop the red Kayenta and Wingate Formations. Impressively deep undercuts have been carved into the lower canyon. Spring and autumn offer the best conditions (summer temperatures can exceed 100°F). Elevations range from 5,640 feet at Burr Trail Road to 4,540 feet at the confluence with Halls Creek to 4,894 feet at the Post.

An information sheet available at the visitors center and trailheads has a small map and route details. Topographic maps of Wagon Box Mesa, Mount Pennell, and Hall Mesa, and the 1:100,000-scale Escalante and Hite Crossing maps are sold at the visitors center. You'll also

CAPITOL REEF

find this hike described in David Day's *Utah's Favorite Hiking Trails* and in the small, spiral-bound *Explore Capitol Reef's Trails,* by the Capitol Reef Natural History Association, available at the visitors center. Carry all water for the trip because natural sources are often dry or polluted.

Upper Muley Twist Canyon

This part of the canyon has plenty of scenery. Large and small natural arches along the way add to its beauty. Upper Muley Twist Road turns north off Burr Trail Road about one mile west from the top of a set of switchbacks. Cars can usually go in half a mile to a trailhead parking area; high-clearance four-wheel-drive vehicles can head another 2.5 miles up a wash to the end of the primitive road. Look for natural arches on the left along this last section. **Strike Valley Overlook Trail** (0.75 mile round-trip) begins at the end of the road and leads to a magnificent panorama of Waterpocket Fold and beyond. Return to the canyon, where you can hike as far as 6.5 miles to the head of Upper Muley Twist Canyon.

Two large arches lie a short hike upstream; Saddle Arch, the second one on the left, is 1.75 miles away. The **Rim Route** begins across from Saddle Arch, climbs the canyon wall, follows the rim (good views of Strike Valley and the Henry Mountains), and descends back into the canyon at a point just above the narrows, 4.75 miles from the end of the road. (The Rim Route is most easily followed in this direction.) Proceed up-canyon to see several more arches. A narrow section of canyon beginning about four miles from the end of the road must be bypassed to continue; look for rock cairns showing the way around to the right. Continuing up the canyon past the Rim Route sign will take you to several small drainages marking the upper end of Muley Twist Canyon. Climb a high, tree-covered point on the west rim for great views; experienced hikers with a map can follow the rim back to Upper Muley Road (no trail or markers on this route). Bring all the water you'll need because there are no reliable sources in Upper Muley Twist Canyon.

Recreation

Fifteen day-hiking trails begin within a short drive of the visitors center. Of these, only Grand Wash, Capitol Gorge, and the short paths to Sunset Point and Goosenecks are easy. The others involve moderately strenuous climbs over irregular slickrock. Signs and rock cairns mark the way, but it's all too easy to wander off if you don't pay attention to the route.

Although most hiking trails can easily be done in a day, backpackers and hikers might want to try longer trips in Chimney Rock/Spring Canyons to the north or Muley Twist Canyon and Halls Creek to the south. Obtain the required backcountry permit (free) from a ranger and camp at least half a mile from the nearest maintained road or trail. (Cairned routes like Chimney Rock Canyon, Muley Twist Canyon, and Halls Creek don't count as trails but are backcountry routes.) Bring a

stove for cooking because backcountry users may not build fires. Avoid camping or parking in washes at any time—torrents of mud and boulders can carry away everything.

HIKING ALONG HIGHWAY 24

Stop by the visitors center to pick up a map showing hiking trails and trail descriptions. These trailheads are located along the main highway through the park and along the Fremont River. Note that the Grand Wash Trail cuts west through the reef to the Scenic Drive.

Chimney Rock Trail

- Distance: 3.5-mile loop

- Duration: 2.5 hours round-trip

- Elevation gain: 540 feet

- Effort: moderate

- Trailhead: 3 miles west of the visitors center, north side of Highway 24

Towering 660 feet above the highway, Chimney Rock (elevation 6,100 feet) is a fluted spire of dark red rock (Moenkopi Formation) capped by a block of hard sandstone (Shinarump Member of the Chinle Formation). The trail leads pretty much straight uphill from the parking lot to a ridge overlooking Chimney Rock, then levels off a bit. Panoramic views take in the face of Capitol Reef. Petrified wood along the trail has been eroded from the Chinle Formation (the same rock layer found in Petrified Forest National Park in Arizona). It is illegal to take any of the petrified wood.

Spring Canyon Route

- Distance: 10 miles one-way

- Duration: 6 hours one-way

- Elevation gain: 540 feet

- Effort: moderate

- Trailhead: Chimney Rock parking lot

Except for its length, this is not a particularly difficult trail. It begins at the top of the Chimney Rock Trail and travels to the Fremont River and Highway 24. The wonderfully eroded forms of Navajo sandstone present a continually changing exhibition. The riverbed is normally dry. (Some maps show all or part of this as "Chimney Rock Canyon.") Check with rangers for the weather forecast before setting off because flash floods can be dangerous, and the Fremont River (which you must wade across) can rise quite high. Normally, the river runs less than knee-deep to Highway 24 (3.7 miles east of the visitors center). With luck you'll have a car waiting for you. Summer hikers can beat the heat with a crack-of-dawn departure. Carry water because this section of canyon lacks a reliable source.

From the Chimney Rock parking area, hike Chimney Rock Trail to the top of the ridge and follow the signs for Chimney Rock Canyon.

DATURA: A PLANT WITH A PAST

As dusk approaches, the huge white flowers of the datura open, and their sweet smell attracts moths, beetles, and wasps. As intoxicating as the datura's fragrance may be, it doesn't hold a candle to the plant itself, which is a potent hallucinogen. It also contains toxic alkaloids, including nerve toxins capable of killing humans and animals.

Nonetheless, datura (also known as jimsonweed) has a rich history of folk use. Many native peoples in the Americas, including the Zuni, Chumash, and even the Aztecs, were familiar with its uses; some regarded it as sacred. It's been used as a shamanic ritual drug, as well as a topical analgesic and even as a sort of medieval Mickey Finn. (Pimps in the Middle Ages used datura to make the prostitutes in their employ more compliant.) Accounts from Jamestown, Virginia, one of the earliest British settlements in North America, report a group of soldiers going insane after eating datura in 1676.

Up until 1968, datura was a component of some over-the-counter asthma medicines; it was banned when it gained popularity among American youth and people began using these medications recreationally. Atropine, an anticholinergic substance often used by ophthalmologists to dilate pupils, is datura's main psychoactive component. It's a central nervous system depressant that mostly causes users to feel drowsy – some report vivid dreams – and also increases heart rate, sometimes to dangerous levels.

In Carlos Castaneda's *The Teachings of Don Juan: A Yaqui Way of Knowledge*, Don Juan warns that datura "is as powerful as the best of allies, but there is something I personally don't like about her. She distorts men. She gives them a taste of power too soon without fortifying their hearts and makes them domineering and unpredictable. She makes them weak in the middle of their great power."

CAPITOL REEF

DESERT VARNISH

Desert varnish streaks sandstone walls.

The dark-colored vertical stripes often seen on sandstone cliff faces across the Colorado Plateau are known as desert varnish. They're mostly composed of very fine clay particles, rich in iron and manganese. It's not entirely known how these streaks are formed, but it seems likely that they're at least partly created by mineral-rich water coursing down the cliffs along the varnished areas and wind-blown clay dust sticking to cliff faces. Bacteria and fungi on the rock's surface may help this process along by absorbing manganese and iron from the atmosphere and precipitating it as a black layer of manganese oxide or reddish iron oxide on the rock surfaces. The clay particles in this thin layer of varnish help shield the bacteria against the drying effects of the desert sun. Prehistoric rock artists worked with desert varnish, chipping away the dark surface to expose the lighter underlying rocks.

Enter the unnamed lead-in canyon and follow it downstream. A sign marks Chimney Rock Canyon, which is 2.5 miles from the start. Turn right 6.5 miles (downstream) to reach the Fremont River. A section of narrows requires some rock-scrambling (bring a cord to lower backpacks), or the area can be bypassed on a narrow trail to the left above the narrows. Farther down, a natural arch high on the left marks the halfway point.

Upper Chimney Rock Canyon could be explored on an overnight trip. A spring (purify before drinking) is located in an alcove on the right side about one mile up Chimney Rock Canyon from the lead-in canyon. Wildlife use this water source, so camp at least a quarter mile away. Chimney Rock Canyon, the longest in the park, begins high on the slopes of Thousand Lake Mountain and descends nearly 15 miles southeast to join the Fremont River.

Sulphur Creek Route

- Distance: 5 miles one-way
- Duration: 3–5 hours one-way
- Elevation gain: 540 feet
- Effort: moderate–strenuous
- Trailhead: across Highway 24 from Chimney Rock parking lot

This moderately difficult hike begins by following a wash across the highway from the Chimney Rock parking area, descends to Sulphur Creek, then heads down the narrow canyon to the visitors center. Park rangers sometimes schedule guided hikes on this route. It's best to hike Sulphur Creek during warm weather because you'll be wading in the normally shallow creek. Three small waterfalls can be bypassed fairly easily; two falls are just below the goosenecks, and the third is about half a mile before the visitors center. Carry water with you. You can make an all-day eight-mile hike in Sulphur Creek by starting where it crosses the highway between Mileposts 72 and 73, five miles west of the visitors center.

Hickman Natural Bridge

- Distance: 1 mile one-way
- Duration: 1.5 hours
- Elevation gain: 380 feet
- Effort: easy–moderate
- Trailhead: 2 miles east of the visitors center on the north side of Highway 24

The graceful Hickman Natural Bridge spans 133 feet across a small streambed. Numbered stops along the self-guided trail correspond to descriptions in a pamphlet available at the trailhead or visitors center. Starting from the parking area (elevation 5,320 feet), the trail follows the Fremont River's green banks a short distance before climbing to the bridge. The last section of trail follows a dry wash shaded by cottonwood, juniper, and piñon pine. You'll pass under the bridge (eroded from the Kay-

enta Formation) at trail's end. Capitol Dome and other sculptured sandstone features surround the site. Joseph Hickman, for whom the bridge was named, served as principal of Wayne County High School and, later, in the state legislature; he and another local man, Ephraim Pectol, led efforts to promote Capitol Reef.

Rim Overlook Trail

- Distance: 2.25 miles one-way
- Duration: 3–5 hours one-way
- Elevation gain: 540 feet
- Effort: moderate–strenuous
- Trailhead: Hickman Natural Bridge Trailhead

A splendid overlook 1,000 feet above Fruita beckons hikers up the Rim Overlook Trail. Take the Hickman Natural Bridge Trail from the parking area, turn right at the signed fork, and hike for about two miles. Allow 3.5 hours from the fork for this hike. Panoramic views take in the Fremont River valley below, the great cliffs of Capitol Reef above, the Henry Mountains to the southeast, and Boulder Mountain to the southwest.

Continue another 2.2 miles from the Rim Overlook to reach **Navajo Knobs.** Rock cairns lead the way over slickrock along the rim of Waterpocket Fold. A magnificent view at trail's end takes in much of southeastern Utah.

◖ Grand Wash Trail

- Distance: 2.25 miles one-way
- Duration: 2 hours
- Elevation gain: negligible
- Effort: easy
- Trailhead: 4.7 miles east of the visitors center on the south side of Highway 24

One of only five canyons cutting completely through the reef, Grand Wash offers easy hiking, great scenery, and an abundance of wildflowers. There's no trail—just follow the dry riverbed. Flash floods can occur during storms. Only a short distance from Highway 24, canyon walls rise 800 feet above the floor and narrow to as little as 20 feet in width (this stretch of trail is known as "The Narrows"). After The Narrows, the wash widens and wildflowers grow everywhere. Cassidy Arch Trailhead (see *Hiking Along the Scenic Drive*) is two miles from Highway 24.

The hike can also be started from a trailhead at the end of Grand Wash Road, off the Scenic Drive.

HIKING ALONG THE SCENIC DRIVE

These hikes begin from trailheads along the Scenic Drive. Drivers must pay $5 to travel this road.

Fremont Gorge Overlook Trail

• Distance: 2.25 miles one-way

• Duration: 2–3 hours

• Elevation gain: 1,000 feet

• Effort: moderate–strenuous

• Trailhead: Fruita blacksmith shop

From the start at the Fruita blacksmith shop, the trail climbs a short distance, then crosses Johnson Mesa and climbs steeply to the overlook about 1,000 feet above the Fremont River. The overlook is not a place for the acrophobic—even people who aren't ordinarily afraid of heights might find it a little daunting.

Cohab Canyon

• Distance: 1.75 miles one-way

• Duration: 2.5 hours

• Elevation gain: 400 feet

• Effort: moderate–strenuous

• Trailheads: across road from Fruita Campground (one mile south of the visitors center) and across Highway 24 from Hickman Natural Bridge Trailhead

Cohab is a pretty little canyon overlooking the campground. Mormon polygamists (cohabitationists) supposedly used the canyon to escape federal marshals during the 1880s. It's possible to hike this trail starting from either trailhead. Starting from the campground, the trail first follows steep switchbacks before continuing along more gentle grades to the top of the reef, 400 feet higher and one mile from the campground. You can take a short trail to viewpoints or continue 0.75 mile down the other side of the ridge to Highway 24.

Another option is to turn right at the top on Frying Pan Trail and head to Cassidy Arch (3.5 miles one-way) and Grand Wash (four miles one-way). The trail from Cassidy Arch to Grand Wash is steep. All of these interconnecting trails offer many hiking possibilities, especially if you can arrange a car shuttle. For example, you could start up Cohab Canyon Trail from Highway 24, cross over the reef on Frying Pan Trail, make a side trip to Cassidy Arch, descend Cassidy Arch Trail to Grand Wash, walk down Grand Wash to Highway 24, then walk (or car-shuttle) 2.7 miles along the highway back to the start (10.5 miles total).

Hiking the Frying Pan Trail involves an additional 600 feet of climbing from either Cohab Canyon or Cassidy Arch Trail. Once atop Capitol Reef, the trail follows the gently rolling slickrock terrain.

Fremont River Trail

• Distance: 1.25 miles one-way

• Duration: 2 hours

• Elevation gain: 770 feet

• Effort: moderate–strenuous

• Trailhead: Fruita Campground amphitheater

The trail passes orchards along the Fremont River (elevation 5,350 feet), and after an easy start it begins the climb up sloping rock to a viewpoint on Miners Mountain of Fruita, Boulder Mountain, and Capitol Reef.

Cassidy Arch

- Distance: 1.75 miles one-way

- Duration: 3 hours

- Elevation gain: 1,150

- Effort: moderate–strenuous

- Trailhead: end of drivable section of Grand Wash Road

- Directions: Turn left off the Scenic Drive 3.6 miles from the visitors center and follow Grand Wash Road to trailhead.

Cassidy Arch Trail begins near the end of Grand Wash Road and ascends the north wall of Grand Wash, then winds across slickrock to a vantage point close to the arch. Energetic hikers will enjoy good views of Grand Wash, the great domes of Navajo sandstone, and the arch itself. The notorious outlaw Butch Cassidy may have traveled through Capitol Reef and seen this arch. Frying Pan Trail branches off Cassidy Arch Trail at the one-mile mark, then wends its

Just a short scramble above Capitol Gorge is a series of natural water tanks, or waterpockets.

© JUDY JEWELL

way across three miles of slickrock to Cohab Canyon (see the *Cohab Canyon* section).

Old Wagon Trail

- Distance: 3.5-mile loop

- Duration: 3 hours

- Elevation gain: 1,000 feet

- Effort: moderate–strenuous

- Trailhead: on Scenic Drive 6 miles south of visitors center, between Grand Wash and Capitol Gorge

Wagon drivers once used this route as a shortcut between Grover and Capitol Gorge. The old trail crosses a wash to the west, then ascends steadily through piñon and juniper woodland on Miners Mountain. After 1.5 miles, the trail leaves the wagon road and continues north for half a mile to a high knoll and the best views of the Capitol Reef area.

◖ Capitol Gorge

- Distance: 1 mile one-way to tanks

- Duration: 1–2 hours

- Elevation gain: 100 feet

- Effort: easy–moderate

- Trailhead: Capitol Gorge parking area

Follow the well-maintained dirt road to the parking area in Capitol Gorge to begin this hike. The first mile downstream is the most scenic: Fremont petroglyphs (in poor condition) appear on the left after 0.1 mile; narrows of Capitol Gorge close in at 0.3 mile; a "pioneer register" on the left soon after consists of names and dates of early travelers and ranchers scratched in the canyon wall; and there are natural water tanks. If you're able to scramble up some rocks and follow a cairn-marked trail across the slickrock, head up out of the wash at the trail marker for the water tanks, about 0.8 mile from the trail. These depressions in the rock collect water and give Waterpocket Fold its name. Back in the wash, listen for canyon wrens—their song starts at a high note and then trills down the scale. From the turnoff to the water tanks, hikers can continue another three miles downstream to Notom Road.

Golden Throne Trail

- Distance: 2 miles one-way
- Duration: 3 hours
- Elevation gain: 1,100 feet to tanks
- Effort: strenuous
- Trailhead: Capitol Gorge parking area

The Golden Throne Trail begins at the trailhead at the end of the drivable part of Capitol Wash. Instead of heading down Capitol Gorge from the parking area, turn left up this trail for a steady climb to dramatic views of the reef and surrounding area. The Golden Throne is a massive monolith of yellow-hued sandstone capped by a thin layer of red rock. This is a good hike to take around sunset, when the rocks take on a burnished glow.

MOUNTAIN BIKING

Ditch the car and get to really know this country with a big loop tour. From Highway 24 near Capitol Reef, take the Notom–Bullfrog Road to Burr Trail Road, then Highway 12 over Boulder Mountain to Highway 24 and back to Capitol Reef. This is definitely the sort of trip that requires some touring experience and a decent level of training. (Boulder Mountain is quite a haul!) Expect the 125-mile loop to take several days.

In the remote northern section of the park, cyclists can ride the challenging Cathedral Canyon Loop. The complete loop is more than 60 miles long. Little water is available along the route, so it's best ridden in spring or fall, when temperatures are low. Contact the visitors center for more information on this and other routes.

CLIMBING

Rock climbing is allowed in the park. Climbers should check with rangers to learn about restricted areas, but registration is voluntary.

THE ORCHARDS OF CAPITOL REEF

Capitol Reef was one of the last places in the West to be discovered by white settlers. First reports came in 1866 from a detachment of Mormon militia pursuing renegade Utes. In 1872, Professor Almon H. Thompson of the Powell Expedition led the first scientific exploration in the fold country and named several park features along the group's Pleasant Creek route. Mormons, expanding their network of settlements, arrived in the upper Fremont Valley in the late 1870s and spread downriver to Hanksville. Junction (renamed Fruita in 1902) and nearby Pleasant Creek (Sleeping Rainbow/Floral Ranch) were settled about 1880. Floods, isolation, and transportation difficulties forced many families to move on, especially downstream from Capitol Reef. Irrigation and hard work paid off with prosperous fruit orchards and the sobriquet "the Eden of Wayne County." The aptly named Fruita averaged about 10 families who grew alfalfa, sorghum (for syrup), vegetables, and a wide variety of fruit. Getting the produce to market required long and difficult journeys by wagon. The region remained one of the most isolated in Utah until after World War II.

Although Fruita's citizens have departed, the National Park Service still maintains the old orchards. The orchards are lovely in late April, when the trees are in bloom beneath the towering canyon walls. Visitors are welcome to pick and carry away the cherries, apricots, peaches, pears, and apples during harvest seasons. Harvest times begin in late June or early July and end in October. You'll be charged about the same as in commercial pick-your-own orchards. You may also wander through any orchard and eat all you want on the spot before and during the designated picking season (no charge).

Climbers must use "clean" techniques (no pitons or bolts) and keep at least 100 feet from rock-art panels and prehistoric structures. Because of the abundance of prehistoric rock art found there, the section of rock wall north of Highway 24 between the Fruita schoolhouse and the east end of Kreuger Orchard (Mile 81.4) is closed to climbing. Other areas closed to climbing are Hickman Natural Bridge and all other arches and bridges, Temple of the Moon, Temple of the Sun, and Chimney Rock.

The harder, fractured sandstone of the Wingate Formation is better suited to climbing than the more crumbly Entrada sandstone. However, the rock is given to flaking, so climbers should use caution. Be sure that chalk matches the color of the rock; white chalk is prohibited.

CAMPGROUNDS

Fruita Campground, one mile south of the visitors center on the Scenic Drive, stays open all year and has drinking water but no showers or hookups ($10). From November to April campers must get their water from the visitors center. The surrounding orchards and lush grass make this an attractive spot. Sites often fill by early afternoon in the busy May–October season. One group campground (by reservation only) and a picnic area are nearby. If you're just looking for a place to park for the night, check out the public land east of the park boundary off Highway 24. Areas on both sides of the highway (about nine miles east of the visitors center) may be used for free primitive camping.

The five-site **Cedar Mesa Campground** is in the park's southern district just off Notom–Bullfrog Road (dirt); campers here enjoy fine views of Waterpocket Fold and the Henry Mountains. Open all year; no water or charge. From the visitors center, go east 9.2 miles on Highway 24, then turn right 22 miles on Notom–Bullfrog Road (avoid this road if it's wet). **Cathedral Valley Campground** serves the park's northern district; it has five sites (no water or charge) near the Hartnet Junction, about 30 miles north of Highway 24. Take either Caineville Wash Road or Hartnet Road. Both roads are dirt and should be avoided when wet. Hartnet has a river ford.

Torrey

Torrey (pop. 166) is an attractive little village with a real Western feel. Only 11 miles west of the Capitol Reef National Park visitors center, at the junction of Highways 12 and 24, it's a friendly and convenient place to stay, with several excellent lodgings and a good restaurant.

Other little towns lie along the Fremont River, which drains this steep-sided valley. Teasdale is a small community just four miles west, situated in a grove of piñon pines. Bicknell, a small farm and ranch town, is eight miles west of Torrey.

OUTFITTERS
Shop for that forgotten piece of gear at **Red River Outfitters** (135 E. Main St., 435/425-3669, www.redriveroutfitter.com). It's mostly a fly shop but also stocks camping gear and outdoor clothing. Guided trips are available. Fishing can be good in the Fremont River and (once the ice melts, sometime in early June) in the lakes on Boulder Mountain, south of town.

You can rent mountain bikes at **Backcountry Outfitters** (junction of Hwy. 12 and Hwy. 24, 435/425-2010 or 866/747-3972, www.ridethereef.com); their main business is guiding people on hiking, canyoneering, mountain biking, or horseback trips.

Hondoo Rivers and Trails (435/425-3519 or 800/332-2696, www.hondoo.com), run by long-time locals, offers guide services for both day trips and multiday backcountry excursions; for a real treat, check out the inn-to-inn trail rides. They also provide shuttle services.

CAPITOL REEF

© W. C. MCRAE

The little village of Torrey boasts an original one-room schoolhouse.

ACCOMMODATIONS
Under $50

There are a few small bunkhouse cabins at the center of town, at the **Torrey Trading Post** (75 W. Main St., 435/425-3716, www.torreytrading post.com, $28). They aren't loaded with frills—the toilets and showers are in men's and women's bathhouses—but the price is right and pets are permitted. The **Capitol Reef Inn and Cafe** (360 W. Main St., 435/425-3271, www.capitol reefinn.com, $48 d, closed in winter) has homey motel rooms and a good café serving breakfast, lunch, and dinner. In the front yard, the motel's owner and his brother have built a kiva resembling those used by Native Americans. It's obviously a labor of love, and a pretty cool place to explore.

In Bicknell, the **Aquarius Motel** (435/425-3835 or 800/833-5379, $47 and up) offers good-sized standard motel rooms, some with kitchens (you supply the kitchenware) and all with wireless Internet access. There's also a somewhat retro café (open daily for breakfast, lunch, and dinner) and a glass-enclosed indoor pool.

$50-75

In a pretty setting three miles south of town, **Cowboy Homestead Cabins** (Hwy. 12, 435/425-3414 or 888/854-5871, www.cowboy homesteadcabins.com, $69) has attractive, modern kitchenette cabins with outdoor gas barbecue grills.

The **Wonderland Inn** (junction of Hwy. 12 and Hwy. 24, 435/425-3775 or 800/458-0216, www.capitolreefwonderland.com, $64 and up), just east of town near the turnoff for Boulder, is a larger motel with an indoor pool, a rather spacious greenhouse, and a restaurant serving breakfast, lunch, and dinner daily.

Farther east, the **Rim Rock Inn** (2523 E. Hwy. 24, 435/425-3388 or 888/447-4676, www.therimrock.net, $59 and up, closed Jan.–Feb.) does indeed perch on a rim of red rock. The motel and its two restaurants are part of a 120-acre ranch, so the views are expansive.

$75-100

Immediately behind downtown Torrey's old trading post and country store in a grove of trees is **Austin's Chuck Wagon Lodge** (12 W. Main St., 435/425-3335 or 800/863-3288, www.austinschuckwagonmotel.com, $69–135, closed Jan.–Feb.), with rooms in an older motel, a newer lodgelike building, or in two-bedroom cabins. There's also a pool and a hot tub.

If you're looking for standard and comfortable motel rooms with perks like high-speed Internet access and an outdoor pool, a good choice is the **Best Western Capitol Reef Resort** (2600 E. Hwy. 24, 435/425-3761, www.bestwestern.com, $90 and up).

In Teasdale, four miles west of Torrey, **Pine Shadows** (125 South 200 West, 435/425-3939 or 800/708-1223, www.pineshadowcabins .net, $69 and up) offers spacious, modern cabins equipped with bathrooms and kitchens in a piñon forest.

Over $100

The lovely **SkyRidge Inn Bed and Breakfast** (950 W. Hwy. 24, 435/425-3222 or 800/448-6990, www.skyridgeinn.com, $109–159) is one mile east of downtown Torrey. The modern inn has been decorated with high-quality Southwestern art and artifacts; all six guest rooms have private baths. SkyRidge sits on a bluff amid 75 acres; guests are invited to explore the land on foot or bike.

The **Lodge at Red River Ranch** (2900 W. Hwy. 24, 435/425-3222 or 800/205-6343, www.redriverranch.com, $140–225) is between Bicknell and Torrey beneath towering cliffs of red sandstone on the banks of the Fremont River. This wonderful wood-beamed lodge sits on a working ranch, but there's nothing rustic or unsophisticated about the accommodations here. The three-story structure is newly built, although in the same grand architectural style as old-fashioned mountain lodges. The great room has a massive stone fireplace, cozy chairs and couches, and a splendid Old West atmosphere. There are 15 guest rooms, most decorated according to a theme, and all have private baths. Guests are welcome to wander ranch paths, fish for trout, or tinker in the gardens and orchards. Breakfast and dinner are served in the lodge restaurant but are not included in the price of lodgings; box lunches can be ordered.

Muley Twist Inn (outside Teasdale, 435/425-3640 or 800/530-1038, www.rof.net/yp/muley, $99–109), an elegantly decorated B&B, is on a 30-acre parcel with great views. It's another really wonderful place to come home to at the end of a day of driving or hiking.

Campgrounds

For campers, **Thousand Lakes RV Park,** one mile west of Torrey on Highway 24 (435/425-3500, $15 tents, $21.50 RVs with full hookups), has sites with showers, a laundry room, and a store, and is open late March through late October. Thousand Lakes also has cabins, ranging from Spartan ($31.50 without linens) to deluxe ($95, sleeps eight, linens provided) and Western-style cookouts on summer weeknights ($12.95–18.50). Right in town, the **Sand Creek RV Park** (540 W. Hwy. 24, 435/425-3577, $12 tents, $16–18 RVs with hookups, Apr.–mid-Oct.) has RV hookups and tent spaces in a pleasant grassy field.

The U.S. Forest Service's **Sunglow Campground** is just east of Bicknell at an elevation of 7,200 feet; sites are open with water mid-May through late October. The surrounding red cliffs really light up at sunset. Several other Forest Service campgrounds are on the slopes of Boulder Mountain along Highway 12 between Torrey and Boulder. These places are all above 8,600 feet and usually don't open until late May or early June.

FOOD

Torrey's restaurant of note is **Cafe Diablo** (599 W. Main St., 435/425-3070, dinner nightly, mid-Apr.–mid-Oct., entrées $20–28). The specialty is zesty Southwestern cuisine, with excellent dishes like fire-roasted pork tenderloin, eggplant-and-poblano-stuffed tamales, and pumpkin-seed trout. This is one of the few places you can order free-range rattlesnake meat, cooked into crabcakelike patties. Because there aren't many restaurants this good in rural Utah, this place is worth a detour.

Another pleasant surprise in this small town is the **Capitol Reef Inn and Cafe** (360

W. Main St., 435/425-3271; breakfast, lunch, and dinner daily; closed in winter, full dinner $10–15), where there's an emphasis on healthy and (when possible) locally grown food. It's easy to eat your veggies here—the 10-vegetable salad will make up for some of the less-nutritious meals you've had on the road.

West of Torrey, in Bicknell, **Alasdair's Stag and Heather Restaurant** (292 W. Main St., Bicknell, 435/425-3289) had not yet opened when we were in the area, but it looked like it might be worth checking out. Chef Alasdair is Scottish, has cooked in upscale European restaurants, and managed a castle hotel in Scotland.

If you're heading east, between Capitol Reef and Hanksville is **Luna Mesa** (Caineville, 435/456-9122, breakfast, lunch, and dinner Mon.–Sat. May–Oct., $3–10), a welcome roadside spot for a burrito or a cold drink.

INFORMATION

The **Fremont River Ranger District** (138 S. Main St., Loa, 435/836-2800, www.fs.fed.us/r4/fishlake/, 8 A.M.–4:30 P.M. Mon.–Fri.) of the Fishlake National Forest has information about hiking, horseback riding, and road conditions in the northern and eastern parts of Boulder Mountain and the Aquarius Plateau.

CANYONLANDS NATIONAL PARK

The canyon country of southeastern Utah puts on its supreme performance in this vast park, which spreads across 527 square miles. The deeply entrenched Colorado and Green Rivers meet in its heart, then continue south as the mighty Colorado through tumultuous Cataract Canyon Rapids. The park is divided into four districts and a separate noncontiguous unit. The Colorado and the Green Rivers form the **River District** and divide Canyonlands National Park into three other regions. **Island in the Sky** lies north between the rivers, the **Maze** is to the west, and **Needles** is to the east. The **Horseshoe Canyon Unit** lies farther to the west. This small parcel of land preserves a canyon on Barrier Creek, a tributary of the Green River, in which astounding petroglyphs and other ancient rock paintings are protected.

Each district has its own distinct character. No bridges or roads directly connect the three land districts and the Horseshoe Canyon Unit, so most visitors have to leave the park to go from one region to another. The huge park can be seen in many ways and on many levels. Paved roads reach a few areas, four-wheel-drive roads go to more places, and hiking trails reach still more, yet much of the land shows no trace of human passage. To get the big picture, you can fly over this incredible complex of canyons (see *Air Tours* under *Recreation* in the *Moab* chapter); however, only a river trip or a hike lets you experience the solitude and detail of the land.

The park can be visited in any season of the year, with spring and autumn the best choices. Summer temperatures can climb into the 100s; carrying (and drinking) lots of water becomes

© W. C. MCRAE

HIGHLIGHTS

Mesa Arch Trail: This easy trail leads to a dramatic cliff-side arch. The sun rising through the arch is a sight to behold – if you have time and energy for just one hike in Canyonlands, this should be it (page 170).

Grand View Trail: This short hike along slickrock cliffs captures the essence of the "Island in the Sky." A sheer mile below the trail, the gorges of the Colorado and Green Rivers join to form Cataract Canyon, and in the distance, the odd promontories of the Needles District punctuate the skyline (page 172).

Upheaval Dome Viewpoint Trail: In the Island in the Sky District, hike to the dome's craterlike rim, created by the impact of an asteroid. From here you'll have a view about 1,000 feet down. A longer trail descends the slickrock and offers even better views (page 172).

BLM Newspaper Rock Historical Monument: This is one of Utah's foremost prehistoric rock-art sites and also one of the most easily accessible. The distinctive petroglyphs here span 2,000 years of human history (page 174).

Cave Spring Trail: The Cave Spring Trail in the Needles District introduces the geology and ecology of the park and passes by an old cowboy line camp. It's also a good introduction to slickrock hiking; rock cairns mark the way and ladders assist hikers on the steep sections (page 175).

Chesler Park: A lovely desert meadow contrasts with the characteristic red and white spires of the Needles District. The trail winds through sand and slickrock before ascending a small pass through the Needles to Chesler Park; the park itself is encircled by a loop trail (page 178).

Land of Standing Rocks: Here, rock spires stand guard over myriad canyons in the Maze District. Land of Standing Rocks is a good place to camp, hike, and generally explore, but it takes some getting to. Be sure to have a high-clearance four-wheel-drive vehicle, a compass, and some good maps (page 182).

Great Gallery Trail: Ghostly life-size pictographs in the Great Gallery are in remote Horseshoe Canyon, just west of the main part of Canyonlands. The hike in to the gallery also offers pleasant scenery and spring wildflowers (page 184).

River-Running through Cataract Canyon: Downstream from its confluence with the Green River, the Colorado River enters Cataract Canyon and picks up speed. The rapids begin four miles downstream and extend for the next 14 miles to Lake Powell. Especially in spring, the 26 or more rapids give a wild ride equal to the best in the Grand Canyon (page 187).

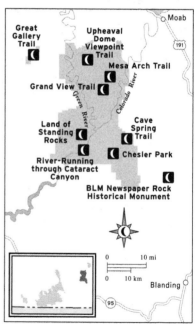

LOOK FOR **(** TO FIND RECOMMENDED SIGHTS, ACTIVITIES, DINING, AND LODGING.

critical then (carry at least one gallon per person per day). Arm yourself with insect repellent from late spring to midsummer. Winter days tend to be bright and sunny, although nighttime temperatures can dip into the teens or even below zero. Visitors coming in winter should inquire about travel conditions because snow and ice occasionally close roads and trails at higher elevations.

PLANNING YOUR TIME

Unless you have a great deal of time, you can't really "do" the entire park in one trip. It's best to pick one section and concentrate on it.

Island in the Sky District

The mesa-top Island in the Sky District has paved roads on its top to impressive belvederes such as Grand View Point and the strange Upheaval Dome. If you're short on time or don't want to make a rigorous backcountry trip, you'll find this district the best choice. It is easily visited as a day trip from Moab. The "Island," which is actually a large mesa, is much like nearby Dead Horse Point on a giant scale; a narrow neck of land connects the north side with the "mainland."

If you're really on a tight schedule, it's possible to spend a few hours exploring Arches National Park, then head to Island in the Sky for a drive to the scenic Grand View overlook and a brief hike to Mesa Arch or the Upheaval Dome viewpoint. A one-day visit should include these elements, plus a hike along the Neck Springs Trail. For a longer visit, hikers, mountain bikers, and those with suitable high-clearance four-wheel-drive vehicles can drop off the Island in the Sky and descend about 1,300 feet to the **White Rim Road,** which follows cliffs of the White Rim around most of the island. Plan to spend at least two to three days exploring this 100-mile-long road.

Needles District

Colorful rock spires prompted the name of the Needles District, which is easily accessed from Highway 211 and U.S. 191 south of Moab. Splendid canyons contain many arches, strange rock formations, and archaeological sites. Overlooks and short nature trails can be enjoyed from the paved scenic drive in the park, and if you are only

here for a day, hike the Cave Spring and Pothole Point Trails. On a longer visit, make a loop of the Big Spring and Squaw Canyon Trails, and hike to Chesler Park. If you have a mountain bike, take a day off from hiking and ride out from the visitors center to the Colorado Overlook.

Drivers with four-wheel-drive vehicles have their own challenging roads through canyons and other highly scenic areas.

Maze District

Few visitors make it over to the Maze District, which is some of the wildest country in the United States. Only the rivers and a handful of four-wheel-drive roads and hiking trails provide access. Experienced hikers can explore the "maze" of canyons on unmarked routes. Plan to spend at least two or three days in this area; even if you're only taking day hikes, it can take a long time to get to any destination here. That said, a hike from the Maze Overlook to the Harvest Scene pictographs is a good bet if you don't have a lot of time. If you have more than one day, head to the Land of Standing Rocks area and hike north to the Chocolate Drops.

Horseshoe Canyon Unit

Horseshoe Canyon Unit, a detached section of the park northwest of the Maze District, is equally remote. It protects the **Great Gallery,** a group of pictographs left by prehistoric Native Americans. This ancient artwork is reached at the end of a series of long, unpaved roads and down a canyon on a moderately challenging hiking trail. Plan to spend a full day exploring this area.

River District

The River District includes long stretches of the Green and the Colorado. River-running provides one of the best ways to experience the inner depths of the park. Boaters can obtain helpful literature and advice from park rangers. Groups planning their own trip through Cataract Canyon need a river-running permit. Flatwater permits are also required. See the *Moab* chapter for information about river outfitters: They offer trips ranging from half a day to several days in length.

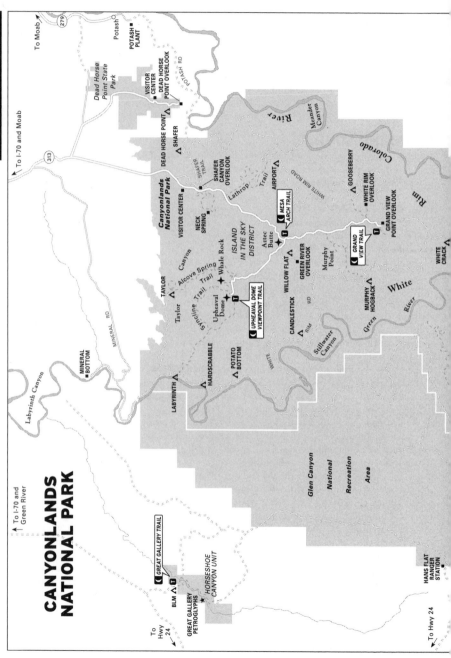

CANYONLANDS NATIONAL PARK

To Moab ↗

To I-70 and Moab ←

To I-70 and Green River ←

To Hwy 24 ↙

To Hwy 24 →

Potash ■ PLANT

POTASH RD

Dead Horse Point State Park

VISITOR CENTER ■
DEAD HORSE POINT OVERLOOK ■

DEAD HORSE POINT ▲
SHAFER ▲

SHAFER TRAIL

SHAFER CANYON OVERLOOK ■

Lathrop Trail

AIRPORT ▲

WHITE RIM ROAD

GOOSEBERRY ▲

WHITE RIM OVERLOOK ■

Meander Canyon

River

Colorado

Rim

Canyonlands National Park

VISITOR CENTER ■

NECK SPRING ▲

MESA ARCH TRAIL ■ ◀ T

ISLAND IN THE SKY DISTRICT

Aztec Butte ▲

GRAND VIEW POINT OVERLOOK ■ T

GRAND VIEW TRAIL ◀ T

WHITE CRACK ▲

TAYLOR ▲

Taylor Canyon

Alcove Spring Trail

Syncline Trail

Taylor Trail

Whale Rock ★

Upheaval Dome

UPHEAVAL DOME VIEWPOINT TRAIL ◀ T

WILLOW FLAT ▲

GREEN RIVER OVERLOOK ■

Murphy Point

White RIM RD

CANDLESTICK ▲

MURPHY HOGBACK ▲

White

River

Green River

Stillwater Canyon

HARDSCRABBLE ▲

POTATO BOTTOM ▲

LABYRINTH ▲

MINERAL RD

MINERAL BOTTOM ■

Labyrinth Canyon

Glen Canyon National Recreation Area

GREAT GALLERY TRAIL ◀ T

BLM ■ ▲ T

HORSESHOE CANYON UNIT

GREAT GALLERY PETROGLYPHS ★

HANS FLAT RANGER STATION ■

279

313

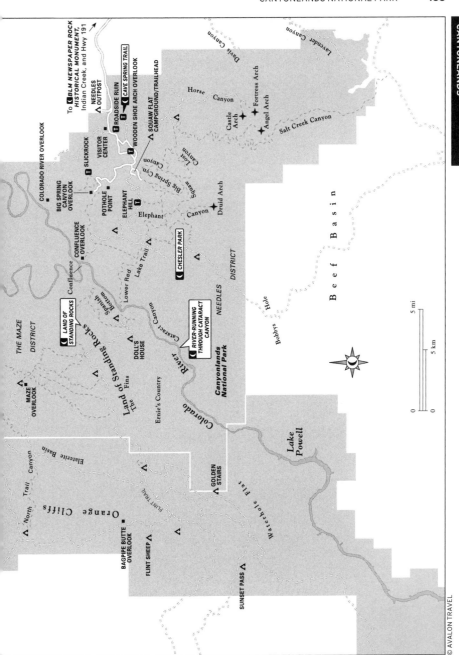

To BLM NEWSPAPER ROCK
HISTORICAL MONUMENT,
Indian Creek, and Hwy 191

NEEDLES
OUTPOST

CAVE SPRING TRAIL

ROADSIDE RUIN

WOODEN SHOE ARCH OVERLOOK

SQUAW FLAT
CAMPGROUND/TRAILHEAD

SLICKROCK

VISITOR
CENTER

COLORADO RIVER OVERLOOK

BIG SPRING
CANYON
OVERLOOK

POTHOLE
POINT

ELEPHANT
HILL

Big Spring Cyn.

Lost Canyon

Squaw Canyon

Horse Canyon

Castle Arch

Fortress Arch

Angel Arch

Salt Creek Canyon

Druid Arch

Elephant Canyon

CONFLUENCE
OVERLOOK

Confluence

CHESLER PARK

Lake Trail

Lower Red Lake Trail

Spanish Bottom

THE MAZE
DISTRICT

LAND OF
STANDING ROCKS

DOLL'S
HOUSE

Cataract Canyon

RIVER-RUNNING
THROUGH CATARACT
CANYON

NEEDLES DISTRICT

Canyonlands
National Park

Beef Basin

Bobbys Hole

MAZE
OVERLOOK

Land of Standing Rocks

The Fins

Ernie's Country

Colorado River

Lake
Powell

Elaterite Basin

FLINT TRAIL

GOLDEN
STAIRS

Waterhole Flat

North Trail Canyon

Orange Cliffs

BAGPIPE BUTTE OVERLOOK

FLINT SHEEP

SUNSET PASS

Davis Canyon

Lavender Canyon

5 mi

5 km

0

0

CANYONLANDS

Exploring the Park

There are four districts and a noncontiguous unit in Canyonlands National Park (www .nps.gov/cany; $10 per vehicle, $5 per bicyclist, motorcyclist, or pedestrian; good for one week in all districts; no fee required to enter Maze or Horseshoe Canyon), each affording great views, spectacular geology, a chance to see wildlife, and endless opportunities to explore. You won't find crowds or elaborate park facilities because most of Canyonlands remains a primitive backcountry park. If your plans include visiting Arches National Park plus Hovenweep and Natural Bridges National Monuments, consider the so-called Local Passport, which for $25 buys entry to each of these federal preserves. Purchase the pass at any park or national monument entry.

Front-country camping is allowed only in established campgrounds at Willow Flat (Island in the Sky) and Squaw Flat (Needles).

Rock climbing is allowed in the park, and permits are not required (unless the trip involves overnight camping); however, it's always a good idea to check in at district visitors centers for advice and information, and to learn where climbing is restricted. Climbing is not allowed within 300 feet of cultural sites.

Pets aren't allowed on trails and must be leashed. No firewood collecting is permitted in the park; backpackers must use gas stoves for cooking. Vehicle and boat campers can bring in firewood but must use grills or fire pans.

The best maps for the park are a series of topographic maps printed on waterproof paper by Trails Illustrated; these have the latest trail and road information. A giant U.S. Geological Survey (USGS) topographic map, *Canyonlands National Park and Vicinity,* has the same 1:62,500 scale at a lower cost, but without the updated information and fancy paper.

VISITORS CENTERS

Since Canyonlands covers so much far-flung territory, separate visitors centers serve each district. One website (www.nps.gov/cany)

serves the whole park and is a good source for current information and permit applications. There are visitors centers at the entrances to the Island in the Sky District (435/259-4712, 8 A.M.–4:30 P.M. daily, open until 6 P.M. Apr.–mid-Oct.) and the Needles District (435/259-4711, 8 A.M.–4:30 P.M. daily, open until 5 P.M. Apr.–mid-Oct.). The Hans Flat Ranger Station (435/259-2652, 8 A.M.–4:30 P.M. daily) is on a remote plateau above the even more isolated canyons of the Maze District and the Horseshoe Canyon Unit. The River District is administered out of the National Park Service Office (2282 SW Resource Blvd., Moab, 435/719-2313). This office can generally handle inquiries for all districts of the park. For backcountry information, or to make backcountry reservations, call 435/259-4351. Handouts from the ranger offices describe natural history, travel, and other aspects of the park.

If you are in Moab, it is most convenient to stop at the Moab Information Center (corner of Main and Center, 435/259-8825 or 800/635-6622), where a national park ranger is usually on duty. All offices have brochures, maps, and books, as well as someone to answer your questions.

TOURS

Outfitters must be authorized by the National Park Service to operate in Canyonlands. See the park's website (www.nps.gov/cany/guided .htm) for a list of authorized outfitters. Most of these guides concentrate on river trips, but some can take you on mountain-bike trips, including vehicle-supported tours of the White Rim 4WD Trail. Most of the guides operating in Canyonlands are based in Moab; see that chapter for more information.

BACKCOUNTRY EXPLORATION

A complex system of fees is charged for backcountry camping, four-wheel-drive exploration, and river-rafting, detailed as follows.

CANYONLANDS NATURAL HISTORY

GEOLOGY

Deep canyons of the Green and Colorado Rivers have sliced through rocks representing 150 million years of deposition. The Paradox Formation, exposed in Cataract Canyon, contains salt and other minerals responsible for some of the folded and faulted rock layers in the region. Under the immense pressure of overlying rocks, the Paradox flows like plastic, forming domes where the rock layers are thinnest and causing cracks or faults as pressures rise and fall. Each of the overlying formations has a different color and texture; they're the products of ancient deserts, rivers, and seas that once covered this land. Views from any of the overlooks reveal that an immense quantity of rock has already been washed downriver toward California. Not so evident, however, is the 10,000 vertical feet of rock that geologists say once lay across the high mesas. The dry climate and sparse vegetation allow clear views of the remaining rock layers and the effects of erosion and deformation. You can read the geologic story at Canyonlands National Park in the 3,500 feet of strata that remain, from the bottom of Cataract Canyon to the upper reaches of Salt Creek in the Needles District.

FLORA AND FAUNA

Extremes of flash flood and drought, hot summers, and cold winters discourage all but the most hardy and adaptable life. Desert grasses, small flowering plants, cacti, and shrubs like blackbrush and saltbush survive on the mostly thin soils and meager eight or nine inches of annual precipitation. Trees either grow in cracks that concentrate rainfall and nutrients or rely on springs or canyon streams for moisture. Piñon pine and juniper prefer the higher elevations of the park, while cottonwoods live in the canyon bottoms that have permanent subsurface water. Tamarisk, an exotic and invasive streamside plant, and willows often form dense thickets on sandbars along the Green and Colorado Rivers. The hanging gardens of lush vegetation that surround cliffside springs or seeps seem oblivious to the surrounding desert.

© W. C. MCRAE

Prickly pear cactus eke out a living in arid juniper shrublands.

The fragile desert ecology can easily be upset. Cattle, especially in the Needles District, once overgrazed the grasslands and trampled cryptobiotic crusts and other vegetation. Increased erosion and growth of undesirable exotic plants like cheatgrass have been the result. Scars left by roads and mines during the uranium frenzy of the 1950s can still be seen, most commonly in the Island in the Sky District.

Fewer than 10 species of fish evolved in the canyons of the Colorado and the Green. These fish developed streamlined bodies and strange features, such as humped backs, to cope with the muddy and varying river waters. Species include Colorado squawfish, humpback chub, bonytail chub, and humpback sucker; most of these live nowhere else. All have suffered greatly reduced populations and restricted ranges as a result of recent dam-building.

Of the approximately 65 mammal species living in the park, about one-third are rodents and another third are bats. You're most likely to see chipmunks, antelope ground squirrels, and rock squirrels, which are often active during the day. Most other animals wait until evening to come out and feed; in the morning, look for tracks of mule deer, bighorn sheep, coyotes, gray foxes, badgers, porcupines, spotted skunks, beavers, black-tailed jackrabbits, wood rats, kangaroo rats, and many species of mice.

Except for the main campgrounds at Willow Flat (Island in the Sky) and Squaw Flat (Needles), you'll need a permit for backcountry camping. There is a $15 fee for a backpacking permit and a $30 fee for a vehicle permit (also required for mountain bikes). Each of the three major districts has a different policy for backcountry vehicle camping, so it's a good idea to make sure that you understand the details. Backcountry permits will also be needed for any trips with horses or stock; check with a ranger for details.

It's possible to reserve a backcountry permit in advance; for spring and fall travel to popular areas like Island in the Sky's White Rim Trail or the Needles backcountry, this is an extremely good idea. Find application forms on the Canyonlands website. These should be completed and returned at least two weeks in advance of your planned trip. No telephone reservations are accepted.

Back-road travel is a popular method of exploring the park. Canyonlands National Park offers hundreds of miles of exceptionally scenic jeep roads, favorites both with mountain bikers and four-by-four enthusiasts. Park regulations require all motorized vehicles to have proper registration and licensing for highway use (all-terrain vehicles are prohibited in the park); drivers must be licensed. Normally you must have a vehicle with both four-wheel drive and high clearance. It's essential for both motor vehicles and bicycles to stay on existing roads to prevent damage to the delicate desert vegetation. Carry tools, extra fuel, water, and food in case you break down in a remote area.

Before making a trip, drivers and cyclists should talk with a ranger to register and to learn of current road conditions, which can change drastically from one day to the next. Also, the rangers will be more knowledgeable about where to seek help in case you become stuck. Primitive campgrounds are provided on most of the roads, but you'll need a backcountry permit from a ranger. Books on backcountry exploration include local author F. A. Barnes's *Canyon Country Off-Road Vehicle Trails: Island Area* and *Canyon Country Off-Road Vehicle Trails: Canyon Rims & Needles Areas,* and Jack Bikers's *Canyon Country Off-Road Vehicle Trails: Maze Area* (see *Suggested Reading* in the *Resources* chapter for all titles).

One more thing about backcountry travel in Canyonlands: You may need to pack your poop out of the backcountry. Because of the abundance of slickrock and the desert conditions, it's not always possible to dig a hole, and you can't just leave your waste to sit on a rock until it decomposes (decomposition is a very slow process under these conditions). Check with the ranger when you pick up your backcountry permit for more information.

Island in the Sky District

Panoramic views from the "Island" can be enjoyed from any point along the rim; you'll see much of the park and southeastern Utah. Short hiking trails lead to overlooks, Mesa Arch, Aztec Butte, Whale Rock, Upheaval Dome, and other features. Longer trails make steep, strenuous descents from the Island to the White Rim Road below. Elevations on the Island average about 6,000 feet.

Although the massive cliffs in the area look to be perfect for **rock climbing,** in fact much of the rock is not suitable for climbing and the remoteness of the area means that few routes have been explored. One exception is Taylor Canyon, in the extreme northwest corner of the park, which is reached by lengthy and rugged four-wheel-drive roads.

Bring water for all hiking, camping, and travel in Island in the Sky. No services are available, except at the visitors center in emergencies (bottled water is sold).

VISITORS CENTER

Stop here for information about Island in the Sky and to see exhibits on geology and history; books and maps are available for purchase. The visitors center (435/259-4351, 8 A.M.–4:30 P.M. daily except for some winter holidays, telephone reservation information available 8 A.M.–12:30 P.M. Mon.–Fri.) is located just before "the neck" crosses to Island in the Sky. From Moab, go northwest 10 miles on U.S. 191, then turn left and drive 15 miles on Highway 313 to the junction for Dead Horse Point State Park. From there, continue straight seven miles. Many of the park's plants are grown and identified outside the visitors center; look also at the display of pressed plants inside the center.

SHAFER CANYON OVERLOOK

Continue half a mile past the visitors center to this overlook on the left (just before crossing the neck). Shafer Trail Viewpoint, across the neck, provides another perspective half a mile farther. The neck is a narrow land bridge just wide enough for the road, and it's the only vehicle access to the 40-square-mile Island in

the Sky. The overlooks have good views east down the canyon and the incredibly twisting **Shafer Trail Road.** Cattlemen Frank and John Schafer built the trail in the early 1900s to move stock to additional pastures (the "c" in their name was later dropped by mapmakers). Uranium prospectors upgraded the trail to a four-wheel-drive road during the 1950s so that they could reach their claims at the base of the cliffs. Today the Shafer Trail Road connects the mesa top with White Rim Road and Potash Road 1,200 feet and four miles below. High-clearance vehicles should be used on the Shafer. It's also fun to ride this road on a mountain bike. Road conditions can vary considerably, so contact a ranger before starting.

Back on top of the Island, from the neck, follow the paved park road south six miles across Gray's Pasture to a junction. The Grand View Point Overlook road continues south while the road to Upheaval Dome turns west.

GRAND VIEW POINT

Continue south on the park road to a series of incredible vistas over the canyons of the Green and Colorado. The first viewpoint is Buck Canyon Overlook, which looks east over the Colorado River Canyon. Two miles farther is the **Grand View Picnic Area,** a handy lunch stop. Continue one mile on the main road past the picnic area to Grand View Point, perhaps the most spectacular panorama from Island in the Sky. Monument Basin lies directly below, and countless canyons, the Colorado River, the Needles, and mountain ranges are in the distance. The easy, 1.5-mile **Grand View Trail** continues past the end of the road for other vistas from the point.

UPHEAVAL DOME ROAD

Return to the road junction and explore more overlooks and geological curiosities in the western portion of Island in the Sky.

The **Green River Overlook** and **Willow Flat Campground** are just west of the junction on an unpaved road. From the overlook, Soda Springs Basin and a section of the Green River (deeply entrenched in Stillwater Canyon)

Shafer Canyon Overlook, Canyonlands National Park

EARLY EXPLORATION OF THE COLORADO RIVER CANYON

The Dominguez-Escalante Expedition skirted the east edge of the Colorado River Canyon in 1776 in an unsuccessful attempt to find a route west to California. Retreating back to New Mexico, the Spanish explorers encountered great difficulties in the canyons of southern Utah before finding a safe ford across the Colorado River. This spot, known as the "Crossing of the Fathers," now lies under Lake Powell. Later explorers established the Old Spanish Trail through Utah to connect New Mexico with California. The route crossed the Colorado River near present-day Moab and was used 1829–1848, when the United States acquired the western territories. Fur trappers also traveled the canyons in search of beaver and other animals during the early 1800s; inscriptions carved into the sandstone record their passage.

Major John Wesley Powell led the first scientific expedition by boat through the Green and lower Colorado River Canyons in 1869, then repeated most of the journey in 1871–1872. Cowboys brought in cattle during the 1870s. Some of their camps, corrals, and inscriptions still survive, although grazing no longer takes place in the park. Uranium prospectors swarmed through the area with Geiger counters during the 1950s, staking thousands of claims and opening some mines. Most of the jeep roads in use today date from that time.

can be seen below. Small Willow Flat Campground is on the way to the overlook; it's open all year (no water, $10 camping fee).

Continue to the end of the road, 5.3 miles northwest of the junction, for a look at **Upheaval Dome.** This geologic oddity is a fantastically deformed pile of rock sprawled across a crater about three miles wide and 1,200 feet deep. For many years, Upheaval Dome has kept geologists busy trying to figure out its origin. They once assumed that salt of the Paradox Formation pushed the rock layers upward to form the dome. Now, however, strong evidence suggests that a meteorite impact created the structure. The surrounding ring depression (caused by collapse) and the convergence of rock layers upward toward the center correspond precisely to known impact structures. Shatter cones and microscopic analysis also indicate an impact origin. When the meteorite struck, some time in the last 150 million years, it formed a crater up to five miles across. Erosion removed some of the overlying rock—perhaps as much as a vertical mile. The underlying salt may have played a role in uplifting the central section.

The easy **Crater View Trail** leads to overlooks on the rim of Upheaval Dome; the first viewpoint is a half-mile round-trip, the second is one mile round-trip. There's also a small **picnic area** here.

WHITE RIM ROAD

This driving adventure follows the White Rim below the sheer cliffs of Island in the Sky. A close look at the light-colored surface reveals ripple marks and crossbeds laid down near an ancient coastline. The plateau's east side is about 800 feet above the Colorado River. On the west side, the plateau meets the bank of the Green River.

Travel along the winding road presents a constantly changing panorama of rock, canyons, river, and sky. Keep an eye out for desert bighorn sheep. You'll see all three levels of Island in the Sky District, from the high plateaus to the White Rim to the rivers.

Only four-wheel-drive vehicles with high clearance can make the trip. With the proper vehicle, driving is mostly easy but slow and winding; a few steep or rough sections have to be negotiated. The 100-mile trip takes two or three days. Allow an extra day to travel all the road spurs.

FOUR-WHEELING IN CANYONLANDS

© W. C. MCRAE

The 4WD White Rim Road snakes along the base of the Island in the Sky.

For people who think that, just as a dog needs to run free every once in a while, sport-utility vehicles need to occasionally escape the home-to-work-to-store-to-home loop, Canyonlands is a tonic.

Each of the park's three main districts has a focal point for four-wheel-drive travel. In the Island in the Sky, it's the 100-mile-long White Rim Trail. Four-wheelers in the Needles head to Elephant Rock for the challenging climb to a network of roads. The Maze's Flint Trail traverses clay slopes that are extremely slippery when wet. Though all of the park's four-wheel-drive roads are rugged, those in the Maze are especially challenging, and this area is by far the most remote.

Drivers should note that ATVs are not permitted in national parks. All vehicles must be street-legal. The most commonly used vehicles are jeeps. Four-wheel drivers should be prepared to make basic road or vehicle repairs and should carry the following items:

- At least one full-size spare tire

- Extra gas

- Extra water

- Shovel

- High-lift jack

- Chains for all four tires (especially Oct.-Apr.)

Also note that towing from any backcountry area of Canyonlands is very expensive: It's not uncommon for bills to top $1,000.

Permits are required for overnight trips; camping is in designated sites.

Mountain bikers find this a great trip, too; most cyclists arrange an accompanying vehicle to carry water and camping gear. Primitive campgrounds along the way provide convenient stopping places. Both cyclists and four-by-four drivers must obtain reservations and a backcountry permit ($30) for the White Rim campsites from the Island in the Sky visitors center. Find application forms on the Canyonlands website; return the completed application at least two weeks in advance of your planned trip. Questions can be fielded via telephone (435/259-4351, 8 A.M.–12:30 P.M. Mon.–Fri.), but no telephone reservations are accepted. Demand exceeds supply during the popular spring and autumn seasons, when you should make reservations as far in advance as possible. No services or developed water sources exist anywhere on the drive, so be sure to have plenty of fuel and water with some to spare. Access points are Shafer Trail Road (from near Island in the Sky) and Potash Road (Hwy. 279 from Moab) on the east and Mineral Bottom Road on the west. White Rim Sandstone forms the distinctive plateau crossed on the drive.

HIKING
Neck Springs Trail

• Distance: 5-mile loop

• Duration: 3 hours

• Elevation change: 500 feet

• Effort: moderate

• Trailhead: Shafer Canyon Overlook

The trail begins near the Shafer Canyon Overlook and loops down Taylor Canyon to Neck and Cabin Springs, formerly used by ranchers (look for the remains of the old cowboy cabin near Cabin Springs), then climbs back to Island in the Sky Road at a second trailhead half a mile south of the start. A brochure should be available at the trailhead. Water at the springs supports maidenhair fern and other plants. Also watch for birds and wildlife attracted to this spot. Bring water with you as the springs are not potable.

Lathrop Trail

• Distance: 9 miles one-way

• Duration: full day or overnight

• Elevation change: 2,100 feet

• Effort: strenuous

• Trailhead: on the left 1.3 miles past the neck

This is the only marked hiking route going all the way from Island in the Sky to the Colorado River. The first 2.5 miles cross Gray's Pasture to the rim, which affords fantastic vistas over the Colorado River. From here, the trail descends steeply, dropping 1,600 feet over the next 2.5 miles to White Rim Road. Part of this section follows an old mining road past several abandoned mines, all relics of the uranium boom. *Don't enter the shafts because they're in danger of collapse and may contain poisonous gases.* From the mining area, the route descends through a wash to White Rim Road, follows the road a short distance south, then goes down Lathrop Canyon Road to the Colorado River, another four miles and 500 vertical feet. The trail has little shade and can be very hot. Auto traffic may be encountered along the White Rim Road portion of the trail.

◖ Mesa Arch Trail

• Distance: 0.25 mile one-way

• Duration: 30 minutes

• Elevation change: 80 feet

• Effort: easy

• Trailhead: on the left 5.5 miles from the neck

This easy trail leads to a spectacular arch on the rim of the mesa. On the way, the road crosses the grasslands and scattered juniper trees of Gray's Pasture. A trail brochure available at the start describes the ecology of the mesa. The sandstone arch frames views of rock formations below and the La Sal Mountains in the distance. Photographers come here to catch the sun rising through the arch.

Murphy Point

- Distance: 9-mile loop
- Duration: 5–7 hours
- Elevation change: 1,100 feet
- Effort: strenuous
- Trailhead: Murphy Point
- Directions: From the Upheaval Dome junction on the main park road head three miles south. Turn right onto a rough dirt road and follow it 1.7 miles to Murphy Point.

Hikers can take Murphy Trail, which starts as a jaunt across the mesa, then drops steeply from the rim down to White Rim Road. This strenuous route forks partway down; one branch follows Murphy Hogback (a ridge) to Murphy Campground on the four-wheel-drive road, and the other follows a wash to the road one mile south of the campground.

White Rim Overlook Trail

- Distance: 0.75 mile one-way
- Duration: 1 hour
- Elevation change: 25 feet
- Effort: easy
- Trailhead: Grand View Picnic Area

Hike east along a peninsula to an overlook of Monument Basin and beyond. There are also good views of White Rim Road and potholes.

Gooseberry Trail

- Distance: 2.5 miles one-way
- Duration: 5 hours
- Elevation change: 1,400 feet
- Effort: strenuous
- Trailhead: Grand View Picnic Area

Gooseberry Trail drops off the mesa and makes an extremely steep descent to White Rim Road just north of Gooseberry Campground. The La Sal Mountains are visible from the trail.

© W. C. MCRAE

hikers on Grand View Trail, at the southernmost tip of Island in the Sky

(Grand View Trail

- Distance: 1 mile one-way
- Duration: 2 hours
- Elevation change: 50 feet
- Effort: easy
- Trailhead: Grand View Point Overlook

At the overlook, Grand View Trail continues past the end of the road for other vistas from the point, which is the southernmost tip of Island in the Sky. This short hike across the slickrock really gives a feel for the entire Canyonlands National Park. From the mesa-top trail you'll see the gorges of the Colorado and Green Rivers come together, and across the chasm lies the Needles District. Look down to spot vehicles traveling along the White Rim Trail at the base of the mesa.

Aztec Butte Trail

- Distance: 1 mile one-way
- Duration: 1.5 hours
- Elevation change: 200 feet
- Effort: moderate
- Trailhead: Aztec Butte parking area, one mile northwest of road junction on Upheaval Dome Road

It's a bit of a haul up the slickrock to the top of this sandstone butte, but once you get there you'll be rewarded with a good view of the Island and Taylor Canyon. Atop the butte a loop trail passes several Anasazi granaries. Aztec Butte is one of the few areas in Island in the Sky with Native American ruins; shortage of water in this area prevented permanent settlement.

Whale Rock Trail

- Distance: 0.5 mile one-way
- Duration: 1 hour
- Elevation change: 100 feet

- Effort: easy–moderate
- Trailhead: Upheaval Dome Road, on the right 4.4 miles northwest of the road junction

A relatively easy trail climbs Whale Rock, a sandstone hump near the outer rim of Upheaval Dome. In a couple of places you'll have to do some scrambling up the slickrock, which is made easier and a bit less scary thanks to handrails. From the top of the rock, there are good views of the dome.

(Upheaval Dome Viewpoint Trail

- Distance: 2 miles one-way
- Duration: 1.5 hours
- Elevation change: 50 feet
- Effort: easy
- Trailhead: Upheaval Dome parking area

The trail leads to Upheaval Dome overviews; it's one mile to the first overlook and two miles to the second. The shorter trail leads to the rim with a view about 1,000 feet down into the jumble of rocks in the craterlike center of Upheaval Dome. The longer trail descends the slickrock and offers even better views. Energetic hikers can explore this formation in depth by circling it on the Syncline Loop Trail or from White Rim Road below.

Syncline Loop Trail

- Distance: 8-mile loop
- Duration: 5–7 hours
- Elevation change: 1,200 feet
- Effort: strenuous
- Trailhead: Upheaval Dome parking area

Syncline Loop Trail makes a circuit completely around Upheaval Dome. The trail crosses Upheaval Dome Canyon about halfway around from the overlook; walk east 1.5 miles up the canyon to enter the crater itself. This is the only nontechnical route into the center of the dome.

A hike around Upheaval Dome with a side trip to the crater totals 11 miles, and is best done as an overnight trip. Carry plenty of water for the entire trip; this dry country can be very hot in summer. The Green River is the only reliable source of water. An alternate approach is to start near Upheaval Campsite on White Rim Road; hike four miles southeast on through Upheaval Canyon to a junction with the Syncline Loop Trail, then another 1.5 miles into the crater. The elevation gain is about 600 feet.

Alcove Spring Trail

- Distance: 10 miles one-way

- Duration: overnight

- Elevation change: 1,500 feet

- Effort: strenuous

- Trailhead: 1.5 miles southeast of the Upheaval Dome parking area

Another hiking possibility in the area, the Alcove Spring Trail connects with the White Rim Road in Taylor Canyon. Five miles of the 10-mile distance is on the steep trail down through Trail Canyon and five miles is on a jeep road

in Taylor Canyon. (One downside of this trail is the four-wheel-drive traffic, which can be pretty heavy during the spring and fall.) From the Taylor Canyon end of the trail, it's not far to the Upheaval Trail, which heads southeast to its junction with the Syncline Trail, which in turn leads to the Upheaval Dome parking area. Allow at least one overnight if you plan to hike this full loop. Day hikers should plan to turn around after the first five-mile section; this is still a very full day of hiking. Carry plenty of water—the trail is hot and dry.

CAMPGROUNDS

There is only one developed campground in the Island in the Sky District. **Willow Flat Campground** on Murphy Point Road has only 12 sites. The $10-per-night sites are available on a first-come, first-served basis; sites tend to fill up all seasons other than winter. No water or services are available. Rangers present campfire programs here spring through autumn.

Camping is available outside the park at Dead Horse Point State Park (which is also very popular, so don't plan on arriving late to get a spot here) and at primitive BLM campsites along Highway 313.

Needles District

The Needles District showcases some of the finest rock sculptures in Canyonlands National Park. Spires, arches, and monoliths appear in almost any direction you look. Prehistoric ruins and rock art exist in greater variety and quantity here than elsewhere in the park. Perennial springs and streams bring greenery to the desert.

While a scenic paved road leads to the district, this area of the park has only about a dozen miles of paved roads. Needles District doesn't have a lot to offer travelers who are unwilling to get out of their vehicles and hike; however, even a short hike opens up the landscape and leads to remarkable vistas and prehistoric sites.

To reach the Needles District, go 40 miles south from Moab (or 14 miles north of Monticello) on U.S. 191, turn west on Highway 211, and continue 38 miles.

VISITORS CENTER

Stop here (435/259-4711, 8 a.m.–4:30 p.m. daily) for information on hiking, back roads, and other aspects of travel in the Needles, as well as backcountry permits (required for all overnight stays in the backcountry), maps, brochures, and books. Take a moment to look at the little computer-animated slide show on the region's geology—its graphics make it all come clear! When the office isn't open, you'll find information posted outside on the bulletin board.

◖ BLM NEWSPAPER ROCK HISTORICAL MONUMENT

Although not in the park itself, Newspaper Rock lies just 150 feet off Highway 211 on the way to the Needles District. At Newspaper Rock, a profusion of petroglyphs depict human figures, animals, birds, and abstract designs. These represent 2,000 years of human history during which archaic tribes and Anasazi, Fremont, Paiute, Navajo, and Anglo travelers have passed through Indian Creek Canyon. The patterns on the smooth sandstone rock face stand out clearly, thanks to a coating of dark desert varnish. A short nature trail introduces you to the area's desert and riparian vegetation. Picnic areas and a primitive campground (no water, no fee) lie along Indian Creek across the highway.

The cracks in the rock walls around Indian Creek offer **world-class rock climbing.** (Climbers should track down a copy of *Indian Creek: A Climbing Guide,* by David Bloom, for details and lots of pictures.) From U.S. 191 between Moab and Monticello, turn west on Highway 211 and travel 12 miles to Newspaper Rock.

NEEDLES OUTPOST

A general store just outside the park boundary offers a campground (435/979-4007, www.canyonlandsneedlesoutpost.com, $15 tent or RV without hookups, plus $3 for a shower, mid-Mar.–late Oct.), groceries, ice, gas, propane, a café, showers ($7 for noncampers), and pretty much any camping supply that you may have left at home. The turnoff from Highway 211 is one mile before the Needles visitors center.

BIG SPRING CANYON SCENIC DRIVE

The main paved park road continues 6.5 miles past the visitors center to Big Spring Canyon Overlook. On the way, you can stop at several nature trails or turn off on four-wheel-drive roads. The overlook takes in a view of slickrock-edged canyons dropping away toward the Colorado River.

© PAUL LEVY

Newspaper Rock preserves some of the richest, most fanciful prehistoric rock art in Utah.

HIKING

The Needles District includes about 60 miles of backcountry trails. Many interconnect to provide all sorts of day-hike and overnight opportunities. Cairns mark the trails and signs point the way at junctions. You can normally find water in upper Elephant Canyon and canyons to the east in spring and early summer, although whatever what remains is often stagnant by midsummer. Always ask the rangers about sources of water, and don't depend on its availability. Treat water from all sources, including springs, before drinking. Chesler Park and other areas west of Elephant Canyon are very dry; you'll need to bring all water. Mosquitoes, gnats, and deer flies can be pesky from late spring to midsummer, especially in the wetter places, so be sure to bring insect repellent. To plan your trip, obtain the small hiking map available from the visitors center, Trails Illustrated's Needles District map, or USGS topographic maps. Overnight backcountry hiking requires a $15-per-party permit.

Roadside Ruin Trail

- Distance: 0.3-mile loop

- Duration: 20 minutes

- Elevation change: 20 feet

- Effort: easy

- Trailhead: on the left 0.4 mile past the visitors center

This is one of two easy hikes near the visitors center. It passes near a well-preserved granary left by Anasazi. A trail guide available at the start tells about the Anasazi and the local plants.

◖ Cave Spring Trail

- Distance: 0.6-mile loop

- Duration: 45 minutes

- Elevation change: 50 feet

- Effort: easy

- Trailhead: Cave Spring

© PAUL LEVY

tromping through the desert in the Needles District

• Directions: Turn left 0.7 mile past the visitors center and follow signs about one mile to the trailhead.

Don't miss the Cave Spring Trail, which introduces the geology and ecology of the park and goes to an old cowboy line camp. Pick up the brochure at the beginning. The loop goes clockwise, crossing some slickrock; two ladders assist hikers on the steep sections. Native Americans first used these rock overhangs for shelter (faint pictographs still decorate the rock walls). Much later, cowboys used these open caves as a line camp from the late 1800s until the park was established in 1964. The park service has re-created the line camp, just 50 yards in from the trailhead, with period furnishings and equipment. If you're not up for the full hike, or would rather not climb ladders, the cowboy camp and the pictographs are just a five-minute walk from the trailhead.

This trail is a good introduction to hiking on slickrock and using rock cairns to find your way. Signs identify plants along the way.

Pothole Point Nature Trail

• Distance: 0.6-mile loop

• Duration: 40 minutes

• Elevation change: 20 feet

• Effort: easy

• Trailhead: parking area on the left of Big Spring Canyon Overlook Scenic Drive five miles past the visitors center

Highlights of this hike across the slickrock are the many potholes dissolved in the Cedar Mesa sandstone. A brochure illustrates the fairy shrimp, tadpole shrimp, horsehair worm, snail, and other creatures that spring to life when rains fill the potholes. Desert varnish rims the potholes; it forms when water evaporates, leaving mineral residues on the surface of the rocks. In addition to the potholes, you'll enjoy fine views of distant buttes from the trail.

Slickrock Trail

• Distance: 2.4-mile loop

• Duration: 2 hours

• Elevation change: 150 feet

• Effort: easy–moderate

• Trailhead: parking area on the right side of Big Spring Canyon Overlook Scenic Drive 6.2 miles past the visitors center

The Slickrock Trail leads north to a nice overlook of the confluence of Big Spring and Little Spring Canyons. The trailhead is almost at the end of the paved road, where **Big Spring Canyon Overlook,** 6.5 miles past the visitors center, marks the end of the scenic drive but not the scenery.

Confluence Overlook Trail

• Distance: 5.5 miles one-way

• Duration: 5 hours

• Elevation change: 1,250 feet

• Effort: moderate–strenuous

• Trailhead: Big Spring Canyon Overlook

The Confluence Overlook Trail begins at the end of the paved road and winds west to an overlook of the Green and Colorado Rivers 1,000 feet below. The trail crosses Big Spring and Elephant Canyons and follows a jeep road for a short distance. Higher points have good views of the Needles to the south. You might see rafts in the water or bighorn sheep on the cliffs. Except for a few short steep sections, this trail is level and fairly easy; it's the 10-mile round-trip to the confluence and the hot sun that make it challenging. A very early start is recommended in summer because there's little shade. Carry water even if you don't plan to go all the way. This enchanting country has lured many a hiker beyond his or her original goal!

Peekaboo Trail

• Distance: 5 miles one-way

- Duration: 5–6 hours
- Elevation change: 550 feet
- Effort: strenuous
- Trailhead: Squaw Flat Trailhead
- Directions: A road to Squaw Flat Campground and Elephant Hill turns left 2.7 miles past the ranger station. The Squaw Flat Trailhead sits a short distance south of the campground and is reached by a separate signed road. You can also begin from a trailhead in the campground itself.

Peekaboo Trail winds southeast over rugged up-and-down terrain, including some steep sections of slickrock (best avoided when wet, icy, or covered with snow). There's little shade, so carry water. The trail follows Squaw Canyon, climbs over a pass to Lost Canyon, then crosses more slickrock before descending to Peekaboo Campground on Salt Creek Road. Look for Anasazi ruins on the way and rock art at the campground. A rockslide took out Peekaboo Spring, which is shown on some maps. Options on this trail include a turnoff south through Squaw or Lost Canyon to make a loop of 8.75 miles or more.

Squaw Canyon Trail

- Distance: 3.75 miles one-way
- Duration: 4 hours
- Elevation change: 700 feet
- Effort: moderate
- Trailhead: parking area on the left of the main road five miles past the visitors center
- Directions: A road to Squaw Flat Campground and Elephant Hill turns left 2.7 miles past the ranger station. The Squaw Flat Trailhead sits a short distance south of the campground and is reached by a separate signed road. You can also begin from a trailhead in the campground itself.

Squaw Canyon Trail follows the canyon south. Intermittent water can often be found until late spring. You can take a connecting trail (Peeka-

boo, Lost Canyon, and Big Spring Canyon) or cross a slickrock pass to Elephant Canyon.

Lost Canyon Trail

- Distance: 3.25 miles one-way
- Duration: 4–5 hours
- Elevation change: 360 feet
- Effort: moderate–strenuous
- Trailhead: parking area on the left of the main road five miles past the visitors center
- Directions: A road to Squaw Flat Campground and Elephant Hill turns left 2.7 miles past the ranger station. The Squaw Flat Trailhead sits a short distance south of the campground and is reached by a separate signed road. You can also begin from a trailhead in the campground itself.

Lost Canyon Trail is reached via Peekaboo or Squaw Canyon Trail and makes a loop with them. Lost Canyon is surprisingly lush, and you may be forced to wade through water. Most of the way is in the wash bottom, except for a section of slickrock to Squaw Canyon.

Big Spring Canyon Trail

- Distance: 3.75 miles one-way
- Duration: 4 hours
- Elevation change: 370 feet
- Effort: moderate–strenuous
- Trailhead: parking area on the left of the main road five miles past the visitors center
- Directions: A road to Squaw Flat Campground and Elephant Hill turns left 2.7 miles past the ranger station. The Squaw Flat Trailhead sits a short distance south of the campground and is reached by a separate signed road. You can also begin from a trailhead in the campground itself.

Big Spring Canyon Trail crosses an outcrop of slickrock from the trailhead, then follows the canyon bottom to the head of the canyon. It's a lovely springtime hike with lots of flowers,

POTHOLE ECOSYSTEMS

At Canyonlands it's easy to be in awe of the deep canyons and big desert rivers. But the little details of Canyonlands geology and ecology are pretty wonderful, too. Consider the potholes: shallow depressions dusted with wind-blown dirt. These holes, which range from less than an inch to several feet deep, fill after rainstorms and bring entire little ecosystems to life.

Pothole dwellers must be able to survive long periods of dryness, then pack as much living as possible into the short wet periods. Some creatures, like the tadpole shrimp, live only for a couple of weeks. Others, like the spadefoot toad, hatch from drought-resistant eggs when water is present, quickly pass through the critical tadpole stage, then move onto dry land, returning to mate and lay eggs in potholes.

Though pothole dwellers are tough enough to survive in a dormant form during the long dry spells, most are very sensitive to sudden water-chemistry changes, temperature changes, sediment input, being stepped on, and being splashed out onto dry land. Humans should never use pothole water for swimming, bathing, or drinking, as this can change the salinity or pH of a pool drastically. Organisms are unable to adapt to these human-generated changes, which occur suddenly, unlike slow, natural changes. While the desert pothole ecosystems may seem unimportant, they act as an indicator of the health of the larger ecosystems in which they occur.

including the fragrant cliffrose. Outside of summer, you can usually find intermittent water along the way. At canyon's end, a steep slickrock climb leads to Squaw Canyon Trail and back to the trailhead for a 7.5-mile loop. Another possibility is to turn southwest to the head of Squaw Canyon, then hike over a saddle to Elephant Canyon for a 10.5-mile loop.

◖ Chesler Park

- Distance: 3 miles one-way

- Duration: 3–4 hours

- Elevation change: 920 feet

- Effort: moderate

- Trailhead: Elephant Hill parking area or Squaw Flat Trailhead (increases the distance slightly)

- Directions: Drive west three miles past the Squaw Flat campground turnoff on passable dirt roads to the Elephant Hill Picnic Area and Trailhead at the base of Elephant Hill.

The Elephant Hill parking area doesn't always inspire confidence in hikers: Sounds of racing engines and burning rubber can often be heard from above as vehicles attempt the difficult four-wheel-drive road that begins just past the picnic area. However, the noise quickly fades as you hit the trail. Chesler Park is a favorite hiking destination. A lovely desert meadow contrasts with the red and white spires that gave the Needles District its name. An old cowboy line camp is on the west side of the rock island in the center of the park. The trail winds through sand and slickrock before ascending a small pass through the Needles to Chesler Park. Once inside, you can take the Chesler Park Loop Trail (five miles) completely around the park. The loop includes the unusual half-mile Joint Trail, which follows the bottom of a very narrow crack. Camping in Chesler Park is restricted to certain areas; check with a ranger.

Druid Arch

- Distance: 5.5 miles one-way

- Duration: 5–7 hours

- Elevation change: 1,000 feet

- Effort: strenuous

- Trailhead: Elephant Hill parking area or Squaw Flat Trailhead (increases the round-trip distance by two miles)

- Directions: Drive west three miles past the

Squaw Flat campground turnoff on passable dirt roads to the Elephant Hill Picnic Area and Trailhead at the base of Elephant Hill.

Druid Arch reminds many people of the massive slabs at Stonehenge, which are popularly associated with the druids, in southern England. Follow the Chesler Park Trail two miles to Elephant Canyon, turn up the canyon 3.5 miles, then make a steep quarter-mile climb, which includes a ladder and some scrambling, to the arch. Upper Elephant Canyon has seasonal water but is closed to camping.

Lower Red Lake Canyon Trail

• Distance: 9.5 miles one-way

• Duration: 2 days

• Elevation change: 1,000 feet

• Effort: strenuous

• Trailhead: Elephant Hill parking area or Squaw Flat Trailhead (increases the distance slightly)

• Directions: Drive west three miles past the Squaw Flat campground turnoff on passable dirt roads to the Elephant Hill Picnic Area and Trailhead at the base of Elephant Hill.

Lower Red Lake Canyon Trail provides access to the Colorado River's Cataract Canyon. This long, strenuous trip is best suited for experienced hikers and completed in two days. Distance from the Elephant Hill Trailhead is 19 miles round-trip; you'll be walking on four-wheel-drive roads and trails. If you can drive Elephant Hill 4WD Road to the trail junction in Cyclone Canyon, the hike is only eight miles round-trip. The most difficult trail section is a steep talus slope that drops 700 feet in half a mile into the lower canyon. The canyon has little shade and lacks any water source above the river. Summer heat can make the trip grueling; temperatures tend to be 5–10°F hotter than on other Needles trails. The river level drops between midsummer and autumn, allowing hikers to go along the shore both downstream to see the rapids and upstream to the confluence. Undertows and strong currents make the river dangerous to cross.

Upper Salt Creek Trail

• Distance: 12 miles one-way

• Duration: overnight

• Elevation change: 1,650 feet

• Effort: strenuous

• Trailhead: end of Salt Creek Road

• Directions: Drive to the end of the rugged 13.5-mile four-wheel-drive road up Salt Creek to start this hike.

Several impressive arches and many inviting side canyons attract adventurous hikers to the extreme southeast corner of the Needles District. The trail goes south 12 miles up-canyon to Cottonwood Canyon/Beef Basin Road near Cathedral Butte, just outside the park boundary. The trail is nearly level except for a steep climb at the end. Water can usually be found. Some wading and bushwhacking may be necessary. The famous "All-American Man" pictograph, shown on some topographic maps (or ask a ranger), is in a cave a short way off to the east at about the midpoint of the trail; follow your map and unsigned paths to the cave, but don't climb in—it's dangerous to both you and the ruins and pictograph inside. Many more archaeological sites are near the trail, but they're all fragile and great care should be taken when visiting them.

MOUNTAIN BIKING AND FOUR-WHEEL-DRIVE EXPLORATION

Visitors with bicycles or four-wheel-drive vehicles can explore the many backcountry roads that lead to the outback. More than 50 miles of challenging roads link primitive campsites, remote trailheads, and sites with ancient cultural remnants. Some roads in the Needles District are rugged and require previous experience in handling four-wheel-drive vehicles on steep inclines and in deep sand. Be aware that towing charges from this area commonly run over $1,000.

The best route for mountain bikers is the seven-mile-long Colorado Overlook Road, which leaves from near the visitors center. Though very steep for the first stretch, Elephant Hill Road is another good bet, with just a few sandy parts. Start here and do a combination bike/hike to the Confluence Overlook. (It's about eight miles from the Elephant Hill parking area to the confluence; the final half mile is on a trail, so you'll have to lock the bike up and walk this last bit.) Horse Canyon, Peekaboo, and Lavender Canyon are too sandy for pleasant biking.

All motor vehicles and bicycles must remain on designated roads. Overnight backcountry trips with bicycles or motor vehicles require a $30-per-party permit.

Salt Creek Canyon 4WD Road

This rugged route begins near Cave Spring Trail, crosses sage flats for the next 2.5 miles, then heads deep into a spectacular canyon. Round-trip distance, including a side trip to 150-foot-high Angel Arch, is 26 miles. Agile hikers can follow a steep slickrock route into the window of Angel Arch. You can also explore side canyons of Salt Creek or take the Upper Salt Creek Trail (the "All-American Man" pictograph makes a good day-hike destination of 12 miles round-trip).

Horse Canyon 4WD Road turns off to the left shortly before the mouth of Salt Canyon. Round-trip distance, including a side trip to Tower Ruin, is about 13 miles; other attractions include Paul Bunyan's Potty, Castle Arch, Fortress Arch, and side-canyon hiking. Salt and Horse Canyons can easily be driven in four-wheel-drive vehicles. Salt Canyon is usually closed because of quicksand after flash floods in summer and shelf ice in winter.

Davis and Lavender Canyons

Both canyons are accessed through Davis Canyon Road off Highway 211 and contain great scenery, arches, and Native American sites, and both are easily visited with high-clearance vehicles. Davis is about 20 miles round-trip while Lavender is about 26 miles round-trip. Try to allow plenty of time in either canyon because there is much to see and many inviting side canyons to hike. You can camp on BLM land just outside the park boundaries, but not in the park itself.

Colorado Overlook 4WD Road

This popular route begins beside the visitors center and follows Salt Creek to Lower Jump Overlook. Then it bounces across slickrock to a view of the Colorado River (upstream from the confluence). Driving for the most part is easy to moderate, although it's very rough for the last 1.5 miles. Round-trip distance is 14 miles.

Elephant Hill 4WD Loop Road

This rugged backcountry road begins three miles past the Squaw Flat Campground turn-off. Only experienced drivers with stout vehicles should attempt the extremely rough and steep climb up Elephant Hill (coming up the back side of Elephant Hill is even worse!). The loop is about 10 miles round-trip. Connecting roads go to the Confluence Overlook Trailhead (the viewpoint is one mile round-trip on foot), the Joint Trailhead (Chesler Park is two miles round-trip on foot), and several canyons. Some road sections on the loop are one-way. The parallel canyons in this area are grabens caused by faulting where a layer of salt has shifted deep underground. In addition to Elephant Hill, a few other difficult spots must be negotiated.

This area can also be reached by a long route south of the park using Cottonwood Canyon/Beef Basin Road from Highway 211, about 60 miles one-way. You'll enjoy spectacular vistas from the Abajo Highlands. Two *very* steep descents from Pappys Pasture into Bobbys Hole effectively make this section one-way; travel from Elephant Hill up Bobbys Hole is possible but much more difficult than going the other way and may require hours of road-building. The Bobbys Hole route may be impassable at times; ask about conditions at the BLM office in Monticello or at the Needles visitors center.

CAMPGROUNDS

The **Squaw Flat Campground,** about six miles from the visitors center, has 26 sites (many snuggled under the slickrock) and charges a $15 fee. It's open year-round and has water. Rangers present evening programs at the campfire circle on Loop A from spring through autumn.

If you can't find a space in this campground, the private campground at Needles Outpost, just outside the park entrance, is fairly nice. Many people also camp at Newspaper Rock on BLM land.

The Maze District

Only adventurous and experienced travelers will want to visit this rugged land west of the Green and Colorado Rivers. Vehicle access wasn't even possible until 1957, when mineral-exploration roads first entered what later became Canyonlands National Park. Today, you'll need a high-clearance four-wheel-drive vehicle, a horse, or your own two feet to get around. The National Park Service plans to keep this district in its remote and primitive condition. An airplane flight, which is recommended if you can't come overland, provides the only easy way to see the scenic features here.

The names of erosional forms describe the landscape—Orange Cliffs, Golden Stairs, the Fins, Land of Standing Rocks, Lizard Rock, the Doll House, Chocolate Drops, the Maze, and Jasper Canyon. The many-fingered canyons of the Maze gave the district its name. Although it is not a true maze, these canyons give that impression. It is extremely important you have a good map before entering this part of Canyonlands. Trails Illustrated makes a good one, called *Canyonlands National Park Maze District, NE Glen Canyon NRA.*

Getting to the Maze District

Dirt roads to the Hans Flat Ranger Station and Maze District branch off from Highway 24 (across from the Goblin Valley State Park turnoff) and Highway 95 (take the usually unmarked Hite/Orange Cliffs Road between the Dirty Devil and Hite bridges at Lake Powell). The easiest way in is the graded 46-mile road from Highway 24; it's fast, although sometimes badly corrugated. The Hite Road (also called Orange Cliffs Road) is longer, bumpier, and, for some drivers, tedious; it's 54 miles from the

turnoff at Highway 95 to the Hans Flat Ranger Station via the Flint Trail. All roads to the Maze District cross Glen Canyon National Recreation Area. From Highway 24, two-wheel-drive vehicles with good clearance can travel to Hans Flat Ranger Station and other areas near, but not actually in, the Maze District.

Planning an Expedition

Maze District explorers need a $15 backcountry permit for overnight backpacking. Note that a backcountry permit in this district is *not* a reservation. You may have to share a site with someone else, especially in the popular spring months. Those using four-by-fours or mountain bikes for overnight expeditions will need a $30 backcountry permit. Also, as in the rest of the park, only designated sites can be used for vehicle camping. You don't need a permit to camp in the adjacent Glen Canyon NRA or on BLM land. *There are no developed sources of water in the Maze District.* Hikers can obtain water from springs in some canyons (check with a ranger to find which are flowing) or from the rivers; purify all water before drinking. The Maze District has nine camping areas (two at Maze Overlook, seven at Land of Standing Rocks), each with a 15-person, three-vehicle limit.

The Trails Illustrated topographic map of the Maze District describes and shows the few roads and trails here; some routes and springs are marked on it, too. Agile hikers experienced in desert and canyon travel may want to take off on cross-country routes, which are either unmarked or lightly cairned. Extra care must be taken for preparation and travel in both Glen Canyon NRA and the Maze. Always ask rangers beforehand for current conditions. Be sure to leave an itinerary with someone reliable who can contact the rangers if you're overdue. Unless the rangers know where to look for you in case of breakdown or accident, a rescue could take weeks.

🄲 LAND OF STANDING ROCKS

Here, in the heart of the Maze District, strangely shaped rock spires stand guard over myriad canyons. Six camping areas offer scenic places to stay (permit needed). Hikers have a choice of many ridge and canyon routes from the four-wheel-drive road, a trail to a confluence overlook, and a trail that descends to the Colorado River near Cataract Canyon.

Getting to the Land of Standing Rocks takes some careful driving, especially on a three-mile stretch above Teapot Canyon. The many washes and small canyon crossings here make for slow going. Short-wheelbase vehicles have the easiest time, of course. The turnoff for Land of Standing Rocks Road is 6.6 miles from the junction at the bottom of the Flint Trail via a wash shortcut (add about three miles if driving via the four-way intersection). The lower end of the Golden Stairs foot trail is 7.8 miles in; the western end of the Ernies Country route trailhead is 8.6 miles in; the Wall is 12.7 miles in; Chimney Rock is 15.7 miles in; and the Doll House is 19 miles in at the end of the road. If you drive from the south on Hite/ Orange Cliffs Road, stop at the self-registration stand at the four-way intersection, about 31 miles in from Highway 95; you can write your own permit for overnights in the park here.

Tall, rounded rock spires near the end of the road reminded early visitors of dolls—hence the name Doll House. The Doll House is a great place to explore, or you can head out on nearby routes and trails.

NORTH POINT

Hans Flat Ranger Station and this peninsula, which reaches out to the east and north, lie at an elevation of about 6,400 feet. Panoramas from North Point take in the vastness of Canyonlands, including all three districts. From

Millard Canyon Overlook, just 0.9 mile past the ranger station, you can see arches, Cleopatra's Chair, and features as distant as the La Sal Mountains and Book Cliffs. For the best views, drive out to Panorama Point, about 10.5 miles one-way from the ranger station. A spur road goes left two miles to Cleopatra's Chair, a massive sandstone monolith and area landmark.

HIKING
North Canyon Trail

· Distance: 7 miles one-way

· Duration: overnight

· Elevation change: 1,000 feet

· Effort: strenuous

· Trailhead: on North Point Road

· Directions: From Hans Flat Ranger Station drive 2.5 miles east, turn left onto North Point Road, and continue about 1 mile to the trailhead.

This is just about the only trailhead in the Maze District that two-wheel-drive vehicles can usually reach. Hikers can follow the trail down through the Orange Cliffs. At the eastern end of the trail, ambitious hikers can follow four-wheel-drive roads an additional six miles to the Maze Overlook Trail, then one more mile into a canyon of the Maze. Because North Point belongs to the Glen Canyon NRA, you can camp here without a permit.

Maze Overlook Trail

· Distance: 3 miles one-way (to Harvest Scene)

· Duration: 3–4 hours

· Elevation change: 550 feet

· Effort: strenuous

· Trailhead: at end of the road in the Maze District

Here at the edge of the sinuous canyons of the Maze, the Maze Overlook Trail drops one mile into the South Fork of Horse Canyon;

bring a rope to help lower backpacks through one difficult section. Once in the canyon, you can walk around to the Harvest Scene, a group of prehistoric pictographs, or do a variety of day hikes or backpacking trips. These canyons have water in some places; check with the ranger when you get your permit. At least four routes connect with the four-wheel-drive road in Land of Standing Rocks (see the Trails Illustrated map). Hikers can also climb Petes Mesa from the canyons or head downstream to explore Horse Canyon (a dry fall blocks access to the Green River, however). You can stay at primitive camping areas (backcountry permit needed) and enjoy the views.

The Golden Stairs

- Distance: 2 miles one-way

- Duration: 3 hours

- Elevation change: 800 feet

- Effort: moderate

- Trailhead: bottom of Flint Trail, at Golden Stairs camping area

- Directions: Drive the challenging Flint Trail (see *Four-Wheel-Drive Exploration*), a four-wheel-drive route, to its bottom. The top of the Golden Stairs is two miles east of the road junction at the bottom of the Flint Trail.

Hikers can descend this steep foot trail to the Land of Standing Rocks Road in a fraction of the time it takes for drivers to follow roads. The trail offers good views of Ernies Country, the vast southern area of the Maze District, but lacks shade or water. The eponymous stairs are not actual steps carved into the rock, but a series of natural ledges.

Chocolate Drops Trail

- Distance: 4.5 miles one-way

- Duration: 5 hours

- Elevation change: 550 feet

- Effort: strenuous

- Trailhead: Chocolate Drops

- Directions: See the *Land of Standing Rocks* section for driving directions to Land of Standing Rocks Road. The trailhead is just east of the Wall camping area.

The well-named Chocolate Drops can be reached by a trail from the Wall near the beginning of the Land of Standing Rocks. A good day hike makes a loop from Chimney Rock to the Harvest Scene pictographs; take the ridge route (toward Petes Mesa) one direction and the canyon fork northwest of Chimney Rock the other. Follow your topographic map through the canyons and the cairns between the canyons and ridge. Other routes from Chimney Rock lead to lower Jasper Canyon (no river access) or into Shot and Water Canyons and on to the Green River.

Spanish Bottom Trail

- Distance: 1.2 miles one-way

- Duration: 3 hours

- Elevation change: 1,260 feet

- Effort: strenuous

- Trailhead: Doll House, near Camp 1, just before the end of the Land of Standing Rocks Road

This trail drops steeply to Spanish Bottom beside the Colorado River; a thin trail leads downstream into Cataract Canyon and the first of a long series of rapids. **Surprise Valley Overlook Trail** branches right off the Spanish Bottom Trail after about 300 feet and winds south past some dolls to a T junction (turn right for views of Surprise Valley, Cataract Canyon, and beyond); the trail ends at some well-preserved granaries, after 1.5 miles one-way. From the same trailhead, the **Colorado/Green River Overlook Trail** heads north five miles (one-way) from the Doll House to a viewpoint of the confluence. See the area's Trails Illustrated map for routes, trails, and roads.

FOUR-WHEEL-DRIVE EXPLORATION
Flint Trail 4WD Road

This narrow, rough, four-wheel-drive road connects the Hans Flat area with the Maze Overlook, Doll House, and other areas below. The road, driver, and vehicle should all be in good condition before attempting this route. Winter snow and mud close the road from late December into March, as can rainstorms anytime. Check on conditions with a ranger before you go. If you're starting from the top, stop at the signed overlook just before the descent to scout for vehicles headed up (the Flint Trail has very few places to pass). The top of the Flint Trail is 14 miles south of Hans Flat Ranger Station; at the bottom, 2.8 nervous miles later, you can turn left two miles to the Golden Stairs Trailhead or 12.7 miles to the Maze Overlook; keep straight 28 miles to the Doll House or 39 miles to Highway 95.

Horseshoe Canyon Unit

This canyon contains exceptional prehistoric rock art in a separate section of Canyonlands National Park. Ghostly life-size pictographs in the Great Gallery provide an intriguing look into the past. Archaeologists think that the images had religious importance, although the meaning of the figures remains unknown. The Barrier Canyon Style of these drawings has been credited to an archaic culture beginning at least 8,000 years ago and lasting until about A.D. 450. Horseshoe Canyon also contains rock art left by the subsequent Fremont and Anasazi people. The relation between the earlier and later prehistoric groups hasn't been determined.

Call the Hans Flat Ranger Station (435/259-2652) to inquire about ranger-led weekend hikes to the Great Gallery. These are offered as demand justifies on Saturdays and Sundays in spring and early summer. In-shape hikers will have no trouble making the hike on their own, however.

HIKING
C Great Gallery Trail

- Distance: 3.25 miles one-way

- Duration: 4–6 hours

- Elevation change: 800 feet

- Effort: moderate–strenuous

- Trailhead: parking area on canyon's west rim

- Directions: From Highway 24, turn east across from the Goblin Valley State Park turnoff, then continue east 30 miles on a dirt road (keep left at the Hans Flat Ranger Station/Horseshoe Canyon turnoff 25 miles in).

Horseshoe Canyon lies northwest of the Maze District. The easiest and most common way to reach Horseshoe Canyon is from the west and Highway 24. In dry weather, cars with good clearance can reach a trailhead on the canyon's west rim. From the rim and parking area, the trail descends 800 feet in one mile on an old jeep road, which is now closed to vehicles. At the canyon bottom, turn right two miles upstream to the Great Gallery. The sandy canyon floor is mostly level; trees provide shade in some areas.

Look for other rock art along the canyon walls on the way to the Great Gallery. Take care not to touch any of the drawings because they're fragile and irreplaceable. (The oil from your hands will remove the paints.) Horseshoe Canyon also offers pleasant scenery and spring wildflowers. Carry plenty of water. Neither camping nor pets are allowed in the canyon, but you can camp on the rim. Contact the Hans Flat Ranger Station or the Moab office for road and trail conditions.

Horseshoe Canyon can also be reached via primitive roads from the east. A four-wheel-drive road goes north 21 miles from Hans Flat Ranger Station and drops steeply into the canyon from the east side. The descent on this road is so rough that most people prefer to park on the rim and hike the last mile of road. A vehicle barricade prevents driving right up to the rock-art panel, but the 1.5-mile walk is easy. A branch off the jeep road goes to the start of **Deadman's Trail** (1.5 miles one-way), which is less used and more difficult.

The River District

The River District is the name of the administrative unit of the park that oversees conservation and recreation for the Green and Colorado Rivers.

Generally speaking, there are two boating experiences on offer in the park's River District. First are the relatively gentle paddling and rafting experiences on the Colorado and Green Rivers above their confluence. After these rivers meet deep in the park, the resulting Colorado River then tumbles into Cataract Canyon, a white-water destination par excellence with abundant Class III and V rapids.

While rafting and canoeing enthusiasts can plan their own trip to any section of these rivers, by far the vast majority of people sign on with outfitters and let them do the planning and work (a list of recommended outfitters is found in the *Moab* chapter). Do-it-yourselfers must start with the knowledge that permits are required for most trips but are not always easily procured; because these rivers flow through rugged and remote canyons, most trips require multiple days and can be challenging to plan.

No matter how you execute a trip through the Rive District, there are several issues to think about beforehand. There are no designated campsites along the rivers in Canyonlands. During periods of high water, camps can be difficult to find, especially for large groups.

© W. C. MCRAE

Jet-boats and rafts share the Colorado River near the River District.

ENDANGERED FISH OF THE COLORADO RIVER BASIN

Colorado squawfish (Ptychocheilus lucius): Native only to the Colorado and its tributaries, this species is the largest minnow in North America. It has been reported to weigh up to 100 pounds and measure six feet long. Loss of habitat caused by dam construction has greatly curtailed its size and range. Fishers often confuse the smaller, more common roundtail chub (Gila robusta) with the Colorado squawfish; the chub is distinguished by a smaller mouth extending back only to the front of the eye.

Humpback chub (Gila cypha): Scientists first described this fish only in 1946 and know little about its life. This small fish usually weighs less than two pounds and measures less than 13 inches. Today the humpback chub hangs on the verge of extinction; it has retreated to a few small areas of the Colorado River, where the water still runs warm, muddy, and swift. The bonytail chub (Gila robusta elegans) has a similar size and shape, but without a hump; its numbers are also rapidly declining.

Humpback or razorback sucker (Xyrauchen texanus): This large sucker grows to weights of 10–16 pounds and lengths of about three feet. Its numbers have been slowly decreasing, especially above the Grand Canyon. They require warm, fast-flowing water to reproduce. Mating is a bizarre ritual in the spring: When the female has selected a suitable spawning site, two male fish press against the sides of her body. The female begins to shake her body until the eggs and spermatozoa are expelled simultaneously. One female can spawn three times, but she uses a different pair of males each time.

During late summer and fall, sandbars are usually plentiful and make ideal camps. There is no access to potable water along the river, so river runners need to either bring along their own water or be prepared to purify river water.

While it's possible to fish in the Green and Colorado Rivers, these desert rivers don't offer much in the way of fish varieties that most people consider edible. You'll need to bring along all your foodstuffs.

Also, the park requires all river runners to carry out their solid human waste. Specially designed portable toilets that fit into rafts and canoes can be rented from most outfitters in Moab.

RIVER-RUNNING ABOVE THE CONFLUENCE

The Green and Colorado Rivers flow smoothly through their canyons above the confluence of the two rivers. Almost any shallow-draft boat can navigate these waters: canoes, kayaks, rafts, and powerboats are commonly used. Any travel requires advance planning because of the remoteness of the canyons and the scarcity of river access points. No campgrounds, supplies, or other facilities exist past Moab on the Colorado River or the town of Green River on the Green River. All river-runners must follow park regulations, which include carrying life jackets, using a fire pan for fires, and packing out all garbage and solid human waste. The river flow on both the Colorado and the Green Rivers averages a gentle 2–4 miles per hour (7–10 mph at high water). Boaters typically do 20 miles per day in canoes and 15 miles per day in rafts.

The Colorado has one modest rapid called the Slide, which is 1.5 miles above the confluence, where rocks constrict the river to one-third of its normal width; the rapid is roughest during high water levels in May and June. This is the only difficulty on the 64 river miles from Moab. Inexperienced canoeists and rafters may wish to portage around it. The most popular launch points on the Colorado are the Moab Dock (just upstream from the U.S. 191 bridge near town) and the Potash Dock (17 miles downriver on Potash Road, Highway 279).

On the Green, boaters at low water need to watch for rocky areas at the mouth of Millard Canyon (33.5 miles above the confluence, where a rock bar extends across the river) and at the mouth of Horse Canyon (14.5 miles above the confluence, where a rock and gravel bar on the right leaves only a narrow channel on the left side). The trip from the town of Green River through Labyrinth and Stillwater Canyons is 120 miles. Launch places include Green River State Park (in Green River) and Mineral Canyon (52 miles above the confluence; reached on a fair-weather road from Highway 313).

No roads go to the confluence. The easiest return to civilization for nonmotorized craft is a pick-up by jet-boat from Moab by Tex's Riverways (435/259-5101, www.texsriverways .com) or Tag-A-Long Tours (800/453-3292, www.tagalong.com). A far more difficult way out is hiking either of two trails just above the Cataract Canyon Rapids to four-wheel-drive roads on the rim.

Park rangers require that boaters above the confluence obtain a $20 **backcountry permit** either in person from the Moab office or by mail (at least two weeks in advance). River notes on boating the Green and Colorado are available on request from the Moab office (435/259-3911). Bill and Buzz Belknap's *Canyonlands River Guide* has river logs and maps pointing out items of interest on the Green

River below the town of Green River and all of the Colorado from the upper end of Westwater Canyon to Lake Powell. Don Baar's *A River Runner's Guide to Cataract Canyon* also has good coverage.

◖ RIVER-RUNNING THROUGH CATARACT CANYON

The Colorado River enters Cataract Canyon at the confluence and picks up speed. The rapids begin four miles downstream and extend for the next 14 miles to Lake Powell. Especially in spring, the 26 or more rapids give a wild ride equal to the best in the Grand Canyon. The current zips along (up to 16 mph) and forms waves more than seven feet high! When the excitement dies down, boaters have a 34-mile trip across Lake Powell to Hite Marina; most people either carry a motor or arrange for a power boat to pick them up. Depending on how much motoring is used, the trip through Cataract Canyon can take 2–5 days.

Because of the real hazards of running the rapids, the National Park Service requires boaters to have proper equipment and a $30 **permit.** Many people go on a commercial trip in which everything has been taken care of (check the list of outfitters in the *Moab* chapter). Private groups must contact the Canyonlands River Unit far in advance for permit details (2282 SW Resource Blvd., Moab, UT 84532, 435/259-3911).

Additional Southeast Utah Sights

In addition to Arches and Canyonlands, this corner of Utah contains several scenic and culturally significant sites that deserve a detour. Following are some suggestions on other sites and itineraries to make this part of your journey pleasant and fulfilling.

DEAD HORSE POINT STATE PARK

The land drops away in sheer cliffs from this lofty perch west of Moab (435/259-2614, www

.stateparks.utah.gov, $7-per-vehicle day-use fee). Nearly 5,000 square miles of rugged canyon country lie in the distance. Two thousand feet below, the Colorado River twists through a gooseneck on its long journey to the sea. The river and its tributaries have carved canyons that reveal a geologic layer cake of colorful rock formations. Even in a region of impressive views around nearly every corner, Dead Horse Point stands out for its exceptionally breathtaking panorama. You'll also see below

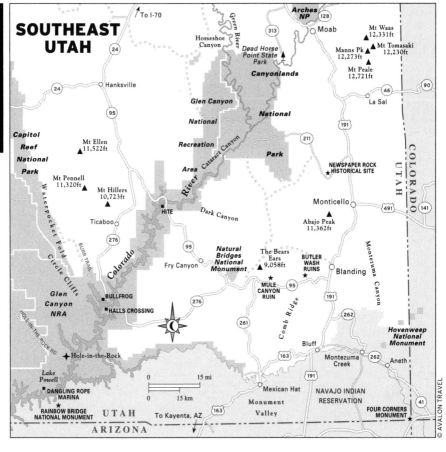

you, along the Colorado River, the result of powerful underground forces: Salt, under pressure, has pushed up overlying rock layers into an anticline. This formation, the Shafer Dome, contains potash that is being processed by the Moab Salt Plant. You can see the mine buildings, processing plant, and evaporation ponds (tinted blue to hasten evaporation).

A narrow neck of land only 30 yards wide connects the point with the rest of the plateau. Cowboys once herded wild horses onto the point, then placed a fence across the neck to make a 40-acre corral. They chose the desirable animals from the herd and let the rest go.

According to one tale, a group of horses left behind after such a roundup became confused by the geography of the point. They couldn't find their way off and circled repeatedly until they died of thirst within sight of the river below. You may hear other stories of how the point got its name.

Besides the awe-inspiring views, the park also offers a visitors center (with displays), a campground, a picnic area, a group area, a nature trail, and hiking trails. The point has become popular with hang gliders. If you are lucky in timing your visit, you may see one or more crafts gliding back and forth above

© W. C. MCRAE

Dead Horse Point State Park rises above the Colorado River.

or below the viewpoint. Dead Horse Point is easily reached by paved road, either as a destination itself or as a side trip on the way to the Island in the Sky District of Canyonlands National Park. From Moab, head northwest 10 miles on U.S. 191, then turn left 22 miles on Highway 313. The drive along Highway 313 climbs through a scenic canyon and tops out on a ridge with panoramas of distant mesas, buttes, mountains, and canyons. Several rest areas are along the road.

Visitors Center and Campground

Stop here for registration and exhibits about the park. Staff can answer questions and provide checklists of local flora and fauna. A short slide presentation is given on request. In summer, rangers give talks at the amphitheater behind the visitors center. Books, maps, posters, postcards, T-shirts, charcoal, ice, and soft drinks are available for purchase. Open 8 A.M.–6 P.M. daily in summer (May 16– Sept. 15) and 9 A.M.–5 P.M. the rest of the year. A short nature trail introduces the high-desert

country and its plants. Continue 1.5 miles on the main road to viewpoints and picnic areas on the point itself. Primitive trails connect the point with several other overlooks, the visitors center, and the campground. Ask for a map at the visitors center.

Kayenta Campground (reservations 800/ 322-3770, www.reserveamerica.com, $15 camping fee, $7 additional fee for reservations), just past the visitors center, offers sites with water and electric hookups but no showers. The campground nearly always fills up during the main season. Either make reservations ahead of time or try to arrive by early afternoon to ensure a space. Winter visitors may camp on the point; no hookups are available, but the restrooms have water.

HOVENWEEP NATIONAL MONUMENT

Delve into the region's cultural history and architecture at remote Hovenweep National Monument (970/749-0510, www.nps.gov/ hove/, $6 per vehicle, $3 per person), where the Anasazi built many impressive masonry buildings during the early to mid-1200s, near the end of their 1,300-year stay in the area. A drought beginning in A.D. 1274 and lasting 25 years probably hastened their migration from this area. Several centuries of intensive farming, hunting, and woodcutting had already taken their toll on the land. Archaeologists believe the inhabitants retreated south in the late 1200s to sites in northwestern New Mexico and northeastern Arizona. The Ute word *Hovenweep* means "deserted valley," an appropriate name for the lonely high-desert country left behind. The Anasazi at Hovenweep had much in common with the Mesa Verde culture, although the Dakota sandstone here doesn't form large alcoves suitable for cliff-dweller villages. Ruins at Hovenweep remain essentially unexcavated, awaiting the attention of future archaeologists.

The Anasazi farmers had a keen interest in the seasons because of their need to know the best time for planting crops. Astronomical stations (alignments of walls, doorways, and tiny openings) allowed the sun priests to determine the equinoxes and solstices with an accuracy of one or two days. This precision also may have been necessary for a complex ceremonial calendar. Astronomical stations at Hovenweep have been discovered at Hovenweep Castle, House of Square Tower Ruins, and Cajon Ruins.

Getting to Hovenweep

One approach from U.S. 191 between Blanding and Bluff is to head east nine miles on Highway 262, continue straight six miles on a small, paved road to Hatch Trading Post, then follow the signs for 16 miles. A good way in from Bluff is to go east 21 miles on the paved road to Montezuma Creek and Aneth, then follow the signs north for 20 miles. A scenic 58-mile route through Montezuma Canyon begins five miles south of Monticello and follows unpaved roads to Hatch and on to Hovenweep; you can stop at the BLM's Three Turkey Ruin on the way. From Colorado, take a partly paved road west and north 41 miles from U.S. 666 (the turnoff is four miles south of Cortez).

tower-like Anasazi grain silos at Hovenweep National Monument

© W. C. MCRAE

Visitors Center

Hovenweep National Monument protects six groups of villages left behind by the Anasazi. The sites lie near the Colorado border southeast of Blanding. Square Tower Ruins Unit, where the visitors center is located, has the most ruins and the most varied architecture. In fact, you can find all of the Hovenweep architectural styles here. The visitors center (970/749-0510, 8 A.M.–4:30 P.M. year-round) has a few exhibits on the Anasazi and photos of local wildlife. A ranger can answer your questions, provide brochures and handouts about various aspects of the monument, and give directions for visiting the other ruin groups. Related books can also be purchased.

There's also a small **campground** near the visitors center ($10 per site, no reservations). Mesa Verde National Park (970/529-4465, www.nps.gov/meve) administers Hovenweep.

Square Tower Ruins

This extensive group of Anasazi towers and dwellings lines the rim and slopes of Little Ruin Canyon, located a short walk from the visitors center. Obtain a trail-guide booklet from the ranger station. You can take easy walks of less than half a mile on the rim or combine all the trails for a loop of about two miles with only one up-and-down section in the canyon. The booklet has good descriptions of Anasazi life and architecture and of the plants growing along the trail. You'll see towers (D-shaped, square, oval, and round), cliff dwellings, surface dwellings, storehouses, kivas, and rock art. Keep an eye out for the prairie rattlesnake (a subspecies of the Western rattlesnake), which is active at night in summer and during the day in spring and autumn. Please stay on the trail; don't climb the fragile ruin walls or walk on rubble mounds.

Other Ruins

These ruins are good to visit if you'd like to spend more time in the area. You'll need a map and directions from a ranger to find them because they aren't signed. One group, the Goodman Point, near Cortez, Colorado, has relatively little to see except unexcavated mounds.

Holly Ruins group is noted for its Great House, Holly Tower, and Tilted Tower. Most of Tilted Tower fell away after the boulder on which it sat shifted. Great piles of rubble mark the sites of structures built on loose ground. Look for remnants of farming terraces in the canyon below the Great House. A hiking trail connects the campground at Square Tower Ruins with Holly Ruins; the route follows canyon bottoms and is about eight miles round-trip. Ask a ranger for a map and directions. Hikers could also continue to Horseshoe Ruins (one mile farther) and Hackberry Ruins (just beyond Horseshoe). All of these lie just across the Colorado border and about six miles (one-way) by road from the visitors center.

Horseshoe Ruins and **Hackberry Ruins** are best reached by an easy trail (one mile round-trip) off the road to Holly Ruins. Horseshoe House, built in a horseshoe shape similar to Sun Temple at Mesa Verde, has exceptionally good masonry work. Archaeologists haven't determined the purpose of the structure. An alcove in the canyon below contains a spring and a small shelter. A round tower nearby on the rim has a strategic view. Hackberry House has only one room still intact. Rubble piles and wall remnants abound in the area. The spring under an alcove here still has a good flow and supports lush growths of hackberry and cottonwood trees along with smaller plants.

Cutthroat Castle Ruins were remote even in Anasazi times. The ruins lie along an intermittent stream rather than at the head of a canyon like most other Hovenweep sites. Cutthroat Castle is a large multistory structure with both straight and curved walls. Three round towers stand nearby. Look for wall fragments and the circular depressions of kivas. High-clearance vehicles can go close to the ruins, about 11.5 miles (one-way) from the visitors center. Visitors with cars can drive to a trailhead and then walk to the ruins (1.5 miles round-trip on foot).

Cajon Ruins are at the head of a little canyon on Cajon Mesa in the Navajo Reservation in Utah, about nine miles southwest of the visitors center. The site has a commanding view across the San Juan Valley as far as Monument Valley. Buildings include a large multiroom structure, a round tower, and a tall square tower. An alcove just below has a spring and some rooms. Look for pictographs, petroglyphs, and grooves in rock (used for tool grinding). Farming terraces were located on the canyon's south side.

BETWEEN CANYONLANDS AND CAPITOL REEF

Just south of Blanding, Highway 95—here labeled the "Trail of the Ancients" National Scenic Byway—heads west across a high plateau toward the Colorado River, traversing Comb Ridge, Cedar Mesa, and many canyons. This is remote country, so fill up with gas before leaving Blanding because you can't depend on finding gasoline until Hanksville, which is 122 miles away. Fry Lodge and Hite and the other Lake Powell marinas do have gas and supplies, but their schedules are limited.

Cedar Mesa and its canyons have an exceptionally large number of prehistoric Anasazi sites. Several ruins lie just off the highway, and hikers will discover many more. If you would like to explore the Cedar Mesa area, be sure to drop in at the **Kane Gulch Ranger Station** (435/587-1532, www.blm.gov/utah/monticello), four miles south of Highway 95 on Highway 261. Bureau of Land Management (BLM) staff issue the permits required to explore the Cedar Mesa backcountry at $2 for day use and $8 per person for overnight stays in Grand Gulch, Fish Creek Canyon, and Owl Creek Canyon. The number of people permitted to camp at a given time is limited, so call ahead. BLM people will also tell you about archaeological sites and their values, current hiking conditions, and where to find water.

Butler Wash Ruins

Well-preserved pueblo ruins left by the Anasazi lie tucked under an overhang across the wash 11 miles west on Highway 95 (between Mileposts 111 and 112) from U.S. 191. At the trailhead on the north side of the highway, follow cairns for half a mile through juniper and piñon pine woodlands and across slickrock to the overlook.

Comb Ridge

Geologic forces have squeezed up the earth's crust in a long ridge running 80 miles south from the Abajo Peaks into Arizona. Sheer cliffs plunge 800 feet into Comb Wash on the west side. Engineering the highway down these cliffs took considerable effort. A parking area near the top of the grade offers expansive panoramas across Comb Wash.

Arch Canyon

This tributary canyon of Comb Wash has spectacular scenery and many Native American ruins. Much of the canyon can be seen on a day hike, but two to three days are needed to explore the upper reaches. The main streambeds usually have water (purify before drinking). To reach the trailhead, turn north 2.5 miles on a dirt road in Comb Wash (between Mileposts 107 and 108 of Highway 95), go past a house and water tank, then park in a grove of cottonwood trees before a stream. This is also a good place to camp. The mouth of Arch Canyon lies just to the northwest (it's easy to miss). Sign in at the register here. Look for a Native American ruin just up Arch Canyon on the right. More ruins lie tucked under alcoves farther up-canyon.

Arch Canyon Overlook

A road and short trail to the rim of Arch Canyon provide a beautiful view into the depths. Turn north four miles on Texas Flat Road (County 263) from Highway 95 between Mileposts 102 and 103, park just before the road begins a steep climb, and walk east on an old jeep road to the rim. This is a fine place for a picnic, although there are no facilities or guardrails. Texas Flat Road is dirt but okay when dry for cars with good clearance. Trucks can continue up the steep hill to other viewpoints of Arch and Texas Canyons.

Mule Canyon Ruin

Archaeologists have excavated and stabilized this Anasazi village on the gentle slope of Mule Canyon's South Fork. A stone kiva, circular tower, and 12-room structure are all visible, and all were originally connected by tunnels. Cave Towers, two miles to the southeast, would have been visible from the top of the tower here. Signs describe the ruin and periods of Anasazi development. Turn north 0.3 mile on a paved road from Highway 95 between Mileposts 101 and 102. Hikers can explore other ruins in the North and South Forks of Mule Canyon; check with the Kane Gulch Ranger Station for advice and directions. You might see pieces of pottery and other artifacts in this area. Please leave *every* piece in place so that future visitors can enjoy the discovery, too. Federal laws also prohibit the removal of artifacts.

NATURAL BRIDGES NATIONAL MONUMENT

Streams in White Canyon and its tributaries cut deep canyons, then formed three impressive bridges, now protected as Natural Bridges National Monument (435/692-1234, www.nps .gov/nabr/, $6 per vehicle or $3 per pedestrian or bicyclist). Silt-laden floodwaters sculpted the bridges by gouging tunnels between closely spaced loops in the meandering canyons. You can distinguish a natural bridge from an arch because the bridge spans a streambed and was initially carved out of the rock by flowing water. In the monument, these bridges illustrate three different stages of development, from the massive, newly formed Kachina Bridge to the middle-aged Sipapu Bridge to the delicate and fragile span of Owachomo. All three natural bridges will continue to widen and eventually collapse under their own weight. A nine-mile scenic drive has overlooks of the picturesque bridges, Anasazi ruins, and twisting canyons. You can follow short trails down from the rim to the base of each bridge or hike through all three bridges on an 8.6-mile loop.

Ruins, artifacts, and rock art indicate a long occupation by tribes ranging from archaic groups to the Anasazi. Many fine cliff dwellings built by the Anasazi still stand. In 1883, prospector Cass Hite passed on tales of the huge stone bridges that he had discovered on a trip up White Canyon. Adventurous travelers, including those on a 1904 *National*

© PAUL LEVY

Owachomo Bridge is the most fragile and elegant of the monument's bridges.

Geographic magazine expedition, visited this isolated region to marvel at the bridges. The public's desire for protection of the bridges led President Theodore Roosevelt to proclaim the area a national monument in 1908. Federal administrators then changed the original bridge names from Edwin, Augusta, and Caroline to the Hopi names used today. Although the Hopi never lived here, the Anasazi of White Canyon very likely have descendants in the modern Hopi villages in Arizona.

Visitors Center

From the signed junction on Highway 95, drive 4.5 miles on Highway 275 to the visitors center (435/692-1234, 8 A.M.–5 P.M. daily, elevation 6,505 feet). Monument Valley Overlook, two miles in, offers views south across a vast expanse of piñon pine and juniper to Monument Valley and distant mountains. A slide show in the visitors center illustrates how geologic forces and erosion created the canyons and natural bridges. Exhibits introduce the people who once lived here, as well as the area's geology, wildlife, and plants. Outside, labels identify common plants of the monument.

Rangers can answer your questions about the monument and surrounding area. If asked, staff will provide details on locations of ruins and rock-art sites. You can purchase regional books, topographic and geologic maps, postcards, and slides. Checklists of birds, other wildlife, and plants are available, too.

The Bridge View Drive is always open during daylight hours, except after heavy snowstorms. A winter visit can be very enjoyable; ice or mud often close the steep Sipapu and Kachina Trails, but the short trail to Owachomo Bridge usually stays open. Pets aren't allowed on the trails or in the backcountry at any time.

Other than the small but popular campground at the national monument, the nearest accommodations and café are at Fry Canyon, 26 miles northwest of the visitors center on Highway 95. The closest gas station is 40 miles east near Blanding or 50 west miles at Hite.

Photovoltaic Array

A large solar electric-power station sits across the road from the visitors center. This demonstration system, the largest in the world when constructed in 1980, has 250,000 solar cells spread over nearly an acre and produces up to 100 kilowatts. Batteries, located elsewhere, store a two-day supply of power. The monument lies far from the nearest power lines, so the solar cells provide an alternative to continuously running diesel-powered generators.

Bridge View Drive

This nine-mile drive begins its one-way loop just past the campground. You can stop for lunch at a picnic area. Allow about 1.5 hours for a quick trip around. To make all the stops and do a bit of leisurely hiking takes most of a day. The crossbedded sandstone of the bridges and canyons is part of the 265-million-year-old Cedar Mesa Formation.

Sipapu Bridge viewpoint is two miles from the visitors center. The Hopi name refers to the gateway from which their ancestors entered this world from another world below. Sipapu Bridge has reached its mature or middle-aged stage of development. The bridge is the largest in the monument and has a span of 268 feet and a height of 220 feet. Many people think Sipapu is the most magnificent of the bridges. Another view and a trail to the base of Sipapu are 0.8 mile farther. The viewpoint is about halfway down on an easy trail; allow half an hour. A steeper and rougher trail branches off the viewpoint trail and winds down to the bottom of White Canyon, which is probably the best place to fully appreciate the bridge's size. Total round-trip distance is 1.2 miles with an elevation change of 600 feet.

Horse Collar Ruin, built by the Anasazi, looks as though it has been abandoned for just a few decades, not 800 years. At 3.1 miles from the visitors center, a short trail leads to an overlook. The name comes from the shape of the doorway openings in two storage rooms. Hikers walking in the canyon between Sipapu and Kachina Bridges can scramble up a steep rock slope to the site. Like all ancient ruins, these are fragile and must not be touched or entered. Only with such care will future generations of visitors be able to admire the well-preserved structures. Other groups of Anasazi dwellings can be seen in or near the monument, too; ask a ranger for directions.

The **Kachina Bridge** viewpoint and trailhead are 5.1 miles from the visitors center. The massive bridge has a span of 204 feet and a height of 210 feet. A trail, 1.5 miles round-trip, leads to the canyon bottom next to the bridge; the elevation change is 650 feet. Look for pictographs near the base of the trail. Some of the figures resemble Hopi kachinas (spirits) and inspired the bridge's name. Armstrong Canyon joins White Canyon just downstream from the bridge; floods in each canyon abraded opposite sides of the rock fin that later became Kachina Bridge.

The **Owachomo Bridge** viewpoint and trailhead are 7.1 miles from the visitors center. An easy walk leads to Owachomo's base—a half-mile round-trip with an elevation change of 180 feet. Graceful Owachomo spans 180 feet and is 106 feet high. Erosive forces have worn the venerable bridge to a thickness of only nine feet. Unlike the other two bridges, Owachomo spans a smaller tributary stream instead of a major canyon. Two streams played a role in the bridge's formation. Floods coming down the larger Armstrong Canyon surged against a sandstone fin on one side while floods in a small side canyon wore away the rock on the other side. Eventually a hole formed, and waters flowing down the side canyon took the shorter route through the bridge. The name *Owachomo* means "flat-rock mound" in the Hopi language; a large rock outcrop nearby inspired the name. Before construction of the present road, a trail winding down the opposite side of Armstrong Canyon provided the only access for monument visitors. The trail, little used now, connects with Highway 95.

Natural Bridges Loop Trail

- Distance: 8.6-mile loop
- Duration: 5–6 hours

- Elevation change: 500 feet
- Effort: moderate–strenuous
- Trailhead: Sipapu Bridge

A canyon hike through all three bridges can be the highlight of a visit to the monument. Unmaintained trails make a loop in White and Armstrong canyons and cross a wooded plateau. The trip is easier if you start from Sipapu and come out the relatively gentle grades at Owachomo. You can save 2.5 miles by arranging a car shuttle between Sipapu and Owachomo Trailheads. Another option is to go in or out on the Kachina Bridge Trail midway to cut the hiking distance in half. On nearing Owachomo Bridge from below, a small sign points out the trail, which bypasses a deep pool. The canyons remain in their wild state; you'll need some hiking experience, water, proper footwear, a compass, and a map (the handout available at the visitors center is adequate). The USGS 7.5-minute topographic maps also cover this area.

When hiking in the canyons, keep an eye out for natural arches and Native American writings. Try not to step on midget faded rattlesnakes or other living entities (such as the fragile cryptobiotic soil). And beware of flash-flood dangers, especially if you see big clouds billowing in the sky in an upstream direction. You don't need a hiking permit, although it's a good idea to talk beforehand with a ranger to find out current conditions. Overnight camping within the monument is permitted only in the campground. Backpackers, however, can go up or down the canyons and camp outside the monument boundaries. Note that vehicles can't be parked overnight on the loop drive.

Campgrounds

Drive 0.3 mile past the visitors center and turn right into the **Natural Bridges Campground,** set in a forest of piñon pine and juniper. Sites stay open all year and cost $10. Obtain water from a faucet in front of the visitors center. Rangers give talks several evenings each week during the summer season. The campground is often full, but there is a rather grim designated overflow area near the intersection of Highway 95 and Highway 261. RVs or trailers more than 21 feet long must use this parking area.

NATURAL BRIDGES TO BULLFROG MARINA BY FERRY

Eight miles west of the entrance to Natural Bridges National Monument, travelers must make a decision: whether to continue on Highway 95 to cross the Colorado by bridge at Hite or to follow Highway 276 to the Halls Crossing Marina and cross the river—at this point tamed by the Glen Canyon Dam and known as Lake Powell—by car ferry.

Obviously, the ferry is the more exotic choice, and both Halls Crossing and Bullfrog marinas offer lodging and food, which are a relative scarcity in this remote area. Crossing the Colorado on the ferry also makes it easy to access Bullfrog–Notom Road, which climbs for 60 miles through dramatic landscapes on its way to Capitol Reef National Park's otherwise remote Waterfold Pocket. The road ends at Notom, just four miles from the eastern entrance to Capitol Reef Park on Highway 24. Drivers can also turn west on the Burr Trail and follow back roads to Boulder, near the Escalante River Canyon.

Glen Canyon National Recreation Area

Lake Powell lies at the center of Glen Canyon National Recreation Area (520/608-6404, www.nps.gov/glca, $15 per vehicle or $7 per pedestrian or bicyclist for seven days, no charge for passing through Page on U.S. 89), a vast land covering 1.25 million acres in Arizona

---

GLEN CANYON EMERGES

When the Glen Canyon Dam was completed in 1963, the Colorado River backed up behind it, forming Lake Powell and submerging Glen Canyon. Just before the remote canyon disappeared, Sierra Club president David Brower took a trip into the area and realized what a huge mistake it had been not to fight this dam. (The Sierra Club had focused its energy on preventing a dam in Dinosaur National Monument, and Glen Canyon had been a pawn in the politics that saved Dinosaur.)

Particularly spectacular, and soon to be flooded, was a spot called the Cathedral in the Desert, where sandstone walls rose nearly 200 feet and a waterfall misted the air. These remarkable canyons were memorialized in a book by Brower and photographer Eliot Porter, *The Place No One Knew.*

Years passed, and Lake Powell was marketed as a recreational "jewel in the desert," where you could rent a houseboat and spend the week jet-skiing across the huge lake.

Then came the drought. After six years of drought, by the spring of 2005 water levels in Lake Powell had dropped about 150 feet, revealing slot canyons, cliffs, and waterfalls that had been underwater for more than 40 years. Among these was the Cathedral in the Desert. It became possible to rent a motorboat at Bullfrog and head up the Escalante River and into Clear Creek Canyon to visit the Cathedral. You could actually get out of the boat and walk on the ground, gazing up at a waterfall.

As heavy spring rains and snowmelt poured down into the lake, side canyons began to fill with water. The lake deepened, and you could no longer walk in the Cathedral. But there is some question about how long or how deeply the Cathedral and other features, such as natural bridges, Anasazi structures, and rock art will be submerged. The Bureau of Reclamation claims that once the effects of the drought have passed, all will be back to business as usual. But Richard Ingebretsen, of the Glen Canyon Institute (www.glencanyon.org), maintains that it's not so much the drought that has drained Lake Powell as it is downstream demand for water, which is not likely to let up. Time, of course, will tell. But it's hard not to think that the ghost of Edward Abbey isn't doing a little gleeful monkey-wrenching.

and Utah. When the Glen Canyon Dam was completed in 1964, conservationists deplored the loss of remote and beautiful Glen Canyon of the Colorado River beneath the lake waters. In terms of beauty and sheer drama, Glen Canyon was considered the equal of the Grand Canyon. Today, we have only words, pictures, and memories to remind us of its wonders. On the other hand, the 186-mile-long lake now provides easy access to an area most had not even known existed. Lake Powell is the second-largest human-made lake within the United States. Only Lake Mead, farther downstream, has a greater water-storage capacity. Lake Powell, however, has three times more shoreline—1,960 miles—and, when full, holds enough water to cover the state of Pennsylvania one foot deep. Just a handful of roads approach the lake, so access is basically limited to boats—bays and coves offer nearly limitless opportunities for exploration by boaters—or long-distance hiking trails.

Halls Crossing/Bullfrog Ferry Service

At the junction of Highway 276, a large sign lists the departure times for the ferry; note that these may be different than the times listed in the widely circulated flyer or on the website (www.nps.gov/glca/ferry). Confirm the departure times before making the 42-mile journey to Halls Crossing.

The crossing time from Halls Crossing to Bullfrog is 27 minutes (the crossing is only three miles, however). The fare for vehicles smaller than 19 feet 11 inches in length is $20, which includes the driver and all passengers. Bicycles are $5, and motorcycles are $10. Foot passenger fares are $5 per adult, but free for seniors over 65 and children under 5.

During the high summer season, from May 15 to September 14, the ferries run on the hour daily beginning at 8 A.M. The final ferry from Halls Crossing departs at 6 P.M., and the final ferry from Bullfrog departs at 7 P.M. From April 15 to May 14, and from September 15 to October 31, the Halls Ferry begins operation at 8 A.M. and sails every two hours until 4 P.M.

The Bullfrog ferry begins at 9 A.M. and sails every two hours until 5 P.M. The rest of the year, from November 1 through April 14, this same schedule continues, except the final trips of the day are at 2 P.M. and 3 P.M., respectively.

Please note that if drought or downstream demand lowers the level of Lake Powell beyond a certain point, there may not be enough water for the ferry to operate. If this is the case (as it was during the spring of 2005), there will be notices about the ferry's status at just about every park visitors center in southern Utah.

For reservations and information regarding lodging, camping, tours, boating, and recreation at both Halls Crossing and Bullfrog Marina, contact **Lake Powell Resorts & Marinas** (800/528-6154, www.lakepowell.com).

Arriving at Halls Crossing by road, you'll first reach a small store offering three-bedroom units in trailer houses and an RV park. Continue for half a mile on the main road to the boat ramp and **Halls Crossing Marina** (435/684-2261). The marina has a larger store (groceries and fishing and boating supplies), tours to Rainbow Bridge, a boat-rental office (fishing, ski, and houseboat), a gas dock, slips, and storage. The **ranger station** is nearby, although rangers are usually out on patrol; look for their vehicle in the area if the office is closed.

On the western side of the lake, **Bullfrog Marina** (435/684-2233) is more like a small town, with a **visitors center** (435/684-2243), clinic, stores, service station, and a handsome hotel and restaurant. In addition to daily car ferries across to Halls Crossing, the marina offers tours to sights along Lake Powell, including **Rainbow Bridge,** from April 15 to October 31. It also offers boat rentals.

Defiance House Lodge (435/684-3000 or 800/528-6154, www.lakepowell.com) offers comfortable lake-view accommodations and the **Anasazi Restaurant** (open daily in summer for breakfast, lunch, and dinner). Rooms begin at $121 (s or d) in summer (Apr. 1–Oct. 31) and $112 (s or d) in winter. The front desk at the lodge also handles **housekeeping units** (trailers) and an **RV park.** Showers, a laundry room, a convenience store, and a post office are at **Trailer Village.** Ask the visitors center staff or rangers for directions to primitive camping areas with vehicle access elsewhere along Bullfrog Bay.

Bullfrog Marina can be reached from the north via paved Highway 276. It's 40 miles between Bullfrog and the junction with Highway 95. At Ticaboo, 20 miles north of Bullfrog, is another good lodging option. The **Ticaboo Lodge** (435/788-2110 or 800/842-2267, $104 summer) is a new hotel, restaurant, and service-station complex that pretty much constitutes all of Ticaboo.

For more information on Bullfrog/Notom Road, see the *Capitol Reef National Park* chapter.

NATURAL BRIDGES TO LAKE POWELL VIA HIGHWAY 95

If the Lake Powell ferry schedule doesn't match your travel plans, Highway 95 will quickly get you across the Colorado River to the junction with Highway 24 at Hanksville.

Hite

In 1883, Cass Hite came to Glen Canyon in search of gold. He found some at a place later named Hite City and set off a small gold rush. Cass and a few of his relatives operated a small store and post office, which were the only services for many miles. Travelers wishing to cross the Colorado River here had the difficult task of swimming their animals across. Arthur Chaffin, a later resident, put through the first road and opened a ferry service in 1946. The Chaffin Ferry served uranium prospectors and adventurous motorists until the lake backed up to the spot in 1964. A steel bridge now spans the Colorado River upstream from Hite Marina. Cass Hite's store and the ferry site are underwater about five miles down-lake from Hite Marina.

Beyond Hite, on the tiny neck of land between the Colorado River bridge and the Dirty Devil bridge, an unmarked dirt road turns north. Called Hite Road, or Orange Cliffs Road, this long and rugged road eventually

Drought and increasing downstream water use have made Lake Powell very low at Hite.

links up with backcountry routes—including the Flint Trail—in the Maze District of Canyonlands National Park.

The uppermost marina on Lake Powell, Hite lies 141 lake miles from Glen Canyon Dam. It has been hard hit by low water levels in Lake Powell. When water is available, boats can continue up-lake to the mouth of Dark Canyon in Cataract Canyon at low water or into Canyonlands National Park at high water. During times of low water, the boat ramp is often high above the lake. Hite tends to be quieter than the other marinas and is favored by some anglers and families. Facilities include a small **store** with gas, three-bedroom housekeeping units in trailer houses, and a primitive **campground** (no drinking water, free). Primitive camping is also available nearby off Highway 95 at Dirty Devil, Farley Canyon, White Canyon, Blue Notch, and other locations. A **ranger station** (435/684-2457) is occasionally open; look for the rangers' vehicle at other times. Contact **Lake Powell Resorts & Marinas** (800/528-6154, www.lakepowell.com) for accommodation and boat-rental reservations. Reach Hite Marina directly by calling 435/684-2278.

MONTICELLO

This small Mormon town (pop. 1,900) is about 50 miles south of Moab and pretty much its polar opposite. Quiet and relatively non-touristy, it's the best place to stay if you're visiting the Needles District and don't want to camp. Monticello (pronounced mon-tuh-SELL-o) lies at an elevation of 7,050 feet just east of the Abajo Mountains. It's 46 miles east of the entrance to the Needles District of Canyonlands National Park.

Accommodations

Monticello has a number of comfortable and affordable motels. The **Best Western Wayside Inn** (197 E. Central St., 435/587-2261 or 800/633-9700, www.bestwestern.com, $73–80) is an easy place to land after a day of hiking, and it has a pool. The **Monticello Inn** (164 E. Central, 435/587-2274 or 800/657-6622, www.themonticelloinn.com, from $55 d) is a quiet and well-maintained older motel away from the main highway, with very clean rooms and a pleasant setting.

Food

Not only can you get a good cup of coffee and freshly made juice at **Peace Tree Juice Café** (516 N. Main, 435/587-5063, 9 A.M.–5 P.M. daily), but this is the only place this side of Moab that you're likely to get a vegetarian Thai wrap sandwich (and have it taste really good). You'll also find Internet access at this bright and cheery place.

More typical for the area, and a good bet for a big breakfast or dinner, is **MD Ranch Cookhouse** (380 S. Main, 435/587-3299, open for three meals daily), where the Western atmosphere is a part of the appeal. The cowboy cooking is good, too, and includes steaks and buffalo.

Information and Services

The **San Juan County Multi-Agency Visitors Center** (117 S. Main, 435/587-3235 or 800/574-4386, www.southeastutah.com) is on the side of the courthouse (open 8 A.M.–5 P.M. Mon.–Fri. and 10 A.M.–5 P.M. Sat. and Sun. Apr.–Oct., 9 A.M.–5 P.M. Mon.–Fri. Nov.–Mar.).

The **public library** is in the city park (80 N. Main, 435/587-2281).

The **San Juan Hospital** (364 West 100 North, 435/587-2116) is friendly and small, and a good place to repair any camping-related injuries.

ARCHES NATIONAL PARK

A concentration of rock arches of marvelous variety has formed within the maze of sandstone fins at Arches National Park (www.nps .gov/arch), one of the most popular parks in the United States. Balanced rocks and tall spires add to the splendor. Paved roads and short hiking trails provide easy access to some of the more than 1,500 arches in the park. If you're short on time, a drive to the Windows Section (23.5 miles round-trip) affords a look at some of the largest and most spectacular arches. To visit all the stops and hike a few short trails would take all day.

Most of the early settlers and cowboys that passed through the Arches area paid little attention to the scenery. In 1923, however, a prospector by the name of Alexander Ringhoffer interested officials of the Rio Grande Railroad in the scenic attractions at what he called Devils Garden (now known as Klondike Bluffs). The railroad men liked the area and contacted Stephen Mather, who was the first director of the National Park Service. Mather started the political process that led to designating two small areas as a national monument in 1929, but Ringhoffer's Devils Garden wasn't included until later. The monument grew in size over the years and became Arches National Park in 1971. The park now comprises 76,519 acres—small enough to be appreciated in one day, yet large enough to warrant extensive exploration.

PLANNING YOUR TIME

If you only have part of the day to explore, drive the 18-mile length of the main park road

© W. C. MCRAE

ARCHES

HIGHLIGHTS

◖ **Balanced Rock:** An unbelievable spire-upon-spire balancing act rising 128 feet from the desert, Balanced Rock is sure to give your camera a warm-up (page 204).

◖ **Windows Section:** Some of the park's largest arches are here, plus some of its largest crowds. But you have to go: Make it past the first arch and the crowds thin (page 204).

◖ **Delicate Arch Trail:** Perhaps the most dramatic of all the arches, Delicate Arch is beautiful from a distance (from the easily reached viewpoint) but mystical when seen close-up, with canyons and mountains in the distance, after a tough three-mile round-trip hike. Even if you're not up to the hike to Delicate Arch, at least follow the trail across the Salt Wash footbridge and turn left to find this striking but often-overlooked rock-art panel, carved by Ute artists about 400 years ago (page 210).

◖ **Fiery Furnace Trail:** To reach this unusual wonderland of rock mazes, fins, and turrets, hikers must go *mano a mano* with the flaming red rock. If you want to lose the crowds, this is your hike (page 210).

◖ **Devils Garden Loop:** This 7.2-mile loop trail leading to eight named arches and through a landscape of bizarre rock fins is the park's best day-hiking destination (page 211).

◖ **Tower Arch Trail:** This formation in Arch's backcountry is off-limits to the RV set

(you'll need a high-clearance vehicle), and this spire with an arch at its base is one of the park's most beautiful but neglected sights (page 212).

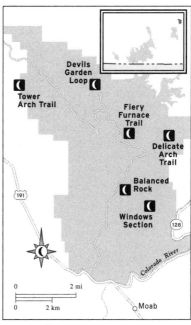

LOOK FOR ◖ TO FIND RECOMMENDED SIGHTS, ACTIVITIES, DINING, AND LODGING.

---

with brief stops at Balanced Rock and the Delicate Arch viewpoint. At the road's end, set out on the Devils Garden trail, but take only the trip to Tunnel and Pine Tree Arches. If you still have some time, stop on the way back out of the park and take a stroll on the Park Avenue trail.

A full day in the park is plenty of time to stop in the visitors center and then hike the full Delicate Arch Trail and explore Devils Garden. (Energetic hikers may want to do the entire 7.2-mile loop in Devils Garden; those who

want less of a workout can walk the mile-long trail to Landscape Arch.)

If you have more than one day to spend, be sure to sign up for a ranger-led hike into the Fiery Furnace area of the park. This will take about half a day; for the other half, head out via car or mountain bike to the Tower Arch Trail.

Though Arches is known more for its day hiking than its backpacking, park rangers can help you put together a backpacking trip and issue the required backcountry permit.

ARCHES

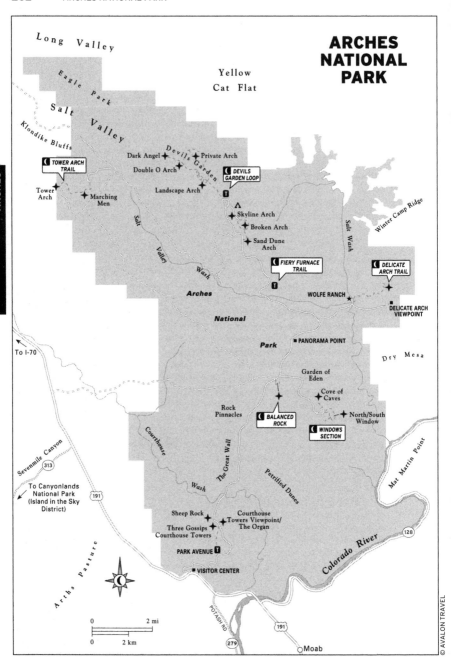

ARCHES NATIONAL PARK

Long Valley

Yellow
Cat Flat

Eagle Park

Salt

Valley

Klondike Bluffs

Dark Angel · Devils Garden · Private Arch
Double O Arch
Landscape Arch · DEVILS GARDEN LOOP

☾ TOWER ARCH TRAIL

Tower Arch
· Marching Men

Skyline Arch
· Broken Arch
· Sand Dune Arch

Salt Valley Wash

Winter Camp Ridge

Salt Wash

☾ FIERY FURNACE TRAIL

☾ DELICATE ARCH TRAIL

Arches

WOLFE RANCH

■ DELICATE ARCH VIEWPOINT

National

■ PANORAMA POINT

Dry Mesa

Park

Garden of Eden

→ To I-70

Cove of Caves

· North/South Window

Rock Pinnacles

☾ BALANCED ROCK

☾ WINDOWS SECTION

Mat Martin Point

Courthouse

The Great Wall

Sevenmile Canyon

313

To Canyonlands National Park (Island in the Sky District)

191

Wash

Petrified Dunes

Sheep Rock
Three Gossips
Courthouse Towers

Courthouse Towers Viewpoint/ The Organ

128

Colorado River

PARK AVENUE 🅣

Arth s Pasture

■ VISITOR CENTER

191

POTASH RD

279

○ Moab

0 ___ 2 mi
0 ___ 2 km

© AVALON TRAVEL

Exploring the Park

The entrance to Arches National Park (435/719-2299, www.nps.gov/arch, $10 per vehicle, $5 bicyclists, motorcyclists, or pedestrians) is five miles north of downtown Moab on U.S. 191.

VISITORS CENTER

Located just past the entrance booth, the expansive new visitors center (8 A.M.–4:30 P.M. daily, with extended hours from spring through fall) provides a good introduction to what you can expect ahead. Exhibits identify the rock layers, describe the geologic and human history, and illustrate some of the wildlife and plants of the park. A large outdoor plaza is a good place to troll for information after hours. A short slide program runs regularly and staff members are available to answer your questions, issue backcountry permits, and sign people up for ranger-led tours in the Fiery Furnace area of the park. Look for the posted list of special activities; rangers host campfire programs and lead a wide variety of guided walks from April through September. You'll also find checklists, pamphlets, books, maps, posters, postcards, and film here for purchase. See the ranger for advice and the free backcountry permit required for overnight trips. The easy 0.2-mile **Desert Nature Trail** begins near the visitors center and identifies some of the native plants. Picnic areas lie outside the visitors center and at Balanced Rock and Devils Garden.

A road guide to Arches National Park, available at the visitors center, has detailed descriptions that correspond to place-names along the main road. Be sure to stop only in parking lots and designated pullouts. Watch out for others who are sightseeing in this popular park. With less than 30 miles of paved road in the park, the traffic density can be surprisingly high in the summer high season.

If your plans include visiting Canyonlands

© W. C. MCRAE

The spires near Park Avenue have fanciful names like Three Gossips and Sheep Rock.

ARCHES

National Park plus Hovenweep and Natural Bridges National Monuments, consider the so-called Local Passport, which for $25 buys entry to all of these federal preserves. Purchase the pass at any of the park or national monument entries.

MOAB FAULT

The park road begins a long but well-graded climb from the visitors center up the cliffs to the northeast. A pullout on the right after 1.1 miles gives a good view of Moab Canyon and its geology. The rock layers on this side of the canyon have slipped down more than 2,600 feet in relation to the other side. Movement took place about six million years ago along the Moab Fault, which follows the canyon floor. Rock layers at the top of the far cliffs are nearly the same age as those at the *bottom* on this side. If you could stack the rocks of this side on top of rocks on the other side, you'd have a complete stratigraphic column of the Moab area—more than 150 million years' worth.

PARK AVENUE

South Park Avenue Overlook and Trailhead are on the left 2.1 miles from the visitors center. Great sandstone slabs form a "skyline" on each side of this dry wash. A trail goes north one mile down the wash to North Park Avenue Trailhead (1.3 miles ahead by road). Arrange to be picked up there or backtrack to your starting point. The large rock monoliths of Courthouse Towers rise north of Park Avenue. Only a few small arches exist now, although major arches may have formed in the past.

◖ BALANCED ROCK

This gravity-defying formation is on the right 8.5 miles from the visitors center. A boulder more than 55 feet high rests precariously atop a 73-foot pedestal. Chip Off the Old Block, a much smaller version of Balanced Rock, stood nearby until it collapsed in the winter of 1975–1976. For a closer look at Balanced Rock, take the 0.3-mile trail encircling it. There's a picnic area across the road. Author Edward Abbey lived in a trailer near Balanced Rock

© W. C. MCRAE

The aptly named Balanced Rock only looks precarious.

during a season as a park ranger in the 1950s; his journal became the basis for the classic *Desert Solitaire.*

◖ WINDOWS SECTION

Turn right onto a paved road 2.5 miles past Balanced Rock. Short trails (0.25–1 mile long one-way) lead from the road's end to some massive arches. Windows Trailhead is the start for North Window (an opening 51 feet high and 93 feet wide), South Window (66 feet high and 105 feet wide), and Turret Arch (64 feet high and 39 feet wide). Double Arch, a short walk from a second trailhead, is an unusual pair of arches; the larger opening—105 feet high and 163 feet wide—is best appreciated by walking inside. The smaller opening is 61 feet high and 60 feet wide. Together, the two arches frame a large opening overhead.

Garden of Eden Viewpoint, on the way back to the main road, has a good panorama of Salt Valley to the north. Under the valley, the massive body of salt and gypsum that's responsible for the arches comes close to the sur-

EDWARD ABBEY: "RESIST MUCH, OBEY LITTLE"

Edward Abbey spent two summers in the late 1950s living in a trailer in Arches National Park. From this experience, he wrote *Desert Solitaire*, which, when it was published in 1968, introduced many readers to the beauties of Utah's slickrock country, and the need to preserve it. In the introduction to this book, he gives a word of caution to slickrock pilgrims:

Do not jump into your automobile next June and rush out to the Canyon country hoping to see some of that which I have attempted to evoke in these pages. In the first place you can't see anything from a car; you've got to get out of the goddamned contraption and walk, better yet crawl, on hands and knees, over the sandstone and through the...cactus. When traces of blood begin to mark your trail you'll see something, maybe.

This sense of letting the outdoors affect you – right down to the bone – pervades Ab-bey's writing. He advocated responding to assaults on the environment in an equally raw, gutsy way. Convinced that the only way to confront rampant development in the American West was by preserving its wilderness, he was a pioneer of radical environmentalism, a "desert anarchist." Long before Earth First!, Abbey's fictional characters blew up dams and created a holy environmentalist ruckus in *The Monkeywrench Gang*. Some of his ideas were radical, others reactionary, and he seemed deeply committed to raising a stir. Abbey's writing did a lot to change the way people think about the American West, its development, and staying true to values derived from the natural world.

Two recent biographies, *Edward Abbey: A Life*, by James M. Cahalan (Tucson: University of Arizona Press, 2001; 357 pages; $27.95), and the less academic *Adventures with Ed*, by Abbey's good friend Jack Loeffler (Albuquerque: University of New Mexico Press, 2002; 308 pages; $24.95), help readers see the person behind the icon.

ARCHES

face. Tiny Delicate Arch can be seen across the valley on a sandstone ridge. Early visitors to the Garden of Eden saw rock formations resembling Adam (with an apple) and Eve. Two other viewpoints of the Salt Valley area lie farther north on the main road.

DELICATE ARCH AND WOLFE RANCH

Drive north 2.5 miles on the main road from the Windows junction and turn right 1.8 miles to the Wolfe Ranch, where a bit of pioneer history survives. John Wesley Wolfe came to this spot in 1888, hoping the desert climate would provide relief for health problems related to a Civil War injury. He found a good spring high in the rocks, grass for cattle, and water in Salt Wash to irrigate a garden. The ranch that he built provided a home for him and some of his family for more than 20 years, and cattlemen later used it as a line ranch. Then sheepherders brought in their animals, which so overgrazed the range that the grass has yet to recover. A trail guide available at the entrance tells about the Wolfe family and features of their ranch. The weather-beaten cabin built in 1906 still survives. A short trail leads to petroglyphs above Wolfe Ranch; figures of horses indicate that Utes did the artwork. Park staff can give directions to other rock-art sites; great care should be taken not to touch the fragile artwork.

Delicate Arch stands in a magnificent setting atop gracefully curving slickrock. Distant canyons and the La Sal Mountains lie beyond. The span is 45 feet high and 33 feet wide. A moderately strenuous three-mile round-trip hike leads to the arch. Another perspective on Delicate Arch can be obtained by driving 1.2 miles beyond Wolfe Ranch. Look for the small arch high above. A steep trail (half a mile round-trip) climbs a hill for the best view.

ARCHES

© PAUL LEVY

This rock art along Delicate Arch Trail was made after the Ute began using horses. Note the dogs along for the hunt.

FIERY FURNACE

Return to the main road and continue three miles to the Fiery Furnace Viewpoint and Trailhead on the right. The Fiery Furnace gets its name from sandstone fins that turn flaming red on occasions when thin cloud cover at the horizon reflects the warm light of sunrise or sunset. Actually, the shady recesses provide a cool respite from the hot summer sun.

Closely packed sandstone fins form a maze of deep slots, with many arches and at least one natural bridge inside. Both for safety reasons, and to reduce impact on this sensitive area, hikers are encouraged to join a ranger-led hike. To visit the Fiery Furnace without a ranger, visitors must obtain a permit at the visitors center.

Rangers lead two- to three-hour hikes into the Fiery Furnace twice each day. Unlike most ranger-led activities, a fee is charged for these hikes ($10 adults, $5 children 6–12 and America the Beautiful Senior Pass holders). Group size is limited, and walks often fill a day or two in advance. Make reservations in person at the visitors center up to seven days in advance.

SKYLINE ARCH

This arch is on the right one mile past Sand Dune/Broken Arch Trailhead. In desert climates, erosion may proceed imperceptibly for centuries until a cataclysmic event happens. In 1940, a giant boulder fell from the opening of Skyline Arch, doubling the size of the arch in just seconds. The hole is now 45 feet high and 69 feet wide. A short trail leads to the base of the arch.

DEVILS GARDEN

The Devils Garden Trailhead, picnic area, and campground all lie near the end of the main park road. Devils Garden offers fine scenery and more arches than any other section of the park. The hiking trail leads past large sandstone fins to Landscape and six other named arches. Carry water if the weather is hot or if you might want to continue past the one-mile point at Landscape Arch. Adventurous hikers could spend days exploring the maze of canyons among the fins.

KLONDIKE BLUFFS AND TOWER ARCH

Relatively few visitors come to the spires, high bluffs, and fine arch in this northwestern section of the park. A fair-weather dirt road turns off the main drive 1.3 miles before Devils Garden Trailhead, winds down into Salt Valley, and heads northwest. After 7.5 miles, turn left on the road to Klondike Bluffs and proceed one mile to the Tower Arch Trailhead. These roads may be washboarded but are usually okay in dry weather for cars; don't drive on them if storms threaten. The trail to Tower Arch winds past the Marching Men and other rock formations; the distance is three miles round-trip. Alexander Ringhoffer, who discovered the arch in 1922, carved an inscription on the south column. The area can also be fun to explore off-trail (map and compass needed). Those with four-wheel-drive vehicles can drive close to the arch on a separate jeep road. Tower Arch has an opening 34 feet high by 92 feet wide. A tall monolith nearby gave the arch its name.

FOUR-WHEEL-DRIVE ROAD

A rough road near Tower Arch in the Klondike Bluffs turns southeast past **Eye of the Whale Arch** in Herdina Park to Balanced Rock on the main park road, 10.8 miles away. The road isn't particularly difficult for four-wheel-drive enthusiasts, although normal backcountry precautions should be taken. A steep sand hill north of Eye of the Whale Arch is difficult to climb for vehicles coming from Balanced Rock; it's better to drive from the Tower Arch area instead.

ARCHES

WHY ARE THERE ARCHES?

The park's distinctive arches are formed by an unusual combination of geologic forces. About 300 million years ago, evaporation of inland seas left behind a salt layer more than 3,000 feet thick in the Paradox Basin of this region. Sediments, including those that later became the arches, then covered the salt. Unequal pressures caused the salt to gradually flow upward in places, bending the overlying sediments as well. These upfolds, or anticlines, later collapsed when ground water dissolved the underlying salt. The faults and joints caused by the uplift and collapse opened the way for erosion to carve hundreds of freestanding fins. Alternate freezing and thawing action and exfoliation (flaking caused by expansion when water or frost penetrates the rock) continued to peel away more rock until holes formed in some of the fins. Rockfalls within the holes helped enlarge the arches. Nearly all arches in the park eroded out of Entrada sandstone.

Eventually all the present arches will collapse, but we should have plenty of new ones by the time that happens. The fins' uniform strength and hard upper surfaces have proved ideal for arch formation. Not every hole in the rock is an arch. The opening must be at least three feet in one direction, and light must be able to pass through. Although the term *windows* often refers to openings in large walls of rock, windows and arches are really the same. Water seeping through the sandstone from above has created a second type of arch – the pothole arch. You may also come across a few natural bridges cut from the rock by perennial water runoff.

A succession of rock layers are on display at Arches. The rocks that lie on top of the salt beds – the rocks you actually *see* at Arches – are mostly Entrada sandstone, which is a pretty general category of rock. Within this Entrada Formation are three distinct types of sandstone. The formation's dark red base layer is known as the Dewey Bridge member. It's softer than the formation's other sandstones and erodes easily. Dewey Bridge rocks are topped by the pinkish orange Slick Rock member, the park's most visible rocks. The Slick Rock layer is much harder than the Dewey Bridge, and the combination of the two layers – softer rocks overlaid by harder – is responsible for the differential erosion that forms hoodoos and precariously balanced rocks. The thin top layer of Entrada sandstone is called the Moab Tongue, a white rock similar to Navajo sandstone.

Recreation

Because of its great popularity and easy proximity to Moab, Arches sees a lot of visitors. However, most are content to drive the parkways and perhaps saunter to undemanding viewpoints. You can quickly leave the crowds behind by planning a hike to more outlying destinations. Arches's outback offers magnificent rewards for hikers willing to leave the pavement behind and get dusty on a backcountry trail.

HIKING

Established hiking trails lead to many fine arches and overlooks that can't be seen from the road. You're free to wander cross-country, too, but please stay on rock or in washes to avoid damaging the fragile cryptobiotic soils. Wear good walking shoes with rubber soles for travel across slickrock. The summer sun can be especially harsh on the unprepared hiker—don't forget water, a hat, and sunscreen. The desert rule is to carry at least one gallon of water per person for an all-day hike. Take a map and compass for off-trail hiking. Be cautious on the slickrock because the soft sandstone can crumble easily. Also, remember that it's easier to go up a steep slickrock slope than it is to come back down!

You can reach almost any spot in the park on a day hike, although you'll also find some good overnight camping possibilities. Areas for longer trips include Courthouse Wash in the southern part of the park and Salt Wash in the eastern part. All backpacking is done off-trail. A backcountry permit must be obtained from a ranger before camping in the backcountry.

Backcountry regulations prohibit fires and pets, and allow camping only out of sight of any road (at least one mile away) or trail (at least half a mile away) and at least 300 feet from a recognizable archaeological site or non-flowing water source.

Park Avenue

• Distance: 1 mile one-way

• Duration: 1 hour round-trip

• Elevation change: 320 feet

• Effort: easy–moderate

• Trailhead: Park Avenue or North Park Avenue Trailhead

Get an eyeful of massive stone formations and a feel for the natural history of the park on the easy to moderate Park Avenue trail. The Park Avenue Trailhead, just past the crest of the switchbacks that climb up into the park, is the best place to start. The vistas from here are especially dramatic: The Courthouse Towers, the Three Gossips, and other fanciful rock formations loom above a natural amphitheater. The trail drops into a narrow wash before traversing the park highway at the North Park Avenue Trailhead. Hikers can be dropped off at one trailhead and picked up a half hour later at the other.

The Windows

• Distance: 1-mile loop

• Duration: 1 hour round-trip

• Elevation change: 140 feet

• Effort: easy

• Trailhead: end of Windows Road

Ten miles into the park, just past the impossible-to-miss Balanced Rock, follow signs and a paved road to the Windows Section. A one-mile-round-trip loop along a sandy trail leads to the Windows—a cluster of enormous arches that are impossible to see from the road. Highlights include the **North** and **South Windows** and **Turret Arch.** Unmarked trails lead to vistas and scrambles along the stone faces that comprise the ridge. If this easy loop leaves you eager for more exploration in the area, a second trail departs from just past the Windows parking area and goes to **Double Arch.** This half-mile-long trail leads to two giant spans that are

MORMON TEA

Though it's not the showiest wildflower in the desert, Mormon tea *(Ephedra viridus)* is widespread across southern Utah, and very common in Arches. This broomlike plant is remarkably well adapted to the desert, and many desert-dwelling humans have adapted themselves to enjoy drinking it as a tea.

The branches contain chlorophyll and are able to conduct photosynthesis. The leaves are like tiny scales or bracts; their small size reduces the amount of moisture the plant loses to transpiration. Male and female flowers grow on separate plants.

Native Americans used this plant medicinally as a tea for stomach and bowel disorders as well as for colds, fever, and headaches. Some tribes used it to control bleeding and as a poultice for burns.

Mormon tea is related to Ma-huang, a Chinese herb that is traditionally used to treat hay fever. All parts of the plant contain a small amount of ephedrine, a stimulant that in large concentrations can be quite harmful. Pioneers in southern Utah were mostly Mormons, who are forbidden to drink coffee or similar stimulants. When they learned that drinking the boiled stems of *Ephedra viridus* gave them a mild lift, they approached Brigham Young, the head of the Latter-Day Saints. Young gave the tea his stamp of approval, and the plant's common name grew out of its widespread use by Mormons. (It's also sometimes known as Brigham tea.)

The tea itself is yellowish and, as one local put it, tastes something like what she imagined boiled socks would taste like. To increase the

Mormon tea in bloom

© PAUL LEVY

tea's palatability, it's often mixed with mint, lemon, and sugar or honey. Pioneers liked to add strawberry jam to their Mormon tea.

If you are tempted to try this tea for yourself, make certain not to harvest plants from a national forest. Women who are pregnant or nursing and people with high blood pressure, heart disease, diabetes, glaucoma, or any other health problems should definitely avoid even the small amounts of ephedra present in Mormon tea.

---

joined at one end. These easy trails are good for family groups because younger or more ambitious hikers can scramble to their hearts' content along rocky outcrops.

Delicate Arch Viewpoint

- Distance: 0.25 mile one-way
- Duration: 15–30 minutes
- Elevation change: 100 feet
- Effort: easy–moderate
- Trailhead: one mile past Wolfe Ranch, at end of Wolfe Ranch Road

If you don't have the time or the endurance for the relatively strenuous hike to Delicate Arch, you can view this astonishing arch from a distance at the Delicate Arch Viewpoint. From the viewing area, hikers can scramble up a steep trail to a rim with views across Cache Valley. Even though this is a short hike, it's a good place to wander around the slickrock for a while. It's especially nice to linger around sunset, when the arch captures the light and begins to glow. If you'd rather not scramble around on the slickrock, a short path leads about 100 yards from the parking area to a decent view of the arch.

◖ Delicate Arch Trail

- Distance: 1.5 miles one-way

- Duration: 2 hours

- Elevation change: 500 feet

- Effort: moderate–strenuous

- Trailhead: Wolfe Ranch

For those who are able, the hike to the base of Delicate Arch is one of the park's highlights. Shortly after the trail's start at Wolfe Ranch, a spur trail leads to some petroglyphs depicting horses and their riders and a few bighorn sheep.

Delicate Arch at the end of a 1.5-mile hike

Because of the horses, which didn't arrive in the area until the mid-1600s, these petroglyphs are believed to be the work of Utes.

The first stretch of the main trail is broad, flat, and not especially scenic, except for a good display of spring wildflowers. After about half an hour of hiking, the trail heads up onto the slickrock and the views open up, spanning across the park to the La Sal Mountains in the distance.

Just before the end of the trail, walk up to the small, decidedly un-delicate Frame Arch for a picture-perfect view of the final destination. The classic photo of Delicate Arch is taken late in the afternoon when the sandstone glows with golden hues. Standing at the base of Delicate Arch is a magical moment: The arch rises out of the barren, almost lunar, rock face, yet it seems ephemeral. Views from the arch over the Colorado River valley are amazing.

◖ Fiery Furnace Trail

- Distance: 2-mile loop

- Duration: 2–3 hours

- Elevation change: 250 feet

- Effort: moderate

- Trailhead: Fiery Furnace viewpoint

The Fiery Furnace area is open only to hikers with permits ($2) or to those joining a ranger-led hike. During summer, rangers offer daily two- to three-hour hikes into this unique area (mid-Mar–Oct.; $10 adults, $5 children 6–12 and America the Beautiful Senior Pass holders), and tickets are required. These hikes are popular and are often booked a couple of days in advance, so make reservations in person at the visitors' center up to one week before your planned hike.

Hiking in the Fiery Furnace is not along a trail; hikers navigate a maze of narrow sandstone canyons, and the route through the area is sometimes challenging, requiring hands-and-knees scrambling up cracks and ledges. Navigation is difficult: Route-finding can be

To explore the Fiery Furnace you must join a ranger-led hike.

tricky because what look like obvious paths often lead to dead ends. Drop-offs and ridges make straight-line travel impossible. It's easy to become disoriented. Even if you're an experienced hiker, the ranger-led hikes provide the best introduction to the Fiery Furnace.

Broken and Sand Dune Arches

- Distance: 0.5 mile one-way
- Duration: 45 minutes
- Elevation change: 140 feet
- Effort: easy
- Trailhead: on the right side of the road 2.4 miles past the Fiery Furnace turnoff

A short, sandy trail leads to small Sand Dune Arch (its opening is 8 feet high and 30 feet wide) tucked within fins. A longer trail (one mile round-trip) crosses a field to Broken Arch, which you can also see from the road. The opening in this arch is 43 feet high and 59 feet wide. Up close, you'll see that the arch

isn't really broken. These arches can also be reached by trail from near comfort station number three at Devils Garden Campground. Low-growing Canyonlands biscuitroot, found only in areas of Entrada sandstone, colonizes sand dunes. Hikers can protect the habitat of the biscuitroot and other fragile plants by keeping to washes or rock surfaces.

◖ Devils Garden Loop

- Distance: 7.2 miles round-trip
- Duration: 4 hours
- Elevation change: 350 feet
- Effort: strenuous
- Trailhead: Devils Garden

From the end of the paved park road, a full tour of Devils Garden leads to eight named arches and a vacation's-worth of scenic wonders. This is one of the park's most popular areas, with several shorter versions of the full loop hike that make the area accessible to nearly every hiker. Don't be shocked to find quite a crowd at the trailhead—it will most likely dissipate after the first two or three arches.

The first two arches are an easy walk from the trailhead and lie off a short side trail to the right. **Tunnel Arch** has a relatively symmetrical opening 22 feet high and 27 feet wide. The nearby **Pine Tree Arch** is named for a piñon pine that once grew inside; the arch has an opening 48 feet high and 46 feet wide.

Continue on the main trail to **Landscape Arch** (see separate listing). The trail narrows past Landscape Arch and continues to **Wall Arch,** in a long wall-like fin. A short side trail branches off to the left beyond Wall to **Partition Arch** and **Navajo Arch.** Partition was so named because a piece of rock divides the main opening from a smaller hole. Navajo Arch is a rock-shelter type; perhaps prehistoric Native Americans camped here. The main trail continues northwest and ends at **Double O Arch** (four miles round-trip from the trailhead). Double O has a large oval-shaped opening (45 feet high and 71 feet wide) and a smaller

ARCHES

hole underneath. **Dark Angel** is a distinctive rock pinnacle a quarter mile northwest; cairns mark the way. Another primitive trail loops back to Landscape Arch via **Fin Canyon.** This route goes through a different area of Devils Garden but adds about one mile to your trip (three miles back to the trailhead instead of two). Pay careful attention to the trail markers to avoid getting lost.

Landscape Arch

- Distance: 1 mile one-way
- Duration: 1 hour
- Elevation change: 60 feet
- Effort: easy
- Trailhead: Devils Garden Trailhead

Landscape Arch, with an incredible 306-foot span (six feet longer than a football field), is one of the longest unsupported rock spans in the world. It's also one of the park's more precarious arches to observe up close. The thin arch looks ready to collapse at any moment. Indeed, a spectacular rockfall from the arch on September 1, 1991, accelerated its disintegration, which is the eventual fate of every arch. Now the area directly underneath the arch is fenced off; when you look at the photos of the 1991 rockfall, you'll be happy to stand back a ways.

On the way to Landscape Arch, be sure to take the short side trails to Tunnel and Pine Tree Arches.

◖ Tower Arch Trail

- Distance: 1.75 miles one-way
- Duration: 2.5 hours
- Elevation change: 450 feet
- Effort: moderate–strenuous
- Trailhead: Klondike Bluffs parking area
- Directions: From the main park road, take Salt Valley Road (a dirt road, but usually fine for passenger cars) west 7.7 miles to the Klondike Bluffs turnoff.

Most park visitors don't venture into this area of sandstone fins and big dunes. It's a little bit like Devils Garden, but without the crowds.

After a short but steep climb, the trail levels out and opens up to views of Arches' distinctive sandstone fins and, in the distance, the La Sal and Abajo Mountains. The trail drops down to cross a couple of washes, then climbs onto the fin-studded slickrock Klondike Bluffs. Tower Arch is actually both an arch and a tower, and there's no mistaking the tower for just another big sandstone rock!

Because of the dirt-road access to this hike, it's best to skip it if there's been recent rain, or if rain is threatening.

BIKING

Cyclists *must* stick to established roads in the park. They also have to contend with heavy traffic on the narrow paved roads and dusty, washboard surfaces on the dirt roads. Beware of deep sand on the four-wheel-drive roads, traffic on the main park road, and summertime heat wherever you ride.

One good, not-too-hard ride is along the Willow Flats Road. Allow two or three hours for an out-and-back, starting from the Balanced Arch parking area and heading west.

Perhaps the best bet for relatively fit mountain bikers is the 24-mile ride to Tower Arch and back. From the Devils Garden parking area, ride out the Salt Valley Road (which can be rough). After about 7.5 miles, turn left onto a jeep road that leads to the "back door" to Tower Arch.

Nearby, Bureau of Land Management (BLM) and Canyonlands National Park areas offer world-class mountain biking.

CLIMBING

Rock climbers don't need a permit in Arches, although they should first discuss their plans with a ranger. Most features named on U.S. Geological Survey maps are *closed* to climbing. That means any of the arches and many of the most distinctive towers are off limits. There are still plenty of long-standing routes for advanced climbers to enjoy, although the rock in

Arches is sandier and softer than in other areas around Moab.

Several new climbing restrictions are in place, however. No new permanent climbing hardware may be installed in any fixed location. If an existing bolt or other hardware item is unsafe, it may be replaced. This effectively limits all technical climbing to existing routes or new routes not requiring placement of fixed anchors.

The most commonly climbed faces are along the sheer stone faces of Park Avenue. Another popular destination is Owl Rock, the owl-shaped small tower located in the Windows Section of the park. For more information on climbing in Arches, consult the bible of Moab-area climbing, *Desert Rock,* by Eric Bjørnstad, or ask for advice at **Pagan Mountaineering** (59 S. Main, 435/259-1117, www.paganmountaineering.com), a clothing and recreational gear store in Moab that also offers a climbing guide service.

Note that park officials are undertaking a study to develop a new Climbing Management Plan for Arches, which will likely be in place by summer 2008. The impetus for this new plan came from "unusual climbing activities [that] raised public interest and concern about issues associated with technical rock climbing," according to official statements. In May 2006, Dean Potter, a noted professional rock climber, made a controversial free-solo ascent of Delicate Arch (he had reportedly also made a highline walk between two of the park's Three Gossips a month earlier). These activities clearly contravene park climbing regulations and have apparently led park officials to start the process of creating the new climbing management plan. Check the park website to keep abreast of any further closures or restrictions to climbing in the park.

CAMPGROUNDS

Devils Garden Campground (elevation 5,355 feet, open year-round with water, $15) is near the end of the 18-mile scenic drive. It's an excellent place to camp, with some sites tucked under rock formations and others with great views, but it's *extremely* popular.

The well-organized traveler will plan accordingly and reserve a site in advance for nights March–October. Reservations (877/444-6777, www.recreation.gov, $9 booking fee in addition to camping fee) must be made no less than four days and no more than 240 days in advance. Not all sites are reservable; 24 remain open on a first-come, first-served basis. During the busy spring, summer, and fall seasons, campers without reservations should plan to queue up at the front door of the visitors center at 7:30 A.M. sharp for a chance to fill a campsite.

If you aren't able to score a coveted Arches campsite, all is not lost. There are many BLM campsites within an easy drive of the park. Try the string of primitive BLM campgrounds on Highway 313, just west of U.S. 191 and on the way to Canyonlands National Park's Island in the Sky District. Another cluster of BLM campgrounds is along the Colorado River on Highway 128, which heads northeast from U.S. 191 at the north end of Moab.

ARCHES

MOAB

By far the largest town in southeastern Utah, Moab (pop. 5,500) makes an excellent base for exploring Arches and Canyonlands National Parks and the surrounding canyon country. Moab lies near the Colorado River in a green valley enclosed by high, red sandstone cliffs. The biblical Moab was a kingdom at the edge of Zion, and early settlers must have felt themselves at the edge of their world, too, being so isolated from Salt Lake City—the Mormon city of Zion. Moab's existence on the fringe of Mormon culture and the sizable gentile population give the town a unique character.

In recent years, Moab has become nearly synonymous with mountain biking. The slickrock canyon country seems made for exploration by bike, and people come from all over the world to pedal the backcountry. River trips on the Colorado River are nearly as popular, and a host of other outdoor recreational diversions—from horseback riding to four-wheel jeep exploring to hot-air ballooning—combine to make Moab one of the most popular destinations in Utah.

Moab is also one of the most youthful and vibrant communities in the state; thousands of young people travel to Moab for the recreation, while hundreds of others work here as guides and outfitters. Tanned, fit, and Lycra-covered bodies are the norm here, and the town's brewpubs, bike shops, and cafés do a booming trade.

As Moab's popularity has grown, so have concerns that the town and the surrounding countryside are simply getting loved to death. The landscape has always been a staple in car ads (remember those Chevy pickups balanced on a

HIGHLIGHTS

◖ **Dan O'Laurie Museum:** This fascinating regional museum captures the long history of the Moab area, from dinosaurs to Native American habitation to mining boom, proving that there's a lot more to Moab than just mountain biking (page 218).

◖ **Corona Arch and Bowtie Arch Trail:** This hike doesn't require a lot of exertion, but there's plenty of payback! Three arches are visible from the short trail, including 140-foot-wide Corona Arch, as large as any in Arches National Park (page 222).

◖ **Fisher Towers:** These thin rock columns reach nearly 1,000 feet into the desert air just south of Highway 128, northeast of Moab. Hiking trails loop through the unworldly landscape, ringing the mastlike formations and leading to overlooks of rugged Onion Creek Canyon (page 224).

◖ **Slickrock Bike Trail:** The mountain-bike trail that put Moab on the map requires advanced biking skills and a good level of fitness. Even if you don't qualify on either count, take your bike for a spin along the 2.5-mile Slickrock Trail practice loop, which is a sampler of the challenges and thrills of the longer trail (page 226).

◖ **Air Tours:** It's hard to grasp the scale of Moab's canyon country without getting up above it. Local aviators offer flightseeing trips over Canyonlands National Park and other des-

tinations in southeastern Utah, providing the chance to see this amazing landscape from the viewpoint of an eagle (page 231).

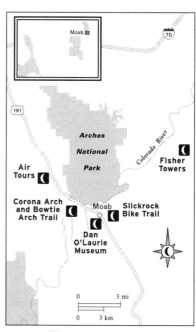

LOOK FOR ◖ TO FIND RECOMMENDED SIGHTS, ACTIVITIES, DINING, AND LODGING.

red-rock pinnacle?); now the landscape sells the "Just Do It" lifestyle for MTV, Nike, and other merchandisers of youth culture. On a busy day, hundreds of mountain bikers form queues to negotiate the trickier sections of the famed Slickrock Trail, and more than 20,000 people crowd into town on busy weekends to bike, hike, float, and party. As noted in an article in *Details* magazine, "Moab is pretty much the Fort Lauderdale of the intermountain West." Whether this old Mormon town and the delicate desert environment can endure such an onslaught of popularity is a question of increasing concern.

PLANNING YOUR TIME

While many people come to Moab because of what it's near, there's certainly enough to do in the town to justify adding an extra day to a park-focused itinerary just for exploring Moab and environs. It's easy to spend a few hours lounging by the hotel pool or shopping for books, crafts, and gifts, and the quality of the food and locally brewed beer has its own appeal, particularly after several days of driving the Utah outback.

Moab is also central for expeditions into the less regulated red-rock canyon country not

MOAB

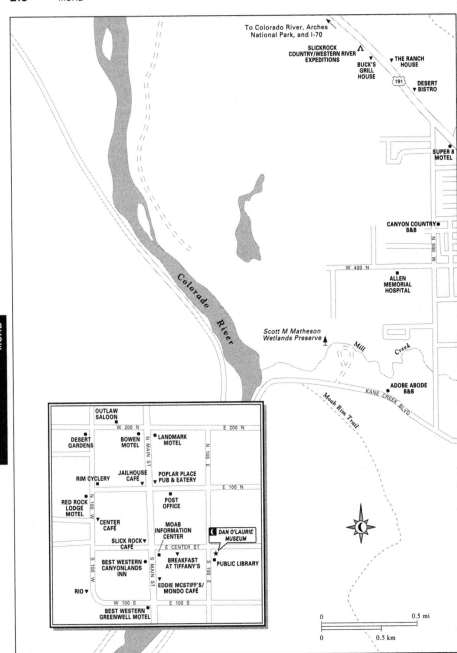

To Colorado River, Arches National Park, and I-70

SLICKROCK COUNTRY/WESTERN RIVER EXPEDITIONS

BUCK'S GRILL HOUSE

THE RANCH HOUSE

191

DESERT BISTRO

SUPER 8 MOTEL

CANYON COUNTRY B&B

N 500 W

W 400 N

ALLEN MEMORIAL HOSPITAL

Scott M Matheson Wetlands Preserve

Mill Creek

Colorado River

ADOBE ABODE B&B

KANE CREEK BLVD

Moab Rim Trail

OUTLAW SALOON

W 200 N

E 200 N

DESERT GARDENS

BOWEN MOTEL

LANDMARK MOTEL

N MAIN ST

N 100 E

RIM CYCLERY

JAILHOUSE CAFÉ

POPLAR PLACE PUB & EATERY

E 100 N

N 100 W

RED ROCK LODGE MOTEL

CENTER CAFÉ

POST OFFICE

MOAB INFORMATION CENTER

DAN O'LAURIE MUSEUM

SLICK ROCK CAFÉ

E CENTER ST

S MAIN ST

S 100 E

BEST WESTERN CANYONLANDS INN

BREAKFAST AT TIFFANY'S

PUBLIC LIBRARY

S 100 W

EDDIE MCSTIFF'S/ MONDO CAFÉ

RIO

W 100 S

E 100 S

BEST WESTERN GREENWELL MOTEL

0   0.5 mi

0   0.5 km

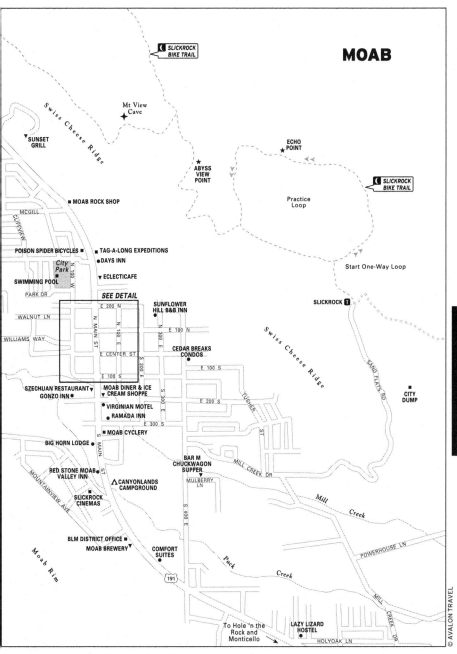

MOAB

MOAB

SLICKROCK BIKE TRAIL

Mt View Cave

Swiss Cheese Ridge

SUNSET GRILL

ECHO POINT

ABYSS VIEW POINT

SLICKROCK BIKE TRAIL

MOAB ROCK SHOP

Practice Loop

MCGILL

CLIFFVIEW

POISON SPIDER BICYCLES

TAG-A-LONG EXPEDITIONS

DAYS INN

City Park

N 100 W

ECLECTICAFE

Start One-Way Loop

SWIMMING POOL

PARK DR

SEE DETAIL

SLICKROCK

E 200 N

WALNUT LN

N MAIN ST

N 100 E

SUNFLOWER HILL B&B INN

N 300 E

E 100 N

WILLIAMS WAY

E CENTER ST

S 200 E

CEDAR BREAKS CONDOS

Swiss Cheese Ridge

E 100 S

E 100 S

SAND FLATS RD

CITY DUMP

SZECHUAN RESTAURANT
GONZO INN

MOAB DINER & ICE CREAM SHOPPE

S 300 E

E 200 S

TUSHER ST

VIRGINIAN MOTEL
RAMADA INN

E 300 S

MOAB CYCLERY

BIG HORN LODGE

S MAIN ST

BAR M CHUCKWAGON SUPPER

MILL CREEK DR

RED STONE MOAB VALLEY INN

CANYONLANDS CAMPGROUND

MULBERRY LN

Mill

MOUNTAINVIEW AVE

SLICKROCK CINEMAS

Creek

BLM DISTRICT OFFICE
MOAB BREWERY

S 400 E

Moab Rim

COMFORT SUITES

POWERHOUSE LN

Puck

MILL CREEK DR

191

Creek

To Hole 'n the Rock and Monticello

LAZY LIZARD HOSTEL

HOLYOAK LN

MOAB

© AVALON TRAVEL

included in the national parks. Take a break from exploring the parks themselves and devote a day to non-park adventures, such as jet-boat tours on the Colorado River, horseback rides in Castle Valley, ATV tours into the backcountry, or even wine-tasting local vintages.

Moab is the most hospitable town in this part of Utah, so don't blow right through. Take time to stop and enjoy its quirky charms.

SIGHTS

It's fair to say that Moab doesn't tempt travelers with a lot of traditional tourist establishments, but all you have to do is raise your eyes to the horizon. The locale is so striking that you'll want to get outdoors and explore, and the astonishing sights of Canyonlands and Arches national parks are just minutes from town. But there's nothing wrong with just enjoying the enthusiastic vibe of the town.

◖ Dan O'Laurie Museum

This regional museum (118 E. Center, 435/259-7985, www.grandcountyutah.net/museum.htm, 10 A.M.–6 P.M. Mon.–Fri. and noon–6 P.M. Sat.–Sun. in summer, 10 A.M.–3 P.M. Mon.–Fri. and noon–5 P.M.

THE ELK MOUNTAIN MISSION

The Old Spanish Trail, opened in 1829 between New Mexico and California, traveled north from Santa Fe into Utah, crossing the Colorado River near present-day Moab. The Mormons under Brigham Young reached Utah in 1847 and by the 1850s were establishing settlements across Utah. Young determined that a Mormon outpost was needed at the Colorado River crossing to control settlement and to proselytize the local Ute tribes.

In 1855, a group of 41 missionaries left the Wasatch Front to explore and build settlements in the Spanish Valley, where Moab now sits. In those days, travel in roadless Utah was challenging – entering Moab Canyon required that wagons be taken apart and lowered by rope down a precipice near today's entry gate to Arches National Park.

By July 15, 1855, the men and 75 head of cattle had arrived in Spanish Valley and construction began on a 64-square-foot stone fort called the Elk Mountain Mission (the fort's walls were north of today's downtown Moab, near the edge of the current Motel 6 parking lot). They also built a corral, planted various crops, and tried to establish friendships with the Ute natives, who controlled a large part of southern Utah. The Spanish Valley area had traditionally been used as a shared common ground for gathering and trading among the Native Americans, particularly the Utes and the Navajos.

Initially the Mormon missionaries found success, tending their abundant gardens and baptizing more than a dozen Utes. However, some of the Utes became concerned about the motives of the new settlers, and tensions between the tribe and the missionaries grew. By early fall, it had become increasingly difficult to keep the peace.

After the Utes started helping themselves to the Mormons' garden produce, such as melons and squash, events quickly escalated. On September 23, 1855, one of the Mormon missionaries was shot by a Ute and a fierce gun battle ensued at the fort. At least two Utes were killed and many more wounded during the hostilities. Two other Mormons, who were returning from a hunting trip, were ambushed and killed. The hay and cornfields surrounding the fort were set ablaze by the Utes.

The next morning, the remaining missionaries abandoned the fort, packing what they could and leaving behind five horses and 25 head of cattle. The three dead missionaries were buried within the walls of the fort.

The Elk Mountain Mission marked one of the rare failures of a Mormon settlement during the church's colonization of the West under Brigham Young. For more than two decades afterward, no permanent settlers lived in the Moab area.

Sat.–Sun. in winter; ages 12 and older $3, families $7) tells the story of Moab's and Grand County's past, from prehistoric and Ute artifacts to the explorations of Spanish missionaries. Photos and tools show pioneer Moab life, much of which centered on ranching or mining; here, too, you'll find displays of rocks and minerals, as well as bones of huge dinosaurs that once tracked across this land. A new resident is a replica of a 120-million-year-old *Gastonia burhei*, an 11-foot-long dinosaur that looks like a cross between a crocodile and a horned toad. Ask for a *Moab Area Historic Walking Tour* leaflet to learn about historic buildings in town.

Hole 'n the Rock

Albert Christensen worked 12 years to excavate his dream home within a sandstone monolith south of town (15 miles south of Moab on U.S. 191, 435/686-2250, www.theholeintherock .com, 8 A.M.–dusk daily in summer, opening at 9 A.M. daily in winter, adults $5, ages 5–10 $3.50). When he died in 1957, his wife Gladys worked another eight years to complete the project. The interior has notable touches like a 65-foot chimney drilled through the rock ceiling, paintings, taxidermy exhibits, and a lapidary room. The 5,000-square-foot, 14-room home is open for tours daily and offers a gift shop, petting zoo, picnic area, and snack bar.

Recreation

Moab sits at the center of some of the most picturesque landscapes in North America. Even the most casual visitor will want to get outdoors and explore the river canyons, natural arches, and mesas. Mountain biking and river tours are the recreational activities that get the most attention in the Moab area, although hikers, climbers, and horseback riders also find plenty to do. If you're less physically adventurous, you can explore the landscape on scenic flights or in Humvees, or follow old mining roads in four-wheel-drive vehicles to remote backcountry destinations.

It's easy to find outfitters and sports rental operations in Moab. It's the largest business segment in town. And there's a remarkable cohesion to the town's operations. It seems that everyone markets everybody else's excursions and services, so just ask the closest outfitter for whatever service you need, and chances are excellent you'll get hooked up with what you want.

The **Moab Information Center** (Main St. and Center St., 435/259-8825 or 800/635-6622, www.discovermoab.com, info@www.discover moab.com) is also a good source for information about the area's recreational options. The center has representatives of the National Park Service, the Bureau of Land Management (BLM), and the U.S. Forest Service on staff, and they can direct

you to the adventure of your liking. The center also has literature, books, and maps for sale. BLM officials can give locations of the developed and undeveloped designated campsites near the Moab Slickrock Bike Trail, Kane Creek, and along the Colorado River; you must use the designated sites in these areas. In addition, **Moab Arts and Recreation** (111 East 100 North, 435/259-6272) sponsors year-round activities for kids; you don't need to be a resident to take part.

To reach most of Moab's prime hiking trails requires a short drive to trailheads. For more options, pick up the *Moab Area Hiking Trails* brochure at the visitors center, and turn to the chapters on Arches and Canyonlands National Parks.

HIKING FROM KANE CREEK SCENIC DRIVE AND U.S. 191 SOUTH

The high cliffs just southwest of town provide fine views of the Moab Valley, highlands of Arches National Park, and the La Sal Mountains.

Moab Rim Trail

• Distance: 6 miles round-trip

MOAB

- Duration: 4 hours round-trip
- Elevation change: 940 feet
- Effort: moderate
- Trailhead: on Kane Creek Boulevard, 2.6 miles northwest of its intersection with U.S. 191 in Moab

If you're hiking, expect to share this route with mountain bikers and four-wheel-drive enthusiasts. The trail climbs northeast 1.5 miles along tilted rock strata of the Kayenta Formation to the top of the plateau west of Moab, with the first of several great views over town and the Spanish Valley. Once on top, hikers can follow jeep roads southeast to Hidden Valley Trail, which descends to U.S. 191 south of Moab—a 5.5-mile trip one-way. Experienced hikers can also head south from the rim to **Behind the Rocks,** a fantastic maze of sandstone fins.

Hidden Valley Trail

- Distance: 2.3 miles one-way to Behind the Rocks overlook
- Duration: 3 hours
- Elevation change: 680 feet

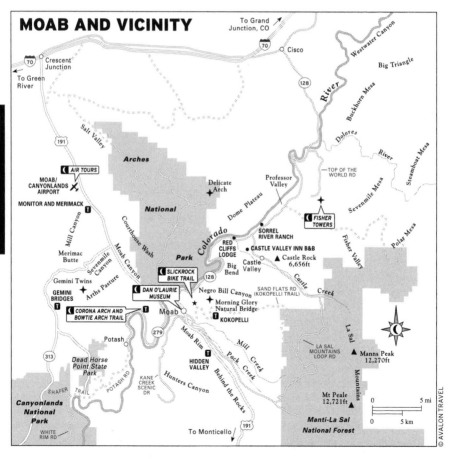

MOAB AND VICINITY

- Effort: moderate
- Trailhead: 3 miles south from Moab on U.S. 191 and right onto Angel Rock Road. After two blocks, turn right onto Rimrock Road and drive to the parking area.

ODD FORMATIONS BEHIND THE ROCKS

A look at the topographic map will show that something strange is going on in the area called **Behind the Rocks.** Massive fins of Navajo sandstone, 100-500 feet high, 50-200 feet thick, and up to one-half-mile long cover a large area. Narrow vertical cracks, sometimes only a few feet wide, separate the fins. The concentration of arches in the area is similar to that in Arches National Park, with over 20 major, named arches and more being discovered each year. Where canyon drainages penetrate the sandstone, pour-offs form into 400- to 1,000-foot-deep, sheer-walled canyons, often exposing perennial springs at the bottom. Behind the Rocks was inhabited extensively by the Anasazi and Fremont people, the two cultures apparently overlapping here. Petroglyph panels, habitation caves, stone ruins, and middens abound throughout the area.

No maintained trails exist, and some routes require technical climbing skills. The maze offers endless routes for exploration. If you get lost (which is very easy to do), remember that the fins are oriented east-west; the rim of the Colorado River Canyon is reached by going west, and Spanish Valley is reached by going east. Bring plenty of water, a topographic map (Moab 7.5-minute), and a compass. Access routes are Moab Rim and Hidden Valley Trails (from the north and east) and Pritchett Canyon (from the west and south). Although it is only a couple of miles from Moab, Behind the Rocks seems a world away. The BLM is considering a possible wilderness designation to protect the solitude and character of this strange country.

You'll see not only a "hidden valley" from this trail but also panoramas of the Moab area and the Behind the Rocks area. The trail ascends a series of switchbacks to a broad shelf below the Moab Rim, then follows the shelf (hidden valley) to the northwest. It then crosses a low pass and follows a second shelf in the same direction. Near the end of the second shelf, the trail turns left to a divide, where you can see a portion of the remarkable fins of Behind the Rocks. The trail continues one-third mile from the divide down to the end of the Moab Rim Trail, with the possibility of loop trails. Instead of turning left to the divide, you can make a short side trip (no trail) to the right for views of Moab.

Hunters Canyon

- Distance: 4 miles round-trip
- Duration: allow 4 hours round-trip
- Elevation change: 240 feet
- Effort: moderate
- Trailhead: on Kane Creek Canyon Road 7.5 miles west of its intersection with U.S. 191 (Hunters Canyon is on the left, one mile beyond the switchbacks).

Hikers along Hunters Canyon enjoy seeing a rock arch and other rock formations in the canyon walls and the lush vegetation along the creek. Off-road vehicles have made tracks a short way up, then you'll be walking, mostly along the creek bed. Short sections of trail lead around thickets of tamarisk and other water-loving plants. Look for Hunters Arch on the right about half a mile up. Most of the water in Hunters Canyon comes from a deep pool surrounded by hanging gardens of maidenhair fern. A dry fall and a small natural bridge lie above the pool. This pretty spot marks the hike's three-mile point and an elevation gain of 240 feet. At this point the hike becomes very brushy. To reach the trailhead from Moab, drive eight miles on Kane Creek Boulevard along the Colorado River and up Kane Creek Canyon. The road is asphalted where it fords

MOAB

Hunters Creek, but the asphalt is usually covered with dirt washed over it by the creek.

You can make a longer hike by going up Hunters Canyon and descending on Pritchett Canyon Road. The road crosses the normally dry creek bed just upstream from the deep pool. To bypass the dry fall above the pool, backtrack 300 feet down the canyon and rock-scramble up a short, steep slope—on your right heading upstream. At a junction just east of there, a jeep road along the north rim of Hunters Canyon meets Pritchett Canyon Road. Walk northeast one-half mile on Pritchett Canyon Road to a spur trail on the left leading to Pritchett Arch. Then continue 4.5 miles on Pritchett Canyon Road to Kane Creek Boulevard. This country is more open and desertlike than Hunters Canyon. A 3.2-mile car shuttle or hike is required for the return to Hunters Canyon Trailhead.

HIKING FROM HIGHWAY 279
Portal Overlook Trail

- Distance: 2 miles to Portal Overlook

- Duration: 3 hours round-trip

- Elevation change: 980 feet

- Effort: moderate

- Trailhead: at JayCee Park Recreation Site on Highway 279, 4.2 miles west of the Highway 279/U.S. 191 junction

The trail switchbacks up a slope, then follows a sloping sandstone ledge of the Kayenta Formation to an overlook. A panorama (the "portal") takes in the Colorado River, Moab Valley, Arches National Park, and the La Sal Mountains. This trail is a twin of the Moab Rim Trail across the river. Expect to share it with many mountain bikers.

◖ Corona Arch and Bowtie Arch Trail

- Distance: 1.5 miles one-way

- Duration: 2 hours round-trip

- Elevation change: 200 feet

- Effort: moderate

- Trailhead: on Highway 279, 10 miles west of the Highway 279/U.S. 191 junction

If you have time for only one hike in the Moab area, this one is especially recommended. The trail leads across slickrock country to two impressive arches. You can't see them from the road, although a third arch—Pinto—is visible. The trail climbs up from the parking area, crosses rail tracks, and follows a jeep road and a small wash to an ancient gravel bar. Pinto (or Gold Bar) Arch stands to the left, although there's no trail to it. Follow cairns to Corona and Bowtie. Handrails and a ladder help in the few steep spots.

Despite being only a few hundred yards apart, each arch has a completely different character and history. Bowtie formed when a pothole in the cliffs above met a cave underneath. It used to be called Paul Bunyan's Potty before that name was appropriated for an arch in Canyonlands National Park. The hole is about 30 feet in diameter. Corona Arch, reminiscent of the larger Rainbow Bridge, eroded out of a sandstone fin. The graceful span is 140 feet long and 105 feet high. Both arches are composed of Navajo sandstone.

HIKING OFF HIGHWAY 128
Negro Bill Canyon

- Distance: 2 miles to Morning Glory Bridge

- Duration: 4 hours round trip

- Elevation change: 330 feet

- Effort: moderate

- Trailhead: on Highway 128, three miles east of junction with U.S. 191

One of the most popular hiking destinations in the Moab Area, the Negro Bill Canyon trail follows a lively stream pooled by beavers and surrounded by abundant greenery and sheer cliffs. The high point of the hike is Morning Glory Natural Bridge, the sixth-longest natural rock span in the country at 243 feet. The

ROCK ART AROUND MOAB

The fertile valley around Moab has been home to humans for thousands of years. Prehistoric Fremont and Anasazi people once lived and farmed in the bottoms of the canyons around Moab. Their rock art, granaries, and dwellings can still be seen here. Nomadic Utes had replaced the earlier groups by the time the first white settlers arrived. They left fewer signs of settlement, but added their artistry to the area's rock-art panels. You don't need to travel far to see excellent examples of native pictographs and petroglyphs.

Golf Course Rock Art Site: Take U.S. 191 south to the Moab Golf Course (approximately 4 miles from the corner of Main and Center in downtown Moab). Turn left and proceed to Spanish Trail Road. Approximately one mile past the fire station, turn right onto Westwater Drive. Proceed half a mile to a small pullout on the left-hand side of the road. Here, an area approximately 30 by 90 feet is covered with human and animal figures, including "Moab Man" and what is popularly referred to as the reindeer and sled.

Kane Creek Boulevard Sites: Kane Creek Boulevard (south of downtown Moab, watch for the McDonald's) follows the Colorado River and leads to a number of excellent rock-art sites. From the junction with U.S. 191 turn west and proceed 0.8 mile to the intersection of Kane Creek Drive and 500 West.

Stay left and continue along Kane Creek Drive approximately 2.3 miles to the mouth of Moon Flower Canyon. Along the rock cliff just beyond the canyon, you will see a rock-art panel behind a chain-link fence (vandalism has been a problem). Continue another 1.2 miles to another rock-art panel, where a huge rock surface streaked with desert varnish is covered with bighorn sheep, snakes, and human forms. For a unique rock-art image, continue on Kane Creek Boulevard past the cattle guard, where the road turns from pavement to graded gravel road. After traveling 1.7 miles from the previous site, or a total of 5.3 miles from the intersection of Kane Creek Drive and 500 West, watch for two pullouts. Down the slope from the road is a large boulder with rock art on all four sides. The most amazing image is of a woman giving birth.

Courthouse Wash Site Although this site is located within Arches National Park, it is accessed from a parking lot off U.S. 191 just north of the Colorado River bridge, one mile north of Moab. A half-mile hike leads to the panel, which is almost 19 feet high and 52 feet long. It has both pictographs and petroglyphs with figures resembling ghostly humans, bighorn sheep, scorpions, and a large beaked bird.

A *Rock Art Auto Tour* brochure is available at the Moab Information Center in Moab.

MOAB

---

trailhead is on the right just after crossing a concrete bridge three miles from U.S. 191. The trail leads up the canyon, along the creek in some places, high on the banks in others.

To see Morning Glory Natural Bridge, head two miles up the main canyon to the second side canyon on the right, then follow a good side trail for half a mile up to the long, slender bridge. The spring and small pool underneath keep the air cool even in summer; ferns, columbines, and poison ivy grow here. William Granstaff was a mulatto who lived in the area about 1877–1881. Modern sensibilities have changed his nickname to "Negro Bill."

Experienced hikers can continue up the main canyon about eight miles and rock-scramble (no trail) up the right side, then drop into Rill Creek, which leads to the North Fork of Mill Creek and into Moab. The total distance is about 16 miles one-way; you'll have to find your own way between canyons. The upper Negro Bill and Rill Canyons can also be reached from Sand Flats Road. The Moab and Castle Valley 15-minute and Moab 1:100,000 topographic maps cover the route. This would be a good overnight trip, although fast hikers have done it in a day. Expect to do some wading and rock-scrambling. Water from the creeks and springs is available in both canyon systems, but be sure to purify it first.

A car shuttle is necessary between the Negro Bill and Mill Creek Trailheads. You can reach Mill Creek from the end of Powerhouse Lane on the east edge of Moab (see the Moab map), but *don't park here.* Vehicle break-ins are a serious problem. Either have someone meet you or drop you off here or park closer to town near houses. A hike up the North Fork offers very pretty scenery. A deep pool and waterfall lie three-quarters of a mile upstream; follow Mill Creek upstream and take the left (north) fork. Negro Bill and Mill Creek Canyons are BLM wilderness study areas.

◖ Fisher Towers

- Distance: 2.2 miles one-way to ridge at trail's end

- Duration: 4 hours round-trip.

- Elevation change: 670 feet

- Effort: moderate

- Trailhead: off Highway 128. At 21 miles east of the Utah 128/U.S. 191 junction, turn right and go 2.2 miles on an improved dirt road to a parking lot.

These spires of dark red sandstone rise 900 feet above Professor Valley. You can hike around the base of these needle rocks on a trail accessed from the BLM picnic area. From the parking lot, the trail goes down a short set of steps and then runs to the left out onto a small slickrock-covered ridge. Follow the ridge away from the main cliffs until just after it narrows and then go left into the ravine through a small cut in the ridge. From the bottom of the ravine, the trail heads steeply up and then begins to wind directly beneath the Fisher Towers. After swinging around the largest tower, the Titan, the trail ascends and ends on a ridge with a panoramic view. Carry water, as much of the trail is exposed and is frequently quite hot.

© W. C. MCRAE

The Fisher Towers are nearly 1,000 feet tall.

HIKING NORTH OF MOAB, OFF U.S. 191
Mill Canyon Dinosaur Trail

- Distance: 0.5 mile round-trip

- Duration: 1 hour

- Elevation change: 50 feet

- Effort: easy

- Trailhead: Drive 15 miles north of Moab on U.S. 191, then turn left at an intersection just north of Milepost 141. Cross the railroad tracks and continue two miles on a dirt road to the Dinosaur Trailhead.

The short Mill Canyon Dinosaur Trail, with numbered stops, identifies the bones of dinosaurs that lived here 150 million years ago. You'll see fossilized wood and dinosaur footprints, too. Pick up the brochure from the Moab Information Center or at the trailhead.

You'll find many other points of interest nearby. A copper mill and tailings dating from the late 1800s lie across the canyon. Half-

MOAB

way Stage Station ruins, where travelers once stopped on the Thompson-to-Moab run, are a short distance down the other road fork. Jeepers and mountain bikers can do a 13- to 14-mile loop to Monitor and Merrimac Buttes (an information sign just off U.S. 191 has a map and details).

BIKING

Moab is the West's most noted mountain-bike destination. In addition to riding the famed and challenging slickrock trails (slickrock is the exposed sandstone that composes much of the land's surface here) that wind through astonishing desert landscapes, cyclists can pedal through alpine meadows in the La Sal Mountains or take nearly abandoned four-wheel-drive tracks into the surrounding backcountry. Beware: The most famous trails—like the Slickrock Bike Trail—are not for beginners. Other trails are better matched to the skills of novices.

It's a good idea to read up on Moab-area trails before planning a trip here (heaps of books and pamphlets are available). You can also hire an outfitter to teach you about the special skills needed to mountain-bike in slickrock country, or join a guided tour. A good place to start is Trails Illustrated's *Bike Map 501*, which covers the Moab area and has mountain-bike routes color-coded according to difficulty. Or pick up a *Moab Area Mountain Bike Trails* map at the Moab Information Center.

Most people come to Moab to mountain-bike between mid-March and late May, and then again in the fall, from mid-September to the end of October. Unless you are an early riser, summer is simply too hot for extended bike touring in these desert canyons. Be prepared for crowds, especially in mid-March, during spring break. The Slickrock Trail alone has been known to attract more than 150,000 riders per year.

MOAB

MOUNTAIN BIKE ETIQUETTE

When mountain biking in the Moab area, don't expect an instant wilderness experience. Because of the popularity of the routes, the fragile desert environment is under quite a bit of stress, and you'll need to be considerate of the thousands of other people who share the trails. By keeping these rules in mind, you'll help keep Moab from being loved to death.

• **Ride only on open roads and trails.** Much of the desert consists of extremely fragile plant and animal ecosystems, and riding recklessly through cryptobiotic soils can destroy desert life and lead to erosion. If you pioneer a trail, chances are someone else will follow the tracks, leading to ever more destruction.

• **Protect and conserve scarce water sources.** Don't wash, swim, walk, or bike through potholes, and camp well away from isolated streams and water holes. The addition of your insect repellent, body oils, suntan lotion, or lubrication from your bike can destroy the thronging life of a pothole.

Camping right next to a remote stream can deprive shy desert wildlife of life-giving water access.

• **Leave all Native American sites and artifacts as you find them.** First, it's against the law to disturb antiquities; second, it's stupid. Enjoy looking at rock art, but don't touch the images – body oils hasten their deterioration. Don't even think about taking potshards, arrowheads, or artifacts from where you find them. Leave them for others to enjoy or for archaeologists to decipher.

• **Dispose of solid human waste thoughtfully.** The desert can't easily absorb human fecal matter. Desert soils have few microorganisms to break down organic material, and, simply put, mummified turds can last for years. Be sure to bury human solid waste at least 6-12 inches deep in sand and at least 200 feet away from streams and water sources. Pack out toilet paper in plastic bags.

If you've never biked on slickrock or in the desert, here are a few basic guidelines. Take care if venturing off a trail—it's a long way down some of the sheer cliff faces! A trail's steep slopes and sharp turns can be tricky, so a helmet is a must. Knee pads and riding gloves also protect from scrapes and bruises. Fat bald tires work best on the rock; partially deflated knobby tires do almost as well. Carry plenty of water—one gallon in summer, half a gallon in cooler months. Tiny plant associations, which live in fragile cryptobiotic soil, don't want you tearing through their homes; stay on the rock and avoid sandy areas.

Dozens of trails thread the Moab area; some of the best and most noted are described as follows.

◼ Slickrock Bike Trail

Undulating slickrock just east of Moab challenges even the best mountain-bike riders; this is not an area in which to learn riding skills. Originally, motorcyclists laid out this route, although now about 99 percent of riders rely on leg and lung power. The practice loop near the beginning allows first-time visitors a chance to get a feel for the slickrock. The "trail" consists only of painted white lines. Riders following it have less chance of getting lost or finding themselves in hazardous areas. Plan on about five hours to do the 9.6-mile main loop, and expect to do some walking.

Side trails lead to viewpoints overlooking Moab, the Colorado River, and arms of Negro Bill Canyon. Panoramas of the surrounding canyon country and the La Sal Mountains add to the pleasure of biking.

To reach the trailhead from Main Street in Moab, turn east 0.4 mile on 300 South, turn right 0.1 mile on 400 East, turn left (east) 0.5 mile on Mill Creek Drive, then left 2.5 miles on Sand Flats Road.

The practice loop also makes an enjoyable 2.5-mile hike. Steep drop-offs into the tributaries of Negro Bill Canyon offer breathtaking views. It's best to walk off to the side of the white lines marking the route. You'll reach the practice loop a quarter mile from the trailhead.

BIKING

More than any other recreational activity, mountain biking has put Utah on the map. Trails in Slickrock Canyon country near Moab attract more than 150,000 biking enthusiasts annually, and now nearly all corners of the state promote their old Forest Service or mining roads as a biking paradise.

Although mountain bikes are prohibited on national park trails, there's almost always great biking just outside the park boundaries. Both Canyonlands and Grand Staircase-Escalante National Monument are laced with dirt roads and jeep tracks ideal for mountain biking.

A good general resource is the *Bicycle Utah Vacation Guide*, which gives general information about bike paths throughout Utah and listings of tour operators, related organizations, and businesses, available free from Bicycle Utah (P.O. Box 738, Park City, UT 84060, 435/649-5806, www.bicycleutah.com).

In general, Utah summers are too hot for mountain biking. The peak season in Moab runs March-May and again September-November.

Kokopelli's Trail

Mountain bikers have linked together a series of back roads through the magical canyons of eastern Utah and western Colorado. You can start on Sand Flats Road in Moab and ride east to Castle Valley (21.1 miles), Fisher Valley (44.9 miles), Dewey Bridge (62.9 miles), Cisco Boat Landing (83.5 miles), Rabbit Valley (108 miles), and Loma (140 miles). Lots of optional routes and access points allow for many possibilities. Campsites along the trail have tables, grills, and outhouses. See *The Utah-Colorado Mountain Bike Trail System, Route 1—Moab to Loma,* by Peggy Utesch, for detailed descriptions. An excellent brochure, *Kokopelli's Trail Map,* is available free at the Moab Information Center.

Gemini Bridges (Bull Canyon) Trail

This 14-mile trail passes through tremendous natural rock arches and the slickrock fins of the Wingate Formation, making this one of the most scenic of Moab-area trails; it's also one of the more moderate trails in terms of necessary skill and fitness. The trail begins 12.5 miles up Highway 313 (the access road to Dead Horse Point State Park), a total of 21 miles—all uphill—from Moab, so you may want to consider a shuttle or arrange a drop-off. Alternatively, a new bike path parallels U.S. 191 from the Colorado River Bridge north of Moab to Highway 313, making this portion of the ride much less stressful, since you don't have to share the road with RVs.

Monitor and Merrimack Trail

A good introduction to the varied terrains of the Moab area, the 13.2-mile Monitor and Merrimack Trail also includes a trip to a dinosaur fossil bed. The trail climbs through open desert and up Usher Canyon, then explores red sandstone towers and buttes across slickrock before dropping down Mill Canyon. At the base of the canyon, you can leave your bike and hike the Mill Canyon Dinosaur Trail before completing the loop to the parking area. Reach the trailhead by traveling 15 miles north of Moab on U.S. 191.

Tours and Rentals

Most of the bicycle rental shops in Moab offer day-long mountain bike excursions, while outfitters offer multiday tours that vary in price depending on the difficulty of the trail and the degree of comfort involved. The charge for these trips is usually between $125–150 per day, including food and shuttles. Be sure to inquire whether rates include bike rental.

Dreamrides Mountainbike Tours (P.O. Box 1137, Moab, UT 84532, 435/259-6419, www .dreamride.com) focuses on leading small, customized group tours. Most packages are three- or five-day tours at roughly $150–200 per day, accommodations extra. **Rim Tours** (1233 S. U.S. 191, 435/259-5223 or 800/626-7335, www.rimtours.com) offers several half-day

A popular mountain bike trail leads to Monitor and Merimack mesas.

(around $85 with two or more cyclists), full-day (around $110 with two or more cyclists), and multiday trips. **Escape Adventures** (operated out of Moab Cyclery, 391 S. Main St., 435/259-7423 or 800/559-1978, www.escape adventures.com) leads multiday trips on mountain bikes; some of the tours combine cycling with rafting, climbing and hiking.

Western Spirit Cycling (478 Mill Creek Dr., 435/259-8732 or 800/845-2453, www.western spirit.com) offers 25 different bicycle tours in the western United States, with about one-third in Utah. Moab-area trips include the White Rim, the Maze, and the Kokopelli Trail.

Rim Cyclery (94 West 100 North, 435/259-5333 or 888/304-8219, www.rimcyclery.com) is Moab's oldest bike and outdoor gear store, offering mountain-bike sales, rentals, and service. Mountain-bike rentals and tours are also available at **Moab Cyclery** (391 S. Main St., 435/259-7423 or 800/559-1978, www.moab cyclery.com) and **Poison Spider Bicycles** (497 N. Main St., 435/259-7882 or 800/635-1792, www.poisonspiderbicycles.com). Expect to pay about $45 per day to rent a mountain bike and about $75–125 to join a group tour.

Shuttle Services

Many mountain-bike trails are essentially one-way, and unless you want to cycle back the way you came, you'll need to arrange a shuttle service to pick you up and bring you back to Moab or your vehicle. Also, if you don't have a vehicle or a bike rack, you will need to use a shuttle service to get to more distant trailheads. **Roadrunner Shuttle** (435/259-9402, www.roadrunnershuttle.com) and **Acme Bike Shuttle** (435/260-2534) both operate shuttle services; depending on distance, the usual fare runs $15–$25 per person. Both companies also shuttle hikers to trailheads or pick up rafters. Roadrunner also serves as a taxi service for groups.

RAFTING AND BOATING

Even a visitor with a tight schedule can get out and enjoy the canyon country on rafts and other watercraft. Outfitters offer both laid-back and exhilarating day trips, which usually require little advance planning. Longer, mul-tiday trips include gentle canoe paddles along the placid Green River and thrilling expeditions down the Colorado River.

You'll need to reserve well in advance for most of the longer trips because the BLM and the National Park Service limit the numbers of trips through the backcountry, and space, especially in high season, is at a premium. Experienced rafters can also plan their own unguided trips, although you'll need a permit for all areas except for the day-long Fisher Towers float upstream from Moab.

The rafting season runs April through September, and jet-boat tours run February through November. Contact the Moab Information Center or the National Park Service office for lists or brochures of tour operators; independent river-runners can also visit the center for Colorado River information, although you'll have to pick up permits from the BLM or national parks offices. Most river-runners obtain their permits by applying in January and February for a March drawing; the Moab Information Center's BLM ranger can advise on this process and provide the latest information about available cancellations.

Rafting and Kayaking Locations

For most of the following, full-day rates include lunch and beverages, while part-day trips include just lemonade and soft drinks. On overnight trips you'll sleep in tents in backcountry campgrounds.

The **Colorado River** offers several exciting options. The most popular day-run near Moab starts upstream near Fisher Towers and bounces through several moderate rapids on the way back to town. Full-day raft trips from Fisher Towers to near Moab generally cost $48–55 per person. Half-day trips run over much the same stretch of river (no lunch, though) and cost around $35–50 per adult.

For a more adventurous rafting trip, the Colorado's rugged **Westwater Canyon** offers lots of white water and several class III–IV rapids near the Utah-Colorado border. These long day trips are more expensive, typically $125–

© W. C. MCRAE

Colorado River Canyon, just outside Moab

and whether you fly, hike, or drive out at the end of the trip.

The **Green River** also offers rafting and canoeing opportunities, although they are milder than those on the Colorado. Trips on the Green make good family outings. Most trips require five days, leaving from the town of Green River and taking out at Mineral Bottom, just before Canyonlands National Park. Highlights of the Green River include Labyrinth Canyon and Bowknot Bend. Costs range $600–850 for a five-day rafting trip.

Rafting or Kayaking on Your Own

The Fisher Towers section of the Colorado is gentle enough for amateur rafters to negotiate on their own. Rent a raft or kayak from one of the rafting outfitters listed in the following section—**Canyon Voyages** and **Navtec Expeditions** are two local rafting companies that rent rafts and kayaks for those who would rather organize their own river adventure. A popular one-day raft trip with mild rapids begins from the Hittle Bottom Recreation Site, 23.5 miles up Highway 128 near Fisher Towers, and ends 14 river miles downstream at Take-Out Beach, 10.3 miles up Highway 128 from U.S. 191. You can rent rafts and the mandatory life jackets in Moab, and you won't need a permit on this section of river.

Experienced white-water rafters with permits can put in at the BLM's Westwater Ranger Station in Utah or at the Loma boat launch in Colorado. A start at Loma adds a day or two to the trip and the sights of Horsethief and Ruby Canyons. Normal takeout is at Cisco, although it's possible to continue 16 miles on slow-moving water through open country to Dewey Bridge.

Daily raft rentals begin at $85 or so; kayaks rent for $35.

Rafting Outfitters

Moab is full of river-trip companies, and most offer a variety of day and multiday trips; in addition, many will combine raft trips with biking, horseback riding, hiking, or four-wheel-drive excursions. Call for brochures or

140 a day. The Westwater Canyon is also often offered as part of multiday adventure packages. The **Dolores River** joins the Colorado about two miles upstream from Dewey Bridge, near the Colorado border. The Dolores River offers exciting white water in a narrow canyon during the spring runoff; the season is short, though, and the river is too low to run by mid-June. With plenty of class III and IV rapids, this trip usually takes two to four days and costs around $400–$700 per person.

The **Cataract Canyon** section of the Colorado River, which begins south of the river's confluence with the Green River and extends to the backwater of Lake Powell, usually requires four days of rafting to complete. However, if you're in a hurry, some outfitters offer time-saving trips that motor (not float) through placid water and slow down only to shoot rapids, enabling these trips to conclude in as little as two days. This is the wildest white water in the Moab area, with big, boiling class III and IV rapids. Costs range $600–1000, depending on what kind of craft, the number of days,

MOAB

check out the many websites at www.discover moab.com/tour.htm. The list below includes major outfitters offering a variety of rafting options. Most of them lead trips to the main river destinations on the Colorado and Green Rivers as well as other rivers in Utah and the West. Inquire about natural-history or petroglyph tours, if these specialty trips interest you.

- **Western River Expeditions,** 435/259-7019 or 866/904-1163, www.westernriver.com

- **Tag-A-Long Expeditions,** 435/259-8946 or 800/453-3292, www.tagalong.com

- **Navtec Expeditions,** 321 N. Main St., 435/259-7983 or 800/833-1278, www.navtec.com

- **Canyon Voyages,** 211 N. Main St., 435/259-6007 or 800/733-6007, www.canyonvoyages.com

- **Adrift Adventures,** 435/259-8594 or 800/874-4483, www.adrift.net

- **Sheri Griffith Expeditions,** 503/259-8229 or 800/332-2439, www.griffithexp.com

Canoeing

Canoeists can also sample the calm waters of the Green River on multiday excursions with **Red River Canoe Company** (497 N. Main St., 800/753-8216, www.redriver canoe.com). It runs scheduled trips to four sections of the river. Red River Canoe also offers trips to calmer stretches of the Colorado and Dolores Rivers. The company also conducts white-water canoe workshops on the Colorado's Professor Valley and combination canoe-and-mountain bike trips. Guided trips range $135–150 per person per day. Red River also rents canoes for around $35 per day including necessary equipment.

Jet-Boat and Motorboat

Guided jet-boat excursions through Canyonlands National Park start around $70 for a half-day trip. **Tag-A-Long Expeditions** and **Adrift Adventures** (see *Rafting Outfitters* for contact information) both offer half-

day trips and full-day combination jet-boat/jeep excursions.

Canyonlands by Night tours leave at sunset in an open motorboat and go several miles upstream on the Colorado River; a guide points out canyon features. The sound and light show begins on the way back; music and historic narration accompany the play of lights on canyon walls ($49 adults, $39 ages 4–12; boats run Apr.–mid-Oct). Package tours with chuckwagon dinners are available. Reservations are a good idea because the boat fills up fast. Trips depart from the Spanish mission–style office just north of Moab, across the Colorado River (435/259-5261, www.canyonlandsbynight.com).

FOUR-WHEEL TOURING

Road tours offer visitors a special opportunity to view unique canyonland arches and spires, indigenous rock art, and wildlife. An interpretive brochure at the Moab Information Center outlines the Moab Area Rock Art Auto Tour, which routes motorists to petroglyphs tucked away behind golf courses and ranches. You might also pick up a map of Moab-area four-wheel-drive trails: four rugged, 15- to 54-mile loop routes through the desert, which take 2.5–4 hours to drive. Those who left their trusty four-by-four and off-road-driving skills at home can take an off-road Jeep tour through a private operator. Most Moab outfitters offer jeep tours, often in combination with rafting or hiking options. **Tag-A-Long Tours** (452 N. Main St., Moab, UT 84532, 435/259-8946 or 800/453-3292, www.tagalong.com) and **Adrift Adventures** (378 N. Main St., 435/259-8594 or 800/874-4483, www.adrift.net) have half-day (starting at $70) and full-day jeep tours (starting at $110) with combination jet-boat or hiking options. Full-day tours include lunch.

You can rent jeeps and other four-wheel-drive vehicles at a multitude of Moab outfits, including **Farabee Jeep Rentals** (1861 N. U.S. 191, 435/259-7734, www.moabjeep rentals.com), **Slick Rock Jeep Rental** (284 N. Main St., 435/259-5678), or **Cliffhanger Jeep Rentals** (1551 N. U.S. 191, 435/259-0889, www.cliffhangerjeeprental.com).

MOAB'S MINING BOOM AND BUST

Moab sits within the Paradox Salt Basin, a geologic formation responsible for the area's famous arch formations and accumulations of valuable minerals relatively near the surface. In addition to significant mineral wealth, mining and oil exploration has provided the region with some of its liveliest history and most colorful characters. Even French scientist Marie Curie, who discovered the element radium in uranium ore in 1898, visited the Moab area in 1899 to inspect a uranium-processing operation near the Dolores River.

Oil exploration in the 1920s caused some excitement in Moab, but nothing like that of the uranium boom that began in 1952. A down-on-his-luck geologist from Texas named Charles Steen struck it rich at his Mi Vida claim southeast of Moab. Steen's timing was exquisite: Uranium was highly sought after by the federal government, primarily for use in Cold War-era atomic weapons and in nuclear power plants. An instant multimillionaire, Steen built a large mansion overlooking Moab and hosted lavish parties attended by Hollywood celebrities (his home is now the Sunset Grill restaurant). The Mi Vida mine alone would ultimately be worth more than $100 million, and it put Moab on the map.

By the end of 1956, Moab was dubbed "The Richest Town in the USA" and "The Uranium Capital of the World." In the wake of Steen's discovery, thousands of prospectors, miners, laborers, and others descended on the area, hoping to cash in on the mother lode. Moab's population tripled in just three years as eager prospectors swarmed into the canyons.

By the mid-1960s, the boom had died out. However, just as uranium played out, mining operations began in 1965 in one of the largest potash deposits in the world (on the Colorado River between Moab and Dead Horse Point), and work continues there today. Other valuable materials mined in the Moab area over the years include vanadium (used in steel processing), lead, gold, copper, and silver, along with helium, natural gas, and oil.

MOAB

ATVS AND DIRT BIKES

As an alternative to four-by-four touring in the backcountry, there's all-terrain vehicle (ATV) and motorcycle "dirt biking," typically but not exclusively geared to the younger generation, or for families. Youths 8–15 years of age may operate an ATV provided they possess an Education Certificate issued by Utah State Parks and Recreation or an equivalent certificate from their home state. Much of the public land surrounding Moab is open to ATV exploration, with thousands of miles of unpaved roads and existing trails on which ATVs can travel. However, ATV and dirt-bike riding is not allowed within either Arches or Canyonlands National Park.

One particularly popular area for ATVs is White Wash Sand Dunes, with many miles of dirt roads in a strikingly scenic location (48 miles northwest of Moab, reached by driving south 13 miles from Exit 175 on I-70, just east of Green River). The dunes are interspersed with large cottonwood trees and bordered by red sandstone cliffs. In addition to the dunes, White Wash is a popular route around three sides of the dunes.

ATVs and dirt bikes are available from a number of Moab area outfitters, including High Point Hummer (281 N. Main St., 435/259-2972 or 877/486-6833, http://moab-utah.com/hummer) and Moab Tour Company (375 S. Main St., 435/259-4080, www.moabtourcompany.us). A half-day dirt bike or ATV rental starts at around $110.

◖ AIR TOURS

You'll have a bird's-eye view of southeastern Utah's incredible landscape from Moab's Canyonland Field with **Redtail Aviation** (P.O. Box 515, Moab, UT 84532, 435/259-7421 or 800/842-9251, www.moab-utah.com/redtail). Flights include Canyonlands National Park (Needles, Island in the Sky, and Maze Districts; $125). Longer tours are available, too.

Rates are based on two or more persons. Flights operate all year. Also based at Canyonlands Field, **Slickrock Air Guides** (435/259-6216 or 866/259-1626, www.slickrockairguides .com) offers a one-hour tour over the Canyonlands area for $125 per person, and $350 for 3.5 hours over Canyonlands, Natural Bridges, Lake Powell, and the Capitol Reef area with a stop for lunch at the Marble Canyon Lodge (not included in rate).

SKY DIVING

If you think the Arches and Canyonlands area looks dramatic from an airplane tour, imagine the excitement of parachuting into the desert landscape. **Skydive Moab** (Canyonlands Fields Airport, 435/259-5867, www.skydive moab.com) offers jumps for both first-time and experienced skydivers. First-timers receive a 30-minute ground schooling, followed by a half-hour flight before a tandem parachute jump with an instructor from 10,000 feet. A tandem skydive, including instruction and equipment, starts at $219 on weekdays, or $239 on the weekend. There are discounts for students or groups of five or more. For experienced skydivers with their own equipment, jumps start at $14 per jump; equipment and parachutes are available for rent.

CLIMBING

The place for rock climbing gear and information is **Pagan Mountaineering** (59 S. Main St., 435/259-1117, www.paganmountaineering .com). The friendly folks here also offer a climbing guide service to the local rock.

HORSEBACK RIDING

Several tour operators, such as **Adrift Adventures** (378 N. Main St., 435/259-7628 or 800/874-4483, www.adrift.net) and the **Moab Adventure Center** (225 S. Main St., 435/259-7019 or 866/904-1163, www.moab adventurecenter.com) offer horseback riding options in conjunction with rafting, hiking and jeep exploration. Red Cliffs Lodge (see *Accommodations;* Milepost 14, Hwy. 128, 435/259-2002 or 866/812-2002, www.redcliffslodge .com) offers horseback rides to nonguests amid the dramatic scenery of Castle Valley. Half-day rides are $60 per person; children must be 8 or older, and an adult must accompany children.

GOLF

The **Moab Golf Club** (2705 SE Bench Rd., 435/259-6488, www.uga.org/clubs/moab) is an 18-hole, par-72 public course set in a green oasis amid stunning red-rock formations. Also offering a driving range and a pro shop, it is open seven days a week, year-round, and green fees are $25 for 18 holes. To get there, go south five miles on U.S. 191, turn left two miles on Spanish Trails Road, then go right on Murphy Lane.

LOCAL PARKS

The **city park** (181 West 400 North, 435/259-8226) has shaded picnic tables, a playground, and an outdoor swimming pool. **Lions Park** offers picnicking along the Colorado River two miles north of town. **Rotary Park,** on Mill Creek Drive, is family-oriented and has lots of activities for kids.

Entertainment and Events

For a town of its size, Moab puts on a pretty good nightlife show, with lots of young hikers, bikers and rafters enjoying their daily conquests in bars and brewpubs. There are also notable seasonal music events, ranging from folk to classical.

NIGHTLIFE

A lot of Moab's nightlife focuses on the town's two brewpubs. The rowdy and well-loved **Eddie McStiff's** (57 S. Main St., 435/259-2337) is right downtown, with 12 handcrafted beers on draft and two outdoor seating areas. The newer and posher **Moab Brewery** (686 S. Main St., 435/259-6333) is more of a restaurant than a bar, but it's a pleasant place to sample good beer—you can also buy its microbrewed beer to go.

The following are private clubs, so you'll need to pay a minimal membership fee to get in. The **Outlaw Saloon** (44 West 200 North, 435/259-2654) doesn't look like much from the outside (it's a Quonset hut), but the bar is spacious, and on weekends DJs spin tunes. The Outlaw is also one of the Moab's few places for late night snacking—there's a "Midnight Menu" served until 12:30 A.M. **Rio Colorado** (2 South 100 West, 435/259-6666) has live music on weekends and a friendly and mellow hippie vibe during the week. The **Sportsman's Lounge** (1991 S. U.S. 191, 435/259-9972) and **Woody's Tavern** (221 S. Main St., 435/259-9323) both have live bands on the weekends.

For a more family-friendly evening out, consider the **Bar-M Chuckwagon's Live Western Show and Cowboy Supper,** a kind of Western-themed dinner theater that includes gunfights, live country music, and other Old West entertainment in addition to a buffet chuckwagon dinner. For more information, see *Food.*

Another long-time tradition for evening entertainment is **Canyonlands by Night,** a cruise on the Colorado River that ends with a sound-and-light presentation along the sandstone cliffs. Dinner packages are available; children under 4 are not permitted per Coast Guard regulations. For more information, see *Recreation.*

For a selection of movies, head for **Slickrock Cinemas** (580 Kane Creek Blvd., 435/259-4441).

EVENTS

To find out about local happenings, contact the Moab Information Center (435/259-8825, www.discovermoab.com). Unsurprisingly, Moab offers quite a few annual biking events. The **Moab Skinny Tire Festival** held the first week of March and the **Moab Century Tour** held in early October are both supported road bike events that benefit the Lance Armstrong Foundation. For information on either, contact www.skinnytirefestival.com or call 435/259-2698. The mountain-bike endurance race event **24 Hours of Moab,** held in mid-October, pits four-person relay teams against the rugged terrain of the Behind the Rocks area. This is one of North America's major events for mountain bikers, bringing more than 500 teams and over 5,000 spectators to Moab. For more information, go to www.grannygear.com/Races/Moab/index.shtml.

Other major annual athletic events include the **Canyonlands Half Marathon and Five Mile Run** in late March (third Saturday).

Moab's most popular annual event, more popular than anything celebrating two wheels, is the **Easter Jeep Safari** (www.rr4w.com/safari.html), which is the Sturgis or Daytona Beach of recreational four-wheeling. Upwards of 2,000 four-wheel-drive vehicles (it's not open just to jeeps, though ATVs are not allowed) converge on Moab for a week's worth of organized back-country touring. "Big Saturday" (the day before Easter) is the climax of the event, when all participating vehicles parade through Moab. Plan well ahead for lodging if you are planning to visit Moab during this event, as hotel rooms are often booked a year in advance.

MOAB

© W. C. MCRAE

Moab's old downtown is filled with boutiques and gift shops.

June kicks up dust at the Spanish Trail Arena (just south of Moab at 3641 S. U.S. 191) with the professional **Canyonlands P.R.C.A. Rodeo** held the second weekend of the month, with rodeo, parade, dance, horse racing, and 4-H gymkhana. August means it's time for the **Grand County Fair,** with agricultural displays, crafts, and arts competitions. Most fair events are held at the Moab Arts and Recreation Center (111 East 100 North) and include a pet parade, a "diaper derby" infant crawl contest, a pie-eating competition, plus live music and entertainment.

The **Moab Music Festival** (435/259-7003, www.moabmusicfest.org) got its start as a classical music festival but soon expanded to include other types of music, including jazz, bluegrass, and folk music. More than 30 artists are currently involved in the festival, which is held the first two weeks of September. Many of the concerts are held in dramatic outdoor settings. The **Moab Folk Festival** (www .moabfolkfestival.com) is the town's other big annual musical event, attracting nationally recognized performers to Moab the first weekend of November.

SHOPPING

Main Street, between 200 North and 200 South, has nearly a dozen galleries and gift shops with Native American art and other gifts. **Back of Beyond Books** (83 N. Main St., 435/259-5154) features an excellent selection of regional books and maps. A good selection of books and maps is also sold at **Times Independent Maps** (5 E. Center St., 435/259-7525).

Accommodations

Moab has been a tourist destination for generations and offers a wide variety of lodging choices, ranging from older motels to new upscale resorts. Luckily, lodgings are relatively inexpensive. The only time when Moab isn't busy is in the dead of winter, from November to February. At all other times, be sure to make reservations well in advance.

If you're having trouble finding a room, **Moab/Canyonlands Central Reservations** (435/259-5125, 800/748-4386, or 800/505-5343, www.moabutahlodging.com) can make bookings at 85 percent of Moab's accommodations, which include area bed-and-breakfasts, motels, condos, cabins, private houses, and luxury vacation homes. Another handy tool is www.moab-utah.com, which has a complete listing of lodging websites for the Moab area.

Summer rates are shown; those in winter typically drop 40 percent.

UNDER $50

The **Lazy Lizard Hostel** (1213 S. U.S. 191, 435/259-6057, www.lazylizardhostel.com) costs just $9 per night for simple dorm-style accommodations. You won't need a hostel card, and all guests share access to a hot tub, kitchen, barbecue, coin-operated laundry, and common room with cable TV. Camping ($6 per person), showers for nonguests ($2), and private rooms ($26 d) are offered, too. New log cabins here can sleep two ($28) to four ($40) people. The Lazy Lizard sits one mile south of town, behind A-1 Storage; the turnoff is about 200 yards south of Moab Lanes.

$50-75

All of the following offer basic but clean motel rooms at reasonable prices. The **Red Rock Lodge Motel** (51 North 100 West, 435/259-5431 or 877/207-9708, $55 d) has rooms with refrigerators and coffeemakers. It also includes a hot tub and a locked bicycle-storage facility.

The **Red Stone Inn** (535 S. Main St., 435/259-3500 or 800/772-1972, $65 d) is a newer, one-story motel; most rooms have efficiency kitchens. Other amenities include a bicycle-maintenance area, covered patio with gas barbecue grill, hot tub, and guest laundry. Motel guests have free access to the hotel pool next door. Pets are permitted only in smoking rooms with a $5-per-night fee. The **Days Inn** (426 N. Main St., 435/259-4468 or 800/329-7466, $68 d) has a pool and complimentary breakfast. For the same price, the **Big Horn Lodge** (550 S. Main St., 435/259-6171 or 800/325-6171) has a pool and restaurant. The **Bowen Motel** (169 N. Main St., 435/259-7132 or 800/874-5439, $67 d and up) is a pleasant, homey motel with an outdoor pool and free continental breakfast. The Bowen offers a variety of room types, including three-bedroom family suites and an 1,800-square-foot, three-bedroom house with full kitchen.

$75-100

The **Landmark Motel** (168 N. Main St., 435/259-6147 or 800/441-6147, www.landmark innmoab.com, $82 d and up) is right in the center of Moab and has a pool and a small waterslide, a hot tub, a guest laundry room, and three family units. At the **Virginian Motel** (70 East 200 South, 435/259-5951 or 800/261-2063, $89 d), more than half the rooms have kitchenettes and pets are permitted. The local **Super 8 Motel** (889 N. Main St., 435/259-8868 or 800/800-8000, $89 d) is north of downtown and has a pool, free high-speed Internet access, and complimentary breakfast, plus a hot tub.

The three two-bedroom cottages that compose **Desert Gardens** (123–127 West 200 North, 435/259-5125 or 800/505-5343) each contain a full kitchen, bath, and living room. The cottages sit in a large shaded yard with access to a hot tub, barbecue, and nicely maintained gardens. A two-night-minimum stay is required.

$100-125

The **Ramada Inn** (182 S. Main St., 888/989-1988 or 435/259-7141, $100 d) has nicely

MOAB

appointed rooms (some with balconies) and a pool, spa, and facilities for small meetings.

South of downtown is the **Comfort Suites** (800 S. Main St., 435/259-5252 or 800/228-5150, $100 d), an all-suites motel with large, nicely furnished rooms complete with microwaves and refrigerators. Facilities include an indoor pool, spa, exercise room, locked bike storage, and a guest laundry room.

Eight blocks from downtown, in a quiet property that backs up to Mill Creek and Nature Conservancy holdings, is **Adobe Adobe** (778 Kane Creek Blvd., 435/259-7716, www.adobeabodemoab.com), a newly constructed adobe inn with large guest rooms done up in handsome Southwest style. The inn also offers high-speed Internet access, a large and tasty breakfast, and a hot tub.

If you want seclusion in a wilderness setting, stay at the **Castle Valley Inn B&B** (in Castle Valley, 18 miles east of Moab, 435/259-7830, www.castlevalleyinn.com, $100 and up). The inn adjoins a wildlife refuge in a stunning landscape of red-rock mesas and needle-pointed buttes. You can stay in one of the main house's five guest rooms or in one of the three bungalows with kitchens. For an additional fee and with advance notice, dinner is available for guests. Facilities include a hot tub. No children or pets are allowed, and a two-night stay is required on weekends. To reach Castle Valley Inn, follow Highway 128 east from Moab for 16 miles and turn south 2.3 miles toward Castle Valley.

$125-150

The centrally located **Best Western Greenwell Motel** (105 S. Main St., 435/259-6151 or 800/528-1234, $125 and up) has a pool, an on-premises restaurant, and some kitchenettes. The **Best Western Canyonlands Inn** (16 S. Main St., 435/259-2300 or 800/528-1234, $125 and up) is also in the heart of Moab, with suites, a pool, a fitness room and spa, a restaurant, and a bike-storage area.

One most interesting accommodations in Moab is the **◖ Gonzo Inn** (100 West 200 South, 435/259-2515 or 800/791-4044, www.gonzoinn.com, $145 d and up). With a look somewhere between an adobe inn and a postmodern warehouse, the Gonzo doesn't try to appear anything but young and hip. Expect large rooms with Day-Glo colors, a pool, and a friendly welcome.

Located in a lovely and quiet residential area, the **◖ Sunflower Hill Bed & Breakfast** (185 North 300 East, 435/259-2974 or 800/662-2786, www.sunflowerhill.com, $145–155 and up) offers high-quality accommodations in one of Moab's original farmhouses and in a newly built garden cottage with patios and balconies. All 12 rooms have private baths, air conditioning, and queen-size beds; there are also two suites. Guests share access to an outdoor hot tub, bike storage, patios, and large gardens. Children are welcome from age eight, and it's open year-round.

GUEST RANCHES

A short drive from Moab along the Colorado River's red-rock canyon is the region's premium luxury guest ranch, the **◖ Sorrel River Ranch** (17 miles northeast of Moab on Hwy. 128, 435/259-4642 or 877/359-2715, www.sorrelriver.com, $279 and up). The ranch sits on 240 acres in one of the most dramatic landscapes in the Moab area—just across the river from Arches National Park and beneath the soaring mesas of Castle Valley. Accommodations are in a series of beautifully furnished wooden lodges, all tastefully fitted with Old West–style furniture. All units have kitchenettes and a patio with porch swing or back deck overlooking the river (some rooms have both). Horseback rides are offered into the arroyos behind the ranch, and kayaks and bicycles can be rented. The ranch's restaurant, the River Grill, has some of the best views in Utah and an adventurous menu offering everything from steaks to grilled duck breast.

Sharing a similar view of the Colorado River and Castle Valley (though three miles closer to Moab) is **Red Cliffs Lodge** (Milepost 14, Hwy. 128, 435/259-2002 or 866/812-2002, www.redcliffslodge.com, from $200 d), a guest ranch and winery combo that offers tents, $30–32 for RVs) is open all year; it has showers, a laundry room, a store, and a pool. Two-person air-conditioned cabins are also available for $42—bring your own bedding. **Slickrock Campground** (one mile north of Moab at 1301-1/2 N. U.S. 191, 435/259-7660 or 800/448-8873, $18 tents or RVs without hookups, $29 with hookups, $34 for cabins with air-conditioning and heat) remains open year-round; it has showers, a store, an outdoor café, and a pool.

Moab Valley RV Resort (two miles north of Moab at 1773 N. U.S. 191 and Hwy. 128, 435/259-4469, tents $20, RVs from $28) is also open all year; it has showers, a pool, a playground, and Wi-Fi access. There's also a selection of cabins available, some simple sleeping rooms, others with bathrooms, fridges, and bedding; prices range $39–69. **Moab KOA** (four miles south of Moab at 3225 S. U.S. 191, 435/259-6682 or 800/562-0372, open Mar.–Nov., $20–29 tents, RVs $26–32, $42–60 cabins) has showers, a laundry room, a store, minigolf, and a pool.

The BLM requires that all camping along the Colorado River (accessible by road above and below Moab), Kane Creek, and near the Moab Slickrock Bike Trail *must* be in developed designated sites (with toilets) or undeveloped designated sites (no restrooms or fee). The following four camping areas are available along Highway 128 for a $10 fee. From the U.S. 191/Highway 128 junction, you'll find JayCee Park at 4.2 miles, Hal Canyon at 6.6 miles, Oak Grove at 6.9 miles, and Big Bend Recreation Site at 7.4 miles. Contact the Moab Information Center for locations of additional campgrounds. You'll also find campgrounds farther out at Arches and Canyonlands National Parks, Dead Horse Point State Park, the La Sal Mountains, and Canyon Rims Recreation Area.

© W. C. MCRAE

Saddle horses await their cowboys at Sorrel River Ranch.

"minisuites" in the main lodge building plus a number of riverside cabins that can sleep up to six. The lodge offers a bar and restaurant, horseback rides, and mountain-bike rentals, and will arrange river raft trips. The lodge is also the headquarters for Castle Creek Winery; there's a tasting room in the lobby.

CAMPGROUNDS

Spanish Trail RV Park (2980 S. U.S. 191, 435/259-2411 or 800/787-2751) is about three miles south of Moab and has showers, laundry, and restrooms; it's open year-round. Sites range from $19 for tents to $25 for hookups. More convenient to downtown, **Canyonlands Campground** (555 S. Main St., 435/259-6848 or 800/522-6848, $21–23 for

MOAB

Food

Moab has the best restaurants in all of southern Utah; no matter what else the recreational craze has produced, it has certainly improved the food. Several Moab-area restaurants are closed for vacation in February, so call ahead if you're visiting in winter.

BREAKFAST AND LIGHT MEALS

Start the day at **Breakfast at Tiffany's** (90 E. Center, 435/259-2553), a happening coffee shop with fresh pastries and a deli. For a traditional breakfast, try the **Jailhouse Café** (101 N. Main St., 435/259-3900). Another favorite is the **Mondo Café** (59 S. Main St., in McStiff's Plaza, 435/259-5551). They serve fresh baked goods, espresso drinks, and sandwiches for lunch. The **Moab Diner & Ice Cream Shoppe** (189 S. Main St., 435/259-4006) is a good place to know about—you'll find the breakfasts old-fashioned and abundant, a Southwestern green-chili edge to the food, and the best ice cream in town. It's open for breakfast, lunch, and dinner. **EclectiCafe** (352 N. Main St., 435/259-6896) has a good selection of organic and vegetarian dishes, mostly with ethnic roots. Open for breakfast and lunch.

CASUAL DINING

Unless otherwise noted, each of the following establishments has a full liquor license. Entrées range $8–15.

For light meals and snacks, try the **Poplar Place Pub & Eatery** (Main St. and 100 North, 435/259-6018), which serves pizza, pasta, and deli sandwiches in a pub atmosphere and is open daily for lunch and dinner. The **(Slickrock Café** (5 N. Main St., 435/259-8004) is another versatile restaurant. Open for breakfast, lunch, and dinner in a historic building downtown, the Slickrock serves up-to-date

---

MOAB AREA WINERIES

Southern Utah is not exactly the first place you think of when you envision fine wine, but for a handful of wine pioneers, the Moab area is the *terroir* of choice. Actually, conditions around Moab are similar to areas of Spain or the eastern Mediterranean, where wine grapes have flourished for millennia. The area's first wine grapes were planted in the 1970s through the efforts of the University of Arizona and the Four Corners Regional Economic Development Commission. The results were positive, as the hot days, cool nights and deep sandy soil produced grapes of exceptional quality and flavor. A fruit-growing cooperative was formed in Moab to grow wine grapes, and by the 1980s the coop was producing wine under the Arches Winery label. As teetotaling Utah's first winery, Arches Winery was more than a novelty – its wines were good enough to accumulate nearly 40 prizes at national wine exhibitions.

Arches Winery was a true pioneer, and now two wineries produce wine in the Moab area. The following are open for wine tasting year-round. In addition, many of Moab's fine restaurants offer wine from these local wineries. **Castle Creek Winery** (formerly Arches Winery, 14 miles east on Hwy. 128 at the Red Cliffs Lodge, 435/259-3332, redcliffslodge.com/winery, noon–5:30 P.M. daily) produces pinot noir, merlot, cabernet sauvignon, chenin blanc, chardonnay, and late-harvest gewürztraminer.

Spanish Valley Vineyards and Winery (6 miles south of Moab at 4710 Zimmerman Lane, 435/259-8134, www.moab-utah.com/spanish-valleywinery, noon–7 P.M. Mon.-Sat.) produces riesling, gewürztraminer, cabernet sauvignon, and syrah.

food at reasonable prices (most dinner main dishes are $9–15), all with a spicy Southwestern or Caribbean kick.

The **Rio Colorado Restaurant** (2 South 100 West, 435/259-6666) can fill the bill for almost any appetite—sandwiches, Mexican food, steak, seafood, chicken, pasta, and salads—and is open daily at 4 P.M. Only one restaurant in town serves Asian food: the **Szechuan Restaurant** (125 S. Main St., 435/259-8984). Fortunately, the food is good, spicy, and inexpensive.

For a Western night out, consider **Bar M Chuckwagon Supper,** located on the banks of Mill Creek just southeast of town (541 S. Mulberry Lane, 435/259-2276, http://barmchuckwagon.com). Tasty cowboy-style cooking is served up from chuck wagons, followed by a variety of live Western entertainment. It's open for dinner only (call to check on times, Apr.–Oct. Mon.–Sat.; beer only). The meal plus entertainment costs $24 for everyone 11 years and older, $12 for younger children.

BREWPUBS

After a hot day out on the trail, who can blame you for thinking about a cold brew and a good meal at a brewpub? Luckily, Moab has two excellent pubs to fill the bill. **Eddie McStiff's** (57 S. Main St., 435/259-2337) was the first brewpub in Moab and is an extremely popular place to sip a cool one or eat a hearty meal of pasta, pizza, steaks, salads, chicken, and Mexican food. The pub is a convivial place to meet like-minded travelers; in good weather there's seating in a nice courtyard. You'll have to try hard not to have fun here (open daily for lunch and dinner; burgers start at $6, grilled salmon is $17).

There's more good beer and maybe better food at the **Moab Brewery** (686 S. Main St., 435/259-6333), although this newer restaurant has yet to attract the kind of scene you'll find at Eddie McStiff's. The atmosphere is light and airy, and the food is good—steaks, sandwiches, burgers, and a wide selection of salads. A jerk-chicken sandwich is $7, prime rib $18. There's deck seating when weather permits.

MOAB

© W. C. MCRAE

Eddie McStiff's on S. Main St., Moab

FINE DINING

The **Sunset Grill** (900 N. U.S. 191, 435/259-7146, open Mon.–Sat. for dinner) is located in uranium king Charlie Steen's mansion, situated high above Moab, with "million-dollar" sweeping views of the valley. Chefs offer steaks, fresh seafood, and a selection of modern pasta dishes ($17–30).

(**Buck's Grill House** (1393 N. U.S. 191, 435/259-5201, dinner nightly) is a steakhouse with a difference. The restaurant features a pleasant Western atmosphere, and the food seems familiar enough—steaks, prime rib, roast chicken, seafood, grilled pork loin—but the quality of the preparation and the side dishes make the difference. This is Western fine dining, with imaginative refinements on standard steakhouse fare. Dishes like pan-fried trout with apricot cilantro mayonnaise, duck tamales, and steaks with barbecue butter are excellent. Entrées range $14–39.

The **River Grill** (at Sorrel River Ranch, 17 miles northeast of Moab on Hwy. 128, 435/259-4642, three meals daily, dinner by reservation only) has a lovely dining room that overlooks spires of red rock and the dramatic cliffs of the Colorado River. The scenery is hard to top, and the food is excellent, with a focus on prime beef and Continental specialties. Fresh fish and other seafood are flown in daily and form the basis for nightly specials.

Moab has two restaurants that feature the most up-to-the-moment cuisine. The **(** **Center Cafe** (60 North 100 West, 435/259-4295) has been a long-time Moab favorite for its international menu and excellent service. The menu is eclectic, with a wide selection of pasta dishes (including several vegetarian choices) and other inventive fare that feature Continental influences and free-range and organic ingredients ($15–28, open Mon.–Fri. for lunch, dinner nightly). There's also a market area for homemade breads, cheeses, and gourmet takeout.

The **(** **Desert Bistro** (1266 N. U.S. 191, 435/259-0756, dinner nightly) has moved to the historic 1896 Ranch House at Moab Springs Ranch on the north end of Moab, where it continues to serve seasonal, sophisticated Southwest-meets-Continental cuisine featuring local meats and game plus fresh fish and seafood. The patio dining here is the nicest in Moab. Main courses range $18–30.

Information and Services

Moab is a small town, and people are generally friendly. Between the Moab Information Center and the county library—and the friendly advice of people in the street—you'll find it easy to assemble all the information you need to have a fine stay.

INFORMATION

The **Moab Information Center** (Main St. and Center St., 435/259-8825 or 800/635-6622, www.discovermoab.com, open 8 A.M.–9 P.M. daily in summer with reduced hours the rest of the year) is the place to start for nearly all local and area information. The National Park Service, the BLM, the U.S. Forest Service, the Grand County Travel Council, and the Canyonlands Natural History Association all are represented here. Visitors needing help from any of these agencies should start at the information center rather than at the agency offices. Free literature is available, and the selection of books and maps for sale is large. Especially useful is the free *Southeastern Utah Travel Guide,* which describes features of and opportunities for recreation in the Arches and Canyonlands National Parks. Included are comprehensive lists of tour operators, places to rent and purchase equipment, and campgrounds.

The **National Park Service office** in Moab (three miles south of downtown at 2282 SW Resource Blvd., Moab, UT 84532, 435/259-7164, 8 A.M.–4:30 P.M. Mon.–Fri.) is headquarters for Canyonlands and Arches National Parks and Natural Bridges

National Monument. The **Manti-La Sal National Forest office** is at the same location (435/259-7155, 8 A.M.–noon and 12:30–4:30 P.M. Mon.–Fri.). The **BLM District office** (82 E. Dogwood or P.O. Box 970, Moab, UT 84532, 435/259-8193, open 7:45 A.M.–4:30 P.M. Mon.–Fri.) is on the south side of town behind Comfort Suites. Some land-use maps are sold here, and this is the place to pick up river-running permits.

SERVICES

The **Grand County Public Library** (25 South 100 East, 435/259-5421, 1–9 P.M. Mon.–Thurs., 1–5 P.M. Fri., and 10 A.M.–2 P.M. Sat.) is a good place for local history and general reading. The library is for local residents, but others can use the services on a daily basis.

The **post office** is downtown (50 East 100 North, 435/259-7427). **Allen Memorial Hospital** provides medical care (719 West 400 North, 435/259-7191). For emergencies (ambulance, sheriff, police, or fire), dial 911.

GETTING THERE

US Airways Express (800/235-9292) provides daily scheduled air service between Canyonlands Field just north of Moab and Salt Lake International Airport, with one direct, round-trip flight Sunday through Thursday and two on Friday. The planes are Beech 1900D, a pressurized aircraft with a capacity of 19 passengers and 2 pilots. The Moab/Canyonlands Airfield is 16 miles north of Moab on U.S. 191.

The only other public transport option to Moab is the ARK Shuttle run by Bighorn Express (888/655-7433, www.bighornexpress.com), which makes one minibus run daily between Moab and Salt Lake City. Advance reservations are required. One-way fare is $65.

For rental cars, contact **Certified Ford** (500 S. Main St., 435/529-6107) or **Thrifty** (711 S. Main St., 435/259-7317 or 800/847-4389), which has an office at the Moab airport. Shuttle services like **Roadrunner Shuttle** (435/259-9402, www.roadrunnershuttle.com) can also pick up and deliver passengers at the airport.

MOAB

Scenic Drives and Excursions from Moab

Each of the following routes is at least partly accessible to standard low-clearance highway vehicles. If you have a four-wheel-drive vehicle, you'll have the option of additional, off-road exploring.

You'll find detailed travel information on these and other places in the books and separate maps by F. A. Barnes, *Canyon Country Off-Road Vehicle Trails: Island Area* (north of Canyonlands National Park) and *Canyon Country Off-Road Vehicle Trails: Arches & La Sals Areas* (around Arches National Park). The BLM takes care of nearly all of this land; staff in the Moab offices may know current road and trail conditions.

UTAH SCENIC BYWAY 279

Highway 279 goes downstream through the Colorado River Canyon on the other side of the river from Moab. Pavement extends 16 miles past fine views, prehistoric rock art, arches, and hiking trails. A potash plant marks the end of the highway; a rough dirt road continues to Canyonlands National Park. From Moab, head north 3.5 miles on U.S. 191, then turn left on Highway 279. The highway enters the canyon at the Portal, 2.7 miles from the turnoff. Towering sandstone cliffs rise on the right, and the Colorado River drifts along just below on the left.

Stop at a signed pullout on the left 0.6 mile past the canyon entrance to see **Indian Ruins Viewpoint,** a small prehistoric Native American ruin tucked under a ledge across the river. The stone structure was probably used for food storage.

Groups of **petroglyphs** cover cliffs along the highway 5.2 miles from U.S. 191, 0.7 mile beyond Milepost 11. Look across the river to see the Fickle Finger of Fate among the sandstone

SEGO CANYON ROCK ART

If you approach Moab along I-70, consider a side trip to one of the premier rock-art galleries in Utah, just a short distance from the freeway junction with U.S. 191 to Moab. Sego Canyon is just three miles past Thompson, reached by taking Exit 185 off I-70. Drive through the slumbering little town and continue up the canyon behind it (BLM signs also point the way). A side road leads to a parking area where the canyon walls close in. Sego Canyon is a showcase of prehistoric rock art – it preserves rock drawings and images that are thousands of years old. The Barrier Canyon Style drawings may be 8,000 years old; the more recent Fremont Style images were created in the last thousand years. Compared to these ancient pictures, the Ute etchings are relatively recent; experts speculate that they may have been drawn in the 1800s, when Ute villages still lined Sego Canyon. Interestingly, the newer petroglyphs and pictographs are more representational than the older ones. The ancient Barrier Canyon figures are typically horned ghostlike beings that look like aliens from early Hollywood sci-fi thrillers. The Fremont Style images depict stylized human figures made from geometric shapes; the crudest figures are the most recent. The Ute images are of buffaloes and hunters on horseback.

U.S. 191. Ahead the canyon opens up where underground pressure from salt and potash have folded the rock layers into an anticline.

At the **Moab Salt Plant,** mining operations inject water underground to dissolve the potash and other chemicals, then pump the solution to evaporation ponds. The ponds are dyed blue to hasten evaporation, which takes about a year. You can see these colorful solutions from Dead Horse Point and Anticline Overlook on the canyon rims.

High-clearance vehicles can continue on the unpaved road beyond the plant. The road passes through varied canyon country, with views overlooking the Colorado River. At a road junction in Canyonlands National Park (Island in the Sky District), you have a choice of turning left for the 100-mile White Rim Trail (four-wheel drive only past Musselman Arch), continuing up the steep switchbacks of the Shafer Trail Road (four-wheel drive recommended) to the paved park road, or returning the way you came.

UTAH SCENIC BYWAY 128

Highway 128 turns northeast from U.S. 191 just south of the Colorado River Bridge, two miles north of Moab. This exceptionally scenic canyon route follows the Colorado for 30 miles upstream before crossing at Dewey Bridge and turning north to I-70. The entire highway is paved. In 1986, a new bridge replaced the narrow Dewey suspension bridge that once caused white knuckles on drivers of large vehicles. The Lions Park picnic area at the turnoff from U.S. 191 is a pleasant stopping place. Big Bend Recreation Site is another good spot 7.5 miles up Highway 128.

A network of highly scenic jeep roads branches off Castle Valley and Onion Creek Roads into side canyons and the **La Sal Mountains Loop Road,** described in the book and separate map *Canyon Country Off-Road Vehicle Trails: Arches & La Sals Areas,* by F. A. Barnes. This paved scenic road goes through Castle Valley, climbs high into the La Sals, then loops back to Moab. Allow at least three hours to drive the 62-mile loop. The turnoff from Highway 128 is 15.5 miles up from U.S. 191.

fins of Behind the Rocks. A petroglyph of a bear is 0.2 mile farther down the highway. Archaeologists think that Fremonts and the later Utes did most of the artwork in this area.

A signed pullout on the right 6.2 miles from U.S. 191 points out **dinosaur tracks** and petroglyphs visible on rocks above. Sighting tubes help locate the features. It's possible to hike up the steep hillside for a closer look.

The aptly named **Jug Handle Arch,** with an opening 46 feet high and three feet wide, is close to the road on the right, 13.6 miles from

Formations in the Castle Valley off Highway 128 were the backdrop for many early Western films.

A graded county road, **Onion Creek Road** turns southeast off the highway 20 miles from U.S. 191 and heads up Onion Creek, crossing it many times. *Avoid this route if storms threaten.* The unpleasant-smelling creek contains poisonous arsenic and selenium. Colorful rock formations of dark red sandstone line the creek. After about eight miles, the road climbs steeply out of Onion Creek to upper Fisher Valley and a junction with Kokopelli's Trail, which follows a jeep road over this part of its route.

The gothic spires of **Fisher Towers** soar as high as 900 feet above Professor Valley. The BLM has a picnic area nearby and a hiking trail that skirts the base of the three main towers. Titan is the tallest.

In 1962, three climbers from Colorado made the first ascent of Titan Tower. The almost-vertical rock faces, overhanging bulges, and sections of rotten rock made for an exhausting 3.5 days of climbing (the party descended to the base for two of the nights). Their final descent from the summit took only six hours.

See the November 1962 issue of *National Geographic* magazine for the story and photos. Supposedly, the name Fisher is not that of a pioneer, but a corruption of the geologic term *fissure* (a narrow crack). An unpaved road turns southeast off Highway 128 near Milepost 21 (21 miles from U.S. 191) and continues two miles to the picnic area.

The modern two-lane concrete **Dewey Bridge** has replaced the picturesque wood-and-steel suspension bridge built in 1916. Here, the BLM has built the Dewey Bridge Recreation Site with a picnic area, trailhead, boat launch, and a small campground. Bicyclists and hikers can still use the old bridge; an interpretive sign explains its history. Drivers can continue on the highway to I-70 through rolling hills nearly devoid of vegetation.

Upstream from Dewey Bridge are the wild rapids of **Westwater Canyon.** The Colorado River cut this narrow gorge into dark metamorphic rock. You can raft or kayak down the river in one day or a more leisurely two days. Camping is limited to a single night. Unlike most desert rivers, this section of the Colorado also offers good river-running at low water levels in late summer and autumn. Westwater Canyon's inner gorge, where boaters face their greatest challenge, is only about 3.5 miles long; however, you can enjoy scenic sandstone canyons both upstream and downstream.

The bumpy four-wheel-drive route **Top-of-the-World Road** climbs to an overlook with outstanding views of Fisher Towers, Fisher Valley, Onion Creek, and beyond. Turn right (east) on the Entrada Bluffs Road (just before crossing Dewey Bridge). After 5.5 miles, keep straight on a dirt road when the main road curves left, then immediately turn right (south) and go uphill 100 yards through a gate (gateposts are railroad ties) and continue about 4.5 miles on the Top-of-the-World Road to the rim. Elevation here is 6,800 feet, nearly 3,000 feet higher than the Colorado River.

KANE CREEK SCENIC DRIVE

This road heads downstream along the Colorado River on the same side as Moab. The four miles through the Colorado River Canyon are paved, followed by six miles of good dirt road through Kane Springs Canyon. This route also leads to several hiking trails (see *Utah Scenic Byway 128*). People with high-clearance vehicles or mountain bikes can continue across Kane Springs Creek to Hurrah Pass and an extensive network of four-wheel-drive trails. The book and separate map *Canyon Country Off-Road Vehicle Trails: Canyon Rims & Needles Areas,* by F. A. Barnes, has detailed back-road information.

LA SAL MOUNTAINS LOOP ROAD

This paved road on the west side of the range provides a good introduction to the high country. Side roads and trails lead to lakes, alpine meadows, and old mining areas. Viewpoints overlook Castle Valley, Arches and Canyonlands National Parks, Moab Rim, and other scenic features. Vegetation along the drive runs the whole range from the cottonwoods, sage, and rabbitbrush of the desert to forests

the La Sal Mountains above the Colorado River

of aspen, fir, and spruce. The 62-mile loop road can easily take a full day with stops for scenic overlooks, a picnic, and a bit of hiking or fishing. Because of the high elevations, the loop's season usually lasts from May to October. Stock up on supplies in Moab because you won't find any stores or gas stations after leaving town. Before venturing off the Loop Road, it's a good idea to check current back-road conditions with the U.S. Forest Service office in Moab. You can also ask them for a road log of sights and side roads.

NEEDLES AND ANTICLINE OVERLOOKS

These viewpoints atop the high mesa east of Canyonlands National Park offer magnificent panoramas of the surrounding area. Now part of the BLM's **Canyon Rims Recreation Area,** these easily accessed overlooks provide the kind of awe-inspiring vistas over the Needles District that you'd need to hike to find in the park itself. The turnoff for both overlooks is at Milepost 93 on U.S. 191, 32 miles south of Moab and seven miles north of Highway 211.

For the **Needles Overlook,** follow the paved road 22 miles west to its end (turn left at the junction 15 miles in). The BLM maintains a picnic area and interpretive exhibits here. A fence protects visitors from the sheer cliffs that drop off more than 1,000 feet. You can see much of Canyonlands National Park and southeastern Utah. Look south for the Six-Shooter Peaks and the high country of the Abajo Mountains; southwest for the Needles (thousands of spires reaching for the heavens); west for the confluence area of the Green and Colorado Rivers, the Maze District, the Orange Cliffs, and the Henry Mountains; northwest for the lazy bends of the Colorado River Canyon and the sheer-walled mesas of Island in the Sky and Dead Horse Point; north for the Book Cliffs; and northeast for the La Sal Mountains. The changing shadows and colors of the canyon country make for a continuous show throughout the day.

For the **Anticline Overlook,** continue straight north at the junction with the Needles road and drive 17 miles on a good gravel road to the fenced overlook at road's end. Here you're standing 1,600 feet above the Colorado River. The sweeping panorama over the canyons, the river, and the twisted rocks of the Kane Creek Anticline is nearly as spectacular as that from Dead Horse Point, only 5.5 miles west as the crow flies. Salt and other minerals of the Paradox Formation pushed up overlying rocks into the dome visible below. Downcutting by the Colorado River has revealed the twisted rock layers. The Moab Salt Mine across the river to the north uses a solution technique to bring up potash from the Paradox Formation several thousand feet underground. Pumps then transfer the solution to the blue-tinted evaporation ponds. Look carefully on the northeast horizon to see an arch in the Windows Section of Arches National Park, 16 miles away.

You can reach **Pyramid Butte Overlook** by a gravel road that turns west off the main drive two miles before Anticline Overlook; the road goes around a rock monolith to viewpoints on the other side (1.3 miles round-trip). Four-wheel-drive vehicles can go west out to **Canyonlands Overlook** (17 miles round-trip) on rough, unmarked roads. The turnoff, which may not be signed, is 0.3 mile south of the Hatch Point Campground turnoff.

There are two campgrounds along the access road—each has water (mid-Apr.–mid-Oct.), tables, grills, and outhouses and charges a $10 fee. **Windwhistle Campground,** backed by cliffs to the south, has fine views to the north and a nature trail; follow the main road from U.S. 191 for six miles and turn left. At **Hatch Point Campground,** in a piñon-juniper woodland, you can enjoy views to the north. Go 24 miles in on the paved and gravel roads toward Anticline Overlook, then turn right and continue for one mile.

BACKGROUND

The Colorado Plateau

Utah's five national parks and the Grand Staircase–Escalante National Monument are all part of the Colorado Plateau, a high, broad physiographic province that includes southern Utah, northern Arizona, southwest Colorado, and northwest New Mexico. This roughly circular plateau, nearly the size of Montana, also contains the Grand Canyon, the Navajo Nation, and the Hopi Reservation.

Created by a slow but tremendous uplift, and carved by magnificent rivers, the plateau lies mostly between 3,000 and 6,000 feet, with some peaks reaching nearly 13,000 feet. Although much of the terrain is gently rolling, the Green and Colorado Rivers have sculpted remarkable canyons, buttes, mesas, arches, and badlands. Isolated uplifts and foldings have formed such features as the San Rafael Swell, Waterpocket Fold, and Circle Cliffs. The rounded Abajo, Henry, La Sal, and Navajo Mountains are examples of intrusive rock—an igneous layer that is formed below the earth's surface and later exposed by erosion.

The Colorado Plateau province is broken down into six physiographic sections: the Grand Canyon, Datil, Navajo, Uinta Basin, Canyon Lands, and High Plateaus. Utah's national parks are spread across the High Plateaus and Canyon Lands sections. The westernmost parks, Zion and Bryce, are in the

© PAUL LEVY

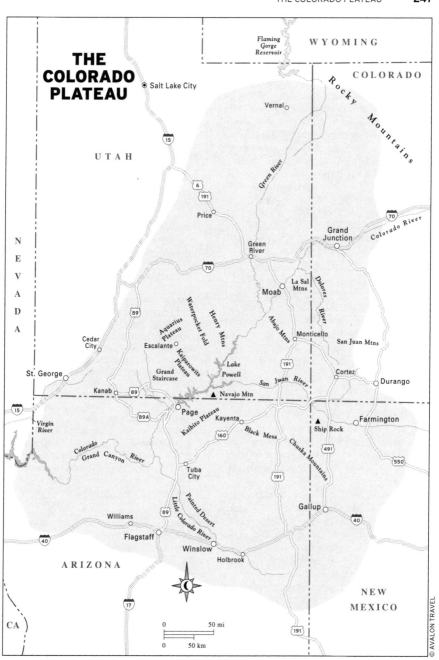

THE COLORADO PLATEAU

WYOMING

Flaming Gorge Reservoir

COLORADO

Rocky Mountains

Salt Lake City

Vernal

UTAH

Green River

Price

Grand Junction

Colorado River

NEVADA

Green River

Moab

La Sal Mtns

Dolores River

Aquarius Plateau

Waterpocket Fold

Henry Mtns

Abajo Mtns

Monticello

San Juan Mtns

Cedar City

Escalante

Kaiparowits Plateau

Lake Powell

191

Cortez

Durango

St. George

Grand Staircase

San Juan River

Kanab

Navajo Mtn

Page

Farmington

Virgin River

Kaibito Plateau

Kayenta

Ship Rock

Colorado River

Grand Canyon

Black Mesa

Chuska Mountains

Tuba City

Williams

Painted Desert

Little Colorado River

Gallup

Flagstaff

Winslow

Holbrook

ARIZONA

NEW MEXICO

CA

0   50 mi
0   50 km

© AVALON TRAVEL

High Plateaus; Capitol Reef, Arches, and Canyonlands are, not surprisingly, in the Canyon Lands section, and the Escalante River forms the dividing line between the two sections.

The High Plateaus (the Paunsaugunt, Markagunt, and Aquarius Plateaus) are lava-topped uplands reaching above the main height of the Colorado Plateau, then dropping off to the south in a series of steps known as the Grand Staircase. Exposed layers range from the relatively young rocks of the Black Cliffs (lava flows) in the north to the increasingly older Pink Cliffs (visible at Bryce), Gray Cliffs (which include the Straight Cliffs of Grand Staircase–Escalante), White Cliffs (Zion's Navajo sandstone), and Vermilion Cliffs (surrounding Kanab, Utah) toward the south.

The Canyon Lands section is noted for its synclines, anticlines, and folds—nongeologists can picture the rock layers as blankets on a bed, and then imagine how they look before the bed is made in the morning. This warping, which goes on deep beneath the earth's surface, has affected the overlying rocks, permitting the development of deeply incised canyons.

GEOLOGY

When you visit any one of Utah's national parks, the first things you're likely to notice are rocks. Vegetation is sparse and the soil is thin, so there's not much to hide geology here. Particularly stunning views are found where rivers have carved deep canyons through the rock layers.

By western U.S. standards, the rocks forming the Colorado Plateau have had it pretty easy. Although faults have cracked and uplifted rocks, and volcanoes have spewed lava across the plateau, it's nothing like the surrounding Rocky Mountains or Basin and Range provinces, both of which are the result of eons of violent geology. Mostly, sediments piled up, younger layers on top of older, then eroded, lifted up, and eroded some more.

The clean, orderly stair steps from the young rocks in Bryce Canyon to the much older Grand Canyon show off the clearly defined layers of rock. Weird crenellations, hoodoos, and arches occur thanks to the way erosion acted on the various rocks, making up this big Colorado Plateau layer cake.

NATURE'S PALETTE

In Utah, you'll get used to seeing a lot of colorful rock formations. The color gives you clues to the composition and geologic history of the rock. In general:

Red rocks are stained by rusty iron-rich sediments washed down from mountains and are a clue that erosion has occurred.

Gray or brown rocks were deposited by ancient seas.

White rocks are colored by their "glue," the limey remains of dissolved seashells that leach down and harden sandstones.

Black rocks are volcanic in origin.

Igneous rocks are the odd rocks out. They are present in the La Sal, Abajo, and Henry Mountains near Canyonlands. These mountains are "laccoliths," formed by molten magma that pushed through the sedimentary layers, leaking deeper into some layers than others and eventually forming broad dome-shaped protuberances, which were eroded into soft peaks, then carved by glaciers into the sharp peaks we see today.

A layer of lava also caps the Paunsaugunt, Markagunt, and Aquarius Plateaus, which have lifted above the main level of the Colorado Plateau. This mostly basalt layer was laid down about 37 million years ago, before the Colorado Plateau began to uplift.

Sedimentation

Water made this desert what it is today. Back before the continents broke apart and began drifting to their present-day locations, Utah was near the equator, just east of a warm ocean. Ancient seas washed over the land, depositing sand, silt, and mud. Layer upon layer, the soils piled up and were—over time—compressed into sandstones, limestones, and shales.

The ancestral Rocky Mountains rose to the east of the ocean, and, just to their west, a troughlike basin formed and was intermittently flushed with sea water. Evaporation caused salts and other minerals to collect on the basin floor; when the climate became wetter, more water rushed in.

As the ancestral Rockies eroded, their bulk washed down onto the basin. The sea level rose, washing in more mud and sand. When the seas receded, dry winds blew sand across the region, creating enormous dunes.

Over time, the North American continent drifted north, away from the equator, but it remained near the sea and was regularly washed by tides, leaving more sand and silt. Just inland, freshwater lakes filled, then dried, and the lakebeds consolidated into shales. During wet periods, streams coursed across the area, carrying then dropping their loads of mud, silt, and sand.

As the ancestral Rockies wore down to mere hills, other mountains rose, then eroded, contributing their sediments. A turn toward dry weather meant more dry winds, kicking up the sand and building it into massive dunes.

Uplift

About 15 million years ago the sea-level plateau began to lift, slowly, steadily, and, by geologic standards, incredibly gently. Some areas were hoisted as high as 10,000 feet above sea level.

Along the western edge of the plateau, underlying faults—like those common in the Basin and Range area—shot through the sedimentary layers. Along these faults, the High Plateaus—the Markagunt, Paunsaugunt, and the Aquarius—rose above the height of the main Colorado Plateau.

Uplift is still occurring. A 1992 earthquake just outside Zion National Park was one strong reminder that the plateau continues to move.

© JUDY JEWELL

In the Kolob Canyons, it's easy to see where the rocks uplifted.

Erosion

As the Colorado Plateau rose, its big rivers carved deep gorges through the uplifting rocks. Today, these rivers—the Green, Colorado, Escalante, Paria, and Virgin—are responsible for much of the dramatic scenery in Utah's national parks.

More subtle forms of erosion have also contributed to the plateau's present-day form. Water percolating down through the rock layers is one of the main erosive forces, washing away loose material and dissolving ancient salts, often leaving odd formations, such as thin fins of resistant rock.

The many layers of sedimentary rocks forming the Colorado Plateau are all composed of different minerals and have varying densities, so it's not surprising that erosion affects each layer a bit differently. For instance, sandstones and limestones erode more readily than the harder mudstones or shales.

Erosion isn't limited to the force of water against rock. Rocks may be worn down or eaten away by a variety of forces, including wind, freezing and thawing, exfoliation (when sheets of rock peel off), oxidation, hydration and carbonation (chemical weathering), plant roots or animal burrows, and dissolving of soft rocks. Rockfalls in Zion, the ever-deepening channel of the Colorado River through Canyonlands, and the slow thinning of pedestals supporting Arches' balanced rocks are all clues that erosion continues unabated.

CLIMATE

The main thing for southern Utah travelers to remember is that they're in the desert.

The high-desert country of the Colorado Plateau lies mostly between 3,000–6,000 feet in elevation. Annual precipitation ranges from an extremely dry 3 inches in some areas to about 10 inches in others. Mountainous regions between 10,000–13,000 feet receive abundant rainfall in summer and heavy snows in winter.

Sunny skies prevail through all four seasons. Spring comes early to the canyon country with weather that's often windy and rapidly changing. Summer can make its presence known in April, although the real desert heat doesn't set in until late May or early June. Temperatures then soar into the 90s and 100s at midday, although the dry air makes the heat more bearable. Early morning is the choice time for travel in summer. A canyon seep surrounded by hanging gardens or a mountain meadow filled with wildflowers provides a refreshing contrast to the parched desert; other ways to beat the heat include hiking in the mountains and river-rafting.

Summer thunderstorm season begins anywhere from mid-June until August; huge billowing thunderstorm clouds bring refreshing rains and coolness. During this season, canyon hikers should be alert for flash flooding.

Autumn begins after the rains cease (usually October) and lasts into November or even December; days are bright and sunny with ideal temperatures, but nights become cold. In all of the parks, evenings will be cool even in midsummer. Think of southern Utah as the lunar

© W. C. MCRAE

Erosion has cut arches and spires out of Bryce Canyon's pink sandstone.

surface: as soon as the sun goes down, all the heat of the day escapes into the atmosphere. Even if the day was baking hot, you'll need a jacket and a warm sleeping bag for the night.

Elevation matters: Bryce Canyon National Park is at 8,000 feet, and will be significantly cooler than nearby Zion, at about 4,000 feet. Bryce is the only park to regularly be covered with enough snow for cross-country skiing or snowshoeing. It's also the park where, during the early spring, a motel room will seem like a good idea to all but the most hardy tent campers. Winter lasts only about two months at the lower elevations. Light snows on the canyon walls add new beauty to the rock layers. Nighttime temperatures commonly dip into the teens, which is too cold for most campers. Otherwise, winter can be a fine time for travel. Heavy snows rarely occur below 8,000 feet.

Flash Floods

Rainwater runs quickly off the rocky desert surfaces and into gullies and canyons. A summer thunderstorm or a rapid late-winter snowmelt can send torrents of mud and boulders rumbling down dry washes and canyons. Backcountry drivers, horseback riders, and hikers need to avoid hazardous locations when storms threaten or unseasonably warm winds blow on the winter snowpack.

Flash floods can sweep away anything in their path, including boulders, cars, and campsites. Do not camp or park in potential flash-flood areas. If you come to a section of flooded roadway—a common occurrence on desert roads after storms—wait until the water goes down before crossing (it shouldn't take long). Summer lightning causes forest and brush fires, posing a danger to hikers who are foolish enough to climb mountains when storms threaten.

The bare rock and loose soils so common in the canyon country do little to hold back the flow of rain or meltwater. In fact, slickrock is effective at shedding water as fast as it comes in contact. Logs and other debris wedged high on canyon walls give proof enough of past floods.

FLORA

Within the physiographic province of the Colorado Plateau, several different life zones are represented.

In the low desert, shrubs eke out a meager existence. Climbing higher you'll pass through grassy steppe, sage, and piñon-juniper woodlands to ponderosa pine. Of all these zones, the piñon-juniper is most common.

But it's not a lock-step progression of plant A at elevation X and plant B at elevation Z. Soils are an important consideration, with sandstones being more hospitable than shales. Plants will grow wherever the conditions will support them, and Utah's parks have many microenvironments that can lead to surprising plant discoveries. Look for different plants in these different habitats: slickrock (where cracks can gather enough soil to host a few plants), riparian (moist areas with the greatest diversity of life), and terraces and open space (the area between riverbank and slickrock, where shrubs dominate). With more than 800 native species, Zion has the greatest plant diversity of any of Utah's parks.

Cactus flowers are brilliant and short-lived.

© PAUL LEVY

evening primrose, a common desert flower

How Plants Survive in the Desert

Most of the plants you'll see in Utah's national parks are well adapted to desert life. Many are succulents, which have their own water-storage systems in their fleshy stems or leaves. Cacti are the most obvious succulents; they swell with stored moisture during the spring, then slowly shrink and wrinkle as the stored moisture is used.

Other plants have different strategies for making the most of scarce water. Some, such as yucca, have deep roots, taking advantage of what moisture exists in the soil. The leaves of desert plants are often vertical, exposing less surface area to the sun. Leaves may also have very small pores, slowing transpiration, or stems coated with a resinous substance, which also slows water loss. Hairy or light-colored leaves help reflect sunlight.

Desert wildflowers are annuals; they bloom in the spring, when water is available, then form seeds, which can survive the dry, hot summer, and die back. A particularly wet spring means a bumper crop of wildflowers.

Even though mosses aren't usually thought of as desert plants, they are found growing in seeps along canyon walls and in cryptobiotic soils. When water is unavailable, mosses dry up; when the water returns, the moss quickly plumps up again.

Junipers have a fairly drastic way of dealing with water shortage. During a prolonged dry spell, a juniper tree can shut off the flow of water to one or more of its branches, sacrificing these branches to keep the tree alive.

Hanging Gardens

Look along Zion's Virgin River canyon for clumps of ferns and mosses lit with maidenhair ferns, shooting stars, monkeyflowers, columbine, orchids, and bluebells. These unexpectedly lush pockets are called "hanging gardens," gemlike islands of plantlife nestled into canyon walls.

Hanging gardens take advantage of a unique microclimate created by the meeting of two rock layers: Navajo sandstone and Kayenta shale. Water percolates down through porous sandstone and, when it hits the denser shale layer, travels laterally along the top of the harder rock and emerges at cliff's edge. These little springs support lush plantlife.

Tamarisk

One of the Colorado Plateau's most common trees, the nonnative tamarisk is also one of the peskiest. Imported from the Mediterranean and widely planted along the Colorado River to control erosion, the tamarisk has spread wildly, and its dense stands have crowded out native trees such as cottonwoods. Tamarisks are notoriously thirsty trees, sucking up vast amounts of water, but they give back little in the way of food or habitat for local wildlife. Their thick growth also increases the risk of fire. The National Park Service is taking steps to control tamarisk.

Cryptobiotic Soil

Over much of the Colorado Plateau, the soil is alive. What looks like a grayish-brown crust is actually a dense network of filament-forming blue-green algae intertwined with soil particles, lichens, moss, green algae, and microfungi. This slightly sticky, crusty mass holds the soil together, slowing erosion. Its spongelike consistency allows it to soak up water and hold it. Plants growing in cryptobiotic soil have a great advantage over plants rooted in dry, sandy soil.

Crytobiotic soils are extremely fragile. Make every effort to avoid stepping on them—stick to trails, slickrock, or rocks instead.

FAUNA

Although they're not thought of as great "wildlife parks" like Yellowstone or Denali, Utah's national parks are home to plenty of animals. Desert animals are often nocturnal and unseen by park visitors.

Rodents

Rodents include squirrels, packrats, kangaroo rats, chipmunks, and porcupines, most of which spend their days in burrows.

One of the few desert rodents out foraging during the day is the white-tailed antelope squirrel, which looks much like a chipmunk. Its white tail reflects the sunlight, and, when it needs to cool down a bit, an antelope squirrel smears its face with saliva (yes, that probably *would* work for you, too, but that's why you have sweat glands). The antelope squirrel lives at lower elevations; higher up you'll see golden-mantled ground squirrels.

Look for rabbits—desert cottontails and jackrabbits—at dawn and dusk. If you're rafting the Green or Colorado River, keep an eye out for beavers.

Kangaroo rats are particularly well adapted to desert life. They spend their days in cool burrows, eat only plants, and never drink water! Instead, a kangaroo rat metabolizes dry food in a way that produces water.

Utah prairie dogs have been given a new lease on life in Bryce National Park. In 1973 the animals were listed as an endangered species and reintroduced to Bryce. Today about 130 animals live in the park—the largest protected population of Utah prairie dogs. Prairie dogs live together in social groups called colonies or towns, which are laced with burrows, featuring a network of entrances for quick pops in and out of the ground. Prairie dogs are preyed on by badgers, coyotes, hawks, and snakes, so a colony will post lookouts, who are constantly searching for danger. When threatened, the lookouts "bark" to warn the colony. Utah prairie dogs hibernate during the winter and emerge from their burrows to mate furiously in early April.

Porcupines are common in Capitol Reef and Zion; although they prefer to live in forested areas, especially the piñon-juniper zone, they sometimes forage in streamside brush. These nocturnal creatures have also been known to visit campsites, where they like to gnaw on sweaty boots or backpack straps.

Bats

As night falls in canyon country, bats emerge from the nooks and crannies that protect them from the day's heat and begin to feed on mosquitoes and other insects. The tiny gray

KNOW YOUR TRACKS

Here's the scenario: You're hiking down a trail and notice fresh, large paw prints. Mountain lion or Labrador retriever? Here's the way to tell the difference: Mountain lions usually retract their claws when they walk. Dogs, of course, can't do this. So if close inspection of the print reveals toenails, it's most likely from a canine's paw.

But about those mountain lions.... In recent years incidents of mountain lion-human confrontations have increased markedly and received much publicity. These ambush hunters usually prey on sick or weak animals but will occasionally attack people, especially children and small adults. When hiking or camping with children in mountain lion territory (potentially all of Utah's national parks), it's important to keep them close to the rest of the family.

If you are stalked by a mountain lion, make yourself look big by raising your arms, waving a big stick, or spreading your coat. Maintain direct eye contact with the animal, and do not turn your back to it. If the mountain lion begins to approach, throw rocks and sticks, and continue to look large and menacing as you slowly back away. In the case of an attack, fight back; do not "play dead."

To put things in perspective, it's important to remember that mountain lions are famously elusive. If you do see one, it will probably be a quick glimpse of the cat running away from you.

Large Mammals

Mule deer are common in all of the parks, as are coyotes. Other large mammals include the predators: mountain lions and coyotes. If you're lucky, you'll get a glimpse of a bobcat or a fox.

If you're hiking the trails of Bryce Canyon early in the morning and see something that looks like a small dog in a tree, it's probably a gray fox. These small (5–10 pounds) foxes live in forested areas and have the catlike ability to climb trees. They're most commonly seen on the connecting trail between the Queen's Garden and Navajo Loop trails. Kit foxes, which are even tinier than gray foxes, with prominent ears and a big bushy tail, are common in Arches and Canyonlands. Red foxes also live across the plateau.

Desert bighorn sheep live in Arches, Canyonlands, and Capitol Reef; look for them trotting across steep, rocky ledges. In Arches, they're frequently sighted along U.S. 191 south of the visitors center. They also roam the talus slopes and side canyons near the Colorado River. Desert bighorns have also been reintroduced in Zion and can occasionally be spotted in steep, rocky areas on the park's east side.

Reptiles

Reptiles are well-suited to desert life. As cold-blooded, or ectothermic, animals, their body temperature depends on the environment, rather than on internal metabolism, and it's easy for them to keep warm in the desert heat. When it's cold, reptiles hibernate or drastically slow their metabolism.

The western whiptail lizard is common in Arches. You'll recognize it because its tail is twice as long as its body. Also notable is the western collared lizard, with a bright green body set off by a black collar.

Less flashy but particularly fascinating are the several species of parthenogenic lizards. All of these lizards are female, and they reproduce by laying eggs that are clones of themselves. Best known is the plateau striped whiptail, but 6 of the 12 species of whiptail present in the area are all-female.

western pipistrelle is common. It flies early in the evening, feeding near streams, and can be spotted by its somewhat erratic flight. The pallid bat spends a lot of its time creeping across the ground in search of food and is a late-night bat (look for it after 10 P.M. in the summer at Capitol Reef). Another common bat (here and across the United States) is the prosaically named big brown bat.

© EMILY ROTH

rattlesnake warming against a rock

The northern plateau lizard is common in areas about 3,000–6,000 feet. It's not choosy about its habitat—juniper-piñon woodlands, prairies, riparian woodlands, and rocky hillsides are all perfectly acceptable. This is the lizard you'll most often see scurrying across your campsite in Zion or Capitol Reef.

Rattlesnakes are present across the area, but, given a chance, they'll get out of your way rather than strike. (Still, it's another good reason to wear sturdy boots.) The midget faded rattlesnake, a small subspecies of the western rattlesnake, lives in burrows and rock crevices and is mostly active at night. Although this snake has especially toxic venom, full venom injections occur in only a third of all bites.

Amphibians

Although they're not usually thought of as desert animals, a variety of frogs and toads live on the Colorado Plateau. Tadpoles live in wet springtime potholes as well as in streams and seeps. If you're camping in a canyon, you may be lucky enough to be serenaded by a toad chorus.

Bullfrogs are not native to the western United States, but since they were introduced in the early 1900s, they have flourished, very likely at the expense of native frogs and toads, whose eggs and tadpoles they eat.

The big round toes of the small, spotted canyon treefrog make it easy to identify—that is, if you can see this well-camouflaged frog in the first place! They're most active at night, spending their days on streamside rocks or trees.

Toads present in Utah's parks include the Great Basin spadefoot, red spotted toad, and western woodhouse toad.

Birds

Have you ever seen a bird pant? Believe it or not, that's how desert birds expel heat from their bodies. They allow heat to escape by drooping their wings away from their bodies, exposing thinly feathered areas (sort of like pulling up your shirt and using it to fan your torso).

The various habitats across the Colorado Plateau, such as piñon-juniper, perennial streams, dry washes, and rock cliffs, allow many species of bird to find homes. Birders will find the greatest variety of birds near rivers and streams. Other birds, such as golden eagles, kestrels (small falcons), and peregrine falcons nest high on cliffs and patrol open areas for prey. Common hawks include the red-tailed hawk and northern harrier; late-evening strollers may see great horned owls. California condors were reintroduced in 1996 to Zion, and while they're still not abundant, their population is steadily increasing.

People usually notice the canyon wren by its lovely song; this small, long-beaked bird nests in cavities along cliff faces. The related rock wren is—as its name implies—a rock collector: It paves a trail to its nest with pebbles, and the nest itself is lined with rocks. Another canyon bird, the white-throated swift, swoops and calls as it chases insects and mates, rather dramatically, in flight. They're often seen near violet-green swallows (which are equally gymnastic fliers) in Canyonlands, Arches, and Grand Staircase–Escalante.

© PAUL LEVY

chukar at Kodachrome Basin State Park

Chukar—chunky game birds introduced for the benefit of hunters in the 1930s—are common at Capitol Reef, where they're often seen on or near the ground, foraging in low-lying shrubs and grasses.

Several species of hummingbird (mostly black-chinned, but also broad-tailed and rufous) are often seen in the summer. Woodpeckers are also common, including the northern flicker and red-naped sapsucker, and flycatchers like Say's phoebe, western kingbird, and western wood-pewee can be spotted too. Two warblers—the yellow and the yellow-rumped—are common in the summer, and Wilson's warbler stops in during spring and fall migrations. Horned larks are present year-round.

Mountain bluebirds are colorful, easy for a novice to identify, and common in Canyonlands and Arches. Look for the American dipper along the Virgin River in Zion. This small, gray bird distinguishes itself from other similar birds by its habit of plunging headfirst into the water in search of insects.

Both the well-known scrub jay and its local cousin, the piñon jay, are noisy visitors to most every picnic. Other icons of western av life—the turkey vulture, the raven, and magpie—are widespread and easily spotte

Fish

Obviously, deserts aren't particularly kno for their aquatic life, and the big rivers of Colorado Plateau are now dominated by n native species such as channel catfish and c Many of these fish were introduced as ga fish. Native fish, like the six-foot, 100-po Colorado pikeminnow, are now uncommo

Spiders and Scorpions

Tarantulas, black widow spiders, and scorpi all live across the Colorado Plateau, and all objects of many a parkgoer's phobias. Altho the black widow spider's venom is toxic, tar tulas deliver only a mildly toxic bite (and ra bite humans), and a scorpion's sting is ab like that of a bee.

ENVIRONMENTAL ISSUES

Utah's national parks have generally b shielded from the environmental issues t play out in the rest of the state, which has ways been business-oriented, with a heavy phasis on extractive industries such as min and logging.

The main environmental threats to the p are the consequences of becoming too popu During the summer, auto and RV traffic clog park roads, with particularly bad snar viewpoint parking areas. Both Zion and Br have made attempts to control park traffic running shuttle buses along scenic drives. Zion, it's mandatory to ride the bus (or y bike) during summer, and it's made a sign cant difference.

Hikers also have an impact, especially wh they tread on fragile cryptobiotic soil. Kill this living soil crust drastically increases e sion in an already easily eroded environme

ORV Overkill

Off-road vehicles, or ORVs (also kno as ATVs—all-terrain vehicles), have ge from being the hobby of a small group of off-road enthusiasts to being one of the fastest-growing recreational markets in the country. Although use of ORVs is prohibited in the national parks, these dune-buggies-on-steroids are having a huge impact on public lands adjacent to the parks and on BLM lands that are currently under study for designation as wilderness. The scope of the issue is easy to measure. In 1979, there were 9,000 ORVs registered in Utah. In 2005, there were 150,000. In addition, the power and dexterity of the machines has greatly increased. Now essentially military-style assault machines that can climb near-vertical cliffs and clamber over any kind of terrain, ORVs are the new "extreme sports" toy of choice, and towns like Moab are now seeing more visitors coming to tear up the backcountry on ORVs than to mountain bike. The problem is that the ORVs are extremely destructive to the delicate natural environment of the Colorado Plateau deserts and canyonlands, and the more powerful, roaring, exhaust-belching machines put even the most remote and isolated areas within reach of large numbers of potentially destructive revelers.

Between the two camps—one which would preserve the public land and protect the ancient human artifacts found in remote canyons, the other which sees public land as a playground to be zipped over at high speed—is the BLM. The Moab BLM office has seemed to favor the ORV set, abdicating its role to protect the land and environment for all. Or so thought an alliance of eight environmental groups called the Southern Utah Wilderness Alliance (SUWA) that took the BLM to court to force it to comply with existing laws and create—and enforce—designated ORV trails in wilderness study areas. While lower courts found in favor of the environmental alliance, in 2004 the U.S. Supreme Court reversed the decision. Meanwhile, the Moab area, the San Rafael Swell near Hanksville, and the Vermilion Cliffs near Kanab are seeing unprecedented levels of ORV activity. Groups like SUWA have regrouped and have developed new strategies to force the BLM to comply with its own responsibility for environmental stewardship of public land. For more information see the SUWA website at www.suwa.org.

Nonnative Species

Nonnative species don't respect park boundaries, and several nonnative animals and plants have established strongholds in Utah's national parks, altering the local ecology by outcompeting native plants and animals.

Particularly invasive plants include tamarisk (salt cedar), cheat grass, Russian knapweed, and Russian olive. Tamarisk is often seen as the most troublesome invader. This thirsty Mediterranean plant was imported in the 1800s as an ornamental shrub and was later planted by the Department of Agriculture to slow erosion along the banks of the Colorado River in Arizona. It rapidly took hold, spreading upriver at roughly 12 miles per year, and is now firmly established on all of the Colorado's tributaries, where it grows in dense stands. Tamarisk consumes a great deal of water and rarely provides food and shelter necessary for the survival of wildlife. It also outcompetes cottonwoods because tamarisk shade inhibits the growth of cottonwood seedlings.

Courthouse Wash in Arches is one of several sites where the National Park Service has made an effort to control tamarisk. Similar control experiments have been established in nearby areas, mostly in small, tributary canyons of the Colorado River.

History

The landscape isn't the only vivid aspect of southern Utah. The area's human history is also noteworthy. This part of the American West has been inhabited for over 10,000 years, and remnants of ancient villages and panels of mysterious rock art lie in now remote canyons. More recently, colonization by Mormon settlers and the establishment of the national parks have brought human history back to this dramatic corner of the Colorado Plateau.

PREHISTORY

Beginning about 15,000 years ago, nomadic groups of Paleo-Indians traveled across the Colorado Plateau in search of game animals and wild plants, but they left few traces.

Nomadic bands of hunter-gatherers roamed the Colorado Plateau for at least 5,000 years. The climate was probably cooler and wetter when these first people arrived, with both food plants and game animals more abundant than today.

Agriculture was introduced from the south about 2,000 years ago and brought about a slow transition to a settled village life. The Fremont culture emerged in the northern part of the region (including present-day Capitol Reef and Arches National Parks and Grand Staircase–Escalante National Monument) and the Anasazi in the southern part (there was a settlement in present-day Zion National Park). In some areas, including Escalante and Arches, both groups lived contemporaneously. Although both groups made pots, baskets, bowls, and jewelry, only the Anasazi constructed masonry villages. Thousands of stone dwellings, ceremonial kivas, and towers built by the Anasazi still stand. Both groups left behind intriguing rock art, either pecked in (petroglyphs) or painted (pictographs).

The Anasazi and Fremont departed from this region about 800 years ago, perhaps because of drought, warfare, or disease. Some of the Anasazi moved south and joined the Pueblo tribes of present-day Arizona and New Mex-

ANASAZI OR ANCESTRAL PUEBLOAN?

As you travel through the Southwest, you may hear reference to the "ancestral Puebloans." In this book, we've chosen to use the more familiar name for these people – the Anasazi. The word *Anasazi* is actually a Navajo term that archaeologists chose, thinking it meant "old people." A more literal translation is "enemy ancestors." For this reason, some consider the name inaccurate. The terminology is in flux, and which name you hear depends on whom you're talking to or where you are. The National Park Service now uses the more descriptive term ancestral Puebloan. These prehistoric people built masonry villages and eventually moved south to Arizona and New Mexico, where their descendants, such as the Acoma, Cochiti, Santa Clara, Taos, and Hopi Mesas, live in modern-day pueblos.

ico. The fate of the Fremont people remains a mystery.

After the mid-1200s and until white settlers arrived in the late 1800s, small bands of nomadic Ute and Paiute moved through southern Utah. The Navajo began to enter Utah in the early 1800s. None of the three groups established firm control of the region north of the San Juan River, where present-day national parks are located.

AGE OF EXPLORATION

In 1776, Spanish explorers of the Dominguez-Escalante Expedition were the first Europeans to visit and describe the region. They had given up partway through a proposed journey from Santa Fe to California and returned to Santa Fe along a route passing through the sites of present-day Cedar City and Hurricane, crossing the Colorado River in a place that is now covered by Lake Powell.

The Old Spanish Trail, used 1829–1848, ran through Utah to connect New Mexico with California, crossing the Colorado River near present-day Moab. Fur trappers and mountain men, including Jedediah Smith, also traveled southern Utah's canyons in search of beaver and other animals during the early 1800s; inscriptions carved into the sandstone record their passage. In 1859, the U.S. Army's Macomb Expedition made the first documented description of what is now Canyonlands National Park. Major John Wesley Powell's pioneering river expeditions down the Green and Colorado Rivers in 1869 and 1871–1872 filled in many blank areas on the maps.

MORMON SETTLEMENT

In 1849–1850, Mormon leaders in Salt Lake City took the first steps toward colonizing southern Utah. Parowan, now a sleepy community along I-15, became the first Mormon settlement in southern Utah, and Cedar City the second—both established in 1851. In 1855, a successful experiment in growing cotton along Santa Clara Creek near present-day St. George aroused considerable interest among the Mormons. New settlements soon arose in the Virgin River Valley; however, poor roads hindered development, and floods, droughts, disease, and hostile Native Americans discouraged some Mormon pioneers, but many of those who stayed prospered by raising food crops and livestock.

Also in 1855, the Elk Ridge Mission was founded near present-day Moab. It lasted only a few months before Utes killed three Mormon settlers and sent the rest fleeing for their lives. Church members had better success during the 1870s in the Escalante area (1876) and Moab (1877).

For sheer effort and endurance, it's hard to beat the efforts of the Hole-in-the-Rock Expedition of 1879–1880. Sixty families with 83 wagons and more than 1,000 head of livestock crossed some of the West's most rugged canyon country in an attempt to settle at Montezuma

Mormon pioneers scratched their names into the rock walls in Capitol Gorge.

Creek on the San Juan River. They almost didn't make it: A journey expected to take six weeks turned into a six-*month* ordeal. The exhausted company arrived on the banks of the San Juan River on April 5, 1880. Too tired to continue just 20 easy miles to Montezuma Creek, they stayed and founded the town of Bluff. The Mormons established other towns in southeastern Utah, too, relying on ranching, farming, and mining for their livelihoods. None of the communities in the region ever reached a large size; Moab is the biggest with a population of 5,500.

NATIONAL PARK MOVEMENT IN UTAH

In the early 1900s, people other than Native Americans, Mormon settlers, and government explorers began to notice that southern Utah was a remarkably scenic place and that it might be developed for tourism.

In 1909, a presidential Executive Order designated Mukuntuweap (now Zion) National Monument, in Zion Canyon. Roads were built to improve the access, and by 1917, a tent camping resort was operating in the canyon. Two years later, Congress passed a bill forming Zion National Park. In the 1920s, the Union Pacific completed a rail line to Cedar City and Zion; Zion Lodge was built; and the technically challenging construction of the Zion–Mt. Carmel Highway, including its impressive 5,613-foot tunnel, began.

Early homesteaders around Bryce took visiting friends and relatives to see the incredible rock formations, and pretty soon they found themselves in the tourism business. In 1923, when Bryce Canyon National Monument was dedicated, the Union Pacific Railroad took over the fledgling tourist camp and began building Bryce Lodge. Tours of the hoodoos proved to be spectacularly popular, and Bryce became a national park in 1928.

Like Bryce and Zion, Arches was also helped along by railroad executives looking to develop their own businesses. In 1929, President Herbert Hoover signed the legislation creating Arches National Monument.

Capitol Reef became a national monument in 1937, thanks largely to one vigorous and enthusiastic local, and for years it was loved passionately by a handful of Utah archaeology buffs, but largely ignored by the federal government, who put it under the administrative control of Zion National Park.

During the 1960s, the National Park Service responded to a huge increase in park visitation nationwide by expanding facilities, spurring Congress to change the status of several national monuments to national parks. Canyonlands became a national park in the 1960s; after a spate of uranium prospecting in the nuclear-giddy 1950s, Capitol Reef and Arches gained national park status in 1971.

As visitors continued to flood the parks during the 1980s and 1990s, park managers realized they needed to develop strategies to deal with the crowds and, especially, the traffic. New trails, campgrounds, and visitors centers were built, and Zion and Bryce have both made attempts to control traffic on their scenic roads.

In 1996, President Bill Clinton used provisions of the National Antiquities Act to establish the Grand Staircase–Escalante National Monument. This vast tract of land, which totals more than 1.8 million acres, is the largest national monument land grouping in the lower 48 states, bringing under federal Interior Department management tracts of land previously administered by the Bureau of Land Management, the National Forest Service, and the state of Utah. Designation as a national monument means that the land is off-limits to specific kinds of development and that the land will be managed to preserve its wilderness characteristics as much as possible. The timing of the designation was apparently motivated by plans to develop a large strip coal mine in the slickrock Escalante River canyons, a well-loved destination for long-distance hikers and adventurers.

The People

One of the oddest statistics about Utah is that it's the most urban of America's western states. Eighty-five percent of the state's population of 2,316,000 citizens live in urban areas, and a full 80 percent reside in the Wasatch Front area.

That means that there aren't many people in remote southern Utah. With the exception of St. George, Kanab, and Moab, there aren't sizable communities in this part of the state. Even the undaunted Mormon settlers found this a forbidding place to settle during their 19th-century agrarian colonization of Utah.

Moab is known as a youthful and dynamic town, and its mountain bikers set more of the civic tone than the Mormon church. However, outside of Moab, most small ranching communities in southern Utah are still deeply Mormon. It's a good idea to develop an understanding of Utah's predominant religion if you plan on spending any time outside of the parks.

LATTER-DAY SAINTS

One of the first things to know is that the term "Mormon" is rarely used by church members themselves. The church's proper title is the Church of Jesus Christ of Latter-Day Saints, and members prefer to be called "Latter-Day Saints," "Saints" (usually this term is just used amongst church members), or "LDS." While calling someone a Mormon isn't *wrong,* it's not quite as respectful.

The religion is based in part on the Book of Mormon, the name given to a text derived from a set of "golden plates" found by Joseph Smith in 1827 in western New York. Smith claimed to have been led by an angel to the plates, which were covered with a text written in "reformed Egyptian." A farmer by upbringing, Smith translated the plates and published an English-language version of the Book of Mormon in 1830.

The Book of Mormon tells the story of the lost tribes of Israel, which, according to Mormon teachings, migrated to North America and became the ancestors of today's Native Americans. According to the Book of Mormon, Jesus also journeyed to North America, and the book includes teachings and prophecies that Christ supposedly gave to the ancient Indians.

The most stirring and unifying aspect of Mormon history is the incredible westward migration made by the small, fiercely dedicated band of Mormon pioneers in the 1840s. Smith and his followers were persecuted in New York and then in their newly founded utopian communities in Ohio, Missouri, and Illinois. After Smith was murdered near Carthage, Illinois, in 1844, the group decided to press even farther westward toward the frontier, led by church president Brigham Young. The journey across the then very Wild West to the Great Salt Lake basin was made by horseback, wagon, or handcart—hundreds of Mormon pioneers pulled their belongings across the Great Plains in small carts. The first group of Mormon pioneers reached the Salt Lake City area in 1847. The bravery and tenacity of the group's two-year migration forms the basis of many Utah residents' fierce pride in their state and religion.

Most people know that LDS members are clean-living, family people who eschew alcohol, tobacco, and stimulants, including caffeine. This can make it a little tough for visitors to feed their own vices (and indeed, it may make what formerly seemed like a normal habit feel a little more sinister). But Utah has loosened up a lot in the past few years, largely thanks to hosting the 2002 Winter Olympics, and it's really not too hard to find a place to have a beer with dinner, though you may have to make a special request. Towns near the national parks are particularly used to hosting non-Saints, and attach virtually no stigma to waking up with a cup of coffee or settling down with a glass of wine.

SOUTHERN UTAH'S NATIVE AMERICANS

It's an oddity of history that most visitors to Utah's national parks will see much more evidence of the state's ancient native residents—in the form of eerie rock art, stone pueblos and storehouses—than they will today's remaining Native Americans. The prehistoric residents of the canyons of southern Utah left their mark on the land, but largely moved on. The fate of the ancient Fremont people has been lost to history, and the abandonment of Anasazi, or Ancestral Puebloan, villages is a mystery still being unearthed by archaeologists. When the Mormons arrived in the 1840s, isolated bands of Native Americans lived in the river canyons. Federal reservations were granted to several of these tribes.

Ute

Several bands of Utes, or Núuci, ranged over large areas of central and eastern Utah and adjacent Colorado. Originally hunter-gatherers, they acquired horses in about 1800 and became skilled raiders. Customs adopted from Plains tribes included the use of rawhide, tepees, and the *travois* (a sled used to carry goods). The discovery of gold in southern Colorado and the pressures of farmers there and in Utah forced the Utes to move and renegotiate treaties many times. They now have the large Uintah and Ouray Indian Reservation in northeast Utah, the small White Mesa Indian Reservation in southeast Utah, and the Ute Mountain Indian Reservation in southwest Colorado and northwest New Mexico.

Southern Paiute

Six of the 19 major bands of the Southern Paiutes, or Nuwuvi, lived along the Santa Clara, Beaver, and Virgin Rivers and in other parts of southwest Utah. Extended families hunted and gathered food together. Fishing and the cultivation of corn, beans, squash, and sunflowers supplemented the diet of most of the bands. Today, Utah's Paiutes have a tribal headquarters in Cedar City and scattered small parcels of reservation land. Southern Paiutes also live in southern Nevada and northern Arizona.

Navajo

Calling themselves Diné, the Navajo moved into the San Juan River area about 1600. The tribe has proved exceptionally adaptable in learning new skills from other cultures: many Navajo crafts, clothing, and religious practices have come from Native American, Spanish, and Anglo neighbors. The Navajo tribe was the first in the area to move away from a hunting and gathering lifestyle, relying instead on the farming and shepherding techniques they had learned from the Spanish. The Navajo have become one of the largest Native American groups in the country, occupying 16 million acres of exceptionally scenic land in southeast Utah and adjacent Arizona and New Mexico. Tribal headquarters is at Window Rock in Arizona.

ESSENTIALS

Getting There

If you're driving from other points in North America, Utah is easy to reach. The parks are east of I-15, which runs from Canada to Mexico, parallel to the Rocky Mountains. And they're south of I-70, which links Denver to I-15.

International travelers flying in to the region have numerous options. Salt Lake City is convenient as a terminus for travelers who want to make a loop tour through the parks. For other travelers, Utah's national parks are best seen as part of a longer American road trip. Many European travelers fly into Denver, rent vehicles or RVs, cross the Rocky Mountains, and explore southern Utah (and perhaps the Grand Canyon) on the way to Las Vegas, from whence they return.

Public transportation, like regularly scheduled flights, is almost nonexistent in southern Utah and the parks. Unless you're on a bicycle, you will need your own vehicle to explore southern Utah.

FROM SALT LAKE CITY

Many tours of Utah's national parks begin in Salt Lake City. Its busy airport and plethora of hotels make it an easy place to begin and end a trip.

Airport

Salt Lake City is a hub for Delta Airlines, and

© PAUL LEVY

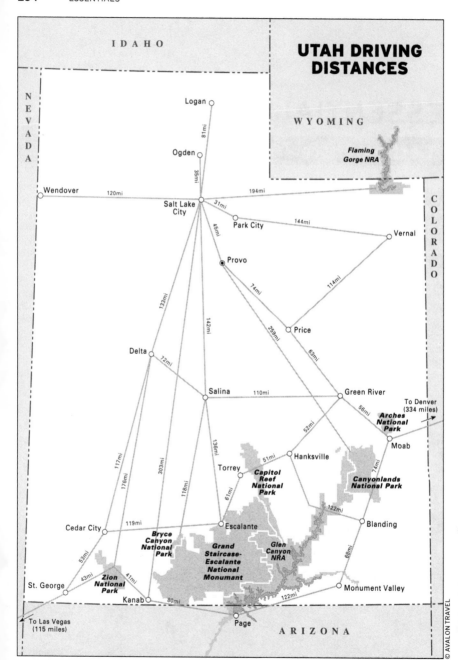

all other major airlines have regular flights into Salt Lake City International Airport (www .slcairport.com). The airport is an easy seven miles west of downtown; reach it via I-80 or North Temple.

SkyWest Airlines (800/453-9417), Delta's commuter line, flies to Cedar City and St. George in Utah and to towns in adjacent states. **US Airways Express** (800/235-9292) provides daily scheduled air service between Canyonlands Field just north of Moab and Salt Lake International Airport, with one direct round-trip flight Sunday–Thursday, two on Friday.

The airport has three terminals; in each you'll find a ground-transportation information desk, a cafeteria, motel/hotel courtesy phones, auto rentals (Hertz, Avis, National, Budget, and Dollar), the Morris Travel office, and a ski-rental shop. Terminal 1 also houses Zion's First National Bank (currency exchange), an ice-cream parlor, and gift shops. The Utah Information Center (801/575-2800) is upstairs in Terminal 2 and is open 24 hours daily (but staffed only during the day). Terminal 3 is dedicated to foreign arrivals and departures.

Train

The only passenger train through Salt Lake City is Amtrak's California Zephyr, which heads west to Reno and Oakland and east to Denver and Chicago four times a week. **Amtrak** (depot at 340 South 600 West, 800/872-7245 for information and reservations, www.amtrak .com) prices tickets as airlines do, with advance-booking, special seasonal, and other discounts available. Amtrak office hours (timed to meet the trains) are irregular, so call first.

Long-Distance Bus

Salt Lake City sits at a crossroads of several major freeways and has good **Greyhound** bus service (160 W. South Temple, 801/355-9579 or 800/231-2222). Generally speaking, buses go north and south along I-15 and east and west along I-80; you won't be able to take the bus to any of Utah's national parks.

Car

From Salt Lake City, it's a long 238-mile drive to Moab, the center for exploring Arches and Canyonlands National Parks. The fastest route takes you south from Salt Lake City on I-15, cutting east at Spanish Fork on U.S. 6/U.S. 89 to Price, south to Green River and I-70, and then to Moab on U.S. 191. Dramatic scenery highlights the entire length of this four-hour drive. To Zion and Bryce, simply take I-15 south from Salt Lake City. Driving time is about four hours.

You'll find all of the major companies and many local outfits eager to rent you a set of wheels. Many agencies have an office or delivery service at the airport: **Avis** (Salt Lake International Airport, 801/575-2847 or 800/331-1212); **Budget** (641 North 3800 West, 801/575-2500 or 800/527-0700); **Dollar** (601 North 3800 West, Salt Lake International Airport, 801/575-2580 or 800/421-9849); **Enterprise** (151 East 5600 South, 801/266-3777, 801/534-1888, or 800/RENT-A-CAR); **Hertz** (Salt Lake International Airport, 775 N. Terminal Dr., 801/575-2683 or 800/654-3131); **National** (Salt Lake City International Airport, 801/575-2277 or 800/227-7368); **Thrifty** (just outside the airport at 15 South 2400 West, 801/265-6677 or 800/847-4389); and **Payless** (1974 W. North Temple, 801/596-2596 or 800/327-3631).

RV and Motorcycle Rentals

Access RV Rental (300 S. U.S. 89, North Salt Lake City, 801/936-1200 or 800/327-6910, www.accessrvrental.com) is a local company with relatively good rates on RV rentals. **Cruise America** is a larger company with RV rentals available (4125 S. State St., 801/288-0930, www.cruiseamerica.com). **El Monte RV** provides rentals out of A-1 Pioneer Moving and Storage (2001 Warm Springs Rd., 888/337-2214, www.elmonterv.com).

Expect to pay $1,000–1,800 per week to rent an RV, depending on the season and the size of the vehicle.

Rent a Harley Davidson motorcycle from **Street Eagle/Bluesky Motorcycle Rentals**

(Sandy Central, Sandy, 801/419-3907, www
.blueskymotorcyclerentals.com). Motorcycles
run $95–200 per day.

Accommodations

With the exception of the two hostels, these
lodgings are all convenient to the airport, and
nearly all offer some form of transportation to
and from the airport. Hotels with the lowest-
number address on West North Temple are
closest to downtown.

If you're driving into town and just want to
find a hotel room *fast,* head south and west of
downtown, where chain hotels proliferate. The
area around 600 South and 200 West is especially fertile ground for midpriced hotels.

Under $50: To find budget accommoda-
tions, you'll have to leave the airport area. **The
Avenues Hostel** (107 F St., 801/363-3855,
www.saltlakehostel.com, $14 dorm, $30–35
private rooms, only half have private baths),
one mile east of Temple Square, offers rooms
with use of a kitchen, TV room, and laundry.
Information-packed bulletin boards list city
sights and goings-on, and you'll meet travelers from all over the world. Reservations (with
first night's deposit) are advised in the busy
summer-travel and winter-ski seasons. Open
8 A.M.–10 P.M. year-round. From downtown,
head east on South Temple Street to F Street,
then turn north two streets.

Directly south of downtown a couple of
miles is the **International Ute Hostel** (21 E.
Kelsey Ave., 801/595-1645, www.international
utehostel.com, $20 dorms, $45 private rooms),
with full access to kitchen facilities and common areas. Kelsey Avenue is the equivalent of
1160 South, just east off State Street.

$50-75: Although it's on the road to the
airport, the **Econo Lodge** (715 W. North Temple, 801/363-0062 or 800/BE-ECONO, $70
d), is also convenient to downtown. The motel
offers a courtesy car to downtown or the airport and has a pool and guest laundry. Of the
many older motor-court motels along North
Temple, the best maintained is the **Overniter
Motor Inn** (1500 W. North Temple, 801/533-
8300 or 800/914-8301, $55 d), with an out-

door pool and clean, basic rooms. Moderately
priced rooms are also available at **Days Inn**
(1900 W. North Temple, 801/539-8538 or
800/329-7466, $62 d) and at the **Motel 6
Airport** (1990 W. North Temple, 801/364-
1053, $51 d), where there's a pool. Closer to
the airport, the **Airport Inn** (2333 W. North
Temple, 801/539-0438, $66 d) has a pool and
guest laundry.

$75-100: Practically next door to the ter-
minal is the **Ramada Salt Lake City Airport**
(5575 W. Amelia Earhart Dr., 801/537-7020
or 800/272-6232, $89 and up), with a pool
and spa.

Over $100: Comfortable rooms, an outdoor
pool, and a better-than-average free continental breakfast make the **Comfort Inn Airport**
(200 N. Admiral Byrd Rd., 801/537-7444 or
800/535-8742, $119 and up) an appealing
place to spend a night.

The **Radisson Hotel Salt Lake City
Airport** (2177 W. North Temple, 801/364-
5800 or 800/333-3333, $139 and up) is an
attractive, lodgelike building with nicely furnished rooms. Guests receive a complimentary
continental breakfast and newspaper, and in
the evenings there's a manager's reception with
free beverages. Facilities include a pool, spa,
and fitness room. Suites come with a loft bedroom area. There's quite a range in room rates,
and package rates and promotions can bring
the rates down dramatically. At the **Airport
Hilton** (5151 Wiley Post Way, 801/539-1515
or 800/999-3736, $124 and up), rooms are
spacious and nicely furnished, and facilities
include two pools, a putting green, a sports
court, and an exercise room and spa. The hotel
even has its own lake.

If you want to really do Salt Lake City in
style, two downtown hotels are good places to
splurge. **Hotel Monaco** (15 West 200 South,
801/595-0000 or 877/294-9710, www.monaco-
saltlakecity.com, $159 and up) occupies a
grandly renovated historic office building in
a convenient spot in the middle of downtown;
on the main floor is **Bambara,** one of the most
sophisticated restaurants in Utah. Rooms are
sumptuously furnished with real élan: This

is no anonymous upscale hotel in beige and mauve. Expect wild colors and contrasting fabrics, lots of flowers, and excellent service. Facilities include an on-site fitness center, meeting rooms, plus concierge and valet services. Each room comes with two-line phones, a CD stereo, in-room fax, printer, and copier, plus an iron and board. Pets are welcome, and if you forgot your own pet, the hotel will deliver a companion goldfish to your room.

A new addition to the Salt Lake hotel scene, the gigantic **Grand America Hotel and Suites** (75 East 600 South, 800/533-3525, www.grand america.com, $250 and up), is Salt Lake City's take on the Vegas fantasy hotel. A block square (that's 10 acres in this land of long blocks), its 24 stories contains 775 rooms, more than half of them suites. Rooms have luxury-level amenities; expect all the perks and niceties that modern hotels can offer.

Camping

Of the several commercial campgrounds around the periphery of Salt Lake City, **Camp VIP** (1350 W. North Temple, 801/328-0224) is the most convenient, located between downtown and the airport. It offers tent and RV sites year-round with showers, swimming pool, game room, playground, store, and laundry. From I-15 northbound, take Exit 311 for I-80; go west 1.3 miles on I-80, exit north for a half mile on Redwood Road (Hwy. 68), then turn right for another half mile on North Temple. From I-15 southbound, take Exit 313 and turn south 1.5 miles on 900 West, then turn right and drive less than a mile on North Temple. From I-80 either take the North Temple exit or Redwood Road (Highway 68), then follow the directions above.

There are two good Forest Service campgrounds in Big Cottonwood Canyon about 15 miles southeast of downtown Salt Lake City and another two up Little Cottonwood Canyon, about 19 miles southeast of town. All have drinking water, and all prohibit pets (because of local watershed regulations).

In Big Cottonwood Canyon, **Spruces Campground** (elevation 7,400 feet, 9.1 miles

up the canyon) is open early June–mid-October. Some sites can be reserved by calling 877/444-6777 or online at www.reserveusa .com. The season at **Redman Campground** (elevation 8,300 feet) lasts mid-June–early October. It's between Solitude and Brighton, 13 miles up the canyon.

Little Cottonwood Canyon's **Tanners Flat Campground** (elevation 7,200 feet, 4.3 miles up the canyon) is open mid-May–mid-October. Reserve a site at 877/444-6777 or www.reserve usa.com. **Albion Basin Campground** lies high in the mountains a few miles past Alta Ski Area (elevation 9,500 feet) and is open early July–late September; go 11 miles up the canyon (the last 2.5 miles are gravel).

Food

If you're going to be camping on your trip through Utah's national parks, you may want to pick up some provisions in Salt Lake City before hitting the road south. Just east of I-15, off I-80 in the Sugar House district, **Wild Oats** (1131 E. Wilmington Ave., 801/359-7913) has a good deli, lots of organic produce, bulk foods, and good bread (likely the last you'll see for a while). It's in a complex that also contains some good restaurants, a camping-supply store, and the brightest, shiniest tattoo parlor you'll ever lay eyes on.

Downtown, stop at **Tony Caputo Market & Deli** (308 W. Broadway, 801/531-8669), an old-style Italian deli brimming with delicious sausages, cheeses, and olives. Don't forget to get a sandwich to go!

For Salt Lake City's best restaurants, you'll need to head downtown. **Lamb's** (169 S. Main, 801/364-7166) claims to be Utah's oldest restaurant. You can still enjoy the classic 1930s diner atmosphere as well as the tasty food. Open for three meals a day (but closed Sun.), Lamb's is an especially good place for breakfast. Dinner entrées are $13–15.

Red Iguana (on the way in from the airport at 736 W. North Temple, 801/322-1489) is one of the city's favorite Mexican restaurants and offers excellent south-of-the-border cooking with a specialty in Mayan and regional foods. Best of all, flavors are crisp, fresh, and earthy. The Red Iguana is very popular, so arrive early—especially at lunch—to avoid the lines.

For fine dining, the **Metropolitan** (173 W. Broadway, 801/362-3472) is easily Salt Lake City's most ambitious restaurant, taking "fusion cuisine" to new lengths. In this high-design dining room (reserve tables near the fireplace-cum-water sculpture), the foods of the world meet and mingle on your plate in preparations that are sometimes unexpected but always stylish. Cuisine like this doesn't come cheap; expect to pay upwards of $10 for appetizers and $25–35 for main dishes. Metropolitan is open nightly for dinner, Monday–Friday for lunch.

At **Bambara** in the Hotel Monaco (202 S. Main, 801/363-5454), the menu emphasizes the freshest and most flavorful of local meats and produce, with preparations in a wide-awake New American style that is equal parts tradition and innovation; entrées range $20–25. At **Martine** (22 East 100 South, 801/363-9328), the antique high-ceilinged dining room is coolly elegant, the cooking and presentation subtly continental. You have a choice of ordering tapas-style ($8–10) or ordering full meals ($23–29). The **Market Street Grill** (48 Market St., near Main and Broadway, 801/322-4668) features fresh seafood plus steak, prime rib, chops, chicken, and pasta. Adjacent is an oyster bar. Entrées run $19–27, though if you arrive before 7 P.M. you can order the early-bird specials for $17. Open daily for breakfast, lunch, and dinner, and for brunch on Sunday.

Utah's oldest brewpub is **Squatters Pub Brewery** (147 W. Broadway, 801/363-2739). In addition to fine beers and ales, the pub serves sandwiches, burgers, and other light entrées in a handsome old warehouse. In summer there's seating on the back deck. Another popular brewpub is the **Red Rock Brewing Company** (254 South 200 West, 801/521-7446), offering pasta, salads, and sandwiches, including an excellent variation on the hamburger (baked in a wood-fired oven inside a bread pocket). There's often a wait to get in the door, but the food and brews are worth it. The Red Rock is unusual for Salt Lake in that it serves food late—till midnight on weekends.

FROM LAS VEGAS

Just because you're going to Utah, don't assume it's best to fly into Salt Lake City. If you're traveling to Zion, Bryce, and/or Grand Staircase–Escalante, consider flying into Las Vegas rather than Salt Lake City. Not only is it closer to these parks, but car rentals are usually about $100 a week cheaper. Even if you have absolutely no interest in gambling, many casino hotels have very good midweek rates.

Airport

McCarran International Airport (5757 Wayne Newton Blvd., 702/261-5743, www.mccarran.com) is just a few minutes south of The Strip (a.k.a. Las Vegas Boulevard South, the six-mile stretch of casinos and hotels).

Las Vegas is well served by all the major airlines, and also by smaller or "no-frills" carriers such as Frontier Airlines (800/432-1359) and Southwest Airlines (800/435-9792), whose bargain prices keep all the other airlines competitive.

The airport has two terminals—Terminal 1 has most of the domestic traffic, while Terminal 2 serves international and charter flights—linked by a shuttle. Exchange foreign currency in Terminal 2; find full-service banking and check-in for some of the larger casino hotels in Terminal 1. Slot machines, of course, are everywhere.

Long-Distance Bus

Greyhound (220 S. Main St., 702/384-9561 or 800/231-2222) serves communities along the I-15 corridor, including St. George.

Car

From Las Vegas, it's just 120 miles northeast on I-15 to St. George, with Zion just 43 miles farther.

It's relatively inexpensive to rent a car in Las Vegas; an economy car will run about $120 per week, before taxes. At the airport, find **Avis** (702/261-5591 or 800/331-1212);

Budget (702/736-1212 or 800/527-0700); **Dollar** (702/739-8403 or 800/800-4000); **Hertz** (702/736-4900 or 800/654-3131); **National** (702/261-5391 or 800/227-7368); **Payless** (702/736-6147 or 800/327-3631); **Sav-mor** (702/736-1234 or 800/634-6779); and **Thrifty** (702/896-7600 or 800/847-4389). A shuttle runs between the airport and the rental office for **Alamo** (6855 Bermuda Rd., 702/263-8411).

RV Rentals

Rent an RV from **Cruise America** (6070 Boulder Hwy., 702/456-6666, www.cruiseamerica .com). **El Monte RV** (13001 Las Vegas Blvd., 888/337-2214 or 702/269-8000, www .elmonterv.com) is another good bet. Rates typically start at about $1,000 a week during the spring, fall, and winter; $1,200 per week during the summer.

Accommodations

For its sheer number of hotel rooms, Las Vegas can't be beat. Even if you have no desire to visit Vegas, it may make sense to spend the first and/or final night of your trip here. During the week, it's relatively easy to find a good rate at a casino hotel. However, beware of weekends if you're watching your pennies: rooms on Saturday nights often cost triple what they cost during the week. Reservation services, such as **Las Vegas Hotels Reservation Service** (800/968-2352, www.lasvegasnevadahotels) or the **Las Vegas Convention and Visitor Authority** (800/332-5334, www.lasvegas24hours.com), may be able to help you find a good deal on a room.

Under $50: If you're looking for a place to call home in Las Vegas, try the **Sin City Hostel** (1208 Las Vegas Blvd. S., 702/868-0222, www.sincityhostel.com), a friendly place in a slightly dodgy neighborhood between downtown and The Strip. Dorm beds start at $19, semiprivate rooms (shared bath) at $39. **USA Hostels Las Vegas** (1322 Fremont St., 702/385-1150 or 800/550-8958, www.usahostels.com/vegas, $15 dorm, $48 and up private) bills itself as a hostel resort, with a large swimming pool, Ja-cuzzi, and a deck with water-misters, a large lounge with free billiards and foosball tables and comfortable couches, DSL Internet access, laundry room, and well-equipped kitchen.

$50-75: About one mile from the airport, and not too far off the south end of The Strip, find the **Ambassador Strip Travelodge** (5075 Koval Lane, 888/844-3131 or 702/736-3600, $49 d and up, much more on weekends). This motel, with an outdoor pool and free continental breakfast, is a good alternative to a casino hotel. In the same price range and also off The Strip near the airport is the **Best Western McCarran Inn** (4970 Paradise Rd., 702/798-5530 or 800/626-7575, $49 d).

Over $100: Most of the major casino hotels (Caesar's Palace, New York New York, The Venetian, etc.) have rooms in this price range. You'll find them listed on reservation services listed above, which makes it easy to locate a room that suits your taste and budget.

If you're looking for lodging that's quintessentially Las Vegas, a bit of a splurge, and convenient to the airport, consider basking in the hip luxury of **Mandalay Bay Resort and Casino** (3950 Las Vegas Blvd. S., 877/632-7400 or 702/632-7777, $140 and up) at the south end of The Strip.

Food

As celebrity chefs from around the country have established outposts in various upscale casinos, Las Vegas has become a destination for fine dining. Nearly every casino hotel has multiple restaurants, sometimes multiple fine dining restaurants. For instance, at the MGM Grand (3799 Las Vegas Blvd. S., 702/891-7374) there's both **Emeril's,** for high-production New Orleans–style seafood, and Joel Robuchon, the eponymous restaurant of the renowned French chef (his only fine dining restaurant in the U.S). And talk about an embarrassment of riches—at the Venetian Hotel (3355 Las Vegas Blvd. S., 702/414-3737), Mr. Lagasse owns the **Delmonico,** a steakhouse that goes well above and beyond your basic rib-eye; Thomas Keller has opened Bouchon with high-end Napa Valley dining; and Mario Batalli has opened an outpost called B&B Ristorante.

Wolfgang Puck's restaurants are nearly ubiquitous in Vegas casinos. **Chinois** (Forum Shops at Caesars Palace, 3500 Las Vegas Ave. S., 702/737-9700, lunch and dinner daily) serves a fusion of Chinese and French cuisines. **Wolfgang Puck Café** (MGM Grand Hotel, 3799 Las Vegas Blvd. S., 702/891-3019, lunch and dinner daily) is Puck's take on American bar-and-grill food.

One of Las Vegas's current hot spots is **Alize** (Palms Hotel, 4321 W. Flamingo Rd., 702/951-7000), with great views and superb French cuisine.

Venture off The Strip to an unlikely looking strip mall to find **Rosemary's** (8125 W. Sahara, 702/869-2251, lunch and dinner), considered to be one of Las Vegas's top restaurants, with its "New American" menu influenced by the chef/owner's time spent in Emeril's kitchen.

Expect main courses at all of these restaurants to be $25–40 and up. Dine less expensively on a selection of appetizers. Cheaper dining can be found at casino buffets, or try **Pink Taco** (Hard Rock Hotel, 4455 Paradise Rd., 702/693-5525) for Mexican food in a hip, freewheeling atmosphere.

Finally, if you want a taste of old Vegas, head up to the 24th floor of Binion's Horseshoe to **Binion's Ranch Steakhouse** (128 E. Fremont St., 702/382-1600), a Las Vegas institution with huge steaks and reasonable prices.

FROM DENVER

Although it may not seem intuitive to start your tour of Utah's national parks in Denver, that's exactly what works best for many folks, especially Europeans who fly from European capital cities to Denver International Airport. From there, it's easy to rent a car or RV and begin a tour that typically includes Rocky Mountain National Park, Utah's five national parks, and the Grand Canyon.

Airport

Locals joke that **Denver International Airport** (DIA, 8500 Peña Blvd., 303/342-2000, www .flydenver.com) is in Kansas; it's actually 23 miles northeast of downtown Denver on CO 470, north of I-70. Major airlines using DIA include American, British Airways, Continental, Delta, and United.

DIA's Jeppesen Terminal has a giant atrium and three concourses connected by a light-rail train. Car-rental counters are in the central terminal atrium between security screening areas.

Car

To drive from Denver to the parks, follow I-70 west, up over the Continental Divide along the Rocky Mountains and down to the Colorado River. Cross into Utah and take I-70 Exit 212 at Cisco. From Denver to Cisco is 297 miles, all on the freeway. From Cisco, follow Highway 128 for 37 highly scenic miles through red-rock canyons to Moab. Allow 5.5 hours of driving time between Moab and Denver.

The following companies have car rentals at DIA or immediately adjacent to it: **Advantage** (303/342-0990 or 800/777-5500); **Avis** (303/342-5500 or 800/331-1212); **Alamo** (24530 E. 78th Ave., 303/342-7373 or 800/462-5266); **Budget** (800/527-0700); **Dollar** (866/434-2226 or 800/800-4000); **Hertz** (303/753-8800 or 800/654-3131); **National** (303/342-0717 or 800/227-7368); **Payless** (303/342-9444 or 800/729-5377); and **Thrifty** (303/342-9400 or 800/367-2277).

RV Rentals

B&B RV (6960 Smith Rd., 303/322-6013, www.bb-rv.com) is a local company. **Moturis Inc.** (5300 Colorado Blvd., Commerce City, 888/295-6837 or 303/295-6837, www.moturis. com) is northeast of downtown Denver and rents both RVs and motorcycles (French, Italian, and German are spoken here). Regional corporations with offices in Denver include **Cruise America** (8950 N. Federal Blvd., 303/650-2865) and **El Monte RV** (6570 N. Federal Blvd., 888/337-2214, www.elmonterv .com), which operates out of Holidays on Wheels RV.

Accommodations

Chain hotels have set up shop in the area surrounding DIA. Almost all offer shuttles to and from the airport.

Under $50: The **Hostel of the Rockies** (1717 Race St., 303/861-7777, $20 dorm, $40 private) is a newly converted hostel in an old and elegant apartment building. Facilities include kitchen, laundry, Internet access, and cable TV.

$50-75: About 12 miles south of the airport, near the intersection of I-70 and Peña Boulevard, is a cluster of chain motels, including **Comfort Inn** (16921 E. 32nd Ave., 303/367-5000, $72 d).

$75-100: The closest lodgings are about six miles from the airport. The **DIA Microtel Inn** (18600 E. 63rd Ave., 303/371-8300 or 800/771-7171, $94 d) offers free breakfast. The **Red Roof Inn** (6890 Tower Rd., 303/371-5300 or 800-REDROOF, $75 d) is easy to find at I-70 Exit 286.

Over $100: The **Hilton Garden Inn Denver Airport** (16475 E. 40th Circle, 303/371-9393, $129 and up) is near the intersection of I-70 and Peña Boulevard, south of the airport. Other comfortable DIA-area hotels include **Comfort Suites** (6210 Tower Rd., 303/371-9300, $129 and up), where all rooms are suites, and the **Fairfield Inn Denver Airport** (6851 Tower Rd., 303/576-9640, $149 d). If you're looking for the classic swank downtown-Denver hotel, try the **Brown Palace** (321 17th St., 303/297-3111 or 800/321-2599, $179 and up), a historic and ornate hotel from Denver's 1890s heyday.

Food

If you're just passing through DIA on your way to Utah, you'll find that there's not a lot of fine dining near the airport (there is a **Wolfgang Puck Express** in Concourse B, 303/342-7611, which is worth knowing about). You'll need to travel into Denver itself if you want to explore the dining scene.

With a large Hispanic population, it's no surprise that Denver has lots of Latin American restaurants, and these are often good and reliable places for inexpensive meals. However, some of Denver's most exciting restaurants are Nuevo Latin American restaurants—where familiar tacos, tortillas, and enchiladas are updated into zippy fine dining. One of the best is **Lola** (1469 S. Pearl St., 720/570-8686), a hip and happening restaurant where main courses like chorizo-stuffed pork chops are under $20. Guacamole is prepared tableside, like Caesar salad in traditional American steakhouses. More upscale is **Tamayo Modern Mexican Cuisine** (1400 Larimer St., 720/946-1433), which is a hybrid of French refinement and zesty Mexican flavors (main dishes $17–26). Views from this rooftop dining room overlook Larimer Square and the Rockies, making it a top spot for margaritas and appetizers (particularly the excellent shrimp tacos).

New American cooking is also popular in Denver. At **Deluxe** (30 S. Broadway, 303/722-1550) the emphasis is on seasonal ingredients and perfect execution of homey foods like pork loin and coleslaw as well as fresh preparations of fish and seafood for around $25. The **Barolo Grill** (3030 E. 6th Ave., 303/393-1040) is a comfortable Northern Italian restaurant with good salads and pasta, and grilled fish, game, and chicken main courses ($15–30). The wine list here is outstanding. Denver is known for its steakhouses, and one of the best is the locally owned **Capital Grille** (1450 Larimer St., 303/539-2500), with swank surroundings, an attentive staff, and excellent steaks, prime rib, and chops ($19–40). For a lighter meal, go to **Falling Rock Tap House** (1919 Blake St., 303/293-8338), one of Denver's top brewpubs, with over 70 brews on tap and tasty pub grub.

Getting Around

For most travelers, getting around southern Utah will require using some form of automobile. Public transport is nonexistent in and between the parks, and distances are great—although the parks cover a relatively compact area, the geography of the land is so contorted that there are few roads that connect the dots. For instance, from Moab to the Arizona border, a distance of nearly 130 miles, only one bridge crosses the Colorado River once it drops into its canyon. Cars are easily rented in gateway cities, and in towns like Moab there is a plethora of Jeep and Humvee rentals as well.

Bicycle touring is certainly an excellent option, but cyclists would need to be in good shape and be prepared for intense heat during summer trips. For detailed information on cycling Utah, read the classic *Bicycle Touring in Utah* by Dennis Coeolo.

STREET NUMBERING AND GRID ADDRESSES

Many towns founded by Mormon settlers share a street-numbering scheme, which can be confusing to first-time visitors but quickly becomes intuitive. A city's address numbering grid will generally have its temple at the center, and have blocks numbered by hundreds out in every direction. For instance, 100 West is a block west of the center of town, then comes 200 West, and so on. In conversation, you may hear the shorthand "4th South," "3rd West," and so on to indicate 400 South or 300 West.

While this street numbering system is a picture of precision, it's also confusing at first. For instance, all addresses have four parts. When you see the address 436 North 100 West, for instance, the system tells you that the address will be found four blocks north of the center of town, on 100 West. One rule of thumb is to remember that the last two segments of an address (300 South, 500 East, 2300 West) are the street's actual name—the equivalent of a single street signifier such as Oak Street or Front Street.

TRAVELING BY RV

Traveling the Southwest national parks in an RV is a time-honored tradition, and travelers will have no problem finding RV rentals in major cities like Denver, Salt Lake City, and Las Vegas, which serve as gateways to the parks of southern Utah. The parks have good campgrounds, and towns like Moab and Springdale have some very spiff campground options with extras like swimming pools and Wi-Fi access. Note that some parks attempt to limit vehicle access—to visit Bryce and Zion, you'll need to leave the RV behind and tour the narrow park roads by free shuttle bus.

DRIVING THE PARKS

During the summer, patience is the key to driving in Utah's national parks. Roads are often crowded with slow-moving RVs, and traffic jams are not uncommon. At Zion, shuttle buses have replaced private vehicles along the scenic Zion Canyon Road, and a voluntary shuttle runs through the main Bryce Canyon amphitheater.

If you're traveling on back roads, especially in the Grand Staircase–Escalante National Monument, make sure you have plenty of gas, even if it means paying top dollar at a small-town gas pump.

Summer heat in the desert puts an extra strain on both cars and drivers. It's worth double-checking your vehicle's cooling system, engine oil, transmission fluid, fan belts, and tires to make sure they are in top condition. Carry several gallons of water in case of a breakdown or radiator trouble. Never leave children or pets in a parked car during warm weather because temperatures inside can cause fatal heatstroke in minutes.

At times the desert has *too much* water, when late-summer storms frequently flood low spots in the road. Wait for the water level to subside before crossing. Dust storms can completely block visibility but tend to be short-lived. During such storms, pull completely off the road, stop, and turn off your lights so as not to confuse other drivers. Radio stations carry frequent weather updates when weather hazards exist.

If stranded, stay with your vehicle unless you're *positive* of where to go for help, then leave a note explaining your route and departure time. Airplanes can easily spot a stranded car (tie a piece of cloth to your antenna), but a person walking is more difficult to see. It's best to carry emergency supplies: blankets or sleeping bags, a first-aid kit, tools, jumper cables, a shovel, traction mats or chains, a flashlight, rain gear, water, food, and a can opener.

Maps

The Utah Department of Transportation prints and distributes a free, regularly updated map of Utah. Ask for it when you call for information or when you stop at a visitors information office. Benchmark Maps' *Utah Road and Recreation Atlas* is loaded with beautiful maps, recreation information, and global positioning system (GPS) grids. If you're planning on extensive backcountry exploration, be sure to ask locally about conditions.

Off-Road Driving

Here are some tips for safely traversing the backcountry in a vehicle (preferably one with four-wheel drive):

- Drive slowly enough to choose a safe path and avoid obstacles such as rocks or giant potholes, but keep up enough speed to propel you through sand or mud.

- Keep an eye on the route ahead of you. If there are obstacles, stop, get out of your vehicle, and survey the situation.

- Reduce the tire pressure if you're driving across sand.

- Drive directly up or down the fall line of a slope. Cutting across diagonally may seem less frightening, but it puts you in a position to slide or roll over.

If you really want to learn to drive your four-wheel-drive rig, consider signing up for a class.

© JUDY JEWELL

Zion's shuttle buses transport visitors along the once-jammed park roads.

SHUTTLES

Both Zion and Bryce parks now offer shuttle bus service during peak summer season along the primary entrance roads to the parks to reduce traffic and vehicular impact on the parks. In Zion, shuttles pick up visitors at various points throughout Springdale and take them to the park gate, where another shuttle runs park visitors up Zion Canyon Road, stopping at trailheads, scenic overlooks, and Zion Lodge. Essentially, private cars are no longer allowed on Zion Canyon Road during peak season. (Registered overnight guests at Zion Lodge can drive their own vehicles to the hotel.)

In Bryce, the shuttle bus picks up visitors at the park gate and drives the length of the main parkway, making stops at all the major trailheads and vista points in addition to campgrounds, Ruby's Inn, and the Bryce Canyon Lodge. The shuttle bus is not required in Bryce, though it is highly recommended.

In both parks, the shuttle-ticket cost is covered in park entrance fees.

TOURS

Bus tours of the southern Utah national parks, often in conjunction with Grand Canyon National Park, are available from several regional tour companies. **Southern Utah Scenic Tours** (P.O. Box 1113, Cedar City, UT 84720, 435/867-8690 or 888/404-8687, www.utah scenictours.com) offers multiday scenic and thematic tours of the Southwest, including the Utah national parks.

Passage to Utah (1338 S. Foothill Dr., Salt Lake City, UT 84108, 801/519-2400 or 800/677-0553, www.passagetoutah.com) leads tours to sights in Utah and the West. With an environmental and recreational focus, Pas-

---

TOURIST INFORMATION

General tourist literature and maps are available from the Utah Travel Council, Council Hall/Capital Hill, Salt Lake City, UT 84114-7420, 801/538-1030, fax 801/538-1399, www.utah.com.

Call or write in advance of your visit to obtain maps and brochures from the parks.

Arches National Park
P.O. Box 907
Moab, UT 84532-0907
435/719-2299
www.nps.gov/arch
archinfo@nps.gov

Bryce Canyon National Park
P.O. Box 170001
Bryce Canyon, UT 84717-0001
435/834-5322
www.nps.gov/brca
Brca_reception _ area@nps.gov

Canyonlands National Park
2282 SW Resource Blvd.
Moab, UT 84532-3298

435/719-2313
www.nps.gov/cany
canyinfo@nps.gov

Capitol Reef National Park
HC 70 Box 15
Torrey, UT 84775-9602
435/425-3791
www.nps.gov/care
CARE_interpretation@nps.gov

Grand Staircase-Escalante National Monument
318 North 100 East
Kanab, UT 84741
435/644-4600
www.ut.blm.gov/monument
escalant@ut.blm.gov

Zion National Park
SR 9
Springdale, UT 84767-1099
435/772-3256
www.nps.gov/zion
ZION_park_information@nps.gov

sage to Utah provides small groups—no more than 10 guests at a time—with near-custom trips through scenic Western landscapes, with frequent stops for hikes, microbrew beers, and other fun diversions that wouldn't make the itinerary in a larger bus tour.

For a truly unusual bus tour, consider the **AdventureBus** (21 E. Kelsey Ave., Salt Lake City, UT 84111, 888/737-5263 in the U.S., 909/633-7225, www.adventurebus.com), a bus that's had most of its seats removed to make six living areas. Guests live on the bus (some meals are also provided) as it makes tours of Utah and other Southwest hot spots.

Recreation

It's difficult to imagine more dramatic landscapes than those found in Utah's national parks. The epic canyons, arches, and needles of sandstone invite you to get out of your vehicle and explore. Hikers will find a variety of trails, ranging from paved all-abilities paths to remote backcountry tracks. Rafts and jet-boats out of Moab provide another means to explore rugged canyons otherwise inaccessible to all but the hardiest trekkers. The sheer rock cliff faces and promontories in the parks provide abundant challenges to experienced rock climbers; be certain to check park regulations before climbing, however, as restrictions may apply.

HIKING

Utah's national parks offer lots of opportunities for hikers and backcountry enthusiasts interested in exploring the scenery on foot. Each of the parks has a variety of well-maintained hiking trails, ranging from easy strolls to multi-day backcountry treks. In fact, much of the Needles and Maze districts in Canyonlands and the most compelling parts of Capitol Reef and Zion are accessible only by foot; visits to remote Anasazi ruins and petroglyphs are among the rewards for the long-distance hiker.

One increasingly popular activity is canyoneering—exploring mazelike slot canyons. Hundreds of feet deep but sometimes only wide enough for a hiker to squeeze through, these canyons are located near Escalante and in the Paria River area. You'll need to be fit to explore these regions—and watch the weather carefully for flash floods.

CAMPING

All of Utah's national parks have campgrounds, with each park keeping at least one campground open year-round. With the exception of Zion's Watchman Campground, no reservations are taken for campsites; it's all first-come, first-served. During the summer and on holiday weekends during the spring and fall, it's best to arrive at the park early in the day and select a campsite immediately. Don't expect to find hookups or showers at National Park Service campgrounds. For these comforts, look just outside the park entrance, where you'll generally find a full-service commercial campground.

Backcountry Camping

Backcountry campers in national parks must stop by the park visitors center for a backcountry permit. Backcountry camping may be limited to specific sites in order to spread people out a bit; if so, a park ranger will consult with you and assign you a campground.

Before heading into the backcountry, check with a ranger about weather, water sources, fire danger, trail conditions, and regulations. Backpacking stores are also good sources of information. Here are some tips for traveling safely and respectfully in the backcountry:

- Tell rangers or other reliable people where you are going and when you expect to return; they'll alert rescuers if you go missing.

- Travel in small groups for the best experience (group size may also be regulated).

AMERICA THE BEAUTIFUL INTERAGENCY PASSES

The U.S. government revamped its year-long park pass system in 2007, doing away with the old Golden Eagle, Golden Age, and Golden Access passes. The new passes are the result of a cooperative effort between the National Park Service, the Forest Service, the U.S. Fish and Wildlife Service, the Bureau of Land Management, and the Bureau of Reclamation.

The basic pass is called the **America the Beautiful – National Parks and Federal Recreational Lands Pass** (good for one year from date of purchase, $80), which is available to the general public and provides access to, and use of, federal recreation sites that charge an entrance or standard amenity fee. Passes can be obtained in person at a park; by calling 888-ASK-USGS (888-275-8747), ext. 1; or at http://store.usgs.gov/pass/.

U.S. citizens or permanent residents age 62 or over can purchase a lifetime version of the America the Beautiful pass for $10. This pass can only be obtained in person at a park. The Senior Pass also provides a 50 percent discount on some fees, such as camping, swimming, boat launch, and specialized interpretive services. The pass is nontransferable and generally does not cover or reduce special recreation permit fees or fees charged by park concessionaires.

U.S. citizens or permanent residents with permanent disabilities are eligible for a free lifetime America the Beautiful Access Pass. Documentation such as a statement from a licensed physician, the Veterans Administration, or Social Security is required to obtain this pass, which can only be obtained in person at a park. Like the Senior Pass, the Access Pass provides a 50 percent discount on some fees.

Volunteers who have amassed 500 service hours with one of the participating federal agencies are eligible for a free one-year pass, which is available through their supervisor.

- Avoid stepping on—or camping on—fragile cryptobiotic soils.

- Use a portable stove to avoid leaving fire scars.

- Resist the temptation to shortcut switchbacks; this causes erosion and can be dangerous.

- Avoid digging tent trenches or cutting vegetation.

- Help preserve old Native American and historic ruins.

- Camp at least 300 feet away from springs, creeks, and trails. Camp at least a quarter-mile from a *sole* water source to avoid scaring away wildlife and livestock.

- Avoid camping in washes at any time; be alert to thunderstorms.

- Take care not to throw or kick rocks off trails—someone might be underneath you.

- Don't drink water directly from streams or lakes, no matter how clean the water appears; it may contain the parasitic protozoan *Giardia lamblia,* which causes giardiasis. Boiling water for several minutes will kill giardia as well as most other bacterial or viral pathogens. Chemical treatments and water filters usually work, too, although they're not as reliable as boiling (giardia spends part of its life in a hard shell that protects it from most chemicals).

- Bathe and wash dishes away from lakes, streams, and springs. Use biodegradable soap and scatter your wash water.

- Bring a trowel for personal sanitation; dig 6–8 inches deep and cover your waste.

- Pack out all your trash, including toilet paper and feminine hygiene items.

- Bring plenty of feed for your horses and mules.

HOW TO CHOOSE AN OUTFITTER

Utah has several outfitters, guides, trail-drive operators, and guest ranches, all of whom promise to get you outdoors and into an Old West adventure. But all outfitting and recreational services are not created equal. The most important consideration in choosing an outfitter is safety; the second is comfort. Make sure you feel confident on both counts before signing on.

Here are some points to ponder while you plan your adventure vacation.

All outfitters should be licensed or accredited by the state and be happy to provide you with proof. This means that they are bonded, carry the necessary insurance, and have money and organizational wherewithal to register with the state. This rules out fly-by-night operations and college students who've decided to set up business for the summer. If you're just starting to plan an excursion, contact the Utah Travel Council at Capital Hill, Salt Lake City, 801/538-1030 or 800/200-1160. The council's website, www.utah.com, contains an extensive network of outfitters and guides.

Many outfitters offer similar trips. When you've narrowed down your choice, call and talk to the outfitters on your short list. Ask lots of questions, and try to get a sense of who these people are; you'll be spending a lot time with them, so make sure you feel comfortable. If you have special interests, like bird- or wildlife-watching, be sure to mention them to your potential outfitter. A good outfitter will take your interests into account when planning a trip.

If there's a wide disparity in prices between outfitters for the same trip, find out what makes up the difference. The cheapest trip may not be the best choice for you. Food is one of the most common areas to economize in. If you don't mind having cold cuts each meal for your five-day pack trip, then maybe the cheapest outfitter is okay. If you prefer a cooked meal, or alcoholic beverages, or a choice of entrées, then be prepared to pay more. On a long trip, it might be worth it. Also be sure you know what kind of accommodations are included in multiday trips. You may pay more to have a tent or cabin to yourself, but again, it may be worth it.

Ask how many years an outfitter has been in business and how long your particular escort has guided this trip. Although a start-up outfitting service can be perfectly fine, you should know what level of experience you are buying. If you have questions, especially for longer or more dangerous trips, ask for referrals.

Most outfitters will demand that you pay a portion (usually half) of your fee well in advance to secure your place, so be sure to ask about cancellation policies. Some lengthy float trips can cost thousands of dollars; if cancellation means the forfeiture of the deposit, then you need to know that. Also, find out what the tipping or gratuity policy is for your outfitter. Sometimes 15 or 20 percent extra is added to your bill as a tip for the "hands." Although this is undoubtedly nice for the help, you should be aware that your gratuities for a week's stay can run into the hundreds of dollars.

- Leave dogs at home; they're not permitted on national park trails.

- If you realize you're lost, find shelter. If you're sure of a way to civilization and plan to walk out, leave a note with your departure time and planned route.

- Visit the Leave No Trace website, www.lnt .org, for more details on responsible backcountry travel.

CLIMBING

Most visitors to Utah's national parks enjoy spotting rock climbers scaling canyon walls and sandstone pillars. But for a few, the whole reason to visit southern Utah is to climb. These folks will need a climbing guide, either the classic and rather hard-to-find *Desert Rock* by Eric Bjørnstad, or *Rock Climbing Utah*, by Stewart M. Green.

Prospective climbers should take note: Just because you're the star of the local rock gym,

© W. C. MCRAE

climbers scaling rock faces near the Needles District

Climbers in the national parks should take care to use clean climbing techniques. Approach climbs via established trails to prevent further erosion of slopes. Camp in park campgrounds or, on multiday climbs, get a backcountry permit. Because white chalk leaves unsightly marks on canyon walls, add red pigment to your chalk. Do not disturb vegetation growing in cracks along your route. Tube or bag human waste and carry it out. Remove all old, worn rope and equipment, but do not remove fixed pins. Make sure your climb is adequately protected by visually inspecting any preexisting bolts or fixed pins. It is illegal to use a power drill to place bolts. Never climb directly above trails, where hikers may be hit by dislodged rocks.

In Canyonlands, even stricter regulations are in place. Here, no new climbing hardware may be left in a fixed location; protection may not be placed with the use of a hammer except to replace existing belay and rappel anchors and bolts on existing routes, or for emergency self-rescue; and unsafe slings must be replaced with an earth-colored sling.

don't think that climbing Zion's high, exposed big walls or Canyonlands' remote sandstone towers is going to be simple. Sandstone poses its own set of challenges; it weakens when wet, so it's wise to avoid climbing in damp areas or after rain. Arches' Entrada sandstone is particularly tough to climb.

Plan to climb in the spring or fall. During the summer, the walls become extremely hot. Some climbing areas may be closed during the spring to protect nesting raptors. Check at the visitors centers for current closures.

Tips for Travelers

Southern Utah may seem a remote, uninhabited and even hostile destination, but it sees hundreds of thousands of travelers each year and has sufficient facilities to ensure that visitors have a pleasant vacation. Before you visit, here are a few tips to ensure that your Utah vacation goes well.

FOREIGN VISITORS
Entering the United States
Citizens of Canada must now provide a passport to enter the United States. However, a visa is not required for Canadian citizens.

Citizens of 28 other countries can enter under a reciprocal visa waiver program. These citizens can enter the United States for up to 90 days for tourism or business with a valid passport; however, no visa is required. These countries include most of Western Europe, plus Japan, Australia, New Zealand, and Singapore. For a full list of reciprocal visa countries (and other late-breaking news for travelers to the U.S.), check out the website at www.travel.state.gov. Visitors on this program who arrive by sea or air must show round-trip tickets back out of the United States within 90 days, and

SAY IT RIGHT!

The following place names are easy to mispronounce. Say it like a local!

Duchesne	du-SHANE
Ephraim	E-from
Hurricane	HUR-aken
Kanab	ke-NAB
Lehi	LEE-hi
Manti	MAN-tie
Monticello	mon-ta-SELL-o
Nephi	NEE-fi
Panguitch	PAN-gwich
Tooele	too-WIL-a
Uinta	u-INT-a
Weber	WE-ber

Escalante poses an unusual problem. Utahans from northern parts of the state pronounce the name of the town and the famous river canyons as es-ka-LAN-tay; however, citizens of the town pronounce it without the final long E, as es-ka-LANT.

they must present proof of financial solvency (credit cards are usually sufficient). If citizens of these countries are staying longer than 90 days, they must apply for and present a visa.

Citizens of countries not covered by the reciprocal visa program are required to present both a valid passport and a visa to enter the United States. These are obtained from U.S. embassies and consulates. These travelers are also required to offer proof of financial solvency and provide a round-trip ticket out of the United States within the timeline of the visa.

Once in the United States, foreign visitors can travel freely among states without restrictions. A few states maintain agricultural checkpoints at state borders to prevent transport of fruit or plants, but Utah is not one of these states.

Customs

U.S. Customs allows each person over the age of 21 to bring in one liter of liquor and 200 cigarettes duty-free into the country. Non-U.S. citizens can bring in $100 worth of gifts without paying duty. If you are carrying more than $10,000 in cash or travelers checks, you are required to declare it.

Currency Exchange and Banking

Outside of Salt Lake City, there are few opportunities to exchange foreign currency or travelers checks in non-U.S. funds at banks or exchanges. Travelers checks in U.S. dollars are accepted at face value in most businesses without additional transaction fees.

By far the best way to keep yourself in cash is by using bank, debit, or cash cards at **ATMs** (automated teller machines). Not only does withdrawing funds from your own home account save in fees, but you also often get a better rate of exchange. Nearly every town in Utah has an ATM. Most ATMs at banks require a small fee to dispense cash. Most grocery stores allow you to use a debit or cash card to purchase food, with the option for a cash withdrawal. These transactions are free to the withdrawer.

Credit cards are accepted nearly everywhere in Utah. The most common are Visa and MasterCard. American Express, Diners Club, and Discover are also used, although these aren't as ubiquitous.

Electricity

As in all of the United States, electricity is 110 volts. Plugs have either two flat or two-flat-plus-one-round prongs. Older homes and hotels may have outlets that only have two-prong outlets, and you may well be traveling with computers or appliances that have three-prong plugs. Ask your hotel or motel manager for an adapter; if necessary, you may need to buy a three-prong adapter, but the cost is small.

TRAVELING WITH CHILDREN

The parks of southern Utah are filled with dramatic vistas and exciting recreation. The parks provide lots of opportunities for adventures, whether it's rafting the Colorado River or hiking to ancient Anasazi ruins, and most children will have the time of their young lives in Utah.

Utah is a family-vacation type of place, and no special planning is required to make a national park holiday exciting for children. Children do receive discounts on a number of things, ranging from motel rooms (where they often stay for free, but inquire about the age restrictions, as they vary from lodging to lodging) to museum admissions. One exception to this family-friendly rule is B&Bs, which frequently don't allow children at all.

Utah law requires all children 4 years old or younger to be restrained in a child safety seat. Child seats can be rented from car-rental agencies—ask when making a car reservation.

SENIORS

The parks and Utah in general are hospitable for senior travelers. The long-standing national-parks-issued Golden Age Passport has been replaced by the America the Beautiful National Parks and Federal Recreational Lands Senior Pass. This is a lifetime pass for U.S. citizens or permanent residents age 62 or over. The pass provides access to, and use of, federal parks and recreation sites that charge an entrance fee or standard amenity. The pass admits the pass holder and passengers in a noncommercial vehicle at per-vehicle fee areas, not to exceed four adults. The pass costs $10 and can only be obtained in person at the park. There is a similar discount program at Utah state parks.

GAY AND LESBIAN TRAVELERS

Utah is not the most enlightened place in the world when it comes to gay issues, but that shouldn't be an issue for travelers to the national parks. Needless to say, a little discretion is a good idea in most public situations, and don't expect to find much of a gay scene anywhere in southern Utah. Moab is notably more progressive than anywhere else in this part of the state, but there are no gay bars or gathering places.

PETS

Unless you really have no other option, it's best not to bring your dog (or cat, or bird, or ferret) along on a national park vacation. Dogs are prohibited on most trails, and for most of the year it's far too hot to leave an animal locked in a car. Additionally, in Zion, private cars are prohibited on the scenic canyon drive, and no pets are allowed on the shuttle buses that drive this route.

ACCESSIBILITY

Travelers with disabilities will find Utah progressive when it comes to accessibility. All of the parks (except Grand Staircase–Escalante National Monument) have all-abilities trails and services. All five national parks have reasonably good facilities for visitors with limited mobility. Visitors centers are all-accessible, and at least a couple of trails in each park are paved or smooth enough for a wheelchair user to navigate with some assistance. Each park has a few accessible campsites.

Most hotels also offer some form of barrier-free lodging. It's best to call ahead and inquire what these accommodations are, however, because these services can vary quite a bit from one establishment to another.

Because the Grand Staircase–Escalante National Monument is almost entirely undeveloped, trails are generally inaccessible to wheelchair users.

CONDUCT AND CUSTOMS
Alcohol and Nightlife

Observant Mormons don't drink alcoholic beverages, and state laws have been drafted to make purchasing alcohol relatively awkward. If going out for drinks and nightclubbing is part of your idea of entertainment, you'll find that only Moab offers much in the way of nightspots. Most towns have a liquor store; outside Moab, don't even expect restaurants to have liquor licenses.

Smoking

Smoking is taboo for observant Mormons, and smoking is prohibited in almost all pub-

UTAH'S DRINKING LAWS

The state's liquor laws are rather confusing and peculiar. Some of Utah's drinking laws were revised in preparation for the 2002 Winter Olympics, but in more remote parts of Utah, don't expect to find it easy to get a drink.

Several different kinds of establishments are licensed to sell alcoholic beverages.

Taverns, which include brewpubs, can sell only 3.2 percent beer (beer that is 3.2 percent alcohol by volume). Taverns can't sell wine, which is classed as hard liquor in Utah. You don't need to purchase food or be a member of a private club to have a beer in a tavern. With the exception of brewpubs, taverns are usually fairly derelict and not especially cheery places to hang out.

Licensed restaurants are able to sell beer, wine, and hard liquor, but only with food orders. Before the Olympics came to town, servers were not allowed to ask you if you cared for a drink; such solicitation was barred by law. Old habits die hard: In many parts of Utah, you'll need to specifically ask for a drink or the drink menu to begin the process. In Salt Lake City, Moab, and Park City, most restaurants have liquor licenses. In other cities and towns, few eating establishments offer alcohol.

Private clubs are essentially the same as bars in other parts of the United States. You can have drinks with or without food during open hours; however, you must be a member to eat or drink in a private club. For travelers, this doesn't present an insurmountable hurdle because you can buy temporary memberships (a two-week membership usually costs around $5). If you're fond of a drink and nightlife, it might well be worth it. Most live-music clubs are private clubs, for instance. Also, club members are able to sign in up to five friends on a nightly basis. You can either ask a friendly-looking stranger to sign you in, or, if you're part of a group, one of you can become a member and sign in the others.

A long-standing Utah law forbids the advertising of alcohol. No signs or notices are allowed to indicate that alcohol is available: You won't see many neon Spud McKenzies in Utah. (The law is only spottily enforced these days.) Although it's pretty obvious that a brewpub will have beer, you won't know whether drinks are served at a restaurant until you ask.

Nearly all towns will have a state-owned liquor store, and 3.2 percent beer is available in most grocery stores. Many travelers find that carrying a bottle of your favorite beverage to your room is the easiest way to enjoy an evening drink. The state drinking age is 21.

lic places. You're also not allowed to smoke on church grounds. Obviously, take care when smoking in national parks and pick up your own butts. Besides the risk of fire, there's nothing that ruins a natural experience more than wind-blown piles of cigarette filters.

Small-Town Utah

If you've never traveled in Utah before, you may find that Utahans don't initially seem as welcoming and outgoing as people in other western states. In many smaller towns, visitors from outside the community are a relatively new phenomenon, and not everyone in the state is anxious to have their towns turned into tourist or recreational meccas. The Mormons are very family- and community-oriented, and if certain individuals initially seem insular and uninterested in travelers, don't take it as unfriendliness.

Mormons are also orderly and socially conservative people. Brash displays of rudeness or use of foul language in public will not make you popular.

Health and Safety

There's nothing inherently dangerous about Utah's national parks, though a few precautions can help minimize what risks do exist. For the most part, using common sense about the dangers of extreme temperatures, remote backcountry exploration, and encounters with wildlife will assure a safe and healthy trip.

HEAT AND WATER

Southern Utah in summer is a *very* hot place. Be sure to use sunscreen, or else you risk having an uncomfortable vacation. Wearing a wide-brimmed hat and good sunglasses, with full UV-protection, can shield you from the sun's harmful effects. Heat exhaustion can also be a problem if you're hiking in the hot sun. In midsummer, try to get an early start if you're hiking in full sun. If you're out during the heat of the afternoon, look for a shady spot and rest until the sun begins to drop.

Drink steadily throughout the day, whether you are thirsty or not, rather than gulping huge amounts of water once you feel thirsty. For hikers, one of the best ways to drink enough is to carry water in a hydration pack (the two top brands are Camelbak and Platypus). These collapsible plastic bladders come with a hose and a mouthpiece, so you can carry your water in your pack, threading the hose out the top of the pack and over your shoulder, which keeps the mouthpiece handy for frequent sips of water. One easy way to tell if you're getting enough to drink is to monitor your urine output. If you're only urinating a couple of times a day, and the color and odor of your urine are both strong, it's time to start drinking more water.

HYPOTHERMIA

Don't think that just because you're in the Utah desert you're immune to hypothermia. This lowering of the body's temperature below 95°F causes disorientation, uncontrollable shivering, slurred speech, and drowsiness. The victim may not even realize what's wrong. Unless corrective action is taken immediately, hypothermia can lead to death. Thus, hikers should travel with companions and always carry wind and rain protection. Space blankets are lightweight and cheap and offer protection against the cold in emergencies. Remember that temperatures can plummet rapidly in Utah's dry climate—a drop of 40°F between day and night is common. Be especially careful at high elevations, where summer sunshine can quickly change into freezing rain or a blizzard. Simply falling into a mountain stream can also lead to hypothermia and death unless proper action is taken. If you're cold and tired, don't waste time! Seek shelter and build a fire, change into dry clothes, and drink warm liquids. If a victim isn't fully conscious, warm him or her by skin-to-skin contact in a sleeping bag. Try to keep the victim awake and offer plenty of warm liquids.

GIARDIA

Giardia, a protozoan that has become common in even the most remote mountain streams, is carried in animal or human waste that is deposited or washed into the water. When ingested, it begins reproducing, causing intense cramping and diarrhea in the host that can become serious and may not be cured without medical attention.

No matter how clear a stream looks, it's best to assume that it is contaminated and to take precautions against giardia by filtering, boiling, or treating water with chemicals before drinking it. A high-quality filter will remove giardia and a host of other things you don't want to be drinking. (Spend a bit extra for one that removes particles down to one micrometer in size.) It's also effective to simply boil your water; 2–5 minutes at a rolling boil will kill giardia even in the cyst stage. Because water boils at a lower temperature as elevation increases, increase the boiling time to 15 minutes if you're at 9,000 feet. Two drops of bleach left in a quart of water for 30 minutes will remove most giardia, although some microorganisms are resistant to chemicals.

HANTAVIRUS

Hantavirus is an infectious disease agent that was first isolated during the Korean War and then discovered in the Americas in 1993 by a task force of scientists in New Mexico. This disease agent occurs naturally throughout most of North and South America, especially in dry desert conditions. The infectious agent is airborne, and in the absence of prompt medical attention, its infections are usually fatal. This disease is called hantavirus pulmonary syndrome (HPS). It can affect anyone, but given some fundamental knowledge, it can also be easily prevented.

The natural host of the hantavirus appears to be rodents, especially mice and rats. The virus is not usually transmitted directly from rodents to humans; rather, the rodents shed hantavirus particles in their saliva, urine, and droppings. Humans usually contract HPS by inhaling particles that are infected with the hantavirus. The virus becomes airborne when the particles dry out and get stirred into the air (especially from sweeping a floor or shaking a rug). Humans then inhale these particles, which leads to the infection.

HPS is not considered a highly infectious disease, so people usually contract HPS from long-term exposure. Because transmission usually occurs through inhalation, it is easiest for a human being to contract hantavirus within a contained environment, where the virus-infected particles are not thoroughly dispersed. Being in a cabin or barn where rodents can be found poses elevated risks for contracting the infection.

Simply traveling to a place where the hantavirus is known to occur is not considered a risk factor. Camping, hiking, and other outdoor activities also pose low risks, especially if steps are taken to reduce rodent contact. If you happen to stay in a rodent-infested cabin, thoroughly wet any droppings and dead rodents with a chlorine bleach solution (one cup per gallon of water) and let them stand for a few minutes before cleaning them up. Be sure to wear rubber gloves for this task, and double-bag your garbage.

The first symptoms of HPS can occur anywhere between five days and three weeks after infection. They almost always include fever, fatigue, aching muscles (usually in the back, shoulders, and/or thighs), and other flulike conditions. Other early symptoms may include headaches, dizziness, chills, and abdominal discomfort (such as vomiting, nausea, and/or diarrhea). These symptoms are shortly followed by intense coughing and shortness of breath. If you have these symptoms, seek medical help immediately. Untreated infections of hantavirus are almost always fatal.

THINGS THAT BITE OR STING

Although travelers in Utah's national parks are not going to get attacked by a grizzly bear, and encounters with mountain lions are rare, there are a few animals to watch out for. Snakes, scorpions, and spiders are all present in considerable numbers, and there are a few key things to know about dealing with this phobia-inducing trio.

Snakes

Rattlesnakes, including the particularly venomous midget faded rattlesnake, are present throughout southern Utah. The midget faded snakes live in Arches and Canyonlands, where they frequent burrows and rock crevices and are mostly active at night. Even though their venom is toxic, full venom injections are relatively uncommon, and, like all rattlesnakes, they pose little threat unless they're provoked.

If you see a rattlesnake, observe it at a safe distance. Be careful where you put your hands when canyoneering or scrambling—it's not a good idea to reach above your head and blindly plant your hands on a sunny rock ledge. Hikers should wear sturdy boots to minimize the chance that a snake's fangs will reach the skin if a bite occurs. Do not walk barefoot outside after dark as this is when snakes hunt for prey.

First aid for rattlesnake bites is an area full of conflicting ideas: to suck or not to suck; to apply a constricting bandage or not; or to take time treating in the field versus rushing to the hospital. Most people who receive medical treatment after being bitten by a rattlesnake live to tell the story. Prompt administration of antivenin is the most important treatment, and the most important aspect of first aid is to arrange transportation of the victim to a hospital as quickly as possible.

Scorpions

A scorpion's sting isn't as painful as you'd expect (it's about like a bee sting), and the venom is insufficient to cause any real harm. Still, it's not what you'd call pleasant, and experienced desert campers know to shake out their boots every morning because scorpions and spiders are attracted to warm, moist, dark places.

Spiders

Tarantulas and black widow spiders are present across much of the Colorado Plateau.

Believe it or not, a tarantula's bite does not poison humans; the enzymes secreted when they bite do turn the insides of frogs, lizards, and insects to a soft mush, allowing the tarantula to suck the guts from its prey. Another interesting tarantula fact: While males live about as long as you'd expect a spider to live, female tarantulas can live for up to 25 years. (Females *do* sometimes eat the males, which may account for some of this disparity in longevity.)

Black widow spiders, on the other hand, have a toxic bite. Although the bite is usually painless, it delivers a potent neurotoxin, which quickly causes pain, nausea, and vomiting. It is important to seek immediate treatment for a black widow bite; although few people actually die from these bites, recovery is helped along considerably by antivenin.

RESOURCES

Suggested Reading

GUIDEBOOKS AND TRAVELOGUES

Benchmark Maps. *Utah Road & Recreation Atlas.* Medford, OR: Benchmark Maps, 2002. Shaded relief maps emphasize landforms, and recreational information is abundant. Use it to locate campgrounds, back roads, and major trailheads, although there's not enough detail to rely on it for hiking.

Huegel, Tony. *Utah Byways: 65 Backcountry Drives for the Whole Family, Including Moab, Canyonlands, Arches, Capitol Reef, San Rafael Swell and Glen Canyon.* Berkeley: Wilderness Press, 2000. If you're looking for off-highway adventure, this is your guide. The spiral-bound book includes detailed directions, human and natural history, outstanding photography, full-page maps for each of the 65 routes, and an extensive how-to chapter for beginners.

Zwinger, Ann. *Wind in the Rock: The Canyonlands of Southeastern Utah.* Tucson: University of Arizona Press, 1986. Well-written accounts of hiking in the Grand Gulch and nearby canyons. The author tells of the area's history, archaeology, wildlife, and plants.

OUTDOOR ACTIVITIES

Adkison, Ron. *Best Easy Day Hikes Grand Staircase–Escalante and the Glen Canyon Region.* Helena, MT: Falcon Publishing, 1998. Features 19 hikes in south-central Utah Canyon Country, including Paria Canyon.

Adkison, Ron. *Hiking Grand Staircase–Escalante and the Glen Canyon Region.* Helena, MT: Falcon Publishing, 1998. The vast Escalante/Glen Canyon area of southern Utah is nearly roadless, and hiking is about the only way you'll have a chance to visit these beautiful and austere canyons. This guide includes detailed information on 59 hikes, including Paria Canyon and Grand Gulch, in addition to the Grand Staircase–Escalante National Monument.

Allen, Steve. *Canyoneering 3.* Salt Lake City: University of Utah Press, 1997. This book provides excellent, detailed descriptions of a variety of hikes in the Grand Staircase–Escalante National Monument, ranging from day hikes to multiday treks.

Barnes, F.A. *Canyon Country Off-Road Vehicle Trails: Canyon Rims & Needles Areas.* Moab: Canyon Country Publications, 1987. Descriptions of backcountry roads and off-road vehicle trails in the Needles area and other public lands south of Moab.

Barnes, F.A. *Canyon Country Off-Road Vehicle Trails: Island Area.* Moab: Canyon Country Publications, 1988. Descriptions of backcountry roads and off-road vehicle trails in the Island in the Sky area.

Barr, Don. *A River Runner's Guide to Cataract Canyon.* Kansas City, KS: Canon Publishers, 1987. A river runner's guide and natural history resource for the Colorado River south of Moab.

Belnap, Bill, and Belnap, Buzz. *Canyonlands River Guide.* Evergreen, CO; Westwater Books, 2006. River map guide to the Colorado and Green rivers, printed on waterproof paper.

Bikers, Jack. *Canyon Country Off-Road Vehicle Trails: Maze Area.* Moab: Canyon Country Publications, 1988. Descriptions of back-country roads and off-road vehicle trails in the Maze area.

Bjørnstad, Eric. *Desert Rock I: Rock Climbs in National Parks.* Helena, MT: Falcon Publishing, 1996. This is a classic climbing guide by one of Utah's most respected climbers.

Bloom, David. *Indian Creek: A Climbing Guide.* Boulder, CO: Sharp End Publishing, 2004. A climber's guide to the area near Needles with such good photos that it will double as a coffee table book.

Campbell, Todd. *Above and Beyond Slickrock.* Salt Lake City: Wasatch Publishers, 1999. Classic guide to mountain biking the slick-rock country of Southeastern Utah.

Coeolo, Dennis. *Bicycle Touring in Utah.* Salt Lake City: Dream Garden Press, 1988. Now out of print, but easy to find online, this book is still the most comprehensive guide to biking Utah.

Crowell, David. *Mountain Biking Moab.* Helena, MT: Falcon Publishing, 2003. A guide to the many trails around Moab, from the most popular to the little explored, in a handy size—small enough to take on the bike with you.

Day, David. *Utah's Favorite Hiking Trails.* Provo, UT: Rincon Publishing Co., 2002. Good simple maps and detailed descriptions of trails all over the state, including many in southern Utah's national parks and monuments.

Green, Stewart M. *Rock Climbing Utah.* Helena, MT: Falcon Publishing, 1998; 538 pages, $26.95. Good detail on climbs in all of Utah's national parks, including many line drawings and photos with climbing routes highlighted.

Kelsey, Michael R. *Canyon Hiking Guide to the Colorado Plateau.* Provo, UT: Kelsey Publishing, 2006. One of the best guides to hiking in southeastern Utah's canyon country. Geologic cross sections show the formations you'll be walking through.

Kelsey, Michael R. *River Guide to Canyonlands National Park.* Provo, UT: Kelsey Publishing, 1991. Explains how to do a trip on the Green and Colorado Rivers and the many hikes and things to see along the way, including lots of local lore. Begins at the town of Green River on the Green and Moab on the Colorado; coverage ends at the confluence area (there's not much on Cataract Canyon).

Lambrechtse, Rudi. *Hiking the Escalante.* Salt Lake City: Wasatch Publishers, 1999. "A wilderness guide to an exciting land of buttes, arches, alcoves, amphitheaters, and deep canyons." Introduction to history, geology, and natural history of the Escalante region in southern Utah. Contains descriptions and trailhead information for 42 hiking destinations. The hikes vary from easy outings suitable for children to a highly challenging four-day backpack trek.

Schneider, Bill. *Best Easy Day Hikes Canyonlands and Arches.* Helena, MT: Falcon Publishing, 2005. Twenty hikes in this popular vacation area, geared to travelers who are short on time or aren't able to explore the canyons on more difficult trails.

Utesch, Peggy. *The Utah-Colorado Mountain Bike Trail System, Route 1—Moab to Loma.* Moab: Canyon County Publications, 1998. A mile-by-mile guide to mountain bike trails along the Utah-Colorado border, with elevation charts and additional useful information.

MEMOIRS

Abbey, Edward. *Desert Solitaire.* New York: Ballantine Books, 1991. A meditation on the Red Rock Canyon Country of Utah.

Abbey brings his fiery prose to the service of the American outback, while excoriating the commercialization of the West.

Childs, Craig. *The Secret Knowledge of Water.* Boston: Back Bay Books, 2001. Childs looks for water in the desert, and finds plenty of it.

Meloy, Ellen. *Raven's Exile.* New York: Henry Holt & Company, 1994. Throughout a summer of Green River raft trips, Meloy reflects on natural and human history of the area.

Zwinger, Ann. *Run, River, Run: A Naturalist's Journey Down One of the Great Rivers of the American West.* Tucson: University of Arizona Press, 1984. An excellent description of the author's experiences along the Green River from its source in the Wind River Range of Wyoming to the Colorado River in southeastern Utah. The author weaves geology, Native American ruins, plants, wildlife, and her personal feelings into the text and drawings.

HISTORY AND CURRENT EVENTS

Dellenbaugh, Frederick S. *A Canyon Voyage: The Narrative of the Second Powell Expedition.* Tucson: University of Arizona Press, 1984. A well-written account of John Wesley Powell's second expedition down the Green and Colorado Rivers, 1871–1872. The members took the first Grand Canyon photographs and obtained much valuable scientific knowledge.

Powell, John Wesley. *The Exploration of the Colorado River and its Canyons.* Mineola, NY: Dover Publications, reprinted 1997 (first published in 1895). Describes Powell's 1869 and 1871–1872 expeditions down the Green and Colorado Rivers. His was the first group to navigate through the Grand Canyon. A description of the 1879 Uinta Expedition is included, too.

Stegner, Wallace. *Beyond the Hundredth Meridian: John Wesley Powell and the Second Opening of the West.* New York: Penguin Books, 1992 (first published in 1954). Stegner's book tells the story of Powell's wild rides down the Colorado River, then goes on from there to point out why the United States should have listened to what Powell had to say about the American Southwest.

ARCHAEOLOGY

Lister, Robert, and Florence Lister. *Those Who Came Before.* Southwest Parks and Monuments, 1983. A well-illustrated guide to the history, artifacts, and ruins of prehistoric Southwest people. The author also describes parks and monuments containing archaeological sites.

Slifer, Dennis. *Guide to Rock Art of the Utah Region: Sites with Public Access.* Albuquerque: University of New Mexico Press, 2000. The most complete guide to rock-art sites, with descriptions of more than 50 sites in the Four Corners region. Complete with maps and directions, and with an overview of rock-art styles and traditions.

NATURAL SCIENCES

Chronic, Halka. *Roadside Geology of Utah.* Missoula: Mountain Press Publishing, 1990. This layperson's guide tells the story of the state's fascinating geology as seen by following major roadways.

Fagan, Damian. *Canyon Country Wildflowers.* Helena, MT: Falcon Publishing, 1998. A comprehensive field guide to the diverse flora of the Four Corners area.

Fleischner, Thomas Lowe. *Singing Stone: A Natural History of the Escalante Canyons.* University of Utah Press, 1999. A former Outward Bound instructor who has guided many city people through the Escalante Canyons, Fleischner knows the area well and lends firsthand vitality to his information on the area's plants, animals, ecology, geology, and prehistory.

Williams, David. *A Naturalist's Guide to Canyon Country.* Helena, MT: Falcon Publishing, 2000. If you want to buy just one field guide, this is the one to get. It's well-written, beautifully illustrated, and a delight to use.

Internet Resources

Although a virtual visit to Utah cannot replace the real thing, you'll find an enormous amount of helpful information online. Thousands of websites cover everything from ghost towns to the latest community news.

The American Southwest
www.americansouthwest.net/utah

Utah Guide provides an overview of national parks, national recreation areas, and some state parks.

Canyonlands Utah
www.canyonlands-utah.com

Good source for information on Moab and the surrounding areas, including Canyonlands and Arches National Parks.

Desert USA
www.desertusa.com

Desert USA's Utah section discusses places to visit and what plants and animals you might meet there. Find out what's in bloom at www.desertusa.com/wildflo/wildupdates.

National Park Service
www.nps.gov

The National Park Service offers pages for all its areas at this site, where a click-on map will take you to Utah's parks. You can also enter this address followed by a slash and the first two letters of the first two words of the place (first four letters if there's just a one-word name); for example, www.nps.gov/brca takes you to Bryce Canyon National Park and www.nps.gov/zion leads to Zion National Park.

Recreation.gov
www.recreation.gov

If a campground is operated by the federal government, this is the place to make a reservation. Again, you can expect to pay a few dollars for this convenience.

Reserve USA
www.reserveusa.com

Use this website to reserve campsites in state campgrounds. It costs a few extra bucks to reserve a campsite, but compare that with the cost of being skunked out of a site and having to resort to a motel room.

State of Utah
www.state.ut.us

The official State of Utah website has travel information, agencies, programs, and what the legislature is up to.

USDA Forest Service
www.fs.fed.us/r4

Utah falls within U.S. Forest Service Region 4. Within southern Utah, the Dixie National Forest (www.fs.fed.us/r4/dixie) is in the southwest and south-central parts of the state, with ranger stations in Cedar City, St. George, Panguitch, and Escalante; the Manti-La Sal National Forest (www.fs.fed.us/r4/mantilasal) is in southeast Utah around Moab and Monticello; and the southern sections of the Fishlake National Forest (www.fs.fed.us/r4/fishlake) are near Torrey.

Utah's Dixie
www.utahsdixie.com

The southwestern Utah city of St. George is the focus of this site, which also covers some of the smaller communities outside Zion National Park.

Utah State Parks
parks.state.ut.us

The Utah State Parks site offers details on the large park system, including links to reserve campsites.

Utah Travel Council
www.utah.com

The Utah Travel Council is a one-stop shop for all sorts of information on Utah. It takes you around the state to sights, activities, events, maps, and offers links to local tourist offices. The accommodations listings are the most up-to-date source for current prices and options.

Zion Park
www.zionpark.com

This will point you to information on Springdale and the area surrounding Zion National Park, with links to lodging and restaurant sites.

Index

www.moon.com

For helpful advice on planning a trip, visit www.moon.com for the **TRAVEL PLANNER** and get access to useful travel strategies and valuable information about great places to visit. When you travel with Moon, expect an experience that is uncommon and truly unique.

HANDBOOKS | METRO | OUTDOORS | LIVING ABROAD

MAP SYMBOLS

≈≈≈	Expressway	【	Highlight	✗	Airfield	⌕	Golf Course
—	Primary Road	○	City/Town	✗	Airport	₽	Parking Area
—	Secondary Road	◉	State Capital	▲	Mountain	▲	Archaeological Site
·······	Unpaved Road	⊛	National Capital	✦	Unique Natural Feature	♠	Church
-------	Trail	★	Point of Interest			⌂	Gas Station
·············	Ferry	•	Accommodation	⟲	Waterfall	⬭	Glacier
—+—+—	Railroad	▾	Restaurant/Bar	▲	Park		Mangrove
≈≈≈	Pedestrian Walkway	▪	Other Location	◘	Trailhead		Reef
⊐⊐⊐⊐	Stairs	Λ	Campground	✗	Skiing Area		Swamp

CONVERSION TABLES

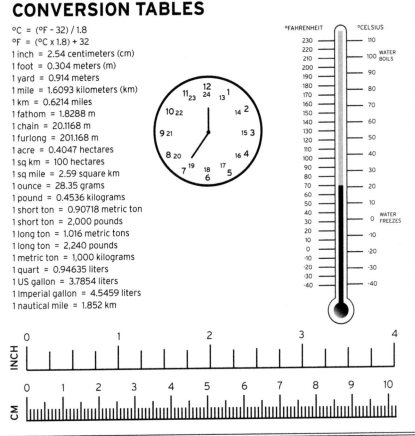

°C = (°F - 32) / 1.8
°F = (°C x 1.8) + 32
1 inch = 2.54 centimeters (cm)
1 foot = 0.304 meters (m)
1 yard = 0.914 meters
1 mile = 1.6093 kilometers (km)
1 km = 0.6214 miles
1 fathom = 1.8288 m
1 chain = 20.1168 m
1 furlong = 201.168 m
1 acre = 0.4047 hectares
1 sq km = 100 hectares
1 sq mile = 2.59 square km
1 ounce = 28.35 grams
1 pound = 0.4536 kilograms
1 short ton = 0.90718 metric ton
1 short ton = 2,000 pounds
1 long ton = 1.016 metric tons
1 long ton = 2,240 pounds
1 metric ton = 1,000 kilograms
1 quart = 0.94635 liters
1 US gallon = 3.7854 liters
1 Imperial gallon = 4.5459 liters
1 nautical mile = 1.852 km

MOON ZION & BRYCE

Avalon Travel
a member of the Perseus Books Group
1700 Fourth Street
Berkeley, CA 94710, USA
www.moon.com

Editors: Cinnamon Hearst, Tiffany Watson
Series Manager: Kathryn Ettinger
Copy Editor: Deana Shields
Graphics Coordinator: Nicole Schultz
Production Coordinator: Darren Alessi
Cover Designer: Nicole Schultz
Map Editor: Albert Angulo
Cartographers: Chris Markiewicz, Kat Bennett,
    Brice Ticen
Cartography Director: Mike Morgenfeld
Indexer: Rachel Kuhn

ISBN-10: 1-59880-009-4
ISBN-13: 978-1-59880-009-8
ISSN: 1540-3823

Printing History
1st Edition – 2003
3rd Edition – March 2008
5 4 3 2 1

KEEPING CURRENT

If you have a favorite gem you'd like to see included in the next edition, or see anything
that needs updating, clarification, or correction, please drop us a line. Send your
comments via email to feedback@moon.com, or use the address above.